This ! ...... return on or before the last ...

28

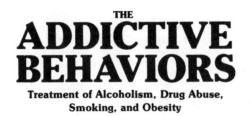

THE
ADDICTIVE
BEHAVIORS
Treatment of Alcoholism, Drug Abuse, Smoking, and Obesity

Other Pergamon Titles of Interest

A Related Journal

THE
ADDICTIVE
BEHAVIORS

Treatment of Alcoholism, Drug Abuse, Smoking, and Obesity

Edited by
William R. Miller
University of New Mexico

PERGAMON PRESS

Oxford • New York • Toronto • Sydney • Paris • Frankfurt

U.K.	Pergamon Press Ltd., Headington Hill Hall, Oxford OX3 0BW, England
U.S.A.	Pergamon Press Inc., Maxwell House, Fairview Park, Elmsford, New York 10523, U.S.A.
CANADA	Pergamon of Canada, Suite 104, 150 Consumers Road, Willowdale, Ontario M2J 1P9, Canada
AUSTRALIA	Pergamon Press (Aust.) Pty. Ltd., P.O. Box 544, Potts Point, N.S.W. 2011, Australia
FRANCE	Pergamon Press SARL, 24 rue des Ecoles, 75240 Paris, Cedex 05, France
FEDERAL REPUBLIC OF GERMANY	Pergamon Press GmbH, Hammerweg 6, Postfach 1305, 6242 Kronberg-Taunus, Federal Republic of Germany

First Edition 1980

British Library Cataloguing in Publication Data

The addictive behaviors.
  1. Drug abuse – Treatment
2. Obesity
I. Miller, William R
616.8'6'06   RC564   80-40169
ISBN 0-08-025203-6

Printed in the United States of America

To my students, whose questioning minds keep alive in me two priceless gifts: the humility of not knowing and the longing to know

Contents

Preface

Ever since I first heard George Miller's 1969 presidential address to the American Psychological Association, "giving psychology away" has been a personal fascination and a challenge. Our research laboratories and journals are filled with exciting and potentially usable findings, many of which will not be applied or will be inexcusably delayed in application because of a failure of communication between researchers and practitioners. Is there not some way in which we can recover these fruits of professional labor and public expenditure and make them accessible to those who really need them, the front-line caregivers and the consumers of mental health services?

It was this desire to communicate usable research findings to practitioners and an interest in the emerging area of "addictive behaviors" that gave rise to the present volume, and to the Taos International Conference on Treatment of Addictive Behaviors upon which its contents were based. Participants in the Taos conference were about equally representative of research and practice. Both practitioners and researchers who attended learned from each other, and a common goal began to evolve: to discover and develop practical and effective therapeutic programs based upon our current knowledge of etiology and treatment-outcome research. You hold in your hands one result of this common interest. In this volume, the invited speakers at the Taos conference attempt to make recent research available and usable to the practitioner who works in the area of addictive behaviors.

The goals of this book are twofold. First, we hope to provide practical guidelines for constructing and choosing treatment programs on rational and empirical bases. Too long our treatment programs have been made up of elements chosen for all the wrong reasons: political expediency, economic advantage, doctrinal adherence, lack of knowledge of alternatives, or "that's the way we've always done it." When no research is available, these may be the only bases upon which to choose treatment methods. There is a rapidly growing body of relevant treatment research, however, and if we are to serve the best interests of our clients, we should know and consider the testimony of this research in forming and reforming our programs. We hope that the material we present here will help you to make use of the valuable research that has accumulated over the past ten years or so.

Secondly, we hope to interest you in some apparent commonalities of those problem areas that have come to be called "the addictive behaviors." We believe that researchers and therapists who work in one area of substance abuse have much to learn from those who work with other addictive disorders. Many

etiological models, research methods, and treatment procedures can be transferred readily from one of these areas to another. The interactions of researchers and practitioners representing the various addictive behaviors at the
Taos conference were rewarding indeed, and we look forward to future occasions for such exchanges.

Certainly a few words of acknowledgment are in order. I am first of all most
appreciative of the work of the contributing authors of this volume. Their
knowledge of their respective fields and their clarity of writing made my tasks
as editor both easy and pleasurable. I also wish to acknowledge the assistance
of the very competent and helpful office staff here in the Department of
Psychology, and especially the efforts of Eleanor Orth, LaNelle Ruebush, and
Joan Block in preparing this manuscript. Thanks are also due to the production
staff at Pergamon Press, and in particular to Ms. Alix Wiles for her efficient
management of this volume. Finally, I am grateful to all those who brought to
Taos their enthusiasm, their expertise, their open-mindedness, and their skis,
creating a memorable professional and personal experience.

I
INTRODUCTION

1

The Addictive Behaviors

William R. Miller

The University of New Mexico
Albuquerque, New Mexico 87131

What do the following have in common: alcoholism, obesity, smoking, drug abuse, and compulsive gambling? Until a few years ago, these were thought of as relatively independent and separate problem areas. Psychologists, psychiatrists, social workers, and other mental health professionals have often specialized in the treatment of *one* of these behaviors, but few have extended their therapy and research efforts to cover more than one or two of these disorders. In addition, specialists in each of these areas have worked in relative isolation from one another, seldom communicating with each other about treatment and research issues.

The past few years, however, have witnessed a remarkable amount of growth and change in professional knowledge within these areas. The emergent concept of "the addictive behaviors" points to possible commonalities among these seemingly diverse problems. There is an increasing awareness that workers in each of these areas have much to learn from one another, and that there may be significant and instructive similarities in etiology, process, and treatment. Several journals are now devoted to the publication of new research, among them *Addictive Behaviors,* which was first issued in 1976, and the older *International Journal of the Addictions.* With the emergence of conferences (Krasnegor, 1979; Miller, 1980) and of volumes such as the present one devoted to the addictive behaviors, treatment and research personnel in these previously separate fields are beginning to benefit from each other's knowledge, wisdom, and experience. It is an exciting time; although there is much accumulated knowledge, it is clear that we are only beginning to scratch the surface, and there are so many fascinating, challenging, and potentially significant avenues to explore.

Common Ground

There are, indeed, some interesting similarities among these problem areas that collectively have come to be known as the addictive behaviors. All involve some form of indulgence for short-term pleasure or satisfaction at the expense of longer-term adverse effects. The four substance abuse disorders considered in this volume—alcoholism, drug abuse, smoking, and obesity—all involve significant health risks expressed primarily as increased probabilities of various chronic diseases. The social costs of addictive behaviors, both in personal expenditures on nonessentials and in costs to the public (e.g., health care, crime control, disability), are enormous if not immeasurable.

Another commonality among the addictive behaviors is that in each case there is no clear single treatment model with demonstrably superior efficacy. Each area has had historically *popular* therapeutic approaches (e.g., Alcoholics Anonymous, methadone maintenance, electrical aversion for smoking control, crash diets), each characterized by the lack of an adequate base of scientific support. The fact is that for each of the addictive behaviors there is a growing array of alternative treatment approaches, including self-help methods. Prior to ten years ago, the primary bases for choosing among these alternatives were unsubstantiated opinion, formal and informal experience, and diatribe. Now, happily, we are beginning to amass a body of scientific research upon which to base sound and rational decisions regarding differential treatment selection. The next four chapters of this volume are devoted to careful reviews of the current status of treatment research on the addictive behaviors. In chapter 2, William Miller and Reid Hester examine scientific support for the confusingly wide range of treatment methods currently available for problem drinkers, including both abstinence-oriented approaches and more recent methods designed to teach moderate drinking. Edward Callahan in chapter 3 evaluates alternative strategies currently available for treating narcotic addiction. In chapter 4, Edward Lichtenstein and Richard Brown provide a helpful and pragmatic guide for the clinician attempting to design an effective program for smoking cessation. Finally, in chapter 5, G. Terence Wilson critically reviews the effectiveness of behavior therapies for treating the obese patient. Each of these four chapters is intended to provide concrete and practical guidelines based upon the most recent scientific literature. These four chapters of part 2, then, serve as an up-to-date handbook on current therapeutic approaches for those who treat the addictive behaviors.

Common Issues

Another common characteristic of the addictive behaviors is the lack of single, simple, and scientifically satisfying models of etiology. How does the problem begin and develop? What causes alcoholism or drug abuse? Are there personality patterns typical of the heavy smoker or of the obese? Each of these areas of addictive behavior has witnessed the enthusiastic overemphasis of single causal factors. The particular popular "cause" has varied with the tenor of the times, but the pattern has remained the same: "Here is the answer! This is the cause! Only treatment directed toward this underlying cause will be effective!" Biologists and behaviorists, sociologists and psychoanalysts, all have been guilty of such etiological chauvinism.

Slowly there is dawning the realization that any comprehensive theory of addictive behavior must be multivariate, taking into account a range of factors. Hereditary predispositions, the physiology of addiction, cognitive expectancies, social-learning patterns—all influence substance use and abuse in important ways. Consequently, the current popular professional pastime is debating the relative importance of etiological factors, with biological elements pitted against psychological elements being a favored joust. In chapter 6, the first of three chapters in part 3 considering common issues in addictive behaviors, Peter Nathan explores some fascinating potential causal factors that may cut across areas, seeking ways in which our understanding of one addictive disorder may shed light on the etiology and process of others.

Likewise, there are important and interesting treatment issues that span the substance abuse disorders. Is abstinence a necessary goal, or is controlled use a feasible or desirable outcome? In the area of obesity, of course, very few professionals advocate total abstinence as a solution. Recent research has explored the feasibility of controlled drinking (Miller & Caddy, 1977), controlled smoking (Frederiksen, Peterson & Murphy, 1976), and even controlled gambling (Dickerson & Weeks, 1979) and controlled opiate use (Harding, Zinberg, Stelmack & Barry, 1980). Is it desirable to arrange for a "substitute substance" as a treatment method? This strategy has been tried in each area: tranquilizers for alcoholics, methadone for heroin addicts, nicotine gum for smokers, satiety-stimulating substances for the obese. A related issue of concern here is the possible transfer of dependence from one substance to another, as may occur when a person discontinues narcotics only to begin heavy use of alcohol or stops smoking but gains a significant amount of weight. In chapter 7, Peter Miller examines some of these pragmatic issues that face practitioners who treat substance abuse disorders.

Perhaps the clearest commonality among the various addictive behaviors is the difficulty of defining an effective and *lasting* intervention. Permanent remission has been the exception, short-term recovery with proximal relapse the rule. Any therapist attempting to meet the challenge of the addictive behaviors must face this quandry: how to help clients maintain their initial gains. It is relatively easy to bring about short-term weight loss or temporary abstinence from alcohol, cigarettes, or drugs. It is not so easy to retain these gains over a long period of time. In their thought-provoking final chapter to this volume, Claudette Cummings, Judith Gordon, and Alan Marlatt propose a new relapse-prevention model that represents an innovative and promising departure from traditional approaches. They posit that the widely accepted disease models of addiction may actually predispose a client to major relapses, and they suggest some alternative strategies for forestalling and foreshortening the infamous ''slips'' that are so characteristic of the addictive behaviors.

Common Transitions

New knowledge brings change, and change brings challenge. The explosion of knowledge in the addictive behaviors is bound to bring about major transitions in treatment and research. Some of these changes are, in fact, already evident.

One has to do with prognosis, the optimism with which treatment is offered. In the recent past, substance abuse disorders have been regarded as largely untreatable personality disturbances, and clients showing addictive behaviors have been labeled as recalcitrant, resistant recidivists. The addictive disorders are rapidly losing their status as hopeless and terminal conditions. The ''DSM-III'' (American Psychiatric Association, 1980)—the newest edition of the American Psychiatric Association's *Diagnostic and Statistical Manual of Mental Disorders*—has removed alcohol and drug abuse from their former classification with the personality disorders. It is interesting that sexual dysfunctions have undergone a similar metamorphosis from refractory personality disturbances to treatable behavior problems as effective treatment methods have become available.

Another transition has to do with the time of intervention. Some traditional alcoholism theorists have held that the alcoholic cannot be treated until he or she ''hits bottom'' and has deteriorated and suffered enough to admit defeat or helplessness. Current priorities are moving toward earlier intervention. The controlled-drinking technologies described in chapter 2 are appropriate for treating the early stages of problem drinking, and there is growing exploration of potential strategies for preventing the development of problem drinking in the first place. Similar prevention efforts targeting the other addictive behaviors have been launched by federal agencies and health maintenance organizations.

Yet another apparent transition regards treatment personnel. Treatment of substance abuse historically has been dominated by the paraprofessional—by the layperson who does not possess advanced training or credentials but who ''has been through it.'' In many states, a personal history of alcoholism with a stated period of continuous abstinence was once the sole sufficient prerequisite for employment as an alcoholism counselor. In some, it was a requirement.

The ideology of "it takes one to treat one" has pervaded the treatment of each of the addictive behaviors to a greater or lesser extent. As the interest and availability of professional personnel in addictive behaviors has increased (usually in direct proportion to the availability of federal funds), disagreements and divisions have arisen regarding the appropriate credentials for treating substance abusers. This has become a controversial issue, particularly in alcohol and drug abuse treatment. It will be a significant challenge for the future to work out cooperative rather than competitive relationships, taking advantage both of the training and expertise of the "professional" and of the experience and cost-effectiveness of the "paraprofessional" (Christensen, Miller & Muñoz, 1978).

Just how much the addictive behaviors have in common remains to be determined. Is it feasible and effective to use similar or even common treatment programs across problem areas? Is dependence transferred from one area to another following the successful treatment of one form of substance abuse? Is "addiction" a useful model for understanding obesity or gambling? Are there common causal factors underlying these various disorders? These and other puzzles of the addictive behaviors will pose worthy Gordian knots for future empirical Alexanders to either untie or cut through.

References

American Psychiatric Association. *Diagnostic and statistical manual of mental disorders.* (3rd ed.) Washington, D.C., Author, 1980.

Christensen, A., Miller, W. R, & Muñoz, R. F. Paraprofessionals, partners, peers, paraphernalia, and print: Expanding mental health service delivery. *Professional Psychology,* 1978, **9**, 249-270.

Dickerson, M. G., & Weeks, D. Controlled gambling as a therapeutic technique for compulsive gamblers. *Journal of Behavior Therapy and Experimental Psychiatry,* 1979, **10**, 139-142.

Frederiksen, L. W., Peterson, G. L., & Murphy, W. D. Controlled smoking: Development and maintenance. *Addictive Behaviors,* 1976, **1**, 193-196.

Harding, W. M., Zinberg, N. E., Stelmack, S. M., & Barry, M. Formerly-addicted-now-controlled opiate users. *International Journal of the Addictions,* 1980, **15**, 47-60.

Krasnegor, N. A. (Ed.) *Behavioral approaches to analysis and treatment of substance abuse.* Washington, D.C., National Institute on Drug Abuse, 1979.

Miller, W. R. (Ed.) *Recent advances in addictions research.* New York: Pergamon Press, 1980.

Miller, W. R., & Caddy, G. R. Abstinence and controlled drinking in the treatment of problem drinkers. *Journal of Studies on Alcohol,* 1977, **38**, 986-1003.

II
TREATMENT APPROACHES AND OUTCOMES

2

Treating the Problem Drinker: Modern Approaches

William R. Miller and Reid K. Hester*

University of New Mexico
Albuquerque, New Mexico 87131

V. A. Hospital
Albuquerque, New Mexico 87131

The well-meaning contention that all ideas have equal merit seems to me little different from the disastrous contention that no ideas have any merit.

Carl Sagan, *Broca's Brain*

*We wish to express special appreciation to our colleagues who read earlier drafts of this chapter and provided their specific and helpful comments—Chad Emrick, Martha Sanchez-Craig, and Betsey Wolff.

Blessed are those who see the size of this chapter but who forgive us our compulsiveness and read it anyhow in search of knowledge, for they shall not be disappointed.

How effectively can problem drinkers be treated? Are some treatment approaches more effective than others? Do certain kinds of problem drinkers respond better than others to treatment in general, or to certain specific therapeutic approaches? Who is best qualified to treat an alcoholic?

These are questions that face any mental health practitioner who comes into contact with problem drinkers—which means virtually every mental health professional. There have been standard accepted answers to these questions. How effective is treatment for alcoholism? Not very. Are some approaches better? No—all treatments are equally ineffective. Do some respond better to treatment than others? Yes—those alcoholics who have "bottomed out" or gone through enough suffering to be motivated for treatment. Who is best qualified to treat alcoholics? Another alcoholic, who's been through it.

These are the easy answers. They continue to be passed down from one year to the next and appear in the most recent writings of some of the most respected professionals in the field. But what support is there for these statements from scientific research? After reading more than 500 treatment outcome studies and writing this chapter, we believe that there is ample reason to question every one of these commonly accepted answers.

So we come to the dual purpose of this chapter: to explain briefly each of the major treatment approaches currently used to help problem drinkers and to carefully examine the evidence regarding the effectiveness of each. We have written this chapter with the practicing professional in mind, highlighting crucial studies and summarizing larger bodies of research, attempting to draw conclusions that will have some practical application for the clinician who must, in the end, decide how to treat each individual.

A brief word about terminology is in order before we begin. You will find us using the terms "problem drinker" and "alcoholic" in seemingly interchangeable fashion. It is our intention, however, to use "problem drinker" as the more generic term, referring to a wider range of individuals—namely, anyone who experiences significant life problems related to their own alcohol use (Cahalan, 1970). We have attempted to use the term "alcoholic," on the other hand, to refer to the more severely disabled end of the continuum of problem drinkers. To be sure, the distinction is often blurred, but this is our intention. All alcoholics are problem drinkers, but not all problem drinkers are alcoholics (Miller & Caddy, 1977).

Average Outcome Rates And "Spontaneous Remission"

Two general kinds of reference points are often discussed in relation to the effectiveness of alcohol treatment programs: average outcome rates and spontaneous remission rates. Both are elusive figures, depending heavily upon how you define and cut the cake.

Average Outcome Rates

There are several ways to calculate average treatment outcome, each producing a slightly different picture. Costello, Biever, and Baillargeon (1977) summarized 80 studies which reported one-year follow-up data and counted "lost" cases as unsuccessful. There is good reason to do the latter, because research has indicated that cases harder to locate in general have poorer outcome (Moos & Bliss, 1978; Wolfe & Holland, 1964). This procedure produces more conservative outcome figures than those which result if abstinence and improved rates are calculated only for those who were located. Defining "success" as the absence of problematic drinking, Costello et al. found success rates to vary between 12% and 45%, with an average of 26%.

Another more common way to cut the cake is to exclude lost cases and to consider only those who could be located and interviewed. In an exhaustive (and probably exhausting) review of research completed between 1952 and 1971, Chad Emrick (1974) catalogued 265 studies, most of which employed this method of outcome calculation. Averaging outcomes across studies, Emrick reported an average abstinence rate of 32%, with an additional 34% rated as "improved," for a total improvement rate of 66%. By weighting studies according to the number of clients treated, Emrick obtained only slightly different figures of 34% abstinent and 33% improved. From this review it might be said that, on the average, 1/3 of those treated will become abstinent, and an additional 1/3 will not abstain but will show improvement. It should be noted, however, that Emrick was including outcome from *all* studies reporting data, regardless of the quality of outcome measures or length of follow-up. The majority of studies report only brief follow-up, if any. This may account for the less optimistic figures reported by Costello et al. (1977).

Other investigators (Gerard, Saenger, & Wile, 1962; Rohan, 1972) have evaluated large samples of treated alcoholics and have reported abstinence rates for one-year follow-up ranging between 18% and 32%, depending upon the stringency of the definition of "abstinence." Improvement was indicated in an additional 12% to 21%.

An issue frequently raised regarding outcome is the lack of evaluation of nondrinking behaviors such as interpersonal and psychological functioning. The majority of studies have relied upon measures of drinking behavior for outcome ratings, although more recent research has begun to incorporate a broader spectrum of variables (e.g., Sobell & Sobell, 1973). Certainly we cannot assume that because a client has modified his or her drinking, improvement will also occur in other areas of life functioning. Nevertheless, most studies to be reviewed in this chapter have relied upon change in drinking pattern to judge outcome, and we regard this as a minimal condition for successful treatment.

Spontaneous Remission

The term "spontaneous remission" refers to recovery without the benefit of formal treatment. The question here, then, is this: What percentage of problem drinkers are likely to recover on their own, if left untreated? It would be helpful to know this in evaluating the relative effectiveness of treatment programs.

There are several problems with the concept of spontaneous remission. In the first place, most studies of "untreated" alcoholics have been of individuals not seeking treatment, or of those beginning treatment but dropping out. Neither sample is likely to be comparable to those individuals who seek and stay in treatment—the group considered in most outcome studies. Emrick (1975) has also pointed out that the term "spontaneous remission" implies that change occurring within therapy is *qualitatively* different from that occurring "naturally" from life processes. It may well be that change inside and outside of therapy proceeds by similar processes (cf. Edwards et al., 1977; Tuchfeld et al., 1976).

Studies which randomly assigned alcoholics to treatment versus no-treatment groups have been rare. Kissin, Platz, and Su (1970a) randomly assigned 41 alcoholics to a no-treatment control condition and found that only two (4.9%) showed improvement. This was lower than the improvement rate (11.2%) among those who dropped out of treatment by the third session ($n = 14$).

Most other studies have evaluated changes in problem drinkers who were not seeking or who refused treatment (Annis & Smart, 1978; Armor et al., 1978; Bailey & Stewart, 1967; Goodwin, Crane, & Guze, 1971; Kendall & Stanton, 1966; Lemere, 1953). Reginald Smart (1976), in an excellent review of this area, constructed a table including a total of nine studies, documenting improvement rates ranging from 4% (Kissin et al., 1968) to 42% (Goodwin et al., 1971). Considering these, plus a recent report by Imber, Schultz, Funderburk, Allen, and Flamer (1976), we calculated an average "remission" (abstinent plus improved) rate of 19% in untreated alcoholics at one year. This is somewhat lower than the remission figures reported by Emrick (1975): 13% abstinent plus 28% improved. These latter figures were based on three studies, however, and Emrick cautions that the quality of measures and length of follow-up were variable.

Summary

Based upon the most recent research, an average of 19% of problem drinkers either not seeking treatment or dropping out of treatment are abstinent or improved a year later. This "spontaneous remission" figure must be regarded cautiously, however, because actual figures have varied widely (4% to 42%). In addition, "spontaneous" recovery within the group most comparable to treated subjects—those seeking treatment but randomly assigned to no treatment—may be much lower. With regard to "average" outcome rates from treatment programs, it appears that 1/3 abstinent and 1/3 improved (but not abstinent) represent reasonable estimates of at least short-term response to treatment. A review restricted to studies with one-year follow-up data, however, suggests that 26% is a representative figure for successful outcome (abstinent plus improved) 12 months after treatment.

Detoxification

Detoxification is the medical process of taking the alcoholic safely through the period of withdrawal from alcohol. It is now well established that alcohol can produce a clear and severe physiological addiction, with a predictable sequence of symptoms occurring when blood-alcohol levels drop during withdrawal. For those individuals who are pharmacologically addicted to alcohol, detoxification is a necessary prerequisite to treatment.

But how many problem drinkers seeking treatment actually require medical detoxification? The percentage will vary, of course, with the population served. Feldman, Pattison, Sobell, Graham, and Sobell (1975) found that only 47% of individuals presenting themselves for acute alcoholism treatment required detoxification and that of these only 19% (9% of the total population) needed inpatient detoxification. It is increasingly clear that for many patients outpatient detoxification is a viable, safe, and cost-effective alternative to standard inpatient care (Rada & Kellner, 1979).

Few professionals think of detoxification alone as a treatment for alcoholism. Chafetz (1967) has opined that "treatment of the acute stage of alcoholism alone is like pouring water into a sieve and being surprised when the floor is wet" (p. 1252). Yet scientific research on the effectiveness of detoxification alone has been sparse. Annis and Smart (1978) reported a follow-up of 522 alcoholics who had had their first admission for detoxification. Six months later, 245 (46.9%) had been rearrested and 271 (52%) had been readmitted one or more times. Drinking behaviors per se were not reported. Annis and Liban (1978) reported a similar three-month follow-up of 70 alcoholics who had been detoxicated, 35 of whom (not randomly chosen) went to a halfway house. Thirteen of 35 matched controls had been rearrested, as compared with two patients from the halfway house. Seventeen of the latter, however, had been readmitted for detoxification (as compared with nine of the controls). Other studies (e.g., Pittman & Tate, 1972) have compared the effectiveness of minimal treatment (including detoxification) with outcome from more extensive treatment programs. These studies will be discussed in a later section of this chapter.

The effectiveness of various medical procedures for safely carrying the alcoholic through acute withdrawal has been comprehensively reviewed in several recent chapters and articles (Gessner, 1979; Hemmingsen, Kramp, & Rafaelsen, 1979; Rada & Kellner, 1979) and will not be elaborated here.

Treatment Approaches Oriented Toward Abstinence

The vast majority of treatment approaches for problem drinkers have set total abstinence from alcohol as a primary goal. We will discuss these approaches first, later turning our attention to a review of the issues and treatment methods associated with an alternative goal of moderation. It is our position that *both* abstinence- and moderation-oriented treatment methods have made substantial contributions to the recovery of problem drinkers, and that selection of appropriate treatment goals and methods should be guided by a knowledge of the findings of current outcome research. It is to this end that we have written this chapter for the alcohol professional.

We will first review those treatment approaches that have been offered primarily as *individual* therapy, notably (a) drug therapies, (b) aversion therapies, (c) hypnosis, (d) psychotherapy, and (e) a few other recent approaches. Discussion will then turn to group methods (including Alcoholics Anonymous) and will conclude with a consideration of family therapies.

The Use of Medications in the Treatment of Problem Drinkers

Disulfiram. Of all the chemical agents that have been used in the treatment of alcoholism, perhaps the most popular has been tetraethylthiuram disulfide or disulfiram (trade name: Antabuse). Originally a chemical used in research with rubber, disulfiram was accidentally discovered to produce a rather violently unpleasant reaction in humans when combined with ordinary beverage alcohol. This reaction, known as the disulfiram-ethanol reaction (DER), is characterized by massive arousal of the autonomic nervous system. The symptoms of the DER include warming and flushing of the face, chest pains and pounding heart, nausea and vomiting, sweating, headache, dizziness, weakness, difficulty in breathing, and a marked drop in blood pressure. As you might expect, this can be quite frightening, and some individuals who have experienced a DER have said that they felt as if they were surely going to die. The precise reason for these symptoms is unclear at the present time. The most common explanation (e.g., Kitson, 1977) is that disulfiram blocks the action of a specific enzyme, aldehyde dehydrogenase, which is involved in the metabolism of the substance acetaldehyde, a metabolic product of alcohol. In the absence of the critical enzyme, acetaldehyde levels build up in the body as long as there is alcohol in the bloodstream. It is uncertain, however, whether the acetaldehyde alone or some other combination of disulfiram and ethanol produces the DER syndrome (Casier & Merlevede, 1962). Disulfiram also alters levels of certain brain chemicals (e.g., dopamine, norepinephrine) involved in neural transmission, which may in turn account for some of the sensitizing effects (Amit & Levitan, 1977; Lake et al., 1977; Rosenfeld, 1960). At any rate, the DER is a most unpleasant experience.

The therapeutic potential of disulfiram was quickly recognized, and by the early 1950s it was in widespread use as a drug for treating alcoholics. It has been promoted as a way of "making a decision once a day instead of hundreds of times a day." As long as the alcoholic continues to take maintenance doses of disulfiram—usually at least twice weekly, if not daily—he or she cannot drink alcohol without risking a DER. It seems, however, that many if not most alcoholics who take disulfiram succumb at least once to the temptation to "try it out," to see whether anything will happen. At the current low maintenance dose (usually 0.5 gm) some individuals find that they are able to have one or two drinks before beginning to experience symptoms of the DER (generally, flushing comes first), although with others one drink may produce a violent reaction. In an attempt to forestall this temptation and perhaps to provide an aversive conditioning trial, early clinics prescribing disulfiram often performed a "challenge" with inpatients, wherein the individual was given disulfiram and then a dose of alcohol—thus experiencing a DER while in the hospital. It was believed that this would dissuade the person from testing the disulfiram again and would also assist the physician in setting the proper maintenance dosage. There is, however, no systematic evidence to indicate that the challenge increases the use or effectiveness of disulfiram (Lundwall & Baekeland, 1971), and it is seldom used in modern practice. Disulfiram itself remains a popular treatment tool.

Side Effects. The professional who includes disulfiram in a treatment package must be concerned with the possibility of side effects. These include skin eruptions, fatigue and drowsiness, headache, impotence, and peculiar aftertastes. These effects do not occur in all patients, seem to be less likely with modern lower-dose levels, and appear to subside over the first few weeks of treatment. Possibly of greater concern is the finding that disulfiram may interfere with normal recovery of serum protein levels (Burnett & Reading, 1970)—perhaps a biochemical substrate of the fatigue that is often observed as a side effect. Other studies have suggested possible deleterious effects of disulfiram upon the central nervous system (Kwentus & Major, 1979; Van Thiel et al., 1977).

Recent research conducted by Dr. William Lijinski (1979) raises additional concern as to the safety of disulfiram. Lijinski found that disulfiram and nitrites (a common substance in human diets, used as a meat preservative) combined to produce cancer of the esophagus in 50% of laboratory animals, whereas no tumors were found in animals receiving only one of these substances. In addition, certain individuals taking disulfiram may develop toxic reactions of varying severity (Goyer & Major, 1979). It is clear that we are only beginning to understand the effects of disulfiram on the body—both therapeutic and otherwise. Finally it should be noted that certain conditions contraindicate the use of disulfiram, including coronary disease, liver disease, diabetes, pregnancy, hypothyroidism, and cerebral damage.

Uncontrolled Studies. Although the literature on disulfiram is quite large, interpretation of findings has been seriously complicated by a number of problems in design and reporting (Lundwall & Baekeland, 1971). Random assignment to disulfiram versus alternatives has seldom been used, producing almost irreparable selection confounds. It is consistently found that patients who voluntarily elect to take disulfiram are substantially different from those who refuse to take it (e.g., Baekeland, Lundwall, Kissin, & Shanahan, 1971; Hoff, 1961; Hoff & McKeown, 1953; Obitz, 1978). It is therefore ambiguous whether successful outcome with disulfiram should be attributed to the drug, to superior motivation of those who take it, or to some other unknown confounding factor. In addition, researchers have often failed to define global outcome descriptors such as ''improved'' or ''successful'' and have frequently failed to specify the period or method of follow-up. Well controlled studies have been few indeed.

An abundance of uncontrolled studies have reported various percentages of successful outcome (ranging from 19% to 89%!) following treatment in multimodal programs in which disulfiram was one component (Baekeland et al., 1971; Baker, Lorei, McKnight, & Duvall, 1977; Bourne, Alford, & Bowcock, 1966; Bowman, Simon, Hine, Macklin, Crook, Burbridge, & Hanson, 1951; Child, Osinski, Bennett, & Davidoff, 1951; Crawford, 1976; Edwards & Dill, 1974; Epstein & Guild, 1951; Ferguson, 1970; Gerrein, Rosenberg, & Manohar, 1973; Hoff, 1961; Hoff & McKeown, 1953; Jacobsen, 1950; Lubetkin, Rivers & Rosenberg, 1971; McClelland, 1974; Martensen-Larsen, 1953; Nørvig & Nielsen, 1956; Ritson, 1969; Shaw, 1951; Wallace, 1952; Wexberg, 1953; Zimberg, 1974). In studies with very large samples, Gerard and Saenger (1966) and Armor, Polich, and Stambul (1978) found elevated improvement rates among patients taking disulfiram as compared with those not taking the drug. Selection biases and the confounding of disulfiram effects with the effects of the treatment components make these studies difficult to interpret. Wexberg (1953), for example, found that patients receiving a standard treatment program *plus* disulfiram shoed a 23% higher remission rate than did patients receiving only standard treatment. Patients *volunterred* to take disulfiram, however, so that differences may be attributable to motivational factors. Hoff (1961) reported that patients accepting disulfiram showed a 76% improvement rate, as compared with 55% among those refusing it.

When he attempted to control for motivation by excluding those dropping out prematurely and lost to follow-up, however, the difference between groups disappeared. Thus, although prognosis seems to be improved for patients who accept and continue to take disulfiram (e.g., Jacobsen, 1950; Ritson, 1969; Wexberg, 1953), this improvement cannot be attributed to the drug on the basis of uncontrolled research.

One interesting question to ask of these outcome data is that of prediction: Of those patients who do take disulfiram, which ones are likely to continue taking it and/or be successful cases? Here, there is some convergence of findings. Individuals who do well with disulfiram appear to be older, with more severe drinking problems, and with fewer psychological complications (Baekeland et al., 1971; Bowman et al., 1951; Hoff & McKeown, 1953). Of course, these characteristics may be associated with successful outcome from *any* abstinence-oriented treatment method and may not be specific to disulfiram. These issues of outcome prediction will be addressed in greater detail later in this chapter.

Controlled Research. Controlled studies of disulfiram have been few. Gallant et al. (1968b) found no difference in success rate at six months among patients receiving group therapy alone, disulfiram alone, group plus disulfiram, or no treatment. In a widely cited study, Wallerstein (1956, 1957, 1958) assigned 178 inpatient alcoholics to one of four treatment groups: (a) disulfiram (including a "challenge" experience of the DER); (b) chemical aversion using emetine (to be discussed later in this chapter); (c) hypnotherapy; and (d) milieu therapy, the basic inpatient program received by all patients. Wallerstein's findings favored disulfiram over alternative approaches. Of those patients in the disulfiram group, 30% were found to be totally abstinent, 15% had had one to several minor slips, and an additional 8% showed reduced alcohol consumption with improved social functioning. This resulted in a total 53% "improved" rate, which compared favorably with the comparable "improved" figures of 24%, 36%, and 26% for groups 2, 3, and 4, respectively.

There are, however, a number of reasons to exercise caution in interpreting Wallerstein's findings. Although patients were alledgedly assigned "randomly" to treatment groups (sequential assignment to groups 1, 2, 3, 4, 1, 2, and so on according to order of admission), several factors raise doubt as to the adequacy of random procedure. Patients showing contraindications to disulfiram or emetine (number unspecified) were, for example, reassigned to another treatment group and remained in the study. In addition, the total group *n*'s, which should have been approximately equal given the described assignment procedure, varied from 39 to 50, with the largest number of patients being in the disulfiram and emetine groups (which should have been the smallest due to exclusions). These differences cannot be accounted for by differential attrition, because all drop-outs are reported to be included in the analyses. In addition to problems in assignment, dependent measures of drinking apparently relied totally upon self-report from an unspecified combination of mail and interview contacts. Follow-up rate was also problematic, with 37% of clients in groups 2, 3, and 4 lost and counted as failures for this reason. Nevertheless, the Wallerstein study remains the best controlled evaluation of oral disulfiram to date.

Disulfiram Implants. Because one of the major problems with oral disulfiram treatment is the discontinuation of medication, the possibility of implanting a long-acting dose of disulfiram has been explored. The usual method is to make a small incision in the lower abdomen and to insert a number of disulfiram tablets (usually about 10) 1-2 cm below the skin within the subcutaneous fat. The incision is then sutured. The entire procedure requires only 15 to 30 minutes (Wilson, 1975).

One major problem with this procedure is that the resulting levels of disulfiram in the bloodstream appear to be quite unpredictable. In general, serum levels tend to be quite low, probably too low to cause a DER in most individuals (Kitson, 1977, 1978). Malcolm et al. (1974) reported that of 58 implanted patients who consumed alcohol, only three experienced a reaction resembling the DER, with the remaining 55 drinking with impunity. Likewise, Wilson et al. (1978) found no detectable serum disulfiram and no DERs in 10 alcoholics challenged with ethanol five days following implant surgery. On the other hand, Wilson and his colleagues (1976, 1978) have reported the occurrence of definite DERs in implant patients drinking at various intervals following discharge. It seems likely, therefore, that there is considerable fluctuation in disulfiram level (both between and within patients) following implant, accounting for the unpredictability of DERs with alcohol consumption (Lewis et al., 1975).

In light of these findings, it is somewhat surprising that the initial outcome evaluations of disulfiram implants have been so favorable. A series of recent uncontrolled studies have reported success rates ranging from 65% to 75%, with implanted patients faring impressively better than comparison groups not receiving implants (Crawford, 1977; Hussain & Harinath, 1972; Kline & Kingstone, 1977; Obholzer, 1974; Whyte & O'Brien, 1974). It should be noted, however, that the cautions that apply to interpretation of uncontrolled studies of oral disulfiram are doubly relevant here. One must question, for example, whether a group volunteering for implant surgery can ever be considered comparable to another group refusing such surgery, regardless of demographic matching. Only adequate control groups with random assignment, preferably including double-blind placebo controls, can circumvent these problems. One such study has been reported (Wilson et al., 1976). In this study, 20 patients were randomly assigned to receive disulfiram or saline implants. Five of the disulfiram and six of the saline implant patients began drinking within the follow-up period (apparently six months). Four of the five disulfiram patients who drank experienced a DER and were subsequently abstinent for at least 90 days. The saline patients, on the other hand, were reported to have continued drinking heavily after their initial episode.

It appears, therefore, that disulfiram implants may increase the probability of sustained periods of abstinence, either through total suppression of drinking or through the occurrence of a DER following drinking. The unpredictability of serum disulfiram levels and the unknown duration of effect (usually reported to be six to eight months) remain important problems in treatment planning.

Summary. It appears that the inclusion of oral disulfiram as a component in a traditional treatment program may significantly elevate improvement rate over that achieved by the same type of program without disulfiram. In situations where patients are given a choice, those electing to take disulfiram fare better than do those who refuse the medication. Disulfiram appears to be particularly successful with older patients having more severe drinking problems but less concomitant psychopathology. Surgical implants of disulfiram likewise appear to enhance improvement in voluntary alcoholic patients.

However, at the present time it is impossible to conclude whether any of these observed effects are due to *specific* action of disulfiram, or to other nonspecific factors such as placebo effect and individual differences in patient motivation. Becker (1979) concludes that, "looking at the whole picture, one is forced to conclude that our current state of knowledge suggests that disulfiram is an 'active placebo' in the usual clinical doses" (p. 297). The efficacy of enforced disulfiram with involuntary patients is unknown at present due to a lack of adequately controlled research. It should be noted that a significant proportion of "improved" or "successful" cases treated with disulfiram have been reported to practice various periods of moderate or attenuated drinking. Both of the most frequently cited studies of oral disulfiram (Gerard & Saenger, 1966; Wallerstein, 1957) regarded as "successful" those clients with moderated drinking and improved social functioning as well as those maintaining continuous abstinence. Controlled drinking has also been reported among some disulfiram implant patients (e.g., Kline & Kingstone, 1977). Future outcome evaluations of disulfiram should therefore carefully assess level and pattern of drinking rather than limiting evaluation to dichotomous status of abstinent vs. drinking (Miller, 1976; Wallerstein, 1957).

Citrated Calcium Carbimide. The toxic side effects of disulfiram have encouraged a search for an alternative drug that would sensitize to alcohol with less risk to the patient. One such alternative chemical is calcium carbimide (also known as cyanamide), a commercial fertilizer and weed killer. The first suggestion of the interaction of this chemical with alcohol came with a 1914 report of workers in a German chemical factory who developed adverse reactions (resembling a mild DER) after drinking and exposure to cyanamide dust (Levy et al., 1967). For human use, calcium carbimide is citrated to slow the absorption process and decrease adverse effects that result when the drug is taken in its raw form (Ferguson, 1956). The resulting substance, citrated calcium carbimide (CCC) does indeed appear to produce a reaction to alcohol similar to the DER, including flushing of the face, headache, and difficulty in breathing (Marconi et al., 1961; Petterson & Kiessling, 1977). CCC differs from disulfiram, however, in that it appears to take effect more quickly (causing an alcohol-CCC reaction within half an hour after administration) and to have a shorter half-life, so that the patient can drink with impunity one day after discontinuing the medication (Bell, 1956). CCC (trade names: Temposil, Abstem) is not currently approved for prescription use in the United States, although it has been manufactured for research use by Lederle Laboratories.

The hope for a less toxic alternative to disulfiram may have been realized in CCC, although more research is needed. Early investigations reported that a majority of patients who had suffered unpleasant side effects from disulfiram failed to show such toxic reactions to CCC (Armstrong & Kerr, 1956; Bell, 1956). In a double-blind evaluation of CCC and disulfiram, Marconi et al. (1960, 1961) found no difference in the total number of complaints of side effects, but when they examined only symptoms that did not occur with placebo and that endured for more than two days, they found that disulfiram produced significantly more of these "serious" side effects. The adequacy of this study must be questioned, however, because patients believed that they were receiving disulfiram throughout the study, and most patients had had prior experience with disulfiram. In addition, alcohol was administered to each patient between one and three times during each drug period, giving patients ample opportunity to observe drug effects. These investigators did find that 20 of 23 patients showed a reaction to alcohol during CCC weeks, as compared with 23 of 23 during disulfiram weeks and only 7 of 23 during placebo weeks.

One consistent difference between CCC and disulfiram appears to be in the severity of cardiovascular effects occurring during an alcohol reaction. Whereas disulfiram characteristically produces a marked drop in blood pressure, chest pains, and EKG abnormalities during the DER, such effects appear to be less common with CCC (Levy et al., 1967; Smith et al., 1957), although they may occur at higher doses of CCC (Lader, 1967). As with disulfiram, adverse symptoms following drinking are relieved by the administration of antihistamines (Smith et al., 1957), a fact that is becoming common knowledge among individuals mandated to disulfiram, who are reported to consume over-the-counter antihistamines in order to be able to continue drinking. Reilly (1976) has reported cases of peripheral neuropathy apparently related to the administration of CCC. Possible risks in the long-term use of CCC are unknown at present.

Serious clinical use of CCC began in the mid-1950s (Armstrong & Kerr, 1956; Bell, 1956; Ferguson, 1956). Because CCC is not an approved medication in the United States, the bulk of research has been conducted in Europe and Japan. Levy, Livingstone and Collins (1967) reported that of 19 patients given CCC, 7 (37%) were known to be abstinent at nine to 14-month follow-up. None of a comparison group of 11 patients receiving disulfiram were known to be abstinent. These investigators also reported that disulfiram produced three times as many side effects as did a placebo, whereas CCC produced fewer symptoms than did a placebo. Griffith Edwards and his colleagues in London (1977) found that two-thirds of their treated patients rated as having "bad or equivocal" outcomes had been given CCC, whereas within the "good" outcome group, only half had received the drug. Thus these two studies, neither of which employed random assignment for CCC, present mixed results.

Certainly the largest volume of research on cyanamide has been produced by a group of investigators at the Kurume University School of Medicine in Japan (Arikawa & Inanaga, 1973; Arikawa, Kotorii & Mukasa, 1972; Arikawa, Naganuma & Oshima, 1972; Mukasa & Arikawa, 1968; Mukasa, Ichihara & Eto, 1964). Their treatment approach has been somewhat unusual in two respects. First of all, their treatment goal has consistently been one of moderation rather than total abstinence. They state that "a forced abstinence by persuasion or threat is an ineffective method in controlling alcoholism. It makes the alcoholic patient 'escape' further toward drinking. Therefore, we do not maintain any negative attitude toward the patient resuming drinking after the administering of the antialcoholic drug" (Arikawa & Inanaga, 1973, p. 11). Secondly, they advocate administration of the drug without the patient's knowledge or consent in a procedure called "Special Therapy" (Arikawa & Inanaga, 1973; Mukasa & Arikawa, 1968; Mukasa et al., 1964). In this method, the members of the problem drinker's family secretly mix CCC (which is colorless, odorless, and tasteless) with his or her food. Dosage level is gradually increased until reaching the maintenance dosage which is "between 20 to 40 mg [daily] to make the patient a moderate drinker" (Arikawa & Inanaga, 1975, p. 11). In a similar procedure known as the "double medication" method, the problem drinker is given a prescription for CCC to be taken voluntarily and, in addition, the family provides secret supplemental doses in the food. The use of deception is justified by these authors because of their finding that very few of their patients voluntarily maintained medication. They conceptualize CCC treatment as a form of aversive counterconditioning that occurs without the patient's awareness, and perhaps without memory (because aversive symptoms occur after drinking).

A recent review of outcome data from these Japanese studies (Pattison, Sobell & Sobell, 1977) reported that of 1,333 patients in three studies (with apparent overlap of patients across studies), 927 (70%) were found to be drinking moderately at follow-up (ranging from three to 72 months), with another 85 (6%) reported as totally abstinent. This overall improvement rate of 76% represents an unprecedented response to a drug therapy for problem drinking and is substantially higher than rates reported from uncontrolled studies of CCC elsewhere. Particularly unusual is the 70% rate of controlled drinking. One possible explanation for this unusually favorable response to CCC may lie in racial factors. Oriental people have been found in recent research to be particularly sensitive to alcohol consumption, possibly due to differing rates of alcohol and acetaldehyde metabolism (Hanna, 1978). Many orientals report symptoms similar to those of a mild DER upon consuming even moderate amounts of alcohol. A drug which further raises acetaldehyde levels by interfering with aldehyde dehydrogenase, then, might be expected to have a more substantial effect within an oriental population. This interesting possibility remains as a subject for future comparative research.

Summary. CCC has been explored as an alternative to disulfiram, but is not currently available by prescription in the United States. Research suggests that it produces fewer toxic side effects than does disulfiram, and appears to place less stress on the cardiovascular system if the patient does consume alcohol. The only extensive research on the effectiveness of CCC has been conducted in Japan; reports indicate high rates of moderate drinking outcomes but low rates of abstinence.

Metronidazole. Metronidazole (trade name: Flagyl) was first used in 1959 for the treatment of urinal and vaginal infections (especially trichomoniasis). One of its side effects, however, appeared to be a metallic taste in the mouth and aversion to the taste of alcohol. With these side effects in mind, Taylor (1964) conducted a clinical trial of metronidazole in the treatment of alcoholics. She reported 90% abstinence in 50 alcoholics for a period of two to five months. Semer et al. (1966) reported on a pilot study using metronidazole and noted that 24 of 26 alcoholics were abstinent for two to five months. In addition, they reported a decrease in anxiety, insomnia, and obesity and increases in work efficiency and appetite (without considering the possibility that the changes may have been due to the period of abstinence per se rather than drug effects).

These early reports of successful treatment of alcoholism with metronidazole received extensive coverage in the lay media, and demand for the drug increased rapidly. Further studies with adequate controls, however, failed to replicate the high success rates noted above.

Platz et al. (1970) in a double-blind study found that patients taking metronidazole had significantly ($p < .05$) more abstinent periods during the second half of treatment than did patients taking placebos. Their findings are difficult to interpret, however, due to the lack of follow-up data.

Lysoff (1972) reported on a double-blind study in which patients were given either metronidazole or placebo during the four weeks of inpatient therapy and were then all given the drug after discharge. Of 83 patients 17 (21%) were lost to follow-up, 40 (48%) were considered failures (i.e., drinking), and 26 (31%) were abstinent. Of these 26, a total of 19 had received the drug during the initial four weeks. Unfortunately, these results were confounded by all patients receiving metronidazole upon discharge from inpatient treatment.

Merry and Whitehead (1968) compared 600 mg. metronidazole dosage plus the standard hospital therapy to the latter alone and found no additional benefits in the maintenance of abstinence for the 30 days of the experiment when the experimental group was compared with (a) its own abstinence rate for the previous 30 days in therapy and (b) the control group.

In a single-blind study, Lowenstam (1969) compared metronidazole to a placebo (Thiamine) in addition to the standard therapy. He reported a nonsignificant but slight trend towards better outcome with the placebo group ("outcome" was evaluated during the course of treatment). One of his conclusions was that if motivated, clients will do as well on placebo as on metronidazole. In 1969, Lal used a single-blind study and attempted to substitute a placebo for metronidazole (and vice versa after two to three months) for a period of one to three months. Because of a high relapse rate (12 of 27 in the drug group within two weeks of discharge), the crossover design was only done on 13 patients. At six-month follow-up, only four of 27 (15%) in both the experimental and the control group (routine hospital therapy) were abstinent.

Well designed double-blind studies have also tended to disconfirm the effectiveness of metronidazole in the treatment of alcoholism. Tyndel, Fraser, and Hartlieb (1969) compared patients on two different dose schedules of metronidazole with two dose-matched placebo groups. Results were compromised by a 53% ($n = 23$) drop-out rate within the first month of treatment, but the overall improvement rate was approximately equal for both drug and placebo groups. They concluded that metronidazole was no more effective than a placebo in decreasing desire for and intake of alcohol, and that motivation to remain abstinent probably played a significant role in the successful outcome.

Gallant et al. (1968a) compared the drug at 1 g/day to chlordiazepoxide at 40 mg/day in a double-blind study with a three- and six-month follow-up. They found nonsignificant differences between metronidazole and chlordiazepoxide groups and noted that success rates for both groups were comparable to those of their standard inpatient program.

Penick and his associates (1969, 1971) randomly assigned 100 patients into either a metronidazole (750 mg/day) or a placebo group. At six-month follow-up on the first 50 patients, nine of 21 (42%) drug and 15 of 23 (65%)

placebo patients were considered successes, i.e., abstaining with only an occasional drink. At a four-year follow-up (Penick et al., 1971) they found that five of 50 (10%) drug and nine of 50 (18%) placebo subjects had been abstinent four years; one placebo subject was drinking moderately. Eleven of these 14 had not been in any other therapy and three had been attending A.A.

One well controlled double-blind study reporting positive findings is that of Swinson (1971), who found significantly more improvement among individuals receiving metronidazole than among those receiving placebo. Prior to one-year follow-up, there had been no significant differences, but at one year 50% of the drug group versus 8% of the placebo group who were still in treatment were improved. If one counts drop-outs as failures, these percentages decline to 32% and 3%, respectively.

Egan and Goetz (1968) compared 23 subjects receiving metronidazole with 23 given placebo and found identical rates of drop-outs ($n=6$), relapses ($n=16$) and successes ($n=1$) for each group during the six months of therapy. Other controlled studies have similarly found no significant advantage of metronidazole over placebo (Egan & Goetz, 1968; Kaplan et al., 1972; Linton & Hain, 1967; Lysoff, 1972).

Summary. Controlled studies of metronidazole have reported mixed results, with the majority finding no difference between drug and placebo in helping individuals to achieve and maintain abstinence (cf. Goodwin & Reinhard, 1972; Rada & Kellner, 1979). Metronidazole appears to have fallen into disuse, with the most recent controlled studies reported in 1972. Use of this drug may be further curtailed by the finding, reported as a warning in the 1980 *Physicians' Desk Reference*, that metronidazole produces cancer in laboratory animals.

Psychotropics. Given the heterogeneous nature of alcoholic populations, it is not surprising that some percentage will show concomitant psychopathology ranging from mild to severe. Psychotropic medications are those intended to directly influence mental state and to alleviate symptoms such as depression and anxiety. Psychotropics have been used extensively in the detoxification process (Gessner, 1979; Rada & Kellner, 1979), but our attention here will be devoted to their longer-term use with problem drinkers in an effort to reduce or eliminate alcohol abuse. The underlying assumption here is that if certain psychiatric symptoms are alleviated, the excessive use of alcohol will also abate. Unfortunately, the majority of evaluative studies have examined *only* the impact of drugs upon psychological measures such as depression scales or the Minnesota Multiphasic Personality Inventory, without directly assessing changes in drinking behavior. Follow-up periods have also typically been short, usually a few weeks following the onset of treatment. Summarizing methodology in this area, Baekeland (1977) wrote, ''Drug treatment of alcoholism has been one of the most carelessly and mechanically treated areas of research, careless because of the enormous proliferation of uncontrolled studies, mechanical because of the blind application of double blind techniques with utter disregard of many other equally important methodological requirements (p. 471).''

The number of studies of pharmacotherapy for alcoholism is genuinely overwhelming. Rather than attempting to review the methodology and findings of each report, we propose instead to summarize the results of major research, presenting representative or critical studies as appropriate.

Minor Tranquilizers. Next to alcohol, the minor tranquilizers represent some of the most widely used and abused drugs in our society. These drugs have been prescribed for alcoholics primarily because of their "antianxiety" action which calms without the heavy sedation typical of barbiturates, and with less apparent risk of pharmacologic addiction.

The first thing one notices in reviewing research on minor tranquilizers, of which chlordiazepoxide (trade name: Librium) is the most commonly used, is an extraordinarily high drop-out rate, averaging 47% in the studies we reviewed. Many studies have simply excluded these cases in calculating success rates.

Overall, the findings of controlled and comparative studies of minor tranquilizers do not paint an optimistic picture of their effectiveness with problem drinkers. Abstinence and improvement rates tend to be comparable across drug and placebo or no-drug groups (Bartholomew & Guile, 1961; Carlsson & Fasth, 1976; Charnoff et al., 1963; Mooney et al., 1961; Rosenberg, 1974; Shaffer et al., 1963). Both Gerard and Saenger (1966) and Mayer and Myerson (1971) found lower improvement rates (on drinking measures) within groups receiving tranquilizers than among patients receiving no medication. Hoff (1961), on the other hand, found better improvement on drinking measures in a Librium-treated group, as compared with a matched control at three to twelve month follow-up. The absence of random assignment in these studies, however, renders the comparability of groups uncertain. At any rate, current data do not support minor tranquilizers as an effective adjunct in alcoholism treatment, and limited evidence suggests that their effect may be a negative one in certain populations.

Tranquilizer/Antidepressant Combinations. The outlook for combinations of antianxiety and antidepressant medications is only slightly brighter. Kissin and Gross (1968) reported a "success" rate of 28% with a Librium/Tofranil combination, compared with rates of 19% for Librium alone, 0% for Tofranil alone, and 12.5% for placebo. Unfortunately, the criteria for success were not stated. In a subsequent study (Kissin et al., 1970b), the tranquilizer-antidepressant combination was found to produce "total or near abstinence" in 16%, compared with 22% in psychotherapy, 22% in standard hospital treatment, and 6% for untreated controls. Length of follow-up was stated as "one year after registration." Shaw et al. (1975), using the same drug combination, found few differences in comparison to a placebo group on measures of depression. One important consideration is pointed out in a study by Baekeland and Lundwall (1975) who found no significant differences between drug-combination and placebo groups. When patients actually *taking* adequate doses of medication were compared with patients faithfully taking placebo, however, significant differences emerged. This factor of patient compliance is one that is seldom recognized and controlled for in drug research in this area, and may account in part for the generally dismal lack of effectiveness that has been reported.

Antidepressants. The data on antidepressants look a bit more promising. Four studies (Akiskal et al., 1974; Butterworth, 1971; Shaffer et al., 1964; Wilson et al., 1970) have reported significant improvement in groups receiving antidepressant medication, although outcome measures have largely been limited to indices of depression. Akiskal et al. (1974) reported four depressed subjects with concomitant secondary alcoholism to be "symptom free" at one- to two-year follow-up. Otherwise, the impact of antidepressant medication upon drinking behavior has been unspecified. It appears that certain antidepressant medications are at least effective in alleviating depressive symptoms in alcoholics.

Antipsychotics. Uncontrolled studies employing antipsychotic medications to treat alcoholics (Fox & Smith, 1959; Gerard & Saenger, 1966; Lowenstam, 1967) have reported improvement rates ranging from 16% to 88%! Fox and Smith (1959), for example, used promazine routinely "to block the overflow of tension from the thought process to the physical system (p. 771)" and reported some or good progress in 39% of their patients. As is frequently the pattern, however, double-blind controlled studies (Butterworth & Watts, 1974, Turek et al., 1973) have not reported impressive results. In general, all groups (including placebo) have tended to improve on various measures of psychopathology, with few or no significant differences between groups. Drinking data are again not reported in most studies. In the absence of supporting data, treating nonpsychotic alcoholics with major tranquilizers seems a bit like hunting shrew with an elephant gun.

Lithium. Studies of lithium treatment of alcoholics, like those of the antianxiety drugs, have been troubled by high drop-out rates (averaging 48%). If one considers those who do remain in treatment, however, there are indications that depressed alcoholics receiving lithium drink significantly less and have had fewer relapses at follow-up in comparison to patients receiving only placebo (Kline et al., 1974; Merry et al., 1976). Young and Keeler (1977) have urged caution in interpreting such findings, however. They note that their data on 15 alcoholics with bipolar affective disorder (10 of whom relapsed) indicate that patients who are lost to follow-up may be unlocated because of excessive drinking. The high attrition rates reported in lithium studies to date suggest caution in drawing conclusions about the drug's effectiveness with alcoholics.

Other Drugs. A variety of other medications have been employed in treating alcoholics. Emetine, apomorphine, and succinylcholine have had specific applications in aversion therapy, to be discussed later. Anorexigenic agents have been tried without marked success (e.g., Krasner et al., 1976). Propranolol has shown mixed but encouraging success in relieving symptoms of anxiety and depression in alcoholics (Rada & Kellner, 1979). Multivitamin therapy has also received mixed support (Gerard & Saenger, 1966; Hoff, 1961; Rada & Kellner, 1979), with the principal benefits being those accruing from vitamin supplementation, rather than any marked influence upon drinking behavior.

Summary. In the most comprehensive review of the drug literature to date, Rada and Kellner (1979) conclude that "No drug has been conclusively shown to attenuate drinking in controlled studies, and there is little evidence that the elimination of target symptoms improves the recidivism rate. Presently there appears to be a discrepancy between clinical practice and research findings" (p. 129). Indeed, in spite of the very mixed nature of the literature, psychotropic drugs retain their status as one of the most common treatment methods for problem drinkers (Pattison, 1977). Neither the absolute effectiveness of psychotropic medications nor their implicit strategy—to modify drinking by alleviating affective states—has been validated (cf. Mottin, 1973). Pattison (1977) has observed, "The fact that an acute alcoholic patient manifests anxiety, depression, and cognitive dysfunction does not mean that these transient disturbances are basic syndromes with specific target symptoms requiring intensive psychotropic medication" (p. 263). Perhaps with increasingly careful differential diagnosis, subclasses of alcoholics will be identified for whom certain medications will prove therapeutic (Winokur et al., 1970, 1971). In the meantime, the routine prescription of psychotropic medications for problem drinkers remains a practice without scientific support.

Hallucinogens. In the late 1950s through the 1960s lysergic acid diethylamide (LSD) enjoyed a flurry of popularity as a treatment for alcoholism. LSD was hypothesized to help the alcoholic develop insight, break down inappropriate defenses, produce marked personality changes and make her or him more amenable to psychodynamic psychotherapy. Actual procedures varied somewhat. Smith (1958) reported that the therapist present took an attitude of exhortation, persuasion, and suggestion to help the alcoholic "hit bottom" artifically while on LSD. Pahnke et al. (1970) described three other types of LSD therapy: (a) "psycholytic" in which low doses were accompanied by psychoanalysis; (b) "psychedelic" chemotherapy (i.e., LSD with minimal or no therapy), and (c) psychedelic-peak therapy in which large doses were given to achieve a "peak" experience with intense psychotherapy before and after. Most studies tended to use moderate to high doses of LSD in combination with dynamic psychotherapy.

Early uncontrolled studies reported abstinence rates following LSD treatment ranging from 38% at 14-month follow-up (O'Reilly & Funk, 1964) to 94% at six-month follow-up (Chwelos et al., 1959), with an average abstinent-plus-improved rate of about 53% (Bryce, 1970; Chandler & Hartman, 1960; Cheek & Holstein, 1971; Eisner & Cohen, 1958; MacLean, MacDonald, Byrne & Hubbard, 1961; Pahnke et al., 1970; Smith, 1958).

These uncontrolled studies of LSD were soundly criticized on methodological grounds by Smart and Storm (1964). Following this article, there was a small explosion of well controlled studies on LSD, which eventually rang the death knell for its use as a treatment for alcoholics. The pattern of results in these studies (Bowen, Soskin, & Chotlos, 1970; Denson & Sydiaha, 1970; Hollister, Shelton, & Krieger, 1969; Smart, Storm, Baker, & Solursh, 1966; Johnson, 1969, 1970; Ludwig, Levine, & Stark, 1970; Ludwig, Levine, Stark, & Lazar, 1969) illustrates the hazards of developing a treatment technique on the basis of uncontrolled studies. Typically, LSD subjects showed marked short-term improvements on personality measures and increased levels of abstinence. When compared to placebo drug and non-drug controls, however, there were no significant differences on measures of drinking behaviors or psychosocial adjustment.

Two controlled studies, however, did not fit this pattern of results. Jensen and Ramsay (1963) reported an abstinence plus improved rate of 74% (46/62) for LSD and 41% (12/29) for a control group of alcoholics at six-to 18-month follow-up. The combination of a non-randomized assignment into treatment groups and a 47% (26/55) lost to follow-up rate for the control group, however, make the results uninterpretable. Tomsovic and Edwards (1970) reported a significant difference in abstinence rates for nonschizophrenic alcoholic volunteers who either did or did not receive LSD. Fourteen (44%) and three (11%) respectively, were abstinent at one year. When the LSD group was compared to a control group who had not volunteered to take LSD, there were no significant differences between groups. In addition, a dropout rate of 37% to 42% for the groups brings into question the overall frequency of abstinence for patients in this study on the whole.

A single study of the shorter-acting hallucinogen dipropyltryptamine (DPT) was conducted by Soskin, Grof, and Richards (1973). Using a within-subjects design, they conducted an average of eight psychotherapeutic interviews with each of the 18 patients given either placebo or DPT in a double-blind design. Both therapists and patients indicated that greater progress was made during DPT interviews, as compared with placebo. No effect upon drinking behavior was noted, however. Poor outcome with DPT (75% unimproved) has been reported by Faillace et al. (1970).

Summary. Although early studies of the use of LSD as a treatment for alcoholics reported positive results, controlled studies have found equally positive treatment outcomes within control groups. Following these reports there was a rapid demise in the use of LSD with alcoholics, and we found no reports of its use in the literature since 1971. This serves as one more historical lesson that controlled studies of treatment techniques are necessary to establish the efficacy of any therapeutic intervention.

Aversion Therapies

As applied to problem drinking, the aversion therapies attempt to interrupt drinking behavior by creating an aversion or distaste for alcoholic beverages. This therapeutic approach was originally based upon Pavlovian concepts of conditioning (Kantorovich, 1930), although, as we shall see, there is now substantial reason to question whether classical conditioning is in fact the basis for the effectiveness of these methods. Aversion therapy has usually, although not always (Lovibond & Caddy, 1970), been employed toward a goal of total abstinence.

Procedurally, the aversion therapies are relatively simple. Conditioning stimuli (in this case, alcohol beverages) are repeatedly paired with an unconditioned stimulus which is powerfully unpleasant. The desired effect is for the unpleasantness of the unconditioned stimulus to generalize and become associated with the sight, smell, and taste of alcohol. A variety of unconditioned stimuli have been used and we will review these separately within this section: (a) chemical agents such as emetine, apomorphine and succinylcholine; (b) electrical stimulation; and (c) aversive imagery.

Nausea-Producing Drugs. Voegtlin, Lemere, and their associates at Shadel Hospital in Seattle, Washington, began using emetine aversion for alcoholics in 1935 (Voegtlin, 1940). The typical procedure consists of an intramuscular injection of emetine hydrochloride, producing nausea and vomiting. Prior to the onset of nausea, the patient is given alcoholic drinks to consume and later vomit. The cycle of emesis and consumption of alcohol continues for about 30 minutes per session. A patient typically receives about five aversive conditioning sessions on an inpatient basis, with additional "boosters" scheduled at various invervals after discharge, depending upon the institution. The object of the treatment is to provide the alcoholic with a temporary, involuntary "time-out" from alcohol abuse by creating an aversion to the taste, sight, and smell of alcohol. During this time-out, the alcoholic has the opportunity to rearrange his or her life and develop behavioral patterns which are incompatible with alcohol abuse.

Interestingly, the process of chemical aversion appears to proceed not according to standard classical conditioning rules, but rather through the mechanism of taste aversion, a phenomenon clearly demonstrated in animal learning in which the delay between CS and UCS can be as long as several hours (Baker & Cannon, 1979; Boland et al., 1978). Other recent experimental research suggests that the critical pairing is between sickness and the *taste* of beverages, and that attempts to pair sickness with the state of intoxication itself may even be countertherapeutic (Revusky et al., 1979).

Between 1940 and 1950, the Shadel Hospital group published numerous treatment outcome studies which reported abstinence rates in their patients ranging from 60% (Lemere & Voegtlin, 1950) to 70% at one year (Voegtlin & Broz, 1949), with most reporting rates in the low 60s (Lemere et al., 1942; Voegtlin, 1940; Voegtlin, Lemere, Broz, & O'Hollaren, 1941, 1942).

More recently, Wiens, Montague, Manaugh, and English (1976) reported a 63% abstinence rate at one year with a 92% follow-up rate for 261 patients at the Raleigh Hills Hospital in Portland, Oregon. Similar outcomes are not unexpected, however, since both hospitals share a common ancestry, have relatively similar treatment programs and have tended to treat clients with similar characteristics.

Neuberger, Matarazzo, Schmidt, and Pratt (in press) reported one year follow-up results of 275 and 290 patients treated in 1975 and 1976 respectively at the Raleigh Hills Hospital in Fair Oaks, California. They reported an abstinence rate (allowing for one "slip") of 107 (39%) and 146 (50%) for the two respective samples. These rates are substantially lower than those found by Wiens et al. (1976); the poorer results may have been a result of the characteristics of the Neuberger et al. sample. In their groups only 35% and 39% of the 1975 and 1976 samples, respectively, were employed as compared to 92% in the Wiens study. In addition the Fair Oaks samples, by comparison with the Portland sample, were "not as stable maritally, . . . included some medicare recipients and consumed more alcohol per day" (p. 8). In a post-hoc analysis, total abstinence rates of married, employed, and both married and employed clients were 55%, 66%, and 75% respectively for the combined Fair Oaks samples.

In vivid contrast, Wallerstein's (1957) study comparing emetine aversion, milieu therapy, disulfiram, and hypnotherapy reported an abstinence rate of only 4%, with an additional 20% improved at three to 24 months within the emetine group. In addition, it appears that virtually all of these had required reconditioning, which introduces a motivational confound into the results.

Thimann (1949) and Miller, Dvorak, and Turner (1960) have reported total abstinence rates of 51% and 49% respectively, but they failed to describe client characteristics. Because of this, comparisons between these and the studies done at Shadel and Raleigh Hills Hospitals are difficult.

Although abstinence rates between 60% and 70% in the Shadel and Raleigh Hills studies appear to be relatively good treatment outcomes for one year, it would be overstepping the limits of the data to conclude that chemical aversive conditioning should yield similar results for all alcoholics. Voegtlin and his associates (Voegtlin, 1940, 1947a, b; Voegtlin & Broz, 1949) and Wiens et al. (1976) repeatedly stress the importance of patient characteristics as factors in successful treatment outcome with chemical aversive conditioning. Voegtlin and Broz (1949) reported that marital status (married patients did better), length of drinking history independent of age (longer histories tended to remain abstinent longer), and type of occupation and financial status (the higher the status/job, the better the prognosis) were important factors in treatment outcome at Shadel Hospital. Lemere (1947) noted that poor results had been achieved with patients less than 30 years old. He also discussed aspects of the program which tended to increase its success rate. One factor was that the hospital was for alcoholics only, creating feelings of sanctuary and community with other patients instead of shame. He also noted the low rate of neuroses once patients were sober, the voluntary nature of the program, and the substantial fee for treatment.

Relatedly, Lemere and Voegtlin (1950) reported that 100 charity cases (i.e., no fee) had been treated with discouraging results and concluded that "conditioned-reflex" therapy is of value primarily to advantageously circumstanced types of alcoholic patients. To conclude then that chemical aversive conditioning should be used with all alcoholics is clearly inappropriate. Although reported success rates have been high, the treatment outcome studies described above are lacking in control groups and are confounded by expectancy factors and by select samples which have relatively good prognosis and might benefit equally from other types of treatment interventions.

Other agents have been used to induce nausea. Apomorphine was employed in the early Shadel studies, but has largely been discarded in favor of emetine because of the undesirable hypnotic and tranquilizing side-effects of apomorphine and because of comparatively poorer outcomes (Beil & Trojan, 1977; Feldman, 1950; Halvorsen & Mertensen-Larsen, 1978; Schlatter & Lal, 1972). Baker and Cannon (1979) caution against the potential toxic effects of emetine at high doses and describe an alternative and medically conservative procedure that produces equivalent nausea by using syrup of ipecac and low doses of emetine (cf. Baker et al., 1978). Baker and Cannon also provided the first clear experimental verification that chemical aversion does indeed produce a conditioned taste aversion to the tastes of alcohol beverages. Boland, Mellor, and Revusky (1978) advocated the use of lithium as the aversive agent because it has a shorter half-life than does emetine and appears to produce more robust taste aversions in animals. In a pilot study with 25 patients, they found an abstinence rate of 36% at six months following aversion treatment with lithium (47% if only patients who became sick are counted), as compared with a 12% rate within a comparable control group treated with citrated calcium carbimide (discussed earlier). The high toxicity of lithium and the fact that it does not produce a dependable nausea response make the relative utility of this drug as a UCS questionable, however (Baker & Cannon, 1979).

Summary. It appears that emetine aversive conditioning has been used with relative success within certain patient populations having intact jobs and marriages, middle class or higher socioeconomic status and sufficient motivation to pursue an expensive and unpleasant treatment program. Abstinence rates within this group tend to be between 60% and 70% at one year. Effectiveness within other populations is less clear.

Succinylcholine. During the 1960s, succinylcholine (Scoline) was used on an experimental basis in an attempt to create an aversion to alcohol by pairing it with a traumatic event. Succinylcholine is a curare-like drug which produces a total paralysis of the muscles, including those involved in breathing. Just prior to injection the patient is given alcohol to see, smell, and taste. The drug is given intravenously in a dose sufficient to produce apnea for about 60 seconds, a highly terrifying experience. Sanderson, Campbell, and Laverty (1963) reported preliminary results of a clinical trial of succinylcholine with 12 alcoholics. They noted a 50% abstinence rate over an unspecified period of time. Further investigations reported much poorer results, with abstinence rates ranging from 9.5% to 40% (Clancy et al., 1967; Farrar et al., 1968; Holzinger et al., 1967; Laverty, 1966; Madill et al., 1966). The highest rate (40%) was found in a single-blind study by Clancy et al. (1967), who also reported a 35% abstinence rate at one year in a placebo group. The drug treatment group was not significantly different from the placebo group in either abstinence or improvement rate at one year. In view of this relatively large placebo/expectancy factor, the poor outcomes in most studies, and the drastic nature of the treatment, succinylcholine aversion therapy has fallen into justifiable disuse.

Electrical Aversion. Because of the rather extreme unpleasantness of chemical aversion and because of medical contraindications to the use of emetine, various writers have advocated the use of electric shock as an alternative unconditioned stimulus. Shock as the UCS offers a range of technical advantages including greater control over onset, intensity and duration, greater feasibility of repeated trials within one session, and greater amenability to partial schedules of reinforcement, all of which theoretically should improve maintenance (Franks, 1970; McGuire & Vallance, 1964; Rachman, 1965; Rachman & Teasdale, 1969). Studies using electrical aversion have varied widely with regard to the intensity and duration of shock used, the conditioning paradigm employed, and the site to which shock was delivered (e.g., fingers, feet, leg, face). (Electrical aversion should not be confused, however, with electroconvulsive therapy in which current is passed through the brain.)

The earliest published report of electrical aversion with alcoholics appeared in Russia in 1930 (reported by Razran, 1934). In this report, Kantorovich described the use of shock aversion to suppress drinking behavior. In comparison to ten control subjects treated by "hypnotherapy and medication," 20 aversion subjects (apparently not randomly assigned) showed longer periods of time until relapse (mean of three months as opposed to 11 days for controls). At three months following treatment, however, only 25% remained abstinent.

Electrical aversive counterconditioning has received extensive investigation in the intervening 50 years. A variety of uncontrolled group and case studies have reported improvement rates ranging from 0% to about 60% (Blake, 1965, 1967; Ciminero et al., 1975; Claeson & Malm, 1973; Hsu, 1965; McGuire & Vallance, 1965; Michaelsson, 1976; Miller & Hersen, 1972; Morosko & Baer, 1970). Once again, however, nonrandomized designs yield results that are difficult to interpret because of the motivational confound inherent in selection for aversive treatment procedures such as disulfiram and electrical counterconditioning. Fortunately, a number of studies have employed randomized or matching designs to compare alternative forms of shock aversion with each other or with other treatment approaches. Several studies have found that treatment programs which include electrical counterconditioning procedures produce favorable outcomes by comparison with "conventional" approaches (Glover & McCue, 1977; Hallam et al., 1972; Lovibond, 1975; Vogler et al., 1970), though others have found no significant difference in effectiveness (McCance & McCance, 1969). Miller (1978a) reported that clients receiving only electrical aversion improved more slowly but did not differ significantly from those receiving two alternative treatment programs focusing on self-control. In these controlled studies, improvement rates have ranged from 20% to 60%.

What accounts for the wide range of outcome observed in these studies? Several relevant factors have been explored. Miller, Hersen, Eisler, and Hemphill (1973) randomly assigned subjects to high versus low levels of shock intensity and found no significant difference in efficacy. These findings are consistent with the clinical literature in general, in that studies employing very severe shock intensities and durations (e.g., Hsu, 1965) show no better outcome than do those employing milder shock levels or shock intensities under the control of the clients themselves (e.g. Miller, 1978). More severe shock intensities do appear, however, to lead to higher rates of client drop-out from treatment (e.g., Devenyl & Sereny, 1970; Hsu, 1965).

The use of periodic booster sessions has been found to be associated with improved outcome (e.g., Vogler et al., 1970), although lack of random assignment renders these results equivocal because of the selection factor involved in whether or not patients return for booster sessions.

The type of conditioning stimulus (e.g., looking at or holding the beverage, sniffing it, sipping, swallowing, etc.) appear to have relatively little impact upon outcome as long as actual beverages are used. Studies which have employed pictures or slides of beverages as the sole conditioning stimuli, however, have had uniformly poor outcome (e.g., Hedberg & Campbell, 1974; MacCulloch et al., 1966). There is probably something to be said for delivering shocks at unpredictable intervals spaced throughout the chain of drinking behaviors. Certainly it is clear that a variety of beverages should be used if generalization is desired, because counterconditioning of a single type appears to generate avoidance of that beverage alone, with a consequent shift to alternative drinks (Ciminero et al., 1975; Quinn & Henbest, 1967).

Explorations of alternative shock paradigms have yielded interesting re-sults. Vogler and his colleagues (1970) randomly assigned clients to *escape conditioning* (in which they could terminate shock by spitting out the beverage), *pseudoconditioning* (in which equivalent shocks were delivered randomly), and *sham conditioning* groups (same procedure but no shocks delivered). A one-year follow-up of these groups (Vogler, et al., 1971) revealed no significant differences between escape conditioning and pseudoconditioning groups, though both groups that received shocks fared better than did the sham group. Similarly, Devenyl and Sereny (1970) found no difference between two groups receiving *punishment paradigm* conditioning (contingent but nonescapable shock) and two groups receiving *backward conditioning* (UCS preceding CS), although the study was plagued by a high drop-out rate and uniformly dismal outcome. Lain and Schoenfield (1974), using viewing time of alcoholic-stimulus slides as their dependent measure, failed to find differences in conditioning among four groups: classical paradigm, avoidance paradigm, random shock and no-shock controls. Similar findings were reported by Holmes (1972) who used actual beverages as stimuli. These studies question whether in fact classical conditioning is the critical element in electrical aversion therapy. Numerous studies have failed to find evidence of a conditioned emotional response or have found such response to be unrelated to outcome or treatment (Hallam & Rachman, 1972; Hallam et al., 1972; MacCulloch et al., 1966; Regester, 1971). Interestingly, several investigators have reported that the "conditioned aversion" resulting from electrical aversive counterconditioning, when it does occur, is experienced not as anxiety, but rather as a *distaste* for alcohol or a loss of *desire* to drink (e.g., Lovibond & Caddy, 1970). It appears that a classical conditioning model does not account well for the pattern of outcome resulting from electrical aversion therapy.

In an important unpublished study, Marlatt (1973) randomly assigned inpatient alcoholics to four alternative forms of electrical aversion: (1) punishment paradigm, (2) escape conditioning, (3) avoidance conditioning, and (4) noncontingent punishment. A fifth group, also randomly assigned, received only the normal inpatient hospital treatment program given to all patients. Results from three-month follow-up are instructive. If the criterion for "success" is total abstinence, the groups did not differ significantly. The largest percentage of abstainers was found, in fact, in the "hospital control" group. If abstinent or improved patients are counted, all groups appear to be equally efficacious. Over all groups, 21% of patients were abstinent, but an additional 64% were rated as improved. However, if one considers still a third outcome criterion—the *degree* of reduction in drinking—the pattern is quite different. The punishment paradigm group showed the greatest reduction by far (94%), with the escape, avoidance, noncontingent, and control groups showing reductions of 69%, 65%, 23%, and 42% respectively. Preliminary 12-month follow-up data reflected similar trends. This study, then, supports the use of punishment paradigm over alternative forms of electrical aversion. Consistent with these findings, studies reporting the highest rates of improvement have been those employing either a punishment (Claeson & Malm, 1973; Hallam et al., 1972; Miller, 1978) or an escape paradigm (Blake, 1967; Lunde et al., 1970).

Marlatt's study also points to another important and often overlooked aspect of this approach. This is the fact that shock aversion appears to produce a relatively high rate of nonabstinent "improved" cases, even when the treatment goal has been total abstinence. In a number of studies of electrical aversion, the percentage of cases showing moderated drinking has exceeded the percentage of abstinent outcomes (Bhakta, 1971; Glover & McCue, 1977; Hallam et al., 1972; Lovibond, 1975; Marlatt, 1973; Miller, 1978). Clearly it is essential, in evaluating outcome, to consider successful moderation as well as abstinence. The failure to do so may account for some of the wide variability in reported outcomes.

In 1970, Lovibond and Caddy introduced a variation of electrical aversive counterconditioning in a study that proved to be a milestone in the treatment of problem drinking. Although the goal in this and several subsequent studies was moderation rather than total abstinence, they will be discussed here because of their implications for electrical aversive counterconditioning. Noting that shock aversion tended to reduce desire for alcohol, they reasoned that problem drinkers might be trained to lose their desire to drink *beyond* a moderate level of intoxication. They allowed their clients to consume alcohol sufficient to raise blood alcohol to 65 mg%, and then began a program of punishment paradigm shock aversion, requiring clients to continue drinking and receiving shocks contingent upon drinking behaviors. This method was combined with several other treatment components to be described later in this chapter, and yielded "complete success" in 21 of 28 cases, with three additional cases "improved." A randomly assigned comparison group received noncontingent shocks, but unfortunately a high differential drop-out rate in this group (eight of 13) prevented the authors from completing the comparison. Nevertheless, the total improvement rate of 86% at 12 months is impressive.

Attempts to replicate these findings have been mixed. Caddy and Lovibond (1976) and Lovibond (1975) have reported similarly encouraging improvement rates of 85% and 80% respectively, although the rates of "complete success" were lower than before (38% at 12 months and 59% at one to nine months, respectively). Ewing and Rouse (1976), on the other hand, were spectacularly unsuccessful in their attempt to teach controlled drinking. In long-term follow-up interviews from 27 to 55 months following treatment, no patients were found to be maintaining consistent controlled drinking (although nine of 14 were reported to be abstaining!). Several methodological problems cloud interpretation of this study, however. Of 25 patients beginning the program, only 14 completed six or more sessions—a drop-out rate of 44%. The authors also apparently considered a patient to be relapsed if he or she had a single period of excessive drinking, because outcome is reported in terms of the "poorest" rating during any follow-up block. Nevertheless, these findings are so discrepant from the reports of other investigators that they merit consideration, especially in light of the length of follow-up.

A second team of investigators (Maxwell et al., 1974) likewise failed to replicate the positive findings of Lovibond and Caddy (1970). Caddy (1975) has criticized this study as failing to replicate the precise treatment program originally employed by Lovibond and Caddy. Although not fully described in the original report, Lovibond and Caddy's program included a number of additional self-control components that appear, from subsequent research, to be critical elements. Caddy and Lovibond (1976) have more fully described all of the components of their original approach.

Because electrical aversion has been most often offered to clients as one element in a multimodal treatment program (a la Lovibond & Caddy, 1970), one might ask whether the shock aversion component is either necessary or sufficient to successful treatment outcomes. Several studies have examined this question and have come to a fairly consistent conclusion. Caddy and Lovibond (1976) randomly assigned clients to versions of their multimodal program with and without the electrical aversion component. They found that removal of the shock aversion component resulted in a modest decline in overall improvement rate (60% versus 80% for the full program) and, although a statistical contrast of these two groups was not reported, it appears that the difference would not have been significant. Similarly, Vogler, Compton, and Weissbach (1975) found that a multimodal program including electrical aversion produced better results (though not significantly better in most cases) on all outcome measures than did a group receiving "alcohol education and behavioral counseling" that required about half as much therapist contract. The former group showed an 80% reduction in alcohol consumption, as compared with a 42% reduction in the latter condition. Vogler et al. (1977b) reported similar findings for a population of nonalcoholic problem drinkers: a group receiving electrical aversion showed no greater improvement than did two other groups receiving similar multimodal programs but without aversion therapy. In a very similar study, Miller (1978a) compared a behavioral counseling condition with a more extensive treatment program that included electrical aversion in the manner of Lovibond and Caddy. In this study, the group *not* receiving electrical aversion showed superior outcome (though again not significantly) at three-month follow-up, with differences disappearing by 12-month follow-up. In both the Miller and the Vogler studies, clients in the multimodal conditions received everything given to the "behavioral counseling" clients, *plus* electrical aversion and several other elements. The contribution of shock aversion to the effectiveness of multimodal programs for problem drinkers appears to be minimal at best, and in certain cases may even exert a negative influence.

One final form of electrical aversion therapy must be considered before we proceed to the examination of other forms of counterconditioning. Sobell and Sobell (1973b), in their landmark study, included the use of electric shocks contingent upon overdrinking behaviors in an avoidance learning paradigm. In a procedure piloted earlier by Schaefer (1972; Mills, Sobell & Schaefer, 1971), clients were instructed in certain "rules" for moderate drinking (e.g., maximum sip size, minimum spacing of sips) and received shocks for rule violations. This method was applied within a complex multimodal program. Clients with a goal of abstinence and those with a goal of controlled drinking both showed greater initial improvement than did their respective control groups, replicating earlier pilot data (Schaefer, 1972). Over three years of follow-up, however, this significant difference held up only for those clients with a goal of controlled drinking (Caddy, Addington, & Perkins, 1978). Once again the relative contribution of the shock contingency within this complex treatment program is unknown. The fact that most patients in this study received very few or no shocks would question whether any kind of counter-conditioning occurred. Furthermore, both Miller (1978a) and Vogler and his colleagues (1975) have reported no significant difference in effectiveness between behavioral treatment programs with and without a shock contingency training program modeled after that of Sobell and Sobell (1973b).

A Comparison of Chemical and Electrical Aversion. In 1978, Jackson and Smith reported a two year follow-up study of patients who had received either chemical or electrical aversion at Shadel Hospital. They reported that 57% of the patients receiving chemical and 55% of the patients receiving electrical aversion had been abstinent without receiving further treatment apart from scheduled "booster" sessions. Although this would appear to indicate that the two treatment methods are equally effective, the results are con-founded by a nonrandomized assignment of patients into the two treatment groups. Patients were given electrical conditioning if chemical aversion was medically contraindicated. Consequently, the former group was significantly older and tended to have more severe health problems. This constituted a sample selection bias in favor of the electrical aversion group because older alcoholics and those with more severe health problems tend to do better with a goal of abstinence than do younger, healthier alcoholics. In addition, the study is further confounded by low follow-up rates for both groups. The follow-up rates of 55% and 58% for the chemical and electrical aversion groups respec-tively not only make comparisons between the two groups difficult, but also bring into question the overall rates of abstinence for the two groups because abstinence rates were only calculated on the basis of those who responded to mailed questionaires.

Summary. The status of electrical aversion as a treatment technique for problem drinkers is uncertain at present. It appears that electrical aversion

(EA) produces greater improvement than can be attributed to no treatment or conventional treatment alone, and that controlled drinking outcomes are fairly common following EA, even when the identified goal of therapy is total abstinence. Alternative treatment methods may be equally effective, however, without invoking some of the unpleasant concomitants and side-effects of EA (e.g., high drop-out rate). As an approach to abstinence, EA appears to be relatively ineffective in comparison to alternative methods. As one component within a multimodal program for training controlled drinking, EA seems to be of minimal value. It may be, however, that EA is an effective adjunct for *certain* clients, and with those clients the availability of booster sessions may be beneficial.

One factor hampering the effective use of EA is our current lack of understanding as to *why* it seems to work for certain individuals. The traditional explanation that a conditioned emotional response is established by classical conditioning has been found to be lacking. Rather, clients report something more akin to a mild taste aversion for alcohol, and a decreased desire for it, although such experiences do not appear to be necessary to a successful outcome. It may be that critical changes in cognitive processes and/or structures, (e.g., cognitive dissonance, valence of labeling, causal attribution) account for the impact of EA, as has been hypothesized to be the case for aversion therapy's cognitive cousin, covert sensitization, to which we now turn our attention.

Covert Sensitization. Covert Sensitization (CS), or verbal aversion therapy, is a technique which involves verbally guided imagery of alcohol and drinking scenes which are associated with unpleasant feelings, usually imagined nausea and vomiting. Various specific procedures have been described (Anant, 1967; Cautela, 1966, 1967, 1970) which either do or do not have the subject imagine tasting the alcohol before becoming nauseous. The rationale for CS is similar to that of emetine chemical aversion in that the ostensible goal is to develop a conditioned aversion to alcohol. Raymond (1964) has concluded that the important component in taste aversion conditioning is feelings of nausea and not actual vomiting. Although both occur with emetine aversion, only the former typically occurs with CS, thereby making the implementation of CS easier and perhaps more useful with a broader range of subjects.

Uncontrolled Studies. A number of case studies (Anant, 1968b); Cautela, 1966; Smith & Gregory, 1976; Tepfer & Levine, 1977) have reported complete abstinence in their subjects following CS therapy for periods of time ranging from six months (Smith & Gregory, 1976) to 23 months (Anant, 1968b).

Uncontrolled studies with samples sizes greater than one have reported more variable results. Miller (1959) used CS within a hypnotic state as an adjunct to group and social therapy and disulfiram. He reported an abstinence rate for 150 alcoholics at one year to be 62%.

Anant (1967) reported results with 26 alcoholics who had received CS therapy. Fifteen had been treated in small groups and 11 were treated individually. Of the 26, a total of 25 had completed the program and all had been abstinent for a period of time ranging from eight to 15 months. However, a further report (Anant, 1968a) noted that seven of the 15 treated in groups had been lost to follow-up. Three of the remaining eight were abstinent and five were drinking less frequently. Data on the 11 treated individually were not specified.

Elkins (1977) reported results of 22 subjects who had received CS as an adjunct to an alcoholism rehabilitation program at the Augusta VA Medical Center. His work has been particularly noteworthy in that he has measured autonomic responses, made behavioral observations, and utilized subjective reports to determine the onset and intensity of nausea experienced. Using these measures, he has been able to discriminate those subjects who develop conditioned nausea (i.e., become nauseous to images of alcohol alone) from those who are only able to develop nausea upon demand (i.e., become nauseous only while imagining feeling ill and vomiting). Given these distinctions, Elkins and Murdock (1977) reported that 22 of 24 alcoholics were able to develop demand nausea and of these 15 developed conditioned nausea whereas seven remained at the demand-nausea stage. The conditioned-nausea alcoholics remained abstinent significantly longer ($\overline{X} = 14.9$ months) than did the demand-nausea alcoholics ($\overline{X} = 3.7$ months). In a further report (Elkins, 1977), 30.8% of the conditioned-nausea subjects were found to be abstinent for a period of time ranging from five to 62 months, whereas none of the demand-nausea subjects had remained abstinent. When controlled drinking criteria were applied as outcome measures, however, 11 of 13 (88%) of the conditioned- and 5 of 6 (83%) of the demand-nausea patients were in remission (i.e., not abusing alcohol).

Controlled Studies. Maletzky (1974) has reported results of alcoholics treated with CS "assisted" by valeric acid, a foul-smelling fluid. Subjects were randomly assigned into either the routine halfway house treatment which included disulfiram, group, and individual therapy (to compensate for the time the experimental Ss spent in CS therapy) or CS with valeric acid. During treatment, Ss would smell the valeric acid as an aid in the development of nausea. At six months, the CS group had significantly fewer urges to drink, had consumed fewer drinks, and had been on fewer reports for drunken behavior by authorities (this was a military program) than had the controls.

Ashem and Donner (1968) randomly assigned clients into either a CS treatment or a waiting list control group and reported that 6/15 (40%) of those treated were abstinent at six months, whereas none of the control clients were abstinent.

Hedberg and Campbell (1974) compared CS, electrical aversion (EA), systematic desensitization (SD), and behavioral family therapy (BFT) by randomly assigning problem drinkers into treatment groups with a goal of either abstinence or controlled drinking. With abstinence as the treatment goal, rates for abstinence and "much improved" at six months were: 9/10 in the BFT group, 9/10 in the SD group, 9/14 in the CS group and 0/4 in the EA group. (The EA group had a drop-out rate of 67%, making it the least effective treatment.) Thus CS was found to be less effective than either SD or BFT, but compared favorably with EA. It is noteworthy that this study used Cautela's (1966) procedures which usually do not include having the subject imagine *tasting* the alcohol, a component which Elkins (1979) believes is important in the process of developing a conditioned aversion.

Piorkowsky and Mann (1975) reported no significant differences in treatment outcome when insight therapy, CS, or systematic desensitization were compared. A high drop-out rate (65%) and a low abstinence rate (21%) present difficulties in interpretation.

Wilson and Tracy (1976) compared CS and electrical aversion in a single subject, multiple baseline study. Baselines following treatment revealed no significant differences between treatments, but neither treatment was very effective in suppressing drinking. The purpose of the treatments however, was apparently to suppress drinking, which is different from attempting to develop an aversion in alcoholics who are already abstinent. Drinking occasions may have provided opportunity for the continual extinction of any conditioned aversion. In support of the usefulness of this distinction, Elkins (in press) has presented results of animal studies which suggest that "acquisition of therapeutic alcohol aversions should be enhanced by a preconditioning period of alcohol abstinence."

Summary. Research data are inadequate to reach firm conclusions regarding covert sensitization. Controlled studies suggest that CS is more effective than no treatment. When only abstinent outcomes are considered, success rates range around 40%. Moderate drinking outcomes may also occur, however, and raise "success" percentages when included in outcome evaluation. The extent of establishment of a conditioned response to alcohol may be predictive of response to CS.

Hypnosis

References to the use of hypnosis in the treatment of alcoholism date as far back as 1899 (Moll, 1899, cited in Edwards, 1966). Both early and more recent uncontrolled clinical trials have tended to report good results, with abstinence rates ranging from 40% (Palez, 1952) to 76% (Gabrynowicz, 1977).

In an early comparison of the efficacy of hypnotherapy to emetine, antabuse and milieu therapy, Wallerstein (1957) reported that 14 of 39 hypnotherapy patients (36%) were "improved" (i.e., abstinent, plus "much or mildly improved" categories) at three to 24 months (therapy seems to have involved emotional catharsis and covert behavioral rehearsal of desirable behaviors.) Another 14 were rated as unimproved and 11 (28%) were lost to follow-up and also considered unimproved. This outcome was better than that of emetine aversion therapy (24% improved) and milieu therapy (26% improved), but less favorable than that found for disulfiram treated patients (53% improved). Other controlled studies have failed to support the effectiveness of hypnosis as an adjunct treatment (Edwards, 1966; Jacobson & Silfverskiöld, 1973; Smith-Moorhouse, 1969). All three of these studies reported nonsignificant differences between groups receiving hypnosis and control groups receiving standard treatment packages.

Higher success rates reported by the uncontrolled studies may be attributable to other aspects of the particular treatment program and/or prognostic characteristics of the alcoholics treated. For example, Gabrynowicz's (1977) "hypnotic" program description included Transactional Analysis, education, and continuing support groups, a therapy similar to the rational-emotive approach and homework assignments of autohypnotic relaxation twice daily. In addition, the program was oriented to a self-help perspective, with responsibility for designing the treatment contract and for change resting with the client. Because many of these specific treatment components are relatively effective approaches themselves, the 76% success rate cannot be credited to hypnosis alone. With regard to the other factor—pretreatment prognostic characteristics of the clients—Edwards (1966) found that patients with good outcomes at one year had significantly higher scores on a measure of social stability than did alcoholics with poor outcomes. This was true regardless of whether or not the patient received hypnosis.

Still another complicating factor is that goals and techniques vary greatly from one hypnotist to another. Smith-Moorhouse (1969) made only positive posthypnotic suggestions, whereas Jacobson and Silfverskiöld (1973) suggested an indifference to alcohol, and Miller (1976) attempted to develop an aversion to alcohol by pairing it with prior experiences of nausea and vomiting (essentially covert sensitization). The point here is that methods called "hypnosis" encompass a wide range of approaches.

One possible reason for a relative lack of consistent results and for poor results in the controlled studies may lie, in part, in the way in which the concept of hypnosis has been presented to the subjects. Traditionally, it has been described as a giving over of personal control to the hypnotist, who makes suggestions to the "unconscious mind" regarding future thoughts, feelings, and actions. The client is seen as being in a passive role and lacking in personal control, and the treatment may appear to have magical qualities. Recent literature in the area of self-control and cognitive behavior modification (e.g. Meichenbaum, 1977) would argue that this type of perspective (i.e., externally imposed changes with little active involvement on the part of the client) would not result in long-term success because the person has not acquired any new behavioral skills or adaptive cognitive processes to deal with intraper-

sonal and interpersonal pressures that may lead to relapse (cf. chapter 8 by
Cummings, Gordon and Marlatt in this book). Contemporary hypnosis researchers (e.g., Barber, Spanos, & Chaves, 1974; Katz, 1979) have suggested reconceptualizations of the hypnotic process that are more consistent
with self-control.

Summary. ''Hypnosis'' is a term that applies to numerous therapeutic
methods, and better specification of procedure is needed in order to judge
effectiveness. Present controlled research does not support the value of hypnosis as an adjunct in the treatment of alcoholism, but it would be premature to
dismiss hypnotic techniques as valueless on the basis of current data.

Psychotherapy

Perhaps the most significant obstacle in interpreting the psychotherapy outcome literature is a general ambiguity as to exactly *what* was done in therapy.
Many alcoholism treatment studies state simply that patients received ''individual and group psychotherapy.'' The content, procedures, and leadership of
such ''psychotherapy'' are so variable that one is at a loss to try to reconstruct
the treatment process.

Most psychotherapy for alcoholics seems, however, to have derived from
psychoanalytic models. The central assumption here is that alcoholism is a
symptom of an underlying unconscious conflict, with the implication that the
conflict rather than the symptom should be treated. Speculations about the
precise nature of the unconscious conflict have varied, but popular hypotheses
regarding the function of alcohol abuse have included: (a) a defense against
depression due to unfulfilled oral dependence needs—hence, a fixation at the
early oral stage of psychosexual development; (b) a defense against latent
homosexuality; (c) a defense against anxiety due to the impending break-
through of unconscious impulses; and (d) self-destructive behavior as a result of
introjected matricidal wishes related to unresolved hostile-dependent attach-
ment to the mother (DeVito et al., 1970; Fenichel, 1945; Silber, 1970). Others
have emphasized the importance of ''grief work'' in psychotherapy with
alcoholics, to work through the symbolic loss of the bottle (Bellwood, 1975;
Lynn, 1976). More recently, alternative psychodynamic formulations have
entered the field, including the game theory of transactional analysis (Steiner,
1971) and communication systems theory which emphasizes the role of alcohol in stabilizing the family structure (Steinglass et al., 1971). All share the
assumption that the key to resolution of the symptom (alcoholism) lies in the
achievement of some critical insight into intrapsychic dynamics.

In spite of the persistent contention that psychotherapy for alcoholism is
''alive and well,'' (Lynn, 1976; Zimberg et al., 1978), there seems to be a
consensus that intensive psychotherapy is not a treatment of choice for alcoholics (Ewing, 1974; Lynn, 1976; Moore, 1963; Shea, 1954). Alcoholics
are generally unpopular patients among psychotherapists (Hayman, 1956;

Selzer, 1967) and are rather consistently diagnosed as having personality disorders (De Vito et al., 1970; Miller, 1976), with less than optimal prognosis in psychotherapy. Gerard, Saenger, and Wile (1962) found that abstinence does not bring insight, nor is insight necessary to the maintenance of abstinence. There is also increasing evidence that other life problems tend to remit rather than worsen when alcohol abuse is alleviated, a trend opposite to that which might be expected from psychodynamic theories (Miller, Hedrick, & Taylor, 1979).

None of the above addresses what is the critical issue for purposes of this review: do insight-oriented psychotherapies bring about improvement in the drinking habits of alcoholics? Uncontrolled outcome studies of "psychotherapy" with alcoholics have reported findings ranging from dismal (Moore & Ramseur, 1960) to promising within better-prognosis populations (Pfeffer & Berger, 1957; Zimberg, 1978), with approximately 28% of patients improved on the average. Hoff (1961) found that the addition of disulfiram substantially improved the outcome of a psychotherapy-treated population, but did not evaluate whether psychotherapy made a significant contribution beyond the effects achieved by disilfiram alone. Bruun (1963) did compare psychotherapy (group) with disulfiram alone, however, and found no significant difference in efficacy, with both producing less than 19% total improvement. Hill and Blane (1967), in an exhaustive review of research on psychotherapy for alcoholism conducted between 1952 and 1963, noted that no firm conclusions could be drawn because "The bulk of the studies are gross retrospective surveys, usually with large groups of patients, as if quantity substituted for quality; with reliance on unreliable and unvalidated superficial measures and with inadequate follow-up procedures" (p. 100).

Three subsequent controlled studies have included psychotherapy as one treatment condition. Levinson and Sereny (1969) compared three inpatient groups receiving individual psychotherapy with three other groups treated on the same ward but receiving only the ward routine, occupational, and recreational therapy. The latter group showed a recovery rate twice that of the psychotherapy-treated group, with no significant differences reflected in improvement on psychological tests. These findings must be interpreted cautiously, however, because patients apparently were assigned sequentially rather than randomly to treatment groups.

In the two remaining studies, patients were assigned at random to insight-oriented psychotherapy versus alternative treatment methods. In both studies, insight therapy was conducted by fully trained professionals who were "believing" practitioners in this model—an essential condition for findings to be interpretable. Pomerleau and his colleagues (1978) compared insight therapy with a form of behavioral self-control training (to be discussed later in this chapter). Both were offered in small group format. The behavioral treatment program yielded a total improvement rate of 72% at 12-month follow-up, compared to a 50% improvement rate for the insight group. It is noteworthy that the lower success rate in the insight group is attributable primarily to a high drop-out rate, which reportedly peaked when therapy touched upon confrontation of critical personal issues. Brandsma and his colleagues (in press) randomly assigned patients to insight therapy, to one of two forms of cognitive behavior therapy, to Alcoholics Anonymous, or to an untreated control group. All treated groups showed greater improvement than did the control group, with differences dissipating over longer periods of follow-up and with professionally-led treatments showing a slight advantage over Alcoholics Anonymous. (This study will be discussed further in a subsequent section on A.A.) No significant differences were observed between insight-oriented psychotherapy and rational behavior therapy. It should be noted, however, that rational behavior therapy in many ways resembles insight therapy in focusing upon cognitive processes. Nevertheless, the authors were able to successfully demonstrate, via blind ratings of samples from tape recordings of sessions, that the treatment procedures used in these two conditions were quite distinguishable.

Some writers have suggested that although psychotherapy may not be an optimal method for modifying drinking habits, it may have a beneficial effect upon related psychopathology and thus may improve *maintenance* of sobriety, at least for some subset of the total population (Blane, 1977; Ewing, 1974; Lynn, 1976; Moore, 1963). Fortunately, this is a testable hypothesis (Miller, in press), but unfortunately no studies to date have evaluated the value of psychotherapy as an aftercare measure. The literature reviewed above does not support superior maintenance or generalization of gains when psychotherapy is used as the primary treatment strategy. The chapter by Cummings, Gordon and Marlatt in Part III of this volume reviews current research on approaches to maintenance of gains and relapse prevention.

Summary. Present research indicates that insight-oriented psychotherapy does not represent a treatment of choice for alcoholics. Controlled research has pointed to a high drop-out rate and lower or at best equivalent effectiveness in comparison to alternative treatment methods (cf. Gomes-Schwartz et al., 1978). One possible reason for the poor response of alcoholics to insight therapies is a well-documented (albeit partially reversible) pattern of deficits in cognitive abstraction and memory abilities associated with chronic alcohol use (Eckardt et al., 1978; Hester, 1979; Miller & Orr, in press). In addition, psychotherapy, in general, is a long-term undertaking, and current research does not support the superiority of long-term intensive interventions over less extensive and expensive alternatives (cf. Christensen et al., 1978; Edwards et al., 1977). The length of psychotherapy and degree of professional training required for its administration, combined with the somewhat unfavorable outcome literature reviewed above, do not bode well for the cost-effectiveness of psychotherapy as a primary treatment modality for alcoholism. The possibility remains, of course, that psychotherapy might represent an optimal intervention for a certain selected subset of alcoholics (Moore, 1963), but no data are presently available to guide us in this selection process.

Alcoholics Anonymous

Now in its 45th year of existence, A.A. represents one of the most widespread and longstanding approaches to the treatment of alcoholism. Because the philosophy and historical roots of A.A. have been described in detail elsewhere (Alcoholics Anonymous, 1955; Alibrandi, 1978; Blumberg, 1977; Leach & Norris, 1977) and are probably familiar to most readers, we will not expound upon them here. It is noteworthy, however, that the common perhaps unusually consistent and unified across a wide variety of socioeconomic settings. All groups use the same reference materials, employ similar meeting settings. All groups use the same reference materials, employ similar meeting formats, and are led by recovering alcoholic peers. One might therefore be more confident in generalizing research findings from one A.A. group to another than would be justifiable for more amorphous and variable approaches such as "group therapy" or "psychotherapy."

Unfortunately, there have been relatively few interpretable findings to generalize. Attempts to evaluate the effectiveness of A.A. have met with formidable if not insurmountable methodological problems, among them the very anonymity of members which precludes systematic follow-up evaluation. Most studies have failed to include control groups (a near impossibility because of the availability of A.A. to all who are interested), have relied almost entirely upon self-report (often via mailed questionnaires) and upon abstinence as the sole criteria for success, have been plagued by sizable attrition rates and large selection confounds, and have failed to use single-blind designs, thus remaining open to criticisms of interviewer bias (particularly when the investigators have been "insiders"—members of A.A. themselves).

Almost a quarter of a century ago, Wallerstein (1957) wrote that "self-help activities of alcoholics as most typically exemplified by Alcoholics Anonymous have not, as yet, been adequately evaluated" (p. 5). Summarizing justifiable conclusions from research in the intervening 20 years, Bebbington (1976) states that "it appears that the state of our knowledge has not improved beyond what we know from clinical experience: that many go to A.A. and that some do very well and attribute their success to their attendance" (p. 579).

In spite of a lack of supporting scientific evidence, A.A. has received widespread uncritical acclaim (Emrick, Lassen, & Edwards, 1977). As recently as 1974, Madsen described A.A. as "the only continuing and successful group dealing with alcoholism" (p. 156). Although acknowledging that A.A. is not for everyone, Madsen further states, "Yet in comparison with other therapies, its success rate is nearly miraculous" (p. 195). Still more recently, Father Joseph C. Martin, in his keynote address to the First Annual Training Institute on Addictions, referred to A.A. as "medicine's crowning glory" and the world's greatest therapy ("Father Joseph Martin," 1980). The "big book" of A.A. (Alcoholics Anonymous, 1955) itself makes bold claims of efficacy:

Of alcoholics who came to A.A. and realy (sic) tried, 50% got sober at once and remained that way: 25% sobered up after some relapses, and among the remainder, those who stayed on with A.A. showed improvement. Other thousands came to a few A.A. meetings and at first decided they didn't want the program. But great numbers of these—about two out of three—began to return as time passed. [p. xx]

This claims a 75% permanent abstinence rate, with some additional improved cases among those "who really tried." No research or source for these claims is provided, and one is left, in addition, with an unclear definition of "really trying." A point made by Dr. Luther Cloud in a National Council on Alcoholism press release regarding the Rand Report is also well taken here: "research leading to new knowledge regarding alcoholism . . . should be conducted with the utmost care, scrutinized by the scientific community and published in scientific literature before it is submitted for public consumption" (Armor et al., 1978, pp. 232-233).

What then *are* the data regarding the effectiveness of Alcoholics Anonymous? What can we answer to the question, "Does A.A. really work?" (Leach, 1973).

One major problem in interpreting the literature on A.A. is what Campbell and Stanley (1963) have termed a "multiple treatment interference" confound. Seldom has A.A. been studied as the sole approach to treatment. The majority of empirical studies, controlled and uncontrolled, have evaluated complex treatment programs that have included A.A. as one element (The Alcoholic Felon, 1974; Browne-Mayers et al., 1973; Costello et al., 1976; D. Edwards et al., 1977; Fitzgerald et al., 1971; Kish & Hermann, 1971; Levitt & Weedman, 1973; Manos, 1975; Mayer & Myerson, 1971; Moos et al., 1978; Papas, 1971; Pursch, 1976; Ritson, 1968; Rohan, 1972; Rossi, 1970; Rossi et al., 1963; Selzer & Holloway, 1957; Tomsovic, 1970; Vallance, 1965; Willems et al., 1973). On the average these studies have reported total improvement rates (abstinent cases plus others rated as "improved") between 40% and 50%. The problem, however, is to determine what contribution A.A. makes as one component within these multimodal programs. How important is A.A. as part of treatment?

One approach is to ask whether the extent to which an individual participates in A.A. meetings predicts the degree of his or her success in treatment. The evidence here is quite mixed. Some investigators have found favorable outcome to be associated with A.A. attendance (Armor et al., 1978; Bateman & Petersen, 1971; Browne-Mayers et al., 1973; Kish & Hermann, 1971; Robson et al., 1965; Rossi, 1970; Tomsovic, 1970; Zimberg, 1978). Others (Haberman, 1966; Ritson, 1968) have reported that *prior* exposure to A.A. improved prognosis. A study by Robson, Paulus, and Clarke (1965) exemplifies these positive findings. Two matched groups were studied: an "experimental" group that participated in at least five sessions of an outpatient rehabilitation program, and a self-selected "control" group that attended fewer than five sessions. A.A. was available to all patients. The experimental group was found to show more improvement in severity of drinking problem and in other areas of life functioning than did the control group, although percentage of abstinent cases did not differ. Of greater interest here was the finding of a difference between those individuals who attended 11 or more meetings of A.A. (22% of all cases) and those who did not. Within the experimental group, 71% of *regular* A.A. attenders were rated as improved (by nonblind raters at 10 to 46 month follow-up) versus 57% of those not attending A.A. more than ten times. Within the control group, the comparable figures were 70% versus 37%. One might conclude from data such as these that A.A. makes a substantial contribution to treatment, particularly among the "control" patients who dropped out of the outpatient program. The correlational design of such studies does not justify this conclusion, however. It may be that some third factor such as patient "motivation" accounts for both A.A. attendance and successful outcome. Unintentional interviewer bias must also be considered because ratings were apparently done with knowledge of A.A. attendance. This study, like most, relied upon unverified patient self-reports for outcome data. Beyond these methodological problems, attribution of success to A.A. within multimodal programs is further called into doubt by the fact that numerous studies have found no relationship between degree of participation in A.A. and overall treatment outcome (Belasco, 1971; Davidson, 1976; Ditman, 1967; Imber et al., 1976; Mayer & Myerson, 1971; McCance & McCance, 1969; Pattison et al., 1968; Rohan, 1972; Selzer & Holloway, 1957; Zimberg, 1974). Costello and his colleagues (1976) reported that the overall effectiveness of their intermediate care unit was nearly doubled (from 18% to 33% improved at one year) when the unit converted from an exclusively A.A. oriented model to a multimodal therapeutic milieu that included A.A. as one element.

Thus, on the basis of present data, we cannot conclude whether or not A.A. makes a significant contribution to multimodal treatment programs. In light of this absence of supporting data, it is interesting that A.A. has been the single most popular treatment component within hospital programs for alcoholism (Moore & Buchanan, 1966).

A different question regards the effectiveness of A.A. *alone*. What happens to alcoholics who attend A.A. as the primary or sole road to recovery? Several studies have attempted to address this question directly.

One approach has been the *questionnaire study*. The typical methodology here has been to distribute questionnaires to those attending all or selected A.A. meetings within a certain geographic area over a given period of time. Attendees are asked to complete the questionnaire and to return it anonymously, reporting data such as length of current abstinence, number of relapses since first joining A.A., and length of membership in A.A. Leach (1973) reviewed four major studies of this type. With reasonable consistency these studies have indicated that of those responding, about 9% have been abstinent for ten years or more, 15% for five to ten years, 33% for one to five years, and 43% for less than one year. Subsequent surveys have yielded similar results (Leach & Norris, 1977; Norris, 1978). The obvious major problem with these studies, even if self-report is assumed to be honest, is the selection factor. These data do not reflect the status of (a) those who attended one or more meetings and then discontinued their attendance; (b) those who for various reasons (some of them related to outcome) did not attend the meetings at which questionnaires were distributed; and (c) those who elected not to return the questionnaire.

Rarest and perhaps most instructive of all are longitudinal studies which, unlike the cross-sectional questionnaire studies, employ follow-up methodology to study treatment outcome. Two "internal" evaluations (conducted by participants in A.A.) are reported by Bill C. (1965) and by Jindra and Forslund (1978). The former studied 393 persons who attended ten or more meetings of A.A. in a southwestern city, according to the club log books and the author's "personal knowledge." Data collection methods are not specified, except to say that most information was collected by personal interview. Bill C. reported that at one-year follow-up, 31% had remained totally abstinent, 12% had stayed mostly sober with minor slips, 9% were not sober but were still in A.A., 5% were dead, 5% were in prison or mental institutions, and 38% were lost to follow-up. By assuming that at least 10% of the latter (lost) category had also stayed sober, Bill C. arrived at a total figure of 47% sobriety at one year. From retrospective data, he concluded that the probability of staying sober two years given one year of sobriety is 70%, and that the probability of three years given two years is 90%. Even with the two apparent methodological problems of possible interviewer bias and exclusion of those who attended fewer than ten times, this remains one of the most informative studies available regarding the effectiveness of A.A.

Jindra and Forslund (1978) studied 62 A.A. "members" (with membership defined by group consensus within A.A.) who attended 105 meetings of two A.A. groups in a western city. Once again, "brief attenders" were excluded from the sample. At 30-month follow-up, 23% had been abstinent for ten years or more, 21% had maintained abstinence for five to ten years, 15% had been abstinent for one to five years, 10% were not in A.A., 10% had had slips, one was drinking while continuing to attend A.A. meetings, two (3%) had died, and 18% were unavailable for interview. This overall known abstinence rate of 58% is the most optimistic empirical report of A.A. outcome so far. As before, selection factors, interviewer bias, reliance upon self-report, possibility of patients having received other treatment, and the absence of control groups must be considered in interpreting these findings.

Controlled Research. The first controlled evaluation of A.A. was reported by Ditman and Crawford (1966; Ditman et al., 1967). Individuals convicted of alcohol-related offenses were randomly assigned by the court to one of three conditions: (a) clinic treatment; (b) A.A. alone (mandated to attend five meetings within 30 days); or (c) probation alone, with no special treatment. No significant differences among groups were observed at follow-up of 12 months, with the following percentages found to be "successful" (no new arrests): 32% for clinic patients, 31% for those assigned to A.A., and 44% in the untreated group. Only those for whom both local and state police records were available at follow-up were included in analyses, and specific data regarding drinking behavior were not provided. Further, few would regard mandated attendance at five meetings to be an adequate test of the efficacy of A.A.

In an admirably thorough and extensive study, Brandsma, Maultsby, and Welsh (in press) have contributed the only methodologically adequate evaluation of A.A. to date. Alcoholics were randomly assigned to one of five treatment conditions: (a) insight therapy; (b) rational behavior therapy conducted by a professional; (c) rational behavior therapy conducted by a paraprofessional; (d) A.A.; and (e) a control group that received only a list of other available community services. All treatments were administered on an outpatient basis, by appropriately trained persons who were "believers" in their respective models. Screening, intake, termination and follow-up assessment procedures were extensive, covering a wide range of drinking variables and measures of general functioning. Of 532 patients screened, 197 initiated treatment, and of these a final sample of 104 completed at least ten sessions and some otucome measures (the requirements to be included in this study). Although there is an obvious amount of motivational screening occurring in this reduction, pretreatment selection preceded random assignment and thus applied equally to all groups. All patients were classifiable as alcoholics according to criteria described by the National Council on Alcoholism (1972), showed clear signs of life problems related to drinking, and reported a formidable level of alcohol consumption (mean of 14.9 ounces of ethanol per day when drinking). Most notably, 87% of the final sample were from the lowest social classes, probably because the primary source of referrals was from the courts following conviction for driving while intoxicated (cf. Miller, 1978a).

The findings of this study are, needless to say, complex. To summarize relevant conclusions: (a) all treatments combined showed more improvement on a variety of measures as compared with the control group, with the magnitude of differences decreasing over longer periods of follow-up; (b) of the four treatment groups, A.A. showed the highest drop-out rate (68%, compared with 57% in other groups); (c) A.A. appears to have shown the least improvement of the treated groups—A.A. treated patients were significantly more likely to binge at three-month follow-up than were control subjects or those in other treatment groups, and at all follow-up points A.A. showed fewer if any significant differences from the control condition in comparison to the other treatment groups.

Some aspects of this study suggest the advisability of caution in interpreting these results. Follow-up assessment apparently relied upon the self-report of patients without collecting corroborative data. This may be a particular problem within a court-referred population where patients may perceive possible consequences of honest versus dishonest reporting. The drop-out rate was also quite high, although 78% of all patients did complete all four follow-up interviews (three, six, nine, and 12 months). Nor can any one study be definitive. The fact that the majority of patients in this study were court mandated may suggest merely that A.A. may not be optimally effective as a *coerced* program (cf. Ditman et al., 1967). Nevertheless, the weaknesses of this study are characteristic of all studies reveiwed earlier in this section, and overall the Brandsma project remains the soundest from a methodological standpoint of all studies reported to date that have evaluated the efficacy of Alcoholics Anonymous.

It would seem that a fruitful direction for future research would be an attempt to identify the type of person for whom A.A. represents the most promising approach. Numerous writers (e.g., Belasco & Trice, 1969; Canter, 1966; Trice & Roman, 1970) have suggested that A.A. may work best for a certain kind of individual. A.A. attendance has been found to be associated with higher authoritarianism and lower educational levels (Canter, 1966; Ditman et al., 1967), with affiliative and dependency needs (Trice & Roman, 1970) and with a relative lack of related psychopathology (Gerard et al., 1962). Curlee (1967, 1971) has suggested that women may have greater difficulty than do men in identifying with the group spirit of A.A. (cf. Davidson, 1976), a sentiment that has given rise to a similar organization more oriented to the unique needs of the female alcoholic, "Women for Sobriety" (Kirkpatrick, 1978). Tournier (1979) opined that A.A. is poorly suited to the needs of *early*-stage problem drinkers (cf. Miller & Caddy, 1977; Trice & Roman, 1970). Given the rather consistently reported high drop-out rate from A.A.—numerous researchers have reported that only 5 to 15% of their patients have remained in A.A. after one year (Armor et al., 1978; Belasco & Trice, 1969; Browne-Mayers et al., 1973; Dubourg, 1969; Kish & Hermann, 1971; McCance & McCance, 1969; Tomsovic, 1970)—it would seem highly desirable to be able to identify *beforehand* whether or not a given individual is likely to respond favorably.

Finally, we wish to emphasize that alcoholism professionals and A.A. members probably have much to learn from each other. An unfortunate polarization has tended to separate these two groups, emphasizing differences to the exclusion of similarities. Recently, Burt (1975) has suggested that in terms of actual treatment procedures, A.A. and behavior therapists may have much in common. The A.A. program is a complex one, and typically has an impact upon the participant's life extending far beyond the meetings themselves (Davidson, 1976; Henry & Robinson, 1978). Bassin (1975) described the A.A. "chip" system that clearly resembles an operant token reinforcement system, accompanied by an impressive amount of social reinforcement for sobriety. Burt (1975) has pointed to other similarities, including the vicarious learning involved in A.A. public testimonials and the behavioral contracting aspects of the A.A. sponsorship system. Peter Miller (1978) has discussed possible applications of behavioral social skills training to the accomplishment of steps five and six of the A.A. Twelve Steps. Last but not least are the therapeutic benefits of *being* a model (Christensen et al., 1978) inherent in the "twelfth stepping" behaviors of helping other alcoholics to sobriety. The enormous advantages of so extensive a self-help system cannot be overlooked: daily contact with thousands of alcoholics to whom traditional treatment is undesirable or unavailable, long-term maintenance by A.A. group support following treatment, the low cost of this treatment approach (Christensen et al., 1978; Dumont, 1974; Stuart, 1977). It is our hope that the future will see collaborative research and treatment efforts that will expand the effectiveness and influence of A.A. as well as other treatment approaches.

Summary. Although A.A. remains the most widespread and popularly known approach to alcoholism treatment, its effectiveness is not supported by adequate scientific data at the present time. Bold claims of efficacy made by A.A. and its advocates do not correspond to current research findings. Although some studies report a correlation between A.A. attendance and favorable outcome, such correlational data cannot be interpreted as causal, and an equal number of studies have found no relationship between A.A. involvement and improvement. High drop-out rates from A.A. appear to be characteristic. Longitudinal follow-up studies of A.A. outcome have been few and have suffered from serious methodological flaws. The most extensive and careful study to date (Brandsma et al., in press) does not support past claims of the superiority of A.A. over alternative approaches. Bebbington (1976) has suggested, from a review of current literature, that 26% may represent a reasonable *minimum* figure for the effectiveness rate of A.A., although even this estimate was based on a study that may have overestimated efficacy due to methodological problems. The internal evaluation studies of Bill C. (1965) and Jindra and Forslund (1978), containing design flaws and biases likely to inflate the rate of reported favorable outcomes, suggest an *upper bound* for the effectiveness of A.A. in the vicinity of 50% abstinent at one year. Probably the actual "success rate" lies somewhere between these two figures, but available data do not justify a more precise estimate. Certainly an exclusive or preferential reliance upon A.A. as a treatment model for *all* problem drinkers is not justified by our present knowledge.

Group Therapies

Group approaches to the treatment of alcoholism arose in the 1940s following World War II, in part due to a need for more efficient methods for treating large numbers of individuals (Hartocollis & Sheafor, 1968). The term "group therapy," like "psychotherapy," subsumes a wide range of procedures and theoretical orientations (Battegay, 1977; Blume, 1978a; Doroff, 1977; Sands & Hanson, 1971; Scott, 1976). Although many studies simply state that "group psychotherapy" was administered, there are numerous detailed descriptions of various group techniques for treating alcoholism including psychodrama (Blume, 1978b; Blume et al., 1968; Weiner, 1967), reality therapy (Bratter, 1974), interactional group process (Brown & Yalom, 1977; Yalom, 1974), marathon group (Dichter et al., 1971), transactional analysis (Steiner, 1971), experiential group (Mullan & Sangiuliano, 1967; Trudel, 1978), patient-led group (Schaul et al., 1971) and group hypnotherapy (Scott, 1966).

According to Moore and Buchanan (1966), "group psychotherapy" has been the second most common technique employed in hospital alcoholism programs (78% of programs reported using it), with A.A. representing the most often used method (cf. Ford, 1976). Like A.A., group approaches have received widespread if uncritical acclaim. Fox (1967) stated that "Group therapy is perhaps the most effective type of treatment for the alcoholic aside from A.A." (p. 773). Summarizing the state of the art, Doroff (1977) observed that "In recent years there appears to have emerged a consensus among the scientific and professional community to the effect that among the various psychotherapies a group approach seems to offer the brightest promise" (p. 236).

Whatever the basis for this confidence, it is not to be found in the present treatment outcome literature (Hartocollis & Sheafor, 1968; Parloff & Dies, 1977; Pattison, 1977). Although a large number of studies have included group psychotherapy among the procedures evaluated, common methodological problems cloud the interpretation of findings. The precise nature of group procedure is often unspecified, and different techniques often overlap heavily. There is, for example, considerable interface between psychodrama and current behavior therapy procedures such as assertion training and behavior rehearsal (Blume et al., 1978b; Kelly, 1978). Group techniques are seldom used alone, raising the familiar multiple-treatment confound. Overlap is common between group therapy and A.A., itself a group method, but differing from traditional groups in its self-help format and the recommendation of *permanent* membership (Hartocollis & Sheafor, 1968; Pursch, 1976). Dropout rates are frequently high, and follow-up methods have tended to rely upon questionnaires and other self-report methods. In 1968, Hartocollis and Sheafor summarized their review of group therapy outcome literature by saying, "Although all reports of group psychotherapy with alcoholic patients are positive, if not enthusiastic, the fact remains that the results reported are mainly a matter of the impression of the authors from their own experience" (p. 21). We turn our attention now to a brief review of outcome research in this area, with emphasis on studies completed within the past ten years.

Outcome Research. The vast majority of studies represent uncontrolled reports of outcome from various group therapies, usually contained as one element within a multimodal treatment program (Belasco & Trice, 1969; Brown & Yalom, 1977; Browne-Mayers et al., 1973; Clancy et al., 1965; Davidson, 1976; Dichter et al., 1971; Edwards, Bucky et al., 1977; Fitzgerald et al., 1971; Gliedman et al., 1956; Hartman, 1971; Kish & Hermann, 1971; Knox, 1972; Levitt & Weedman, 1973; MacDonough, 1976; Madden & Kenyon, 1975; Papas, 1971; Simpson & Webber, 1971; Tomsovic, 1970; Van-Dijk & Van-Dijk-Koffeman, 1973; Willems et al., 1973; Wolff, 1968). Improvement rates (defined in various ways after periods of follow-up varying from immediate to four years) have ranged from 0% (MacDonough, 1976) to 82% (Browne-Mayers et al., 1973), with an approximate average of 38% of cases rated as either abstinent or improved.

Controlled and comparative studies have been fewer. Pattison, Brissenden, and Wohl (1967) found that patients randomly assigned to receive psychoanalytically-oriented group psychotherapy in addition to other treatment components did not differ on a wide range of outcome measures from patients receiving only the standard psychiatric ward program. Difference trends that did exist seemed to favor the "control" group. Likewise, Zimberg (1974) found no difference between a group receiving individual and group psychotherapy plus medication and another group receiving brief supportive therapy from an internist in addition to the regular hospital program. Again, the differences that were found favored the brief therapy group.

Other studies have compared group therapy with alternative approaches, often using standard group treatment as a "control" condition. No significant differences have been found between group therapies and electrical aversive counterconditioning (McCance & McCance, 1969; Miller, Hersen, Eisler, & Hemphill, 1973) or multimodal abstinence-oriented behavior therapies (Caddy et al., 1978; Vogler et al., 1975), with existing trends in these studies indicating group therapy patients to be less improved. Wallerstein (1957) found less improvement among patients treated by group milieu therapy than among those assigned (at random) to disulfiram or hypnotherapy. Bruun (1963) found no differences between a group ($n=203$) receiving psychotherapy and a random control group ($n=100$) receiving disulfiram only.

In a study employing "random" assignment, Kissin, Platz, and Su (1970a) compared the effectiveness of psychodynamic group psychotherapy, drug therapy (tranquilizer + antidepressant), rehabilitation ward therapy (where the principal treatment method was group psychotherapy), and no treatment. Unfortunately, these authors permitted patients in certain groups to change their group assignment following randomization. Psychotherapy patients, for example, could elect to switch to the drug therapy group or to no treatment, an option which more than half of the psychotherapy patients exercised. Of 129 patients initially assigned to psychotherapy, 62 remained (some of whom transferred into psychotherapy from the rehabilitation ward, again exercising their option). Of these 62, a total of 22 patients (35.5%) were considered "successful" at one-year follow-up (as compared with 21.2% in the drug group, 15.2% on the rehabilitation ward, and 4.9% in the delayed treatment control group). Each of these percentages was based only on the total number of patients who remained in their respective treatment conditions.

Four studies have compared alternative group methods. Ends and Page (1957) compared groups based upon learning theory, client-centered, and psychoanalytic frameworks with a "social discussion" group intended as a control. The same therapists administered all groups in this study. Greatest improvement in alcohol consumption (at the 12- to 18 month follow-up conducted by interviewers blind to group membership) was shown by the client-centered group, followed by the psychoanalytic group and, at some distance, by the control and learning groups. A similar pattern of outcome was reflected in patient responses to a Q-sort measure. Tomsovic (1976) found that alcoholics treated in a closed encounter group showed slightly greater gains in self-concept than did those treated in a more traditional open and eclectic group. No assessment of impact upon drinking was offered. Wood and his colleagues (in press) reported slightly greater overall improvement among alcoholics treated in a psychodrama group than among those treated in traditional small group therapy, although assignment in this study was not random. Pomerleau et al. (1978) randomly assigned problem drinkers to insight-oriented group treatment or to a behaviorally-oriented group, each conducted by fully qualified professionals trained in these respective models. The behavioral group showed greater reduction in drinking and a higher overall percentage of improvement (72% versus 50%), although the differences fell short of statistical significance. A highly significant difference was observed in drop-outs from behavioral (11%) versus insight groups (43%). Drop-out from insight groups peaked at the point of greatest confrontation in sessions.

Finally, group therapy is often recommended as an aftercare procedure for alcoholics who have received more extensive prior treatment. As with the A.A. literature reviewed above, current group therapy research does not provide clear empirical support for the efficacy of groups as aftercare. Kirk and Masi (1978) found the voluntary use of individual and group aftercare to be related to slightly *higher* rates of rehospitalization for alcoholism. Interpretation of such results must be cautious, however, because patients perceiving themselves to be in greater need of additional therapy may be more likely to remain in contact with the treatment program (cf. W. R. Miller, 1978). More conclusive findings would be provided by a study in which patients were randomly assigned, following treatment, to various aftercare alternatives including a group receiving no additional treatment. This design would be relatively easy to employ within a standard treatment setting (Miller, in press) and would provide better information regarding the cost-effectiveness of alternative aftercare plans.

Summary. Group therapy is widely acclaimed and commonly used as a primary treatment technique for alcoholics, usually in concert with other therapeutic methods. Numerous alternative models for conducting group therapy exist, and there are few data to recommend one method over another. In general, the outcome of group treatment for alcoholism has been inconsistent, with improvement rates averaging around 40%. Comparative and controlled studies have provided no support for the popular belief that group methods represent a superior approach for treating alcoholics. Some studies have failed to find differences between group-treated and control patients, or have favored alternative approaches over traditional group methods. All in all, the data are inconclusive at present. If any advantage is to be seen for group approaches, it would be a cost-effectiveness advantage, given no absolute differences in outcome among alternative treatments. This may be particularly true of minimal-intervention, education groups such as those described by Taylor and Miller (1979), Loranger (1972), and Vogler et al. (1975).

Halfway Houses

The halfway house concept arose in the 1950s in an attempt to ease the transition of alcoholic patients from intensive inpatient care to community readjustment (Rubington, 1977, 1979). Halfway houses vary widely in structure and content of program, but in general are characterized by a small patient population (usually less than 25), brief patient stay (from a few days to a few months), emphasis on Alcoholics Anonymous to maintain abstinence, minimal rules and regulations, and the absence of professionally trained personnel (Baker, Sobell, Sobell, & Cannon, 1976; Donahue, 1971; Donahue & Donahue, 1975; Ogborne & Smart, 1976; Ozarin & Witkin, 1975; Rubington, 1967, 1970, 1977).

Research on the efficacy of halfway houses has been characterized by the same methodological weaknesses that have clouded evaluation of other treatment approaches, particularly a lack of adequate control groups and a large sample attrition at follow-up (Ogborne & Smart, 1976). Donahue and Donahue (1975) reported that 41% of their sample of halfway house residents were abstinent at the time of discharge, but no follow-up data were provided. Rubington (1977) estimated that on the average about 20% of halfway house clients remain abstinent for six months or longer following discharge. Outcome has typically been judged dichotomously—abstinent versus drinking—and level and pattern of alcohol consumption have seldom been evaluated. Ogborne (1978) reported that a "fair proportion" of former residents reported shifting from steady to periodic drinking following discharge.

Comparative evaluations have been few (Ogborne & Smart, 1976). Annis and Liban (1979) compared 35 halfway house residents with 35 other alcoholics matched on factors known to be predictive of outcome. Halfway house graduates showed significantly fewer alcohol-related arrests but significantly more readmissions in comparison to controls. Combining arrests and admissions to form an index of documented drunkenness, Annis and Smart found no significant difference between groups. Smart (1978c) found no difference in effectiveness between inpatient and halfway house facilities, nor were the 35% who accepted treatment found to differ significantly in outcome from the 65% who declined to enter treatment in these facilities. Pattison et al. (1969) likewise found no differences in efficacy among an inpatient, an outpatient, and a halfway house facility.

Characteristics of individuals who respond successfully to halfway house treatment resemble those depicting successful outcome in general—social stability, age, and perhaps length of stay (Ogborne & Smart, 1976). Rubington (1979) reported that two halfway houses with a more ''home-like'' atmosphere produced longer stays and lower readmission rates among residents than did two other houses with more institutional atmospheres. This study was correlational in design, however, and no statistical analyses of data were reported.

Summary. On the basis of present data there is no reason to believe that halfway houses significantly improve patient outcome in comparison to no treatment or to alternative treatments.

Family Therapy

Family therapy includes a broad range of theoretical approaches and therapeutic interventions. Specific techniques have included a concurrent group for spouses of alcoholics, family group meetings excluding the alcoholic, couples groups, and conjoint family therapy (i.e., seeing the couple and/or family all together). In addition, the theoretical orientations which are the basis for family therapy have been diverse. Some researchers have based their therapy upon the premise that alcoholism is a cause of marital discord whereas others view alcohol abuse as a consequence of the marital disruption. More recent theoretical models have placed less importance on etiological issues and have focused more upon an operant analysis of behaviors within the family structure. In view of the vast differences in theoretical models and therapeutic interventions, all of which come under the heading of family therapy, a short summary of the treatment outcome studies for the entire area will be presented, accompanied by a more detailed discussion of recent theoretical models and interventions which show promise.

Treatment Outcome Studies. In general, both controlled and uncontrolled treatment outcome studies have reported positive and adaptive changes in functioning within the family structure in addition to abstinence rates ranging from about 45% (Gallant et al., 1970; Smith, 1969) to 80% at six months

(Hedberg & Campbell, 1974). With many family therapy studies, however, the goal of treatment is to bring about changes within the family structure and thereby improve the quality of life for the alcoholic and her or his family (Davis et al., 1974; Paolino, McCrady, & Kogan, 1978). In defense of this prioritization of treatment goals, Burton and Kaplan (1968) cited Hill and Blane's (1967) conclusion that improvement in drinking behaviors is not necessarily associated with improved adjustment in most areas and that such a notion remains an empirical question. Conversely, however, Burton and Kaplan (1968) found that group counseling of couples focusing on interpersonal problems, when successful, was associated with decreased drinking or abstinence.

Smith (1969) offered concomitant and separate groups for inpatient alcoholics and their wives and reported an abstinence plus improved rate of 64% at 16 to 22 months. This was compared with a 50% abstinent plus improved rate for the "control group" (husbands of wives who did not attend the group). Because of nonrandom assignment into the two treatment groups, however, the results are confounded and cannot be considered as valid evidence for the efficacy of family therapy.

Cadogan (1973) reported the results of a controlled study with randomized assignment of couples into either an outpatient marital therapy group or a waiting-list control group. All alcoholics had completed an inpatient program prior to outpatient treatment. Alcoholics and their spouses were seen together with other couples in a group and the therapeutic orientation was towards increasing problem-solving skills. At six months, nine of the 20 alcoholics (45%) who were in the experimental condition were abstinent and an additional four of 20 (20%) were "improved." These results were significantly better than those in the control group, in which only two of 20 were completely abstinent and five of 20 "improved."

Corder et al. (1972) reported a study in which the control group received the same inpatient program as did the experimental group with the exception of an intensive four-day training workshop during which the wives resided with the husbands at the residential program. The workshop included two group therapy sessions daily with videotape feedback and analysis of the sessions, videotape presentations of medical and psychological aspects of alcoholism and group discussion of them, group discussion of Transactional Analysis concepts and "game-playing" in alcoholism with role-playing and videotape analysis, talks with a recreational staff person, A.A. and Al-Anon meetings, meetings with other follow-up resources, and homework assignments during the evening hours. Results at six months indicated that eight of 19 experimental group alcoholics were drinking, whereas 17 of 20 control group alcoholics had relapsed. Those who had received the experimental treatment were engaged in significantly more outpatient programs and recreational activities, and were more likely to be employed. Although the experimental group received more attention during the last four days of their program, an attempt was made to control for attention-placebo factors by cutting short their inpatient stay by three days.

Hedberg and Campbell (1974) compared behavioral family counseling with electrical aversion, systematic desensitization, and covert sensitization. At a six-month follow-up, they reported that eight of ten alcoholics (80%) in family counseling who had chosen abstinence has achieved and maintained it. Family therapy compared favorably with the other treatment approaches.

Amir and Eldar (1979) reported on an intensive family-oriented approach for treating alcoholics in Israel. Among the contingencies applied was the removal of the alcoholic's children from the home until the problem drinking was resolved. In one group of 14, seven were found to be abstinent and six others were drinking moderately at follow-up. In a second group of 14, five were abstinent and eight moderate drinkers at six months. This overall success of 93% is noteworthy in spite of the highly selected nature of the sample, although some of the interventions were very specific to the Israeli culture.

Barbara McCrady and her associates (McCrady, Paolino, Longabough, & Rossi, 1979) have reported results of a controlled study comparing (a) the joint inpatient admission of alcoholic and spouse; (b) involvement of the spouse in treatment without admission; and (c) no spouse involvement in the treatment program. All subjects were randomly assigned, and the alcoholic was an inpatient in all conditions. At follow-up (six to eight months), patients and spouses in the joint admission group and patients in the spouse involvement group reported significant decreases in a quantity/frequency measure of alcohol consumption. Spouses in the latter group and patients and spouses in the no-spouse involvement group reported no significant decreases in alcohol consumption. On the other outcome measures, however, significant improvements were reported by all three groups with nonsignificant differences among the groups. These included measures of psychosocial functioning, marital adjustment, emotional status, utilization of aftercare support, and employment status. The findings provide only modest support for the use of joint admissions as a therapeutic intervention.

Structured Family Therapy. Structured family therapy is a more recent theoretical approach which appears to be promising for both therapeutic and research purposes. Within this "systems analysis" perspective, etiology is considered to be less important than is the adaptive function which alcohol abuse plays within the family structure (Finlay, 1974). Alcoholism and family behavior are perceived as being interdependent (Dulfano, 1978; Steinglass, 1979). Steinglass and his associates (Davis et al., 1974; Steinglass, 1976, 1977, 1979; Steinglass et al., 1977) have developed a research project which involved joint admissions of the alcoholic and spouse in small groups for seven to ten days, preceded by two weeks of outpatient groups and followed up by periodic outpatient groups for six months. To investigate the adaptive function of the intoxicated state within the marital structure, Steinglass et al. (1977)

structured the inpatient program so that during seven of the days alcohol was freely available. Behavioral interaction patterns during both intoxicated and sober states were studied and consequently used in group therapy. Self-predictions of behaviors during intoxication proved to be totally unreliable. Often, particular marital issues and certain patterns of expression of affect were seen only during the intoxicated stage. Steinglass noted that interactional behavior while intoxicated was exaggerated or amplified but restricted in range and that behaviors often took on an automated quality. He speculated that for some, the intoxicated state plays a functional role with the marriage. Certain behaviors which may be temporarily adaptive may become associated with the intoxicated state, and the temporary success of the behavior may tend to reinforce the chronic drinking pattern. Because the solution during the intoxicated stage is often only temporary, however, issues of individual pathology, intrafamily and family-environmental conflict continue to recur. Once the adaptive functions of the intoxicated state become known, therapeutic strategies can be devised to teach the family more adaptive skills which they can use to deal with conflict and to bring about longer lasting solutions.

Steinglass (1979) reported a six-month follow-up on eight of the ten couples in his 1977 study. Treatment outcome measures included a detailed drinking behavior measure, a psychiatric symptomatology scale, an individual psychosocial measure, and two measures of marital functioning. Five of the nine alcoholics were drinking less (i.e., from 20% less to total abstention) and eight of nine showed significant changes in pattern and context of drinking. The psychiatric symptomatology scale revealed that all clients were mostly within the normal range of psychiatric outpatients both at pretest and at six-month follow-up. A strong correlation ($r = .91$) was noted between the alcoholic's pre-post drinking changes and pre-post changes in the symptomatology scale of the spouse. Measures of marital functioning showed little improvement except for consistently positive changes in communication. Unfortunately, this positive change was associated with increased behavioral difficulties and decreased marital satisfaction in other areas. Apparently, an intensive six-week program was insufficient to deal effectively with longstanding maladaptive behavioral patterns within the marital structure.

Summary. Controlled evaluations of family therapies have provided modest support for their efficacy relative to alternative approaches and control conditions. The nonrandom assignment of patients in some studies and the absence of appropriate controls (e.g., attention/placebo control) in most studies require conservative conclusions at the present time. Extensive theoretical work and an initial uncontrolled evaluation by Steinglass and his associates suggest that structured family therapy is a method deserving of further exploration in the treatment of problem drinkers. The comparative research of Hedberg and Campbell (1974) also supports behavioral family therapy as a promising approach.

Other Therapeutic Approaches

Many other approaches to treating alcoholics have been tried, each with little or no empirical support at present. Lau (1976) and Sytinsky and Galebskaya (1979) have reviewed literature regarding the use of acupuncture in the treatment of alcoholism and drug addiction. Music therapy has been applied in alcoholism treatment, particularly in continental Europe (e.g., Gaston & Eagle, 1974; Gay & Lecours, 1976). Another form of arts therapies, the use of poetry in treatment, has recently been described by Mazza (1979).

A rather extreme intervention was introduced by Müller, Roeder, and Orthner (1973), who performed surgery on the hypothalamus (a deep structure in the brain, involved in the control of emotion and appetite) of two alcoholics. One relapsed following surgery, and the other remained sober at four-month follow-up. The report of this possible surgical "cure" for alcoholism apparently generated enthusiasm in the popular press as well as a series of inquiries and requests for treatment (Meyer, 1974).

An interesting procedure known as cerebral electrotherapy or "electrosleep" has been used for some years in the Soviet Union, and has recently been explored as a treatment for alcoholism in the Western world. In this technique, low voltage and low intensity electrical current is passed through a portion of the brain, usually one or both frontal lobes. Electrosleep current is substantially lower than that used in standard "electroshock" therapy and does not produce convulsions or other unpleasant effects associated with the latter. Typically, the current is set at a level below that which can be perceived by the subject. The reported therapeutic benefits include improvement in sleep patterns and alleviation of anxiety and depression. Three studies have evaluated electrosleep against a believable placebo control in the treatment of alcoholics. In the placebo control condition, subjects initially feel a brief, mild current and, like treatment subjects, are then told that the current is being turned down below perceptible levels. In the control group, the current is actually turned off. Smith and O'Neill (1975) found a modest difference on self-report mood scales betweeen electrosleep and control subjects following 15 sessions. Tomsovic and Edwards (1973), on the other hand, found no differences on ratings of anxiety and sleep problems using a similar design. McKenzie, Costello, and Buck (1975) employed a balanced placebo design, which includes a group told .that they are receiving electrosleep when, in fact, they are not. These investigators found that improvements in sleep, anxiety, and depression can be attributed in part to specific effects of electrosleep and in part to expectancies. The mechanism for specific effectiveness of electrosleep is unknown, but Rosenthal (1973) has suggested that it may produce changes in brain chemistry (cf. Sytinsky & Galebskaya, 1979, for a similar discussion of acupuncture). The direct impact of electrosleep upon *drinking* behavior has not, to our knowledge, been evaluated.

Given present limitations on therapeutic effectiveness, the introduction and exploration of new alternative treatment procedures for problem drinkers should be encouraged. Enthusiasm for new approaches should be balanced, however, by an awareness of the dangers of premature conclusions regarding effectiveness and of the potential for unforeseen and untoward side effects. There is no substitute for well-controlled follow-up research employing a range of valid outcome measures.

Treatment Methods Oriented Toward Moderation

The concept of moderate drinking as an explicit goal of treatment was relatively ignored prior to 1970, when Lovibond and Caddy published the first report of controlled research with a moderation-oriented treatment procedure. In the ensuing ten years, there has been an encouraging amount of well-designed and controlled research evaluating the efficacy of a variety of treatment methods intended to produce what has come to be called "controlled drinking" (Reinert & Bowen, 1968).

With this trend has come a maelstrom of controversy. Many traditional figures in the alcoholism field have bitterly attacked the concept of controlled drinking, maintaining that a disease model and total abstinence represent the only true hope for alcoholics (Block, 1976; Fox, 1963; Gitlow, 1973). Ruth Fox (1967) has asserted, "Among my own approximately 3,000 patients not one has been able to achieve [moderate drinking], although almost every one of them has tried to" (p. 777). The premature publication of results of the "Rand Report" (Armor et al., 1978) in the popular press, particularly (and falsely) highlighting the suggestion that alcoholics could drink with impunity, raised concerns that the report would cause many alcoholics to abandon successful abstinence, a fear which fortunately does not appear to have been realized (e.g., Hingson et al., 1977).

What these initial emotional responses largely failed to discern is the difference between luring successfully abstinent alcoholics back to drinking and adopting moderation as a goal for certain problem drinkers at the *outset* of treatment (Fine, 1976). No proponent of moderation-oriented therapies has advocated their use with *all* problem drinkers, nor has anyone (including the authors of the Rand Report) suggested that abstainers can safely resume drinking. Rather, it has been maintained that moderation-oriented approaches represent one viable alternative for some problem drinkers.

But for how many? Controlled drinking outcomes are not new to the literature. Early comprehensive studies, in fact, recognized the presence of nonabstinent successful outcomes and routinely reported them (e.g., Gerard &

Saenger, 1962; Wallerstein, 1957). Pattison, Sobell, and Sobell (1977) presented a catalog of 74 studies documenting controlled drinking outcomes. Within studies where the goal of treatment was abstinence but controlled drinking outcomes were reported, approximately 12% of more than 10,000 patients were found to be drinking moderately at follow-up. This figure is somewhat higher than the 5.8% figure reported by Emrick (1974), in part because his admirably extensive review did not include numerous studies that appeared between 1971 and the Pattison review in 1977. Is controlled drinking, then, a realistic goal for only 5 to 15% of patients? Such a conclusion would be misleading because the programs upon which these figures are based were not designed to teach controlled drinking. Rather, they focused on abstinence, and a small percentage of clients "incidentally" became moderate drinkers. A more telling figure would be one reflecting the frequency of moderation outcomes when this was the intention of treatment. Again examining the catalog of studies in the Pattison et al. review, we find 17 studies in which moderation was the explicit goal of treatment. Summing across these studies, 63% of the more than 1,600 patients are reported to be controlled drinkers at follow-up. (This figure is pulled strongly upward by three Japanese cyanamide studies that comprise 83% of the subjects and in which 70% are reported to be controlled drinkers. Without the Japanese studies, the percentage of controlled drinkers drops to 30%, with an additional 11% abstaining.) In a review at the end of this chapter (which incorporates ten more studies not available at the time of the Pattison review), we present summary data to suggest that an average of 33% of clients achieve moderation when this is the goal of treatment, with an additional 31% abstinent or improved as of one year follow-up. This overall improvement figure of 64% is at least comparable to that from abstinence programs (Emrick, 1975). It appears, therefore, that problem drinkers are not being placed at any greater risk of failure within moderation-oriented programs than when the goal of treatment is abstinence. We wish to reemphasize that this is *not* to say that controlled drinking should be adopted as a goal for all problem drinkers. The task before us now is to develop rational means for selecting the optimal treatment modality in each individual case (Miller & Caddy, 1977). Certainly, abstinence remains a viable and conservative recommendation in the interim, while these guidelines are being developed through research (V. Fox, 1976; Nathan, 1976).

The potential advantages of controlled drinking therapies are several. Many problem drinkers, particularly those at earlier stages in problem development, are unwilling to label themselves as "alcoholic" or to consider abstinence as a treatment goal. Moderation-oriented approaches may be more acceptable to such early-stage problem drinkers and may, indeed, be more successful than are traditional methods in such cases (Lovibond, 1975; Miller & Caddy, 1977; Miller & Joyce, 1979). Likewise for the patient who repeatedly fails to respond to an abstinence approach, controlled drinking therapies may offer an effective alternative (Nathan, 1976). Finally, several writers (e.g., Miller & Caddy, 1977; Nagy, 1977) have suggested that even with the resistant client for whom abstinence is ultimately necessary, a trial run through a controlled-drinking program may be beneficial by providing the most direct kind of evidence that moderation is not attainable.

In this section, we will examine alternative treatment procedures that have emerged over the past ten years as avenues toward moderation. The difficult question of diagnosis—how to choose the optimal treatment goal for a given case—will be taken up in our final section on factors predictive of outcome.

Behavioral Self-Control Training

Behavioral self-control training (BSCT) represents an educationally-oriented approach to the treatment of problem drinking. Although the specific content has varied from one clinic to another, BSCT approaches generally have the following common characteristics: (a) an educational program designed to assist individuals in attaining and maintaining a moderate and nonproblematic level of drinking; (b) usually offered on an outpatient basis; and (c) amenable to a variety of presentation formats including group (classroom), individual, and bibliotherapy. In comparison to some alternative approaches described in this chapter, BSCT does not require any special equipment, can be conducted in a standard counseling room or classroom, and does not require the consumption of alcohol beverages within the treatment setting. For these and other reasons to be elaborated below, BSCT also has direct applicability to efforts aimed at the prevention of problem drinking.

Miller and his colleagues (Hamburg et al., 1977; Miller, 1977, 1978a,b; Miller & Muñoz, 1976) have developed and described a comprehensive BSCT program that includes the following elements: (a) *goal-setting*, the determination of specific and appropriate limits for alcohol consumption based upon current knowledge of the effects of ethanol on the body and on behavior, and including external-cue BAC training; (b) *self-monitoring* of alcohol consumption; (c) *rate control training* designed to alter the topography of drinking behavior, using rules similar to those described by Sobell and Sobell (1973); (d) *self-reinforcement training* to encourage ongoing progress; (e) *functional analysis* of drinking behavior, with training in stimulus control procedures; and (f) *alternatives training* designed to teach coping skills to be used in situations where alcohol was previously used to cope (Miller & Mastria, 1977).

This program has been evaluated in a series of five treatment outcome studies conducted over a period of six years in the states of Oregon, California, and New Mexico. In the first of these studies (Miller, 1978a), no significant differences in effectiveness were found between BSCT and two alternative programs, one based on electrical aversive counterconditioning and the other a complex multimodal program incorporating techniques from Lovibond and Caddy (1970) and Sobell and Sobell (1973b) requiring at least three times as much therapist contact. All three programs were found to produce substantial improvement in problem drinking clients at one-year follow-up. A second study (Miller, Gribskov, & Mortell, in press) compared two different approaches to BSCT: a bibliotherapy (minimal therapist contact) condition, and a therapist-administered condition involving ten weekly individual sessions with a paraprofessional. Again, no significant differences were found, with both groups showing good improvement at three-month follow-up. Miller, Pechacek, and Hamburg (in press) conducted an uncontrolled pilot study of BSCT, offered within a classroom setting, and found an improvement rate comparable to that found in the previous two studies. A fourth study (Miller & Taylor, 1980) attempted to replicate the findings of the previous three by assigning problem drinkers to one of four conditions: (1) BSCT bibliotherapy; (2) BSCT individual therapy; (3) BSCT plus relaxation training in individual therapy; and (4) BSCT plus relaxation training in group therapy. Preliminary analyses of one-year and two-year follow-up data confirm previous findings of no significant differences among these groups, with an overall improvement rate of approximately 70%, again consistent with prior studies. In the fifth and most recent study, Miller, Taylor and West (in press) compared BSCT bibliotherapy and BSCT individual therapy with (two more extensive broad-spectrum behavior therapies. Preliminary findings (as of six-month follow-up) again suggest significant improvement in all groups, with no statistically significant differences among groups. Thus, over five studies, various BSCT approaches have produced total improvement rates averaging around 70%, with few differences either between alternative BSCT formats or between BSCT and other (often more extensive) approaches. Overall, these findings point to a possible cost-effectiveness advantage for BSCT methods and particularly for those involving minimal therapist contact.

Alden (1978), using Miller's BSCT program, reported that 70% of her problem-drinking clients were "nonhazardous drinkers" as of treatment termination, with a slight decline in this percentage reflected in preliminary follow-up data. Unlike Miller et al. (in press), she found that an "enriched" multimodal approach produced significantly better outcome than did a basic BSCT program alone. A modest advantage in favor of the enriched program was retained at 12- and 24-month follow-ups (Alden, 1979).

Caddy and Lovibond (1976) found that an enriched BSCT approach produced better improvement (64% at one year) than did an aversion therapy program without self-control instructions (50%), but less improvement than that shown by a group receiving both BSCT and aversion therapy (77%). Unfortunately, specific tests of significance of these contrasts were not reported.

Pomerleau et al. (1978) compared a group BSCT program (including relaxation training and family therapy) with group psychotherapy for problem drinkers and found overall improvement rates of 72% and 50% respectively (not a statistically significant difference).

Vogler and his colleagues (1975, 1977a, 1977b) have compared an educational BSCT program with a much-enriched program including BSCT plus videotape self-confrontation, electrical aversion therapy, and internal cue BAC training. Within both inpatient and outpatient populations, Vogler has found modest differences in effectiveness between groups, with the slight advantage in favor of the more extensive program. In most analyses, however, these differences have failed to reach statistical significance.

Other multimodal inpatient and outpatient programs designed to teach controlled drinking have included the basic elements of BSCT within more complex treatment packages (Baker, Udin, & Vogler, 1975; Ewing & Rouse, 1976; Lovibond, 1975; Lovibond & Caddy, 1970; Sanchez-Craig, 1980; Sobell & Sobell, 1973b). The relative contribution of BSCT within such programs is unclear. In general, the studies reviewed above have found that BSCT alone compares favorably with more extensive programs that include BSCT plus additional elements. The typical finding has been a modest advantage for more extensive interventions, with differences occasionally reaching statistical significance (Alden, 1978; Vogler et al., 1975).

Summary. BSCT appears to be a promising approach in teaching controlled drinking to problem drinkers. Remarkably consistent improvement rates of 60% to 80% have been found across such diverse locations as Pennsylvania, Oregon, Australia, California, New Mexico, and Vancouver, B. C. Patient populations have varied widely in socioeconomic status and have included middle-class self-referrals, patients in state hospitals, and court referrals. It should be noted, however, that *none* of the studies reviewed above has included a randomly assigned no-treatment control group. Thus, the improvement rates cited above, though encouraging, cannot with confidence be attributed to the specific components of BSCT. It is unclear which (if any) of the components of BSCT are necessary or sufficient to produce improvement in problem drinkers. Clients in our clinics have rather consistently reported that self-monitoring has been one of the most valuable parts of the program for them, raising awareness of the amount and pattern of their drinking. The value of self-monitoring alone remains to be confirmed by controlled experimental research (cf. Kennedy et al., 1978; Sobell & Sobell, 1973a).

For a variety of reasons, BSCT may be of value in the primary and secondary prevention of problem drinking as well (Miller & Caddy, 1977; Pomerleau et al., 1975, 1976; Vogler & Caddy, 1973). This approach is amenable to various educational formats and therefore may be made available to persons at earlier stages in the development of problem drinking without the requirement of labeling or seeking "treatment." Many of the components of BSCT (e.g., self-monitoring) are readily applied within a self-help program (Miller, 1978b; Miller & Muñoz, 1976). Finally, the BSCT focus upon moderation of drinking may be acceptable at earlier stages of problem drinking, when individuals may not be receptive to other approaches that require self-labeling as "alcoholic" or lifelong commitment to total abstinence.

Self-Help

Every approach that we have discussed thus far (with the partial exception of Alcoholics Anonymous) has involved a formal treatment process requiring the identification of oneself as having a problem. What about self-help programs? We have no idea how many people successfully cope with overdrinking on their own, let alone how they do it. Most people who come for treatment have taken some measures in an attempt to cope prior to seeking formal help. What do we know about the efficacy of self-help methods?

Numerous self-help books have been published for alcoholics and their relatives, usually with a clear goal of total abstinence (e.g., Alcoholics Anonymous, 1955; Maxwell, 1976; Weston, 1964), although moderation-oriented self-help materials have also begun to appear (Amit et al., 1977; Mertens, 1972; Miller & Muñoz, 1976; Robbins & Fisher, 1973; Winters, 1977). There is increasing professional interest in "bibliotherapy" or "non-prescription therapies," yet relatively little research has been devoted to the evaluation of such self-help treatment approaches (Glasgow & Rosen, 1978; Rosen, 1976).

In our research clinics at Oregon and now in New Mexico, we have used bibliotherapy—simply providing the client with a self-help manual (Miller & Muñoz, 1976) and other self-help materials such as self-monitoring cards—as a "minimum treatment control group" against which to compare the efficacy of other approaches. Our interest in this was sparked when we found that providing a self-help manual appeared to be of value in helping clients to maintain gains they had made during treatment (Miller, 1978a). In three subsequent comparative treatment outcome studies (Miller, Gribskov, & Mortell, in press; Miller & Taylor, 1980; Miller et al., in press), we have found that clients assigned at random to a self-help condition have shown significant gains in their control over drinking, with improvement rates ranging from 50% to 88% (see section on multimodal therapies). Furthermore, we have found, to our surprise, relatively few differences in effectiveness between self-administered and therapist-administered versions of the same treatment (behavioral self-control training) across the three studies. Because our designs have not included no-treatment conditions, we cannot be sure how much of the improvement in self-help groups is due to the materials we provided as opposed to other factors, such as the decision to do something about one's drinking. Everyone in our studies has come to our clinics seeking assistance; thus, our samples are probably not representative of people who might wander into a bookstore and purchase the same self-help materials. Nevertheless, the improvement rates in our self-help groups have compared favorably with more extensive therapist efforts.

In a similar and now controversial study, Edwards and his colleagues (1977) found that a single session of "advice" (basically telling the client that he or she would have to be responsible for making changes in drinking) was not significantly less effective than a traditional treatment program including

A.A., outpatient group psychotherapy, pharmacotherapy with calcium cyanamide, and an option for inpatient services. As will be discussed in a later section, other investigators have also found few differences between minimal and extensive interventions.

We believe that self-help interventions are deserving of further investigation, particularly because of their low cost and their availability to individuals at early stages in problem development, without having to seek treatment or accept a label. It is also likely that there is much we could learn from individuals who have successfully coped with a drinking problem without the assistance of professional resources.

BAC Discrimination Training

Blood alcohol concentration (BAC) is a critical variable in alcohol research and treatment (Matthews & Miller, 1979). It reflects degree of intoxication and impact on the body more accurately than do alcohol consumption data alone. Information regarding the relationships among BAC, alcohol consumption, and probable behavioral effects has been part of many education and treatment programs for problem drinkers.

Internal Cues. One approach to BAC education has been termed ''BAC discrimination training.'' In this method, a breath-alcohol analyzer, such as the Intoximeter, has been used as a biofeedback device to give individuals information regarding their current BAC level. In the typical procedure, the client consumes beverages of unknown alcohol concentration and receives periodic feedback of his or her BAC. The client is asked to attend to subtle proprioceptive and other internal cues in order to establish a relationship between these signs and BAC levels. As a result of this training, the individual is supposed to be able to discriminate her or his BAC level while drinking without feedback.

Lovibond and Caddy introduced this ''internal cue'' training procedure and have included it within a multimodal treatment program designed to teach controlled drinking. The impressive improvement rates from their initial study (86% improved at 12 months and 59% at 24 months following treatment) aroused considerable interest in this method. These investigators have replicated their original findings in two additional studies (Caddy & Lovibond, 1976; Lovibond, 1975), finding comparable multimodal treatment programs to yield improvement rates of 80% at six months and 85% at one- to nine-month follow-up, respectively. Two other research teams, however, have failed to replicate these successful findings (Ewing & Rouse, 1976; Maxwell et al., 1974), although both studies have been roundly criticized on methodological grounds (Caddy, 1975; Sobell & Sobell, 1978).

One question addressed in recent research is whether or not individuals can use internal cues to learn to discriminate their own BAC. Bois and Vogel-Sprott (1974) reported that their nine normal-drinking male subjects learned to discriminate BAC and to self-titrate alcohol dosage in order to maintain a given BAC level. Accuracy of discrimination dropped only slightly when subjects were no longer allowed to know the strength of the beverages they were drinking. The average error at the end of training was less than 10 mg% (mg alcohol per 100 ml blood). Huber, Karlin, and Nathan (1976) likewise were successful in training moderate drinkers to discriminate BAC using an internal cue procedure and found that accuracy did not deteriorate when feedback was withdrawn. Similar accuracy of discrimination (errors less than 10 mg% on the average) among problem drinkers has been reported by Ewing and Rouse (1976), by Lovibond and Caddy (1970), and by Vogler, Weissbach, Compton, and Martin (1977).

On the other hand, Silverstein, Nathan, and Taylor (1974) were unable to train four chronic alcoholics to reach this level of accuracy and reported that the alcoholics' discrimination ability deteriorated when feedback was withdrawn. Lansky, Nathan, and Lawson (1978) reported similar failure with alcoholics trained by the internal cue procedure, with substantial deterioration in accuracy following withdrawal of biofeedback. These studies suggest the possibility of a difference in discrimination ability between alcoholic and nonalcoholic subjects (Rowan, 1978). Lansky, Nathan, Ersner-Hershfield, and Lipscomb (1978) used correlational analyses to study the ability of alcoholic and nonalcoholic subjects to follow *fluctuations* in BAC without knowledge of drink strength and without prior training in BAC discrimination. They found that, indeed, nonalcoholic subjects are better able to monitor changes in BAC than are alcoholics, a finding that may have some interesting implications for the etiology of alcoholism (Caddy, 1978).

Two studies employing placebo designs have contributed further information regarding internal cue training. Maisto and Adesso (1977) allowed heavy-drinking subjects to observe drinks being mixed but deceived some subjects by substituting water for vodka. They found that BAC estimates were accurate only when the actual alcohol content and the subjects' expectations were consistent. Subjects who believed they were consuming alcohol, but in fact were not, gave BAC estimates similar to those of subjects who received alcohol. Henning (1974) employed a full 2 x 2 balanced placebo design, crossing expectancy of receiving alcohol with the actual presence or absence of alcohol in the beverage during training. Like Maisto and Adesso, Henning found that expectancy deceptions generated inaccurate BAC estimates. Henning also reported that the four groups in this study showed equal ability to predict BAC, that three days of training did not substantially improve this ability, and that subjects apparently did not use internal bodily cues to judge BAC level. Here, then, is a curious finding. Internal cue training procedures seem to produce BAC discrimination ability, but subjects (at least nonproblem drinkers) seem to bring some discrimination abilities with them to the experiments and apparently do not use internal cues to make discriminations. That subjects in fact do not depend upon relationships between internal cues and intoxication levels in order to judge BAC is further supported by Bois and Vogel-Sprott (1974) and by Caddy, Sutton, and Lewis (in press).

External Cues. If internal cue training does not work by helping people to attend to internal cues, then what mechanisms have permitted subjects to learn BAC discrimination? The answer may lie in an alternative approach known as "external cue training." In this approach, the individual is provided with a table of BAC (Matthews & Miller, 1979; Miller & Muñoz, 1976), with a calculation device (Compton & Vogler, 1974) or with some simple mathematical rules for estimating BAC based upon the amount of alcohol consumed and the time elapsed. Several clinical teams have included external rather than internal cue training within multimodal treatment programs aimed at controlled drinking, and have reported improvement rates comparable to those of other multimodal programs that have included internal cue procedures (Alden, 1978; Miller, 1977, 1978a, 1978b; Miller & Taylor, 1980; Miller et al., in press; Pomerleau et al., 1978; Sobell & Sobell, 1973b; Vogler et al., 1975, 1977a, 1977b).

Comparing Internal and External Cues. In a laboratory study, Huber, Karlin, and Nathan (1976) compared the accuracy in BAC discrimination of groups trained by internal cues only, by external cues only, and by both internal and external cue procedures. They found that all three groups of moderate drinkers learned to discriminate BAC and remained able to do so after feedback had been withdrawn, with no significant difference among groups even when the strength of drinks was concealed from subjects. This is a curious finding, because externally-trained subjects ostensibly rely upon knowledge of drink strength for accuracy of BAC judgment. The investigators interpret their finding by suggesting that externally-trained individuals may experience some "incidental internal cue training." The failure of Maisto and Adesso's (1977) subjects to learn BAC discrimination under reasonably similar circumstances is puzzling, but may be attributable to the fact that Maisto and Adesso apparently used subjects who were much heavier drinkers than were those in the study by Huber et al. That this may account for differences is further supported by Lansky, Nathan, and Lawson (1978), who compared the BAC estimation accuracy of alcoholics trained only by internal cue procedures with that of alcoholics trained only by external cue methods. When BAC feedback was withdrawn, only externally-trained alcoholics were able to maintain accuracy of BAC estimates during subsequent drinking. It appears that although nonalcoholic moderate drinkers are able to learn BAC discrimination from either external or internal cue training, alcoholics and possibly heavier drinkers benefit only from external cue training (which would be of little or no use within the placebo deception conditions employed by Maisto and Adesso).

The only clinical outcome studies to compare directly internal versus external cue training have been conducted by Vogler and his colleagues (1975, 1977a, 1977b). Vogler, Weissbach, Compton, and Martin (1977) compared two multimodal treatment programs including both external and internal cue BAC training with a more minimal alcohol education program that included external cue BAC training. No significant difference in effectiveness of groups was found. In an earlier study treating more severe alcoholics, Vogler, Compton, and Weissbach (1975, 1977a) found marginally significant differences between a multimodal program including both internal and external cue training and a less extensive alcohol education program that apparently placed little or no emphasis upon BAC training. Caddy and Lovibond (1976) included internal cue training in all three of the treatment packages they compared, but omitted the "self-regulation" component (which emphasized external cue training) from one of the programs. The group randomly assigned to receive the program without external cue training showed the least improvement of the three. Miller (1978a), comparing three alternative treatment packages, found that the group receiving electrical aversion (also the only group not to receive external cue training) showed the least improvement, but that differences among groups disappeared after the aversion group received a self-help manual that included instructions for external cue training (Miller & Muñoz, 1976). In four separate outcome studies, Miller and his colleagues (1977, 1978a; Miller & Taylor, 1980; Miller et al., in press) have found that a self-control training program (including external cue training), with or without therapist assistance, compares favorably with alternative interventions.

Summary. All in all, external cue BAC training appears to be a valuable component within multimodal treatment programs where the goal is controlled drinking, although it is far from clear that it is a necessary component of such programs. External cue training is easily integrated with other control-oriented treatment procedures such as goal-setting and self-monitoring (Matthews & Miller, 1979). Certainly, external cue training is to be preferred over internal cue training for most problem drinkers because: (a) internal cue training involves the use of expensive equipment and requires alcohol consumption within the treatment setting, whereas external cue training is a simple counseling procedure; (b) there is no evidence to suggest superior effectiveness of internal over external cue training; and (c) at least some problem drinkers may be able to benefit from external but not from internal cue training. One limitation on external cue training at the present time is our only modest ability to predict actual BAC from external cues! Most methods take into account body weight, amount consumed, time parameters, and perhaps sex of subject (Matthews & Miller, 1979), but there remains an impressive amount of variance due to other individual differences (e.g., Bois & Vogel-Sprott, 1974; Compton & Vogler, 1975). Although some data are available regarding the individual influence of other factors such as age, drinking history, menstrual cycle, and food in the stomach, only future multivariate research will permit the proper weighting of these many variables to produce optimal predictions of BAC.

Videotape Feedback

Possible applications of tape recording devices to the treatment process were recognized and explored almost as soon as the technology became available. The use of audiotape self-confrontation of patients dates back to the early 1940s and the wire recorder. Pioneer work on videotape self-confrontation followed in the early 1950s (Bailey & Sowder, 1970). The uses of videotape in alcoholism treatment have been varied, and generally have fallen into four classes: (a) taping of an intensive interview (with no alcohol or a moderate dose) exploring significant dynamic material and reviewing the tape with the client at a later time (Feinstein & Tamerin, 1972; Paredes & Cornelison, 1968; Paredes et al., 1969); (b) showing taped interviews with "model patients" who experienced successful outcomes (Baker et al., 1975; Greer & Callis, 1975); (c) using videotape feedback as an aid in behavior rehearsal and the training of social skills (Scherer & Freedberg, 1976); and (d) taping of alcoholics in advanced stages of intoxication or withdrawal and viewing the tape at a later time to confront the patient (now in a sober state) with the severity of his or her alcoholic symptoms, which are typically forgotten or denied (e.g., Faia & Shean, 1976; Schaefer et al., 1971).

The general literature on applications of videotape to psychotherapy has received several reviews (Bailey & Sowder, 1970; Danet, 1968; Griffiths, 1974), with the conclusion that in spite of the usual enthusiastic endorsements by professionals, the value of self-confrontation has not been supported by scientifically acceptable research. There is some evidence, in fact, to suggest that videotape self-confrontation may be harmful to patients, at least if applied in certain ways (Bailey & Sowder, 1970; Schaefer et al., 1971).

In the area of alcoholism treatment, however, an impressive amount of sound research has appeared since the Bailey and Sowder review. Videotape self-confrontation may, in fact, be one of few treatment techniques in this area for which there has been more controlled than uncontrolled research! We will briefly review this recent literature, addressing the four types of applications of videotape listed above.

Adjunct to Psychotherapy. Postulating that alcoholics are characterized by denial, Davis (1972) audiotaped group and individual psychotherapy sessions and played them back at the beginning of each subsequent therapy hour, a technique described earlier by Armstrong (1964). The design of this study was relatively clean, with random assignment to group or individual methods, but, unfortunately, follow-up data relied upon a self-report questionnaire and the criteria for judging improvement were unspecified. A total of 29% of the patients (17% in individual and 42% in group psychotherapy) were described as showing "decreased drinking" at six-month follow-up. Of the 24 patients,

54% (75% in individual and 33% in group psychotherapy) failed to complete the sessions, a rather high drop-out rate, at least in the individual psychotherapy group (cf. Pomerleau et al., 1978). Feinstein and Tamerin (1972) reported administering alcohol to an alcoholic and then conducting a videotaped depth interview in order to elicit dynamically relevant material. The case was unsuccessful. Paredes, Ludwig, Hassenfeld, and Cornelison (1969) used a similar strategy to treat 66 inpatient and outpatient alcoholics, administering a moderate priming dose of alcohol (three to four ounces of vodka). They reported no follow-up data, but indicated that viewing of the tapes elicited strong negative affect in patients, particularly statements indicative of low self-esteem.

All in all, research does not support the use of tape-assisted psychotherapy in the treatment of alcoholism. The few data that are presently available are consistent with findings regarding insight-oriented psychotherapy with alcoholics in general, suggesting low efficacy and a high drop-out rate. The paucity of data requires, however, that judgment be suspended pending further research.

Videotaped Models. In 1966, Goldstein, Heller, and Sechrest suggested that it might be beneficial for new patients to see tapes of "model patients" in order to provide a proper orientation toward treatment and outcome. Greer and Callis (1975) showed taped interviews with successful graduates of an alcoholism program to 34 new admissions to the same program. In comparison to 34 matched controls, the experimental patients were found to show greater gains during treatment on a variety of psychometric measures. No assessment of impact upon drinking behavior and no follow-up data were reported, however. Baker, Udin, and Vogler (1975) compared outcome in four groups constructed by random assignment. The first three groups all received a behavioral counseling package (self-control instructions, functional analysis, alternatives training). One of these groups was also exposed to a series of modeling tapes, and another received videotaped self-confrontation (see below). A fourth group received only the standard hospital program. The group viewing model tapes in addition to receiving behavioral counseling fared no better than did the behavioral-counseling-only group at six-week follow-up (total abstinent plus controlled = 73% vs. 74%) or at six-month follow-up (55% vs. 50%), although both compared favorably with the hospital-control group at six weeks. This latter study suggests no advantage in using modeling tapes, although data are insufficient to draw conclusions as to the value of this procedure.

Videotape in Behavior Rehearsal. As alternative skills training for alcoholics receives increasing attention (Miller & Mastria, 1977), it is likely that videotape will be employed to provide immediate feedback regarding behavior rehearsal performance. Data regarding the value of videotape feedback in the training process are few and unclear at the present time. Scherer and Freedberg (1976), working with an alcoholic population, compared the effectiveness of assertion training with and without videotape feedback and found no difference in impact upon assertiveness behaviors. No drinking data were reported.

Self-Confrontation of Intoxication. The earliest application of videotape with alcoholics was pioneered by the French psychiatrist Carrère (1954, 1958), who developed a procedure called "cinematographic psychoshock." Patients were videotaped in advanced stages of intoxication and withdrawal during the detoxification process, with the hypothesis that the emotional shock of seeing oneself in such a deteriorated condition (normally denied or forgotten when sober) would prevent relapse. Carrère reported that of 65 alcoholics treated with the psychoshock method, 45% remained abstinent and an additional 14% showed considerable improvement (period of follow-up not stated). Further, of the 29 who remained abstinent, 18 had received *only* psychoshock and detoxification. Faia and Shean (1976) used a similar procedure, taping alcoholics upon hospital admission for detoxification. This study included a matched comparison group, but, unfortunately, 52% of the patients were not located for follow-up. Of those found during the year of the study, 95% had relapsed within 60 days.

In addition to these uncontrolled reports, six controlled studies provide further information regarding videotape self-confrontation as a treatment technique. Tim Baker and his colleagues (1975), in a study described above, included one group receiving videotape self-confrontation. Although statistical significance of differences between groups did not hold up at six-month follow-up, the self-confrontation group showed the highest percentage of abstinent plus controlled cases at both six-week and six-month follow-up periods (80% and 65%, as compared with 59% and 47% in the hospital control group). All patients in experimental groups in this study also received behavioral self-control training.

Schaefer, Sobell, and Mills (1971) produced "experimental intoxication" in inpatients by permitting them to consume up to 16 ounces of an alcoholic beverage of their choice. The 36 participating patients were then assigned at random to receive 30-minute, five-minute, or no videotape feedback of their intoxicated behavior. Only 44% of the two videotape groups completed four sessions (again a high drop-out rate) in comparison to 90% of the group who drank without receiving feedback. Within the two videotape groups, 100% of the patients relapsed soon after discharge, as compared with 83% in the no-feedback group and 75% in a nonrandom control group receiving hospital treatment. A one-year follow-up of these groups (Schaefer, Sobell, & Sobell, 1972), however, suggests a possible "sleeper" effect in that 50% of the videotape patients were abstinent or drinking in a controlled manner (as compared with 10% of the no-feedback and 25% of the hospital controls). Videotape-treated patients were also found to seek more additional therapeutic support such as A.A. following hospital discharge. None of the between-group differences were statistically significant, however. The authors suggested that although the videotape treatment may have precipitated a return to drinking in some patients, it may also have raised awareness and motivation for eventual treatment.

Videotape self-confrontation during experimental intoxication has been included as one component of a multimodal treatment program in three other controlled studies (Sobell & Sobell, 1973b; Vogler et al., 1975, 1977b). Reporting on a three-year, double-blind follow-up study of patients treated by Sobell and Sobell (1973b), Glenn Caddy and his colleagues (1978) presented data indicating that a multimodal treatment package including videotape self-confrontation produced significantly better long-term results than did standard hospital treatment only among patients for whom the specified goal of treatment was controlled drinking. Within the abstinence goal groups, however, experimental (multimodal) patients did not show improvement significantly better than that of the hospital control. Although patients in this study were randomly assigned to experimental versus control conditions, they were not assigned at random to abstinence versus controlled drinking goals. Differential response, then, may be attributable in part to pretreatment differences. Nevertheless, the within-goal differences support the effectiveness of the Sobells' multimodal program. Roger Vogler and his colleagues evaluated a very similar multimodal treatment package including videotape self-confrontation with alcoholics (1975) and with problem drinkers (1977b). In both studies, patients receiving the multimodal program were found to be slightly but not significantly more improved on most measures than were patients receiving much more minimal interventions (e.g., an alcohol education program including self-control training). In all three of these studies, patient self-reports were carefully confirmed with collateral sources.

Finally, Lanyon and colleagues (1972) applied a somewhat different technique called "interpersonal aversion" to 15 alcoholics. The patients were videotaped during intensive individual interviews (without alcohol) and then viewed the tapes while two therapists kept up a running commentary of derogatory and confronting remarks. Eight patients undergoing this aversive procedure were also taught systematic desensitization skills, whereas seven were provided only with an equivalent amount of time for discussion. Interestingly, the group provided with desensitization training showed more abstinent cases (5/8) than did either the aversion group without desensitization (1/7) or a nonrandom control group receiving neither treatment (1/7). Outcome data must be questioned, however, because they were based solely upon patient self-report plus the interviewer's judgment as to whether or not the report was "truthful."

Summary. Data are insufficient to determine whether alcoholics are benefitted by the use of videotape as an adjunct to psychotherapy, to provide coping models, or to supply feedback to assist in behavior rehearsal. Data from four well controlled studies are consistent in suggesting a modest but usually not significant advantage for multimodal treatment programs including videotape self-confrontation of intoxicated behavior. The contribution of the videotape component relative to other portions of multimodal packages is difficult to judge. A high drop-out rate, similar to that from confrontive or intensive psychotherapy, seems characteristic. Clearly, videotape self-confrontation can be a powerfully aversive and emotional experience, and the potential for harm to patients should be considered (Bailey & Sowder, 1970; Baker et al., 1975; Feinstein & Tamerin, 1972; Paredes et al., 1969; Schaefer et al., 1971). Present data suggest that if videotape confrontation is used as a motivating device, the patient should also be provided with training in concrete skills for coping with the stress it arouses. Studies that have failed to do so have reported the poorest outcome data (Schaefer et al., 1971; Faia & Shean, 1976). It is not clear whether the self-confrontation experience improves outcome over that which would be accomplished from a self-control training program alone, but it appears that any increment in effectiveness is relatively modest.

Cognitive Therapies

With the rise of behavioral approaches to treatment, interest in personal perceptions and ''cognitive processes and structure'' declined. In recent years, however, interest has been revived and the impact of the individual's cognitions upon her or his behavior is being reassessed (Beck, 1976; Meichenbaum, 1977). Kirkpatrick (1978), for example, has made extensive use of rational-emotive concepts in her innovative program, ''Woman for Sobriety.'' The emerging mixture of cognitive approaches and behavior therapy has come to be called cognitive-behavior modification (CBM). The amount of importance placed on cognitions versus overt behaviors varies. Brandsma, Maultsby, and Welsh (in press) subscribed to the perspective of ''rational-emotive therapy'' in which cognitions or self-statements are seen as the cause of emotional and physiological disturbances. Other positions have attempted to strike more of a balance between cognitive processes and environmental influences on behavior (e.g., Meyers et al., 1976; Sanchez-Craig & Walker, 1974).

Outcome Research. Research on CBM in general (not restricted to alcoholism) is quite recent, but suggests that the combination of approaches may be more effective than either a strict behavioral or a totally cognitive approach alone (Meichenbaum, 1977; Sanchez-Craig, 1976). Within the area of alcoholism, research on CBM is only beginning. Martha Sanchez-Craig and her associates (Sanchez-Craig, 1975, 1976; Sanchez-Craig & Walker, 1974; Walker, Sanchez-Craig, & McDonald, 1974) have described strategies for teaching coping strategies which include cognitive restructuring and the covert rehearsal of adaptive behaviors. Alan Marlatt (see chapter by Cummings, Gordon & Marlatt) has utilized CBM methods in designing relapse prevention strategies for alcoholics.

Hay, Hay, and Nelson (1977) reported a case study with 11-month successful abstinence following six 30-minute sessions in which an alcoholic was taught covert rehearsal of appropriate responses to excessive drinking stimuli. Similarly, positive results with cognitive procedures have been reported in case studies by Sanchez-Craig (1975) and Sanchez-Craig & Walker (1974).

The only controlled evaluation to date has been reported by Brandsma et al. (in press) and compared "rational behavior therapy," insight therapy, A.A., and no treatment. One-year follow-up indicated that all treatment groups showed more improvement than did the control group. Differences among treatment methods were marginal and varied. Rational behavior therapy, whether offered by a professional or by a paraprofessional, was found to be as effective as insight therapy conducted by experienced practitioners. Both had lower drop-out rates and showed slightly better improvement than did A.A. treated clients, although most differences failed to reach statistical significance.

Summary. Outcome data regarding cognitive approaches in the treatment of problem drinking are insufficient to reach substantive conclusions at present. The apparent effectiveness of such approaches in certain other problem areas suggests that their application with problem drinkers should continue to be explored.

Operant Approaches

In the early 1970s, behavioral psychologists began to investigate the influence of environmental contingencies on the drinking behavior of alcoholics. This research is generally called "operant" in that it examines environmental factors that operate to influence behavior. Of particular interest are environmental contingencies that serve to reward or punish a particular response—in this case, drinking.

Also during the early 1970s, a number of inpatient programs began allowing alcoholics access to alcohol under various controlled circumstances. In some cases alcohol was permitted in conjunction with treatment, and in others the focus was upon research alone and treatment was not offered. With rare exceptions (e.g., Miller, 1972), these programs have maintained a formal treatment goal of abstinence, but they are included here because of their implications for moderation-oriented approaches.

One initial concern was the possible detrimental impact of giving alcohol to alcoholics in treatment. In two experiments, both with six-month follow-up data, Faillace, Flamer, Imber, and Ward (1972) and Paredes, Gregory, and Jones (1974) found that administration of alcohol in a controlled manner during treatment did not adversely affect individual or social behavior of patients. To the contrary, Faillace et al. (1972) found that patients given access to alcohol tended to show more improvement on drinking and psychosocial measures following treatment than did those not given alcohol.

Two major projects have examined how different environmental contingencies affect alcoholics' drinking. The first of these is a series of studies conducted by Bigelow, Cohen, Liebson, and their associates at the Baltimore City Hospitals (Bigelow, Cohen, Liebson, & Faillace, 1972; Cohen, Liebson & Faillace, 1972; Cohen, Liebson, Faillace, & Allen, 1971). In one paradigm, these investigators allowed alcoholics to drink, but if they chose to consume more than five ounces of alcohol per day they were restricted to an "impoverished" environment. Under this contingency, alcoholics significantly limited their consumption by comparison with periods in which this contingency was not in effect, regardless of whether these noncontingent periods were in an enriched (Cohen et al., 1971) or an impoverished environment (Cohen et al., 1972). Similarly, Bigelow et al. (1974) found substantial reduction in alcohol consumption when receiving a drink resulted in a ten-to-15-minute "time-out" from social contact in an isolation booth. These studies were among the first to demonstrate that, at least under controlled conditions, diagnosed alcoholics were able to exert some volitional control over amount and pattern of alcohol consumption. Other studies have provided additional data to support the modifiability of alcoholics' drinking behavior by environmental contingencies (Bigelow & Liebson, 1972; Cohen et al., 1971, 1973; Cutter et al., 1970; Goldman et al., 1973; Griffiths et al., 1974; Liebson et al., 1971; Nathan & O'Brien, 1971; Nathan et al., 1970; Ogborne & Collier, 1976; Wilson et al., 1975).

In a second series of studies, Arthur Alterman and his colleagues at the Coatesville V. A. Hospital (Alterman et al., 1974, 1975, 1977, 1978; Gottheil et al., 1971, 1972a, 1972b, 1973, 1975; Skoloda et al., 1975) have reported results of an innovative treatment adjunct called Fixed Interval Drinking Decisions (FIDD). In the FIDD program, inpatients are allowed one drink per hour for four weeks, followed by a week with no alcohol available. This is done in addition to a routine hospital treatment program. In early reports, Gottheil et al. (1971, 1972a) noted that their data did not support the hypotheses of inability to stop drinking and of irresistible craving in alcoholics. Subsequent reports have provided follow-up data on various samples of patients completing this program. In the most extensive report to date, Alterman et al. (1978) detail results of one- and two-year follow-ups. Subjects were divided according to those who abstained, those who drank low to moderate amounts, and those who drank heavily (more than eight ounces per day); first-day and last-day abstainers were also tabulated separately. Of 249 treated patients, 120 (48%) were abstinent at two years. Patients who had abstained on the first and last day of available alcohol were found to be doing about as well as those who had been abstinent throughout treatment. The program-

abstainers and moderate drinkers together showed more favorable outcomes than did those who drank heavily during the program. Overall, there were few differences between abstinent and low-level program drinkers at two years. Relatedly, Thornton et al. (1977) compared results of alcoholics who voluntarily abstained or drank and those of a group who were not allowed alcohol for medical reasons. At six-month follow-up, this latter group was found to be drinking less than those who drank during the program, but not less than those who voluntarily abstained. This suggests that voluntary abstinence in the face of available alcohol may be related to more successful outcome. The provision of opportunities to drink during treatment may be of benefit not only to those who learn to moderate drinking in the process, but also to those who are given a chance to practice refusal of available alcohol (Canter, 1968; Narrol, 1967).

Contingencies need not be attached only to drinking behavior or to moderation goals (e.g., Frederiksen & Miller, 1976). In an uncontrolled study, Bigelow, Strickler, Leibson, and Griffiths (1976) reported results of a contingency contracting procedure for taking disulfiram. Twenty alcoholics contracted to take disulfiram for three months, and failure to appear for scheduled medication resulted in forfeiture of a portion of a security deposit. Of the 2,032 patient days, 95.6% were confirmed as abstinent. Likewise, Peter Miller (1975) arranged for community resources to be provided to ten public drunkenness offenders contingent upon sobriety. During the two months of the experiment, this group had significantly fewer arrests for drunkenness than during the prior two months, and fewer than a randomly assigned control group. Similar differences were found for employment status. In another study, Miller, Hersen, Eisler, and Watts (1974) arranged to administer breath tests to an alcoholic in his natural environment. Tests were given on a random and unannounced basis, and the patient received monetary rewards for "clean" breath samples. Goodwin (1978) and Sanchez-Craig (1980) have advocated contracting for brief periods of abstinence as a prelude either to moderation or to continued abstinence.

Azrin (1976; Hunt & Azrin, 1973) has described a "community reinforcement approach" to treating alcoholics, in which clients are taught to access natural sources of reinforcement from the community in order to support a sober lifestyle. Compared to control group members, those treated by this method have been found to have significantly fewer drinking days, more days of employment, and fewer days of institutionalization.

A rather unsuccessful operant program has been reported by Cheek et al. (1971), who attempted to teach behavior modification skills to the wives of alcoholics. There was a high drop-out rate, and training in operant principles was found to have relatively little impact. This is not surprising, however, in that the program did not involve the alcoholics themselves! Nevertheless, the cooperation of significant others may be of benefit in operant programs. Sulzer (1965) successfully enlisted the aid of two friends of a problem drinker in order to modify drinking behavior.

One additional kind of environmental influence that is relevant here—and that involves the patient's friends or drinking acquaintances—is *modeling*. Several recent studies have shown that the amount and/or pattern of one's drinking is strongly affected by the drinking behavior of those around him or her (Caudill & Marlatt, 1975; Reid, 1978). Lied and Marlatt (1979) found that heavy social drinkers were more influenced by heavy-drinking models than were light social drinkers. Programs designed to modify drinking behavior would do well to consider the importance of modeling influences in the client's environment (e.g., the drinking habits of friends, family).

Summary. Operant research has clearly demonstrated that a variety of environmental factors influence drinking behavior. Alcohol consumption can be modified by contingent reinforcement and punishment as well as by modeling of drinking style. The challenge in using this approach in treatment is to successfully modify the "real world" environment so that changes will generalize beyond the treatment setting. Making alcohol available within the treatment setting (which typically has been alcohol-free) may permit problem drinkers to take responsibility for drinking decisions and to develop coping skills which are useful when alcohol is available in their natural environments. Reports from outcome research on operant methods have been rather consistently positive when the problem drinker is directly involved in treatment, but controlled studies have been few.

Multimodal Treatment Programs

The majority of all treatment programs with an explicit goal of controlled drinking have taken a multimodal approach. Some have used multiple treatment methods, all of which were designed to impact drinking behavior (e.g., Caddy & Lovibond, 1976; Miller, 1978a), whereas others have taken a "broad spectrum" approach (Hamburg, 1975) and have included behavioral methods intended to teach alternative coping skills (e.g., Alden, 1978; Sobell & Sobell, 1973b).

All of the 19 studies summarized in table 2.1 have been discussed elsewhere in this chapter. Together, these studies provide a rather solid base of evaluation research. Of the 19 studies, 15 included and reported results from control or comparison groups, usually with random assignment to treatment conditions. Most included quantified assessment procedures and specified criteria for outcome ratings. In 14 studies, more than 90% of all cases were located at the longest follow-up interval, and only one study located fewer than 80% (this study—Caddy et al., 1978—finding 70% at *three* years posttreatment). Perhaps most remarkably within the context of the alcohol outcome literature, 18 of the 19 studies checked client self-reports against corroborative data sources. Few treatment approaches for problem drinkers have been subjected to the depth and breadth of research reflected in table 2.1.

Table 2.1. Summary of Studies on Treatment with a Goal of Moderation

STUDY	Follow-Up TIME	%LOC	COR?	ACPT	BEGN	COMP	%DROP	I/O	#SES	Treatment COMPONENTS	ABST	C.D.	IMPR	NOTI	LOST	TOT IMP
Alden, 1978	Term	100%	Yes	43	36	31	14%	OPT	10	BACe+SC+SM	−57%—			43%?	0%	57%
									10	BACe+SC+SM+MODi	−88%—			12%?	0%	88%
Baker et al., 1975	6 mo	95%	Yes	40	40	40	0%	IPT	10	BC+SC+VTm+HOSP					0%	} 37%
									10	BC+SC+VTs+HOSP					0%	
									10	BC+SC+HOSP					10%	
									NA	HOSP					10%	?
Caddy et al., 1978 (Follow-up of Sobell & Sobell, 1973)	3 yr	70%	Yes	70	70	20	0%	IPT	17	BC+EA+ED+SC+VTs+HOSP(CD)	15%	20%	15%	25%	25%	50%
						20				HOSP (AB)	15%	0%	10%	45%	30%	25%
						15				BC+EA+ED+SC+VTs+HOSP(AB)	20%	7%	0%?	33%?	40%	27%
						15				HOSP (AB)	13%	0%	33%?	27%?	27%	47%
*Caddy & Lovibond, 1976	6 mo	100%	Yes	69	63	15	25%	OPT	10	BACi+BC+EA+ED+PT+SC+SM	0%	45%	35%	20%	0%	80%
						16	20%	OPT	10	BACi+BC+ED+PT+SC+SM	0%	30%	30%	40%	0%	60%
						13	35%	OPT	10	BACi+EA+ED+PT+SM	0%	20%	10%	70%	0%	30%
Ewing & Rouse, 1976	27-55 mo	100%	Yes	35	35	14	60%	OPT	12g	BACi+EA+ED+SC+SM	64%	0%	0%	36%	0%	64%
Hedberg & Campbell, 1974	6 mo	100%	Yes	59	59	15	0%	OPT	20	RLX, SD	40%	27%	20%	13%	0%	87%
						15	0%	OPT	20	CS, RLX	33%	7%	27%	33%	0%	67%
						4	67%	OPT	20	EA	0%	0%	25%	75%	0%	25%
						15	0%	OPT	20	FAM	53%	33%	13%	13%	0%	87%
Lovibond, 1975	1-9 mo	100%	Yes	29	29	29	0%	OPT	8-10	BACi+BC+EA+ED+PT+SC+SM	0%	59%	26%	15%	0%	85%
				25		16	36%		None	Untreated (Matched)	0%	6%	6%	88%	0%	12%
Lovibond & Caddy, 1970	16-60 wk	100%	Yes	31	31	28	10%	OPT	6-12	BACi+EA+ED+PT+SC	0%	75%	11%	14%	0%	86%
Miller, 1978a	12 mo	83%	Yes	80	65	14	30%	OPT	10	EA+SM	14%	50%	14%	7%	14%	79%
						17	6%	OPT	10	BACe+ED+SC+SM	6%	53%	24%	6%	12%	82%
						15	21%	OPT	10	BACe+EA+ED+SC+SM	7%	47%	7%	13%	27%	60%
*Miller, Gribskov & Mortell in press	3 mo	97%	Yes	35	35	16	0%	OPT	None	BACe+ED+SC+SM	19%	38%	31%	13%	0%	88%
*Miller, Pechacek & Hamburg in press	3 mo	93%	Yes	35	32	15	21%	OPT	10	BACe+ED+SC+SM	7%	60%	13%	13%	7%	80%
				35		28	13%	OPT	10g	BACe+ED+RLX+SC+SM	0%	14%	57%	21%	7%	71%

82

Table 2.1. Continued

STUDY	Follow-Up			Number of Clients				Treatment			Outcome[+]					TOT IMP
	TIME	%LOC	COR?	ACPT	BEGN	COMP	%DROP	I/O	#SES	COMPONENTS	ABST	C.D.	IMPR	NOTI	LOST	
Miller & Taylor 1980	12 mo	93%	Yes	54	48	12	0%	OPT	None	BACe+ED+SC+SM	25%	8%	42%	8%	17%	75%
						11	8%	OPT	10	BACe+ED+SC+SM	0%	27%	18%	45%	9%	45%
						8	33%	OPT	10	BACe+ED+RLX+SC+SM	0%	38%	38%	25%	0%	75%
						10	17%	OPT	10g	BACe+ED+RLX+SC+SM	20%	40%	30%	10%	0%	90%
Miller, Taylor & West, in press	6 mo	83%	Yes	56	45	10	0%	OPT	None	BACe+ED+SC+SM	0%	30%	30%	20%	20%	60%
						11	8%	OPT	6	BACe+ED+SC+SM	9%	36%	27%	27%	0%	73%
						10	17%	OPT	18	BACe+ED+SC+SM+MODp	10%	30%	0%	50%	10%	40%
						10	9%	OPT	18	BACe+ED+SC+SM+MODi	0%	40%	40%	20%	0%	80%
*Pomerleau et al. 1978	12 mo	96%	Yes	46	39	16	11%	OPT	3mo-g	BC+CS+FAM+RLX+SC+SM(CD)	5%	—67%—		11%	5%	72%
*Popham & Schmidt, 1976	12 mo	64%	No	150	150	8	43%	OPT	3mo-g	PT (AB)	14%	—36%—		7%	43%	50%
						"Most"	?	OPT	12+	Group Discussion	6%	12%	28%?	18%?	36%	46%
Schaefer, 1972 (Follow-up of Mills et al., 1971)	12 mo	81%	Yes	26	26	13	0%	IPT	12-14	EA+HOSP	23%	31%		23%	23%	54%
						13	0%	IPT	NA	HOSP	15%	0%		69%	15%	15%
Vogler et al., 1975	12 mo	100%	Yes	59	57	23	23%	IPT	45hr	BACi+BC+EA+ED+SC+VTs+HOSP	30%	35%		35%	0%	65%
Vogler et al., 1977a	12 mo	100%	Yes	39	39	19	27%	IPT	22hr	BC+ED+HOSP	37%	21%		42%	0%	58%
						26	33%	OPT	45hr	BACi+BC+EA+ED+SC+VTs	8%	54%		38%	?	62%
								OPT	22hr	BC+ED	15%	31%		54%	?	46%
Vogler et al., 1977b	12 mo	89%	Yes	277	164	80	26%	OPT	34-40h	BACi+BC+EA+ED+SC+VTs	9%	61%		30%	?	70%
									34-40h	BACi+BC+ED	0%	68%		32%	?	68%
									17-20h	BACe+ED	5%	57%		38%	?	62%
									34-40h	BACe+BC+ED	0%	65%		35%	?	65%

*All drop-outs included in data

[+]Outcome percentages should be interpreted with caution because of differences among studies with regard to client populations and criteria for classification. It should be noted that studies vary widely with regard to percentage of cases reached, and that large loss rates account for elevated "not improved" percentages in certain groups. Drop-out rates also vary widely and should be considered in evaluating data in this table, particularly because drop-outs have not been considered in calculating outcome percentages (except in studies indicated by *). Percentages reported here differ from those reported by the authors in certain studies because of differences in procedures for case classification.

NOTE: See legend on following page.

Legend for Table 2.1

Follow-Up/Number of Clients

TIME   = Length of follow-up upon which data are based
%LOC = Percentage of treated cases (excluding drop-outs) reached at follow-up
COR?   = Self-report data checked against corroborating sources (collaterals, blood tests)
ACPT   = Number of clients accepted for treatment
BEGN   = Number of clients actually beginning treatment program
COMP   = Number of clients completing treatment program
%DROP = Percentage of clients beginning treatment who dropped out before completion (in
           certain cases some clients were placed in dispositions other than "completed" or
           "dropped" (e.g., data unusable, referred, etc.)
I/O   = Inpatient versus outpatient treatment program
#SES   = Length of program or average sessions completed ("g" indicates group sessions)

Treatment Components

BACe = External cue blood alcohol concentration discrimination training
BACi   = Internal cue (biofeedback) blood alcohol concentration discrimination training
BC   = Behavioral counseling (role playing, etc.)
CS   = Covert sensitization
EA   = Electrical aversive counterconditioning or avoidance training
ED   = Alcohol education
FAM   = Family therapy
HOSP = Standard hospital regimen, oriented toward abstinence
MODi = Behavioral alternatives training, individualized to clients
MODp = Behavioral alternatives training, preselected and standardized modules
PT   = Psychotherapy
RLX   = Progressive deep muscle relaxation training
SC   = Self-control training, functional analysis of drinking, stimulus control, etc.
SD   = Systematic desensitization
SM   = Self-monitoring
VTm   = Observation of videotaped model patients
VTs   = Videotape self-confrontation

(AB)   = Treatment program oriented toward abstinence
(CD)   = Treatment program oriented toward controlled drinking

Outcome Percentages

ABST   = Percentage of clients indicated to be totally abstaining as of follow-up (length of
           continuous abstinence required varies from study to study)
C.D.   = Percentage of clients indicated to be controlled drinkers at follow-up. Controlled
           drinking is defined in all cases by adherence to *absolute* standards for moderate
           drinking. These criteria vary from study to study. Some studies do not use this
           classification.
IMPR   = Percentage of clients who do not meet criteria for "controlled drinker" by abso-
           lute standards, but who nevertheless show significant improvement over their
           baseline drinking level. Criteria for improvement vary from study to study.

Legend Table 2.1 Outcome Percentages (continued)

NOTI   = Percentage of clients showing little or no improvement in comparison to pretreat-
            ment drinking levels. (Includes incarcerated clients)
LOST   = Percentage of treated sample not located at follow-up. These cases are included as
            failures in all calculations, except for studies (?) where data regarding number of
            cases lost are not provided. (Includes deceased clients)
TOT IMP = ABST + C.D. + IMPR percentages. Clients who dropped out of treatment prior
            to completion are not included in calculations, except for studies indicated by an
            asterisk (*) where authors did so.

Because these studies have largely been described before, we will limit our discussion here to the consideration of one issue: What is the evidence regarding the relative effectiveness of multimodal or "broad spectrum" approaches versus simpler or drinking-focused methods?

Twelve studies have used random assignment designs to compare simpler drinking-focused treatment programs—in most cases, some form of behavioral self-control training (BSCT)—with more complex and/or more extensive alternative approaches. Sobell and Sobell (1973b) found their multimodal behavior therapy program to be significantly more effective than a standard hospital alcoholism treatment program, a difference which has held up over three years of evaluation (Caddy et al., 1978). Pomerleau et al. (1978) found BSCT to be more effective than group psychotherapy, with differences consisting mostly in differential drop-out rates. When the more *minimal* approach has been BSCT, findings have been mixed. Miller and his colleagues (Miller, 1978a; Miller & Taylor, 1980; Miller, Taylor & West, in press; Miller, Gribskov, & Mortell, in press) have found no significant differences between a bibliotherapy form of BSCT and therapist-administered BSCT or broad-spectrum treatment programs. Alden (1978), on the other hand, found a significant advantage of broad-spectrum over basic BSCT treatment. Vogler and his colleagues (1975, 1977a, 1977b) have compared a minimal educational program resembling BSCT with more extensive and expensive alternative approaches and have consistently found few or no significant differences among groups. Caddy and Lovibond (1976) reported that their complete multimodal package outperformed two alternative and slightly-dismantled versions of the same program. Finally, Baker et al. (1975) reported modest but nonsignificant differences among four treatment programs of varying complexity.

Table 2.2 summarizes the data reported in table 2.1 by summing outcome ratings across studies. Treated subjects have been divided into two groups: those treated by methods closely resembling BSCT (Alden, 1978; Caddy & Lovibond, 1976; Miller, 1978a; Miller, Gribskov & Mortell, in press; Miller, Pechacek & Hamburg, in press; Miller & Taylor, 1980; Miller, Taylor &

Table 2.2.   Outcome of Basic vs. Multimodal Treatment Oriented toward Moderation*

	ABST	C.D.	IMPR	TOT% IMPR	%NOT IMPR	N	LOCATED	
3-6 Month Follow-Up								
Basic BSCT	7%	38%	34%	79%	21%	172	163	(95%)
Multimodal	4%	47%	18%	68%	32%	207	203	(98%)
Combined	5%	43%	25%	73%	27%	379	363	(96%)
12-Month Follow-Up								
Basic BSCT	10%	43%	16%	70%	30%	177	171	(97%)
Multimodal	18%	41%	11%	70%	30%	131	127	(97%)
Combined	13%	42%	14%	70%	30%	308	298	(97%)

*Only studies with explicit goal of controlled drinking are included. Two studies (Mills et al., 1971; Popham & Schmidt, 1976) have been omitted because their treatment methods relied primarily upon standard hospital methods quite dissimilar from the types of procedures used in the 17 other studies included in this table. (Summary data from all 19 studies are represented in table 2.3.) In studies where groups received alternative treatments (Sobell & Sobell, 1973), only those groups treated with a goal of moderation have been included in the summary analyses for this table. For definitions of abstinence (ABST), controlled drinking (C.D.) and improved (IMPR) see footnotes to table 2.1.

West, in press; Pomerleau et al., 1978; Vogler et al., 1975, 1977a, 1977b) and those treated by more extensive multimodal treatment packages (Alden, 1978; Baker et al., 1975; Caddy & Lovibond, 1976; Ewing & Rouse, 1976; Hedberg & Campbell, 1974; Lovibond, 1975; Lovibond & Caddy, 1970; Miller, 1978a; Miller, Taylor & West, in press; Sobell & Sobell, 1973b; Vogler et al., 1975, 1977a, 1977b). Note that different groups from a single study (e.g., Alden, 1978) may cause the study to be represented twice. All subjects were given equal weight, rather than simply averaging outcome percentages across studies with widely varying values of N. This procedure has the liability of giving greater weight to studies with larger N's (e.g., Vogler et al., 1977b), but avoids misleading distortions of data by atypical studies with relatively small samples (e.g., Ewing & Rouse, 1976). There are numerous other pitfalls to averaging across diverse studies (Emrick, 1975), some of which we have noted by caveats in the footnotes to table 2.1. Nevertheless, findings across these studies are sufficiently consistent (see table 2.1) that we believe this summary can be instructive.

Emrick (1975) provided an exhaustive review of alcoholism treatment studies, the majority of which were of programs oriented toward a goal of abstinence. We have attempted in table 2.2 to parallel Emrick's published normative data regarding treatment outcome, examining only studies with a stated treatment goal of controlled drinking. Certain differences are apparent. Whereas Emrick found controlled drinking to be a relatively rare outcome in abstinence-oriented programs, it emerges here as the single most common outcome status. Interestingly, what might be called "byproduct" abstinence outcomes from controlled-drinking programs are approximately as frequent as are ''byproduct'' controlled-drinking outcomes from abstinence programs, as reported by Emrick (1975). The ''total improved'' percentages from controlled-drinking programs are only slightly higher than the 65% figure reported by Emrick to be characteristic of ''more than minimal'' treatment, although the rather minimal BSCT programs summarized in table 2.2 compare favorably with Emrick's total improved figure of 43% for minimal treatment programs. Finally, Emrick's finding of no substantial difference in effectiveness between minimal and more-than-minimal treatment approaches is again reflected in the data of table 2.2 for moderation-oriented approaches.

The finding that minimal treatment approaches (e.g., bibliotherapy) are on the whole only slightly less effective than are more heroic interventions (at least in teaching controlled drinking to problem drinkers—cf. Edwards et al., 1977) has some potential implications for treatment programs. Current data do not support the cost-effectiveness of extensive multimodal treatment programs for *all* clients. Rather than routinely administering expensive broad spectrum treatment to all comers, it would make sense to try to identify that portion of the population likely to benefit differentially from greater expenditures of treatment resources and personnel time. If most clients can benefit from minimal treatment, then staff time and extensive programs can be reserved for those requiring such attention. Perhaps with time and further research, we will be able to identify *a priori* those clients most likely to need broad spectrum services (or those most likely to remain in treatment long enough to receive them). In the meantime, an interim procedure would be to offer a minimal program to all clients (with reasonable exceptions for acute crisis, etc.) and then to offer further services only to those clients who fail to benefit from ''phase one.'' It has been our experience that clients who are going to benefit from BSCT alone do so within six to ten weeks, and that those who have failed to respond within this time are unlikely to attain successful outcome without additional treatment. Such a ''levels of care'' model is likely to improve the cost-effectiveness of treatment programs and to permit staff to devote their time primarily to those clients who need and are most likely to benefit from it.

Summary. Multimodal and broad spectrum approaches may be optimal for certain clients, but on the whole they appear to be no more effective (at least for a majority of clients) than simpler and less costly approaches focusing on behavioral self-control training.

Teaching Alternatives to Problem Drinking

It is an accepted although not established fact that many problem drinkers use alcohol as a coping device for dealing with certain life problems. It is widely believed, for example, that alcohol is a tension-reducing drug and that problem drinkers frequently drink in order to relax. Alcohol is also often described as an avenue to escape, or as a method for coping with depression or frustration.

As a matter of fact, alcohol is a rather poor choice of medications for dealing with such problems. In most cases, it is as likely to exacerbate a negative emotional state (such as tension or depression) as to relieve it, and heavy escape drinking carries a number of clear negative side effects as well. Nevertheless, if people *believe* that alcohol relieves tension or depression or insomnia, they may decide to drink when they need to cope with such states (Wilson, 1978). To make matters worse, it appears that drinkers tend to remember selectively only the early positive emotional effects of alcohol, and not to recall the worsening of negative feeling states that comes with higher levels of blood alcohol (Allman et al., 1972; Mendelson et al., 1964; Steffen et al., 1974; Tamerin & Mendelson, 1969).

If alcohol is used, wisely or not, as a coping mechanism, then it seems reasonable that one strategy for decreasing psychological dependence upon drinking would be to teach the individual alternative skills or "behavioral competencies" for dealing with stressful situations (Bandura, 1969). Behavior therapists have developed a wide range of relevant self-control methods that could be taught to problem drinkers (Miller & Mastria, 1977; Miller & Muñoz, 1976). These skills are equally applicable whether the goal of treatment is abstinence or moderation. We will devote our discussion here to two major areas of alternatives training: (a) relaxation training and systematic desensitization; and (b) social skills training.

Relaxation Training and Systematic Desensitization

Relaxation Training. Training in relaxation skills has been used to help people (a) reduce their overall level of physiological arousal (frequently described as "generalized" or "free-floating" anxiety); (b) reduce craving and urges to drink; (c) get to sleep more easily; and (d) deal with specific environmental factors which result in "anxiety" (e.g., phobias) (Miller & Mastria, 1977). The use of relaxation for the latter purpose is called systematic desensitization, which will be discussed later in this section.

Implicit in the rationale for the use of relaxation training is the tension-reduction theory of alcohol abuse, which posits that alcohol consumption results in reduced levels of "tension" and consequently is reinforcing to the individual (Conger, 1956; Kepner, 1964). More recent research, however, suggests a much more complex relationship between alcohol consumption, physiological arousal and subjective feelings of disturbance (e.g., Steffen et al., 1974).

Nevertheless, researchers and therapists alike have adapted relaxation techniques from other areas for use with alcoholics. These include progressive deep muscle relaxation as developed by Jacobson (Wolpe, 1973), electromyograph (EMG) biofeedback, and Transcendental Meditation (TM). With this diversity of procedures, the first question is whether relaxation training has any impact on drinking behaviors, intrapersonal or interpersonal functioning. The second is whether there are any advantages of one specific technique over another.

Treatment Outcome. Controlled and uncontrolled studies alike have tended to focus only on physiological measures of relaxation. As one exception, however, Rohan (1970) reported abstinence rates for 99 alcoholics who had been in an inpatient program which utilized relaxation training. Of the 99 patients, 31% were abstinent for an average of 11 months. The study lacked controls, however, and 79 patients (39%) who dropped out were not calculated in the abstinence rates.

Passini et al. (1977) reported that his alcoholic sample was able to significantly increase alpha brain wave production with biofeedback training, but that there was no notable correlation between amount of alpha wave increase and decreases on measures of anxiety and psychiatric symptomatology. Improvement on these latter dependent measures may have been due to a placebo effect.

McFarlain et al. (1976) noted significant but equal decreases in self-report measures of anxiety for a muscle relaxation group, a drug placebo group, and a tranquilizer medication group. This study was seriously confounded, however, by a nonrandomized assignment which favored the drug and placebo groups.

Steffen (1975) used a single subject, multiple baseline crossover design to evaluate EMG biofeedback training and an attention placebo group termed "contemplation." Results indicated that while the four alcoholics were receiving EMG training, they achieved lower muscle potential ratings than they did during "contemplation" sessions. Following sessions, however, the opposite pattern was found. Given an opportunity to consume free alcohol, subjects who had just received EMG training maintained lower BACs and reported less subjective disturbance by contrast with periods following placebo treatment, although the total amount of alcohol consumed was equivalent in both conditions.

Parker et al. (1978a, 1978b) randomly assigned 30 alcoholics in a VA program to either a progressive relaxation training, a meditation training group, or a "quiet rest" control group. Upon completion of the three-week training period, all three groups had significantly decreased subjective reports of anxiety and heart rate, but the differences between the groups were nonsignificant. On measures of blood pressure, the meditation group significantly reduced their systolic and diastolic pressures, whereas the progressive relaxation group had a significant decrease only in diastolic pressure and the control group showed increased blood pressure from pre- to post-training levels.

Blake (1965, 1967) reported treatment outcomes for alcoholics who had received either electrical aversion and relaxation training or the former alone. One-year follow-up results indicated a slight but nonsignificant advantage in favor of the combined treatment. Freedberg and Johnston (1978a) randomly assigned 80 alcoholics to receive or not receive relaxation training in addition to a three-week residential treatment program. At one-year follow-up, no significant differences between groups were found on drinking measures, although relaxation subjects showed slightly better improvement on other measures of life functioning.

Miller and Taylor (1980) noted similar modest improvements in outcome when relaxation training was added to a behavioral self-control training (BSCT) program for problem drinkers. They reported ''success'' (abstinent plus considerably plus moderately improved) of 40% for BSCT alone, 75% for BSCT plus relaxation, and 89% for BSCT plus relaxation in a group format. A fourth group, however, receiving bibliotherapy (a self-help manual including relaxation instructions and self-monitoring cards) showed a 75% success rate which was not significantly different from that of the other treatment groups.

Proponents of Transcendental Meditation have claimed that continued practice of TM results in decreased drug abuse. Such causal conclusions tend to be based upon correlational research, however, and overstep the limits of the data. Studies of TM (e.g., Benson, 1974) have typically contained serious methodological flaws that have rendered their findings uninterpretable. Research on TM and addictive behaviors has recently been reviewed by Aron and Aron (1980).

Summary. Controlled studies evaluating relaxation training have reported relatively small increments in positive outcomes as a result of such training. On the basis of very limited comparative research, no particular relaxation procedure appears to be significantly better than any other. Although logically relaxation training would appear to be a treatment of choice for problem drinkers (Hartman, 1973), the data indicate that its contribution is probably a modest one.

Systematic Desensitization. Systematic desensitization (SD) involves the pairing of a relaxed state with specific environmental stimuli or scenes which usually result in feelings of tension or anxiety. The client (usually with a therapist's assistance) delimits distressing themes and develops a hierarchy of scenes ranging from the least to the most anxiety producing. The client then learns a relaxation technique and while relaxed is presented with items in the hierarchy starting with the least stressful. If, during the progression the client signals that he or she is feeling tense, the therapist helps the client to relax until she or he can progress again without feeling tense. Treatment is usually concluded when the client can imagine that which, before treatment, was the most stressful scene, and be relaxed and calm while doing so. Sometimes treatment is extended, however, to include *in vivo* desensitization in which the client actually engages in (rather than just imagining) the behaviors while in a relaxed state.

Treatment Outcome. Kraft and Al-Issa (1967, 1968) have reported on the use of SD in a follow-up of eight alcoholics for 12 to 40 months (Kraft, 1969). All eight were under 35 years of age, and three had a diagnosis of alcoholism "secondary to social anxieties." At follow-up, all were reported to be controlled drinkers, consuming "an occasional pint of beer."

Hodgson & Rankin (1976) reported on an innovative *in vivo* desensitization procedure in which a 43-year-old male alcoholic was given daily primer doses of either 40 or 160 ml of vodka, followed by monitoring of his subjective craving and by objective measures of withdrawal. They reported a gradual extinction on all measures and reported significant improvement at six-month follow-up. Because subjective "craving" is one frequent antecedent of relapse, this unique application of desensitization deserves further attention. Pickens et al. (1973) have reported a similarly successful case study applying stimulus fading of craving-eliciting cues. Sharon Hall (1979) has introduced the related concept of "abstinence phobia" and has advocated the use of desensitization and related techniques to alleviate fears associated with inability to cope with sobriety (cf. Anderson et al., 1973).

Lanyon et al. (1972) reported results on 14 of 15 alcoholics who had been randomly assigned into either an "interpersonal aversion" (IA) plus SD group or an IA plus "placebo" counseling group. The IA treatment involved two experimenters pointing out conflicts and contradictions in a videotaped interview of the client. At six- to nine-month follow-up, 5/7 and 1/7 alcoholics in the experimental and control groups, respectively, were abstinent. The absence of a no-treatment control group leaves open the question of whether SD made patients better or IA alone made them worse.

Hedberg and Campbell's (1974) controlled study compared behavioral family counseling, electrical aversion, covert sensitization, and SD. They reported a combined success rate (goal attained plus much improved at six months) of 90% (9/10) for the abstinence treatment goal group and 80% (4/5) for the controlled drinking goal group receiving SD alone. The SD rates were identical to those of the family counseling group, which with SD was found to be the most effective of the four alternatives.

Summary. The treatment outcome data on SD are more promising than those for relaxation training alone. Cautious optimism is appropriate at this point, based on a small number of positive findings. It appears that SD, unlike relaxation training alone, may be of some value as a component of multi-modal treatment programs for problem drinkers.

Social Skills Training

Within the context of treatment of alcoholics and psychiatric patients, "social skills training" and "assertiveness training" have often been used interchangeably, although assertiveness training might be more appropriately viewed as a subset of social skills training.

Assertiveness has been described as the ability to appropriately express personal rights and feelings, both positive and negative, in the presence of others (Herson, Eisler, & Miller, 1973). The rationale typically put forth for the use of assertiveness training with alcoholics is that a deficit in this skill may lead to intrapersonal and interpersonal conflicts which in turn are associated with relapse. (See chapter by Cummings, Gordon & Marlatt for a detailed discussion of this issue.)

Sturgis, Calhoun, and Best (1979) found that alcoholics who rated high on a self-report scale of assertiveness—the Rathus Assertiveness Schedule (RAS)—were better adjusted than were those who scored low on the RAS. The low-assertive alcoholics reported significantly more trait anxiety on the State-Trait Anxiety Inventory, scored significantly higher on the F validity, Depression, Paranoia, Psychasthenia and Social Introversion scales of the MMPI, and higher on the Neuroticism scale of the Eysenck Personality Inventory (EPI). High-assertive alcoholics scored higher on the extraversion scale of the EPI, the Boredom Susceptibility, and the General and Total Sensation Seeking scales of the Zuckerman Sensation Seeking Scale. In other words, those who reported high levels of assertiveness tended to be better adjusted. A methodological flaw of this study, however, is the lack of a behavioral measure of assertiveness. Miller & Eisler (1977) noted that although alcoholics described themselves as assertive on a self-report measure, behavioral measures indicated a lack of assertive skills in the group. Nevertheless, the Sturgis et al. (1979) study suggests that assertiveness training for some alcoholics might result in a "halo" effect in other areas of intrapersonal and interpersonal functioning. The test of this hypothesis must come, however, from experimental rather than correlational data.

A number of behavioral programs have included assertiveness training to some degree (Hedberg & Campbell, 1974; Miller, Pechacek, & Hamburg, in press; Miller, Stanford, & Hemphill, 1974; Sobell & Sobell, 1973b; Vogler, Compton, & Weissbach, 1975). Lacking experimental groups which did not receive assertiveness training, however, these studies are not able to provide data on its relative effectiveness.

Treatment Outcome. Adinolfi et al. (1976) were among the first to report results of an assertiveness training program with alcoholics. Six alcoholics at a Boston hospital were seen in a group format which included videotape feedback, modeling, behavior rehearsal, individualized role playing dealing with problems of self-esteem, and homework assignments. Follow-up at 11 months revealed that of the six, two who had been abstinent for one year prior to training remained abstinent. Of the four who had been binge drinkers, one was totally abstinent, one had had one three-day drinking episode, one had had four separate one-day episodes, and one had had extended binges which lasted several weeks.

In a study which focused its treatment outcome measures on changes in assertive behaviors, Hirsch et al. (1978) randomly assigned alcoholics to an assertiveness training group which involved ten hours of treatment, a minimal assertiveness training group which included two hours of didactic lectures and group discussion, or a control group which received the routine inpatient treatment. Two weeks after training, the assertiveness training group was significantly more assertive on a self-report, an overt and a covert behavioral measure.

Intagliata (1978) reported results of a controlled study in which the experimental group received problem-solving skills training. After training and before inpatient discharge, the experimental group was slightly, but not significantly, better than the controls on a behavioral problem-solving task, but in an analysis of patients' posttreatment discharge plans, the experimental group was significantly better than controls on all but one of the behavioral ratings. One month after discharge, however, only 14 of 22 subjects contacted in the treatment group had made practical use of their problem-solving skills, and "it was evident that subjects had already forgotten significant portions of the training material" (p. 496). These findings point to the need for additional and continued training on an outpatient basis if gains are to be maintained.

McClelland (1974) reported results of a study in which 52 VA alcoholics received "power motivation treatment" aimed at finding more socially acceptable methods of expressing personal power. At one year, 50% of the experimental group versus 28% of controls who received the standard treatment were "successes" (i.e., drinking less per month and employed at least five out of six months).

Chaney, O'Leary, and Marlatt (1978) have reported one-year follow-up results from a short-term skill training intervention with alcoholics at the Seattle V.A. Hospital. Experimental groups included (a) a skill training group; (b) a discussion group which focused on feelings such as anxiety and anger, which inhibit effective assertiveness; and (c) a control group which received the routine alcohol treatment program. Drinking outcome data followed the model presented by the Sobells (Sobell & Sobell, 1973b), which included number of days voluntarily and involuntarily (e.g., hospitalized or incarcerated) abstinent, number of days controlled drinking, number of days drunk, total number of drinks, and average drinking period length. At one-year follow-up, the skill training group was significantly lower than either control group on total number of days drunk, total number of drinks and average drinking period length. In addition, pretreatment drinking history, demographic data and behavioral measures of assertiveness were analyzed as predictors of treatment outcome. Results indicated that for all outcome measures, the response latency for assertive behaviors was comparable or superior to the most highly predictive drinking history or demographic measures. On the basis of this, Chaney et al. concluded that "this analysis establishes a relationship between ability to respond to problematic drinking-related situations on a verbal role-playing instrument and actual drinking-related behavioral functioning following treatment" (p. 1101).

Freedberg and Johnston (1978b) found a similar pattern of results at one-year follow-up of a controlled study of assertiveness training in employed alcoholics. Abstinence rates at one year for those who did and those who did not receive assertiveness training in a three-week residential program were 36% (n = 20) and 24% (n = 11) respectively. When an improved status is included, the respective favorable outcomes are 72% (n = 40) and 57% (n = 26). Measures of employment status, work productivity, psychosocial functioning, and self-reports of assertiveness revealed similar modest increments in favorable outcomes for those who received assertiveness training.

Summary. Available data generally support the utility of teaching problem drinkers more effective assertion and problem-solving skills. Positive results have been observed both on self-report, overt and covert behavioral measures of target skills and on measures of drinking behavior at follow-up as long as one year. The question remains as to whether skill training is of general benefit or is of differential benefit to certain types of problem drinkers. Hamilton and Maisto (1979) compared four different samples of white male alcoholics with matched nonalcoholic controls and found no differences on a behavioral measure of assertiveness. Alcoholics did, however, report significantly greater *discomfort* in scenes requiring negative assertion (e.g., refusing a request) than did nonalcoholics. These findings suggest that practice in assertion for alcoholics may function more as a desensitizing procedure than as acquisition of new skills. Nevertheless, skill practice appears to be of some benefit in the treatment of problem drinkers (Van Hasselt et al., 1978). Training in certain specific assertive behaviors (e.g., refusing drinks) may be particularly useful (Foy et al., 1976).

Factors Related to Treatment Outcome

The search for general predictors of response to alcoholism treatment has been a long and extensive one, and a review of relevant studies could itself fill a chapter such as this. Fortunately, others have provided informative reviews of this literature (Armor et al., 1978; Baekeland, 1977; Brandsma et al., in press; Gibbs & Flanagan, 1977). Suffice it to say that no consistent individual differences have been found to predict outcome, although most frequently mentioned are variables related to social status and stability (e.g., work history, marital status, socioeconomic status). Gibbs and Flanagan (1977) have suggested that this clear failure to find generalized predictors can probably be attributed to the extraordinary heterogeneity across studies of treatment methods, patient populations, definitions of alcoholism, and chosen predictor variables.

Of greater use to the practitioner would be predictors of *differential* response to alternative treatment strategies. Kissin and his colleagues (1970a), for example, reported that patients with higher education and occupational status tended to select psychotherapy over drug and ward therapies and appeared to respond somewhat better to this approach. Well-designed and controlled studies in this area have been few, however. Cronkite and Moos (1978) found that interactions between patient variables and treatment variables accounted for 23 to 40% of the variance in treatment outcome and suggested that increased attention be paid to matching of patients with appropriate treatments. We will restrict our discussion here to the consideration of three critical predictive issues related to patient/treatment matching: (a) the value of varying amounts of treatment contact; (b) the efficacy of various types of therapists; and (c) criteria for differential assignment to abstinence versus moderation goals in treatment.

Amount of Treatment Contact

There seems to have been an unspoken assumption within the alcoholism treatment field that more treatment is better treatment. The strength of this assumption is reflected in the fact that some studies have chosen to use continued contact (staying in treatment) as the principal or only measure of successful outcome (e.g., Rosenberg et al., 1976). But what basis is there for this belief? Is it, in fact, a service to increase the length and extent of a treatment program?

The only substantive support for this assumption lies in the fact that some studies have reported a correlation between length of treatment contact and success of outcome (e.g., Armor et al., 1978; Smart, 1978b; Smart & Gray, 1978). Such findings from uncontrolled studies are inconclusive, however, because numerous additional factors may account for both length of stay and positiveness of outcome (e.g., patient motivation, severity of problem, social stability). Likewise, there are uncontrolled studies reporting low or even negative correlations between extent and effect of treatment. Gunderson and Schuckit (1978) found positive prognosis to be associated with short (one to five days) as opposed to long hospitalizations (although patients receiving short hospitalization had better prognosis than did those not hospitalized). Ritson (1968) found no significant difference in effectiveness between inpatient and outpatient alcoholism treatment programs and questioned the frequent policy of routine hospitalization of alcoholics. Similarly, Penk,

Charles, and Van-Hoose (1978) reported no significant differences between a day treatment and an inpatient psychiatric program, with both producing equal gains in moderation of alcohol use. Pattison, Coe, and Rhodes (1969) found no significant differences in degree of improvement on dimensions other than alcohol consumption across an inpatient, an outpatient, and a halfway house program. Armor, Polich, and Stambul (1978) reported consistent improvement rates across inpatient, outpatient, and intermediate care facilities at six-month follow-up. Thus, from uncontrolled studies, the data are mixed and afford no firm conclusions.

Findings in controlled studies have been much more consistent. Edwards and Guthrie (1966, 1967) randomly assigned 40 gamma alcoholics (following standard detoxification) to either inpatient or outpatient treatment, with both groups receiving psychotherapy, social work, family consultation, A.A., and prescriptions for calcium carbimide. At six-month (1966) and twelve-month (1967) follow-ups, no significant differences were found between groups, with existing differences favoring the outpatients. Gallant and his colleagues (1973) randomly assigned court-referred chronic drunkenness offenders to outpatient therapy, inpatient treatment, or probation only. They found no significant differences among groups, but their findings are rendered meaningless by the fact that they failed to locate 92% of their sample at one-year follow-up.

Stinson et al. (1979) randomly assigned alcoholics to intensive inpatient care vs. a peer-oriented self-help inpatient program (the latter requiring 40% less staff involvement). The peer-oriented program patients showed significantly greater reduction in drinking behavior at follow-up, with no significant differences between groups on a variety of other measures. Pittman and Tate (1972) assigned alcoholics at random to detoxification only versus detoxification plus three to six weeks of inpatient care. At one-year follow-up, a modest but nonsignificant advantage was observed for the treated group. Willems et al. (1973) compared short-stay (mean of 20 days) with long-stay (50-144 days) inpatients (randomly assigned). At two-year follow-up there were no significant differences between groups. Mosher, Davis, Mulligan, and Iber (1975) allowed their alcoholic patients to complete nine days of inpatient treatment, then randomly assigned them to continue on an inpatient basis for an additional 21 days or to be discharged to outpatient care. The additional inpatient treatment was found to produce no increment in outcome over the outpatient condition at three- or six-month follow-up. Finally, Stein, Newton, and Bauman (1975) used random assignment to determine whether 58 alcoholics should be discharged immediately after detoxification or should be permitted to continue through a 25-day inpatient program including group psychotherapy, A.A., alcohol education, and recreational and occupational therapy. Five interviews were scheduled with each patient over a 13-month follow-up period, and 90% of these face-to-face interviews were successfully completed. On a wide range of outcome measures (including use of other treatment resources, readmissions, and arrest records) no significant differences were found between groups. Thus, controlled research to date rather consistently has found no advantage for patients *in general* treated by inpatient versus more minimal outpatient methods. Whether intensive inpatient care differentially benefits a certain subset of patients remains to be determined.

If inpatient services are of little advantage over outpatient services, what of different *amounts* of treatment offered within a given setting? Again, the findings from controlled research have been surprisingly consistent. A study by Griffith Edwards and his colleagues (1977) provides illustrative results. These investigators randomly assigned 100 married, healthy, and socially stable alcoholic males to one of two treatment conditions: (a) an intensive treatment condition including outpatient psychotherapy, A.A., prescription for calcium cyanamide, and the availability of a private psychiatrist and/or inpatient care; or (b) an "advice" group that received only a single individual session in which the patient was told that he should abstain but that he would have to take responsibility for bringing about change. At both one- and two-year follow-ups, no significant differences were found in success of outcome for the two groups (Edwards et al., 1977; Orford et al., 1976). The two-year follow-up did yield an interesting finding, however: of those patients diagnosed as *gamma* alcoholics, *all* who were rated as having good outcome had received the intensive treatment, whereas of those cases rated as clearly unsuccessful, 80% had received the "advice" treatment. Among patients diagnosed at intake *not* to be gamma alcoholics, the findings were reversed: 65% of those in the good outcome group had received the minimal "advice" treatment, whereas 71% of those rated as clearly unsuccessful had been through the intensive treatment program. These findings suggest that individuals showing more severe symptoms of alcoholism may benefit differentially from intensive treatment efforts, but that such heroic efforts may actually be detrimental to those with less severe symptomatology. This is a valuable and interesting finding that will require replication in future research.

Michael O'Leary and his associates at the Veterans Administration Medical Center in Seattle are currently investigating the role of cognitive abilities in relation to prognosis following treatment. Using neuropsychological measures and a composite index known as the Brain Age Quotient (BAQ), they have found that alcoholics with higher BAQs have fewer relapses, show lower rates of alcohol consumption, and maintain longer periods of abstinence than do patients with lower BAQs (O'Leary, Donovan, Chaney, & Walker, in press). Following this lead, they are currently studying how adaptive abilities, length of treatment, and treatment outcome interact. They hypothesize that alcoholics with significant cognitive impairment will benefit more from a long-term than from a short-term (14-day) program. Alcoholics with higher BAQs, however, may benefit as much from a short-term as from a long-term program. If these hypotheses are supported, neuropsychological assessment procedures may prove valuable aids in planning treatment for problem drinkers (cf. Miller & Orr, in press).

Other studies previously reviewed have pointed to the equivalent efficacy of minimal versus extensive interventions, particularly with earlier-stage problem drinkers (Miller, Gribskov & Mortell, in press; Miller & Taylor, 1980; Miller, Taylor & West, in press; Vogler et al., 1975, 1977a, 1977b). Smart and Gray (1978) found length of treatment to be associated with percentage of successful abstinent cases, but not with overall improvement rates. Ogborne and Wilmot (1979) found no differences at three-month follow-up between skid row men given six months of counseling and a matched control group. Burnum (1974) reported on the success of simple advice to abstain, given by an internist during routine medical consultations. Although alcoholics showed the poorest rate (9%) of compliance with advice (in comparison to the response of smokers, overeaters, and drug abusers), Burnum found that those who did comply did so relatively quickly (advised 1.3 times) whereas repeated advice (average of 7.3 times) was ineffective with noncompliant patients. Perhaps an interim screening measure would be to provide initial advice or other minimal intervention, then to work more intensively with those for whom this is not sufficient within a reasonable period of time (cf. Miller, 1978b, in press).

With regard to detoxification, Feldman, Pattison, Sobell, Graham, and Sobell (1975) found that only 47% of patients seeking acute alcoholism treatment required detoxification, and that of these only 19% required standard inpatient care. The study suggests that the routine provision of inpatient detoxification may be an unwise allocation of resources, burdening staff with an excessive number of patients when such intensive care could be better provided to those genuinely in need of it. Once again, more treatment is not necessarily better treatment!

Summary. Extensive treatment appears to be unnecessary and perhaps detrimental for some patients, and present data do not support the *routine* provision of intensive inpatient or broad-spectrum treatment for all problem drinkers. Differential diagnostic procedures are needed, which in turn will rely upon well-controlled outcome research including a range of predictor variables. Current research suggests that perhaps minimal interventions, rather than "total push" efforts, would be the prudent norm for treatment in this area. More intensive and expensive measures can then be implemented with unresponsive patients, along with research to determine whether such additional efforts yield significant improvement in outcome.

Type of Therapist

"Who is qualified to treat the alcoholic?" This is a question that has been the subject of heated debate from some years (Krystal & Moore, 1963). Kalb and

Propper (1976), in order to stimulate this debate, proposed a sharp distinction between two models of treatment: the "craft" model, in which counselors learn their trade through experience from master counselors, who pass on particular methods; or the "science" model, in which professionals are unified, not by devotion to certain beliefs, but rather by commitment to scientific methodology, with openness to and training in a broad range of alternative interventions. The dichotomy is clearly (and, we believe, intentionally) too simple. In the first place, many well-credentialled professionals have espoused unquestioning loyalty to particular schools of thought regarding therapy. Consider, for example, Dr. Krystal's (1963) contention, unburdened by the weight of data, that "the therapist for the patients addicted to self-medication with alcohol must be able to do effective psychotherapy. Psychotherapy is a technique of treatment in which the patient's unconscious problems are made conscious and the defects of his personality are corrected by working with the pathological manifestations" (p. 711). Paraprofessionals hold no monopoly on dogma. Secondly, we regard as improper Kalb and Propper's contention that "craft vs. science" is an either/or matter in the field of alcohol treatment. To be sure, working models for cooperation among various types of therapists (and therapies) must be developed. We will return to this point later.

But what are the data? Does effective alcoholism treatment *require* the attention of a fully-trained and credentialled professional? Certainly the answer is *no*. The effectiveness of A.A., albeit with a certain subpopulation, supports the efficacy of self-help efforts for some alcoholics. Virtually all of the controlled drinking treatment conducted in our clinics described earlier (Miller, 1977, 1978a; Miller & Taylor, 1980; Miller, Taylor & West, in press) was administered by paraprofessionals with specialized training in particular interventions. Armor and his colleagues (1978) found no significant difference in effectiveness between professional and paraprofessional alcoholism counselors. Volunteer and paraprofessional therapists have been used effectively in alcohol treatment and have allowed clinics to serve a greater number of clients with less cost (Christensen et al., 1978; Manohar, 1973; Staub & Kent, 1973).

Do recovering alcoholics make better paraprofessional counselors than do nonalcoholics? The data here are sparse. Some have found no difference between alcoholic and nonalcoholic counselors (Covner, 1969; Rosenberg et al., 1976). Alcoholic patients have been found to rate alcoholic counselors as higher than nonalcoholics in counseling skills (Lawson, 1976) and to prefer directive to nondirective approaches (Obitz, 1975). Recovering alcoholics have been reported to receive favorable ratings from supervisors (Chalfant et al., 1978) and to show counseling skills equivalent to those of nonalcoholics following training (Buzzetta, 1976). Argeriou and Manohar (1978) compared alcoholic and nonalcoholic counselors working within an outpatient setting and reported that clients of alcoholic counselors were more likely to be abstinent at termination. No difference was observed in the average number of weeks of abstinence between groups, however, and no follow-up was conducted beyond the point of termination. In addition, three of four alcoholic counselors had received training through a specialized alcoholism counselor training program, whereas only one of three nonalcoholic counselors had received such training. On the basis of these few studies, we are inclined to agree with Covner that "a history of alcoholism neither guarantees nor precludes counseling success" (1969, p. 422). An excellent recent review of research on "nonprofessional" therapeutic agents has been provided by Emrick et al. (1977).

The emergence of new alternative treatment methods such as those reviewed earlier in this chapter will have important implications for both professional and paraprofessional therapists. A prescriptive approach (Dimond et al., 1978; Goldstein & Stein, 1976), which matches treatment to patient, seems sounder than one which attempts to select or modify patients to fit a particular therapeutic program. This means that a comprehensive treatment program must be prepared to offer a range of alternative interventions. It is this development which, we believe, will afford a new model for cooperative team efforts. Certain tasks will be best suited to the advanced scientific and clinical training of the professional (Peele, 1976). These include initial screening, diagnosis and patient-needs assessment, determination of optimal treatment modality, program evaluation, and administration of certain more complex therapeutic methods. Paraprofessional counselors, on the other hand, may competently apply well-specified treatment methods for which they have received specialized training, receiving appropriate referrals from professionals who perform screening and supervision. Other types of therapeutic adjuncts (e.g., peer support systems, bibliotherapy) may find their suitable places within this framework as well (Christensen et al., 1978; Glasgow & Rosen, 1978). In this way optimal use is made of staff time, with each team member performing therapeutic services appropriate to his or her level of training and expertise.

Criteria for Abstinence versus Moderation Goals

The advent of treatment approaches oriented toward a goal of moderate drinking has raised a new issue for the therapist: how to determine the most appropriate treatment goal for a given client. Miller and Caddy (1977), noting the paucity of data relevant to this decision, have proposed rational interim guidelines based upon a contraindications model. They have suggested that a treatment goal of moderation is contraindicated if the client shows:
• evidence of progressive liver disease or other medical or psychological problem of sufficient magnitude to render even moderate drinking hazardous to the individual's life and health
• a personal commitment to abstinence, or strong external demands for abstinence

- pathological intoxication
- history of physiological addiction with severe withdrawal symptoms
- use of medication considered dangerous when combined with alcohol
- current successful abstinence following severe problem drinking
- prior failure of competent moderation-oriented treatment

On the other hand, Miller and Caddy suggest, a goal of abstinence is contraindicated if the client shows:

- refusal to consider abstinence as a goal
- strong external demands to drink, or lack of social support for abstinence
- early stage problem drinking without history of physiological addiction
- prior failure of competent abstinence-oriented treatment

These are mostly "common sense" rules for decision-making. Differential assignment to treatment goals could be greatly aided, however, by the availability of data regarding the type of patient most likely to respond favorably to abstinence versus moderation goals.

Fortunately, such data have begun to appear, and a surprising degree of consistency seems to be emerging. These data are of three types: (a) data regarding client *preferences* for treatment goal; (b) predictive data regarding the type of client who becomes a moderate drinker versus an abstainer following abstinence-oriented treatment; and (c) data predicting abstinence versus moderation outcomes following treatment designed to result in controlled drinking.

Relatively little is known about differences between clients who, given a free choice, select moderation versus abstinence goals. Kilpatrick et al. (1978) found no significant differences between these groups with regard to demographic or personality variables. Nevertheless, the client's own preference may be important, as suggested by Miller and Caddy (1977). Caddy et al. (1978) found a 50% improvement rate among clients requesting and assigned to moderation-oriented treatment, as compared with a 25% rate among clients requesting moderation but randomly assigned to abstinence-oriented therapy (Sobell & Sobell, 1973). In another interesting study for which only preliminary results are available, Martha Sanchez-Craig (1980) randomly assigned problem drinkers applying to a "preventive treatment" program into one of two treatment conditions: abstinence-oriented or moderation-oriented. In *both* conditions, clients were advised to maintain a period of total abstinence during the early weeks of treatment. The only difference was with regard to the long-term goal of treatment. Clients assigned to the moderation goal showed a significantly higher rate of compliance with *abstinence* as compared to those assigned to the abstinence goal. Likewise, clients in the moderation goal group, on days when they did drink, drank significantly less than did those assigned to an abstinence goal.

A crucial source of information lies in studies that have examined predictors of various types of treatment outcome. Of special interest here are studies that have examined differential predictors of abstinence versus moderation outcomes (unfortunately lumped together in most studies as "successful" cases) or of controlled versus uncontrolled drinking following treatment (again often combined in older studies and considered jointly as "unsuccessful" cases).

Studies based upon programs where the primary goal was abstinence will be considered first. These studies have reported that individuals who become successful controlled drinkers: (a) were consuming less alcohol at intake (Smart, 1978a); (b) showed less severe symptoms of alcoholism (Armor et al., 1978; Orford, 1973; Orford et al., 1976; Smart, 1978a); (c) were more likely to be married (Levinson, 1977; Smart, 1978a); (d) had a more positive attitude toward abstinence (Orford et al., 1976; Smart, 1978a); (e) were less likely to regard themselves as alcoholics (Orford, 1973); and (f) reported a briefer history of problem drinking prior to treatment (Orford, 1973).

Encouragingly consistent reports have emerged from studies where the treatment goal has been moderation. Combining the client samples of four studies, Miller and Joyce (1979) found that controlled drinkers reported fewer symptoms of alcoholism, had higher income, reported less history of alcoholism in parents, and were more likely to be female in comparison to successful abstainers. In contrast to unsuccessful cases, controlled drinkers were more often female, less likely to label themselves as alcoholic, and reported less education, less parental alcoholism, less previous help, but more life problems related to drinking. Similarly, Popham and Schmidt (1976) found controlled drinkers to be younger, more likely to be female, and drinking less before treatment. Vogler and his colleagues (1977a) found that, in contrast to abstainers, moderate drinkers had a shorter history of problem drinking, had been drinking less at intake, were younger, and had lost fewer work days because of alcohol.

The picture that emerges is clear: individuals who will become successful controlled drinkers show less resemblance to the classic diagnostic picture of alcoholism. They have fewer problems related to drinking and have had them for a shorter period of time, have fewer symptoms and less family history of alcoholism, and drink less. They are more likely to be women, to be younger, and to not regard themselves as alcoholics. It appears that social stability increases the probability of controlled drinking, although this is also a positive prognostic factor for abstinence. With regard to education and income, data are mixed and no clear pattern emerges.

This relationship between severity of problem drinking and outcome is also borne out by the outcome literature. Orford and his colleagues (1976) distinguished patients clearly diagnosable as gamma alcoholics from those clearly nongamma alcoholics and found that, of those individuals with a controlled drinking outcome, *none* were from the gamma alcoholism group, whereas 55% of the abstainers came from the gamma group. Similar findings were reported in the "Rand report" (Armor et al., 1978), where within the "definite alcoholism" group, 46% were found to be abstinent and 16% normal drinkers at 18-month follow-up. By contrast, a group showing less severe symptoms of alcoholism showed a 44% abstinence rate, with 36% found to be "normal drinkers."

We further tabulated the results of 19 outcome studies of treatment programs where the goal was moderation, distinguishing among studies in which the client population was clearly identified as manifesting gamma or chronic alcoholism, those in which clients were clearly less severe problem drinkers, and those in which the population was identified as "alcoholic" but the severity was unclear. The results of our tabulation are summarized in table 2.3. Again, a trend emerges which suggests that the more severe the population being treated, the less probable controlled drinking outcomes are and the more probable abstinence outcomes become.

. **Table 2.3.**   Relationship between Severity of Problem Drinking and Outcome within Treatment Programs with a Goal of Moderation*

Patient Population	Studies	N	%ABST	%C.D.	%IMPR	TOTAL %IMPR
Clear gamma or chronic[1] alcoholic	6	145	26%	25%	3%	53%
Unclear[2]	4	271	10%	24%	26%	61%
Non-gamma problem[3] drinkers	9	349	7%	43%	22%	72%
All populations	19	765	12%	33%	20%	64%

*For definitions of abstinence (ABST), controlled drinking (C.D.) and improved (IMPR) see footnotes to table 2.1:

[1](Baker et al., 1975; Ewing & Rouse, 1976; Schaefer, 1972; Sobell & Sobell, 1973b; Vogler et al., 1975, 1977a)

[2](Caddy & Lovibond, 1976; Hedberg & Campbell, 1974; Lovibond & Caddy, 1970; Popham & Schmidt, 1976)

[3](Alden, 1978; Lovibond, 1975; Miller, 1978a; Miller, Gribskov & Mortell, in press; Miller, Pechacek & Hamburg, in press; Miller & Taylor, 1980; Miller, Taylor & West, in press; Pomerleau et al., 1978; Vogler et al., 1977b)

Thus, it appears that moderation-oriented approaches show greater promise when applied to less severe problem drinkers, whereas abstinence approaches are more effective with more advanced alcoholic populations. The distinction is by no means clearcut. Numerous studies have documented controlled drinking outcomes in clients clearly diagnosable as gamma alcoholics at intake (Caddy et al., 1978; Pattison, Sobell, & Sobell, 1977; Vogler et al., 1975). Nevertheless, the trend is clear, and provides at least the beginning of an empirical procedure for determining optimal treatment goals within a diverse population of problem drinkers.

Conclusions and Discussion

The literature on the effectiveness of various approaches in the treatment of problem drinkers has been growing at a rapid rate. In preparing this review, we were particularly encouraged to note an increase, in recent years, in the number of well-designed studies and in the use of adequate assessment procedures. Certainly, more controlled research is needed in all areas, but the field of alcohol treatment is at last accumulating a usable body of knowledge regarding treatment outcome. We are, happily, well past the point where all treatment approaches can be regarded as equally valid and effective.

To summarize the volume of research reviewed above is a difficult if not dangerous task. We recall Dumas' famous caveat, "All generalizations are dangerous—even this one!" Nevertheless, we will attempt to abstract the current state of knowledge from research regarding various approaches, with the assumption that the reader will check our conclusions against his or her own based upon the research we have reviewed, and with the knowledge that some of our conclusions will almost certainly prove incorrect as further research emerges.

Summary of Conclusions

The Average Fate of Problem Drinkers. From the most extensive reviews available, it appears that when problem drinkers are treated, approximately one-third become abstinent and an additional one-third show substantial improvement without abstinence. These figures are based upon short-term follow-up, however, and data from studies with longer follow-up suggest that, on the average, only 26% of those treated remain abstinent or improved after one year. As for untreated problem drinkers, our best estimate is that about 19% are abstinent or improved after one year. These figures provide a very rough baseline against which to compare the efficacy of various treatment approaches.

Medication. Selected medications have a definite place in the detoxification process, although it appears that they are not necessary in many cases. As long-term treatment, however, medication is more questionable. Drugs intended to "substitute" for alcohol (e.g., tranquilizers) yield outcome rates at or below those attributable to spontaneous remission. Certain psychotropic medications, particularly antidepressant drugs and lithium, may be useful in the treatment of concomitant psychiatric and psychological disorders, but they appear to have relatively little impact upon drinking.

The antidipsotropic or "protective" drugs intended to forestall alcohol consumption appear somewhat more promising. Voluntary acceptance of disulfiram appears to be associated with elevated improvement rates, although this may be due to a selection factor. Disulfiram implants have received little use in the United States and their effectiveness appears to be attributable to placebo and motivational factors rather than to the unpredictable levels of disulfiram in the bloodstream. Recent research questions the safety of disulfiram as a medication and alternative protective drugs have been explored. The protective effects of metronidazole are doubtful and its carcinogenic properties render it questionable as a medication. Citrated calcium carbimide may produce fewer side effects than does disulfiram, but its efficacy has not been established.

After a period of initial enthusiasm, the use of hallucinogens (LSD) in the treatment of alcoholism has declined rapidly with the finding that gains were no greater than those attributable to placebo.

Aversion Therapies. Aversion therapy using nausea-inducing drugs has been found to produce consistently high abstinence rates (averaging between 60% and 70% at one-year) well above "average" outcome figures and rates attributable to spontaneous remission. Controlled research is notably absent in this area, however, and the success of this approach may be restricted to populations with greater social stability and financial resources.

Apnea-producing drugs, such as succinylcholine, are extremely dangerous, and produce improvement rates that are generally inferior to those observed with nausea aversion. Use of this method is no longer justifiable.

Electrical aversion therapy has been found to produce improvement rates higher than those attributable to no treatment or conventional treatment, usually with a larger percentage of moderate drinking outcomes than has been observed following nausea aversion. In comparison to other treatment approaches, however, electrical aversion has been found to be relatively ineffective and its contribution within multimodal programs is minimal at best. Its effect appears to be a moderate decrease in the desirability of alcohol tastes, rather than the classically conditioned anxiety that it was originally thought to produce.

Covert sensitization appears to produce outcome rates roughly comparable to those observed in other aversion therapies, although studies have been too few to draw conclusions at this time. The fact that this form of aversion therapy requires no administration of physically aversive stimuli (shock, vomiting) recommends it as a medically if not humanely preferable alternative if future research supports its efficacy.

Hypnosis. The term "hypnosis" describes a wide range of different therapeutic procedures. Some forms resemble covert sensitization and are modestly supported. Current research does not support the efficacy of other forms of hypnosis as an adjunct in alcoholism treatment, although further research is warranted.

Psychotherapy. Traditional insight-oriented psychotherapy is rather clearly not a treatment of choice for problem drinkers. Drop-out rates are very high, and improvement rates for those who remain are, at best, comparable to average outcome figures. Individual psychotherapy is also an expensive and long-term undertaking that does not compare favorably with the cost-effectiveness of alternative methods.

Alcoholics Anonymous. A. A. is perhaps the most popular and most widely acclaimed method for treating alcoholics. Research to support claims of efficacy has been both sparse and flawed. Uncontrolled studies suggest an abstinence rate between 26% and 50% at one-year, which compares favorably with average outcome data. A recent controlled evaluation failed to support A. A. as more effective than no treatment, and relative to other approaches A. A. was equally effective at best. Drop-out rates from A. A. are characteristically high, suggesting that it may be optimal for a certain type of alcoholic individual.

Group Therapies. After A. A., group therapies are the most common method for treating alcoholics. Group methods have varied widely, as have improvement rates, which average around 40% at short-term follow-up. There is no evidence to support traditional group methods as a superior approach in alcoholism treatment. Insight-oriented group psychotherapy appears to be no more effective than is individual psychotherapy. Cost-effectiveness considerations may hold an advantage for group approaches, all else being equal.

Family Therapies. Both behavioral family therapy and structured (systems) family therapy have received modest support from uncontrolled research. One controlled study found behavioral family therapy to be more effective than aversion therapies. Initial findings have been promising, but more controlled research is necessary before conclusions can be drawn.

Controlled Drinking Therapies. Overall, controlled drinking therapies have produced total improvement rates comparable to those produced by abstinence-oriented methods. The pattern is different, however, with about one-third becoming totally controlled drinkers and an additional one-third abstinent or improved.

Behavioral self-control training (BSCT) has received consistent support in ten controlled studies, producing improvement rates ranging between 60% and 80%. BSCT is a complex package, however, and the relative importance of its components is unknown. Self-monitoring may be an important element. BSCT appears to be amenable to and effective as a self-help method as well.

Blood alcohol discrimination training using external cues has been a common element in BSCT. It appears that whereas social drinkers can learn to discriminate BAC from internal cues with biofeedback, alcoholics are unable to do so and rely upon external cues instead. The extent to which BAC training contributes to BSCT or multimodal programs is unknown.

Videotape self-confrontation has been found to produce modest increments in improvement in four controlled studies. It is also clear, however, that this procedure can have powerfully aversive effects upon clients and may result in a high drop-out rate. The relative contribution of videotape self-confrontation within a multimodal program (where it has typically been used) is not known, nor is it clear whether the apparently small increments in positive outcome outweigh the potential risks involved.

Cognitive-behavior therapies are a relatively recent addition to the armamentarium of the alcoholism therapist. Several case studies and one controlled evaluation support the effectiveness of these methods, but it is really too soon to tell what contribution they will make to abstinence- as well as control-oriented treatment.

Operant approaches have been employed mostly within inpatient settings. Exposure of alcoholics to alcohol while in treatment (requiring choices of to drink or not to drink) appears not to decrease the success of treatment, but neither is the value of such procedure established. It appears that if environmental contingencies can be modified, the problem drinker may be assisted in attaining abstinence or moderation.

Finally, multimodal treatment programs have been the most common approach in teaching moderate drinking to problem drinkers. Controlled research has very consistently found no advantage or very minimal advantage in multimodal and broad-spectrum approaches over simpler and less expensive methods such as BSCT. It may be that a certain subset of problem drinkers will benefit differentially from more extensive interventions, but as a *general* approach multimodal programs are not justifiable from a cost-effectiveness standpoint.

Teaching Alternative Skills. Teaching behavioral alternatives to alcohol is a logical and relatively recent addition to treatment programs. Relaxation training alone appears to be of little value, but systematic desensitization (which includes relaxation) has been found in initial comparative evaluations to be promising as a treatment adjunct. Likewise, the inclusion of social skills training within alcoholism treatment has received support in several controlled studies. The volume of data does not justify firm conclusions at the present time, however, and we advocate a stance of cautious optimism regarding the utility of training in alternative skills.

Predictors of Outcome. Controlled studies have very consistently found that extensive and long-term treatment programs, whether oriented toward abstinence or toward moderation, are no more effective than are briefer and less expensive approaches. It appears that individuals showing more severe symptoms characteristic of gamma alcoholism may benefit differentially from more extensive interventions.

With regard to the type of therapist, present data do not indicate substantial differences in the effectiveness of professional versus paraprofessional therapists or of alcoholic versus nonalcoholic counselors.

Significant headway has been made during the past few years toward the development of guidelines for selection of treatment goal. Although the distinction is by no means complete, successful controlled drinkers have rather consistently been found to be those showing less severe symptoms of problem drinking at intake, whereas successful abstainers have been found more often to show advanced symptomatology resembling that characteristic of gamma alcoholism. This relationship has held whether the goal of treatment has been abstinence or moderation. Outcome data from treatment programs with an explicit goal of moderation suggest that they have been more successful with clients in earlier stages of the development of problem drinking.

Discussion: Implications for Treatment Planning

First of all, it is clear that certain treatment methods are not supported by research to date, which has suggested that they are ineffective, uneconomical, or unjustifiably hazardous for problem drinkers. These methods include the use of tranquilizers (except during detoxification,) metronidazole, LSD, succinylcholine, insight-oriented psychotherapy, and routine multimodal treatment. Whether any of these methods might be useful for defined subsamples of problem drinkers remains to be seen.

The majority of treatment procedures for problem drinkers warrant a "Scotch verdict" of unproved at the present time. The absence of adequately controlled research or inconsistency of findings regarding most currently-used methods leave us uncertain of their effectiveness. Ironically, the most widely accepted and commonly used treatment techniques currently fall into this category of "unproved," largely due to a lack of appropriate evaluation research.

Certain procedures, however, can be regarded as tentatively supported in that the weight of present uncontrolled and controlled research points to their efficacy. For several of these, including disulfiram, electrical aversion, videotape self-confrontation, and chemical (nausea) aversion, there is some question as to whether the risks, costs, or discomfort involved outweigh the attendant benefits. Behavioral self-control training and broad spectrum approaches including desensitization and social skills training have received sufficiently consistent support from outcome studies to be considered as tentatively supported, and no significant risks or side effects have been noted. Nevertheless, no treatment method has been shown to be consistently superior to the absence of treatment or to alternative treatments in a sufficient number of well-controlled studies to warrant "established" status. We have learned much about the effectiveness and ineffectiveness of various approaches and this knowledge is helpful in planning modern treatment programs, but there is still much to be learned.

If a program intends to offer comprehensive treatment services for problem drinkers, it seems clear that a range of alternative interventions must be offered. Predictive data, for example, suggest that for early stage problem drinkers, moderation-oriented methods may be optimal, whereas more advanced alcoholics may be best served by effective abstinence-oriented approaches. The consistent finding that extensive and intensive interventions are

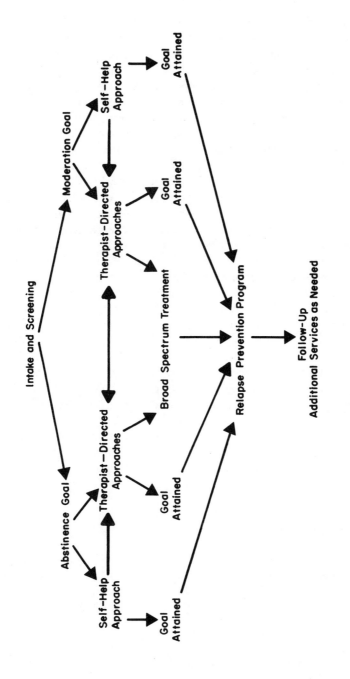

Fig. 2.1. Integrated outpatient program.

no more effective in general than are more minimal treatments suggests that it would be unwise policy to routinely provide multimodal, long-term, or broad-spectrum treatment for *all* clients. Rather, both minimal and more intensive alternatives should be available, with the latter used selectively. The offering of multiple modalities within the comprehensive treatment setting permits cross-referral within the center, decreasing the chances of losing the client in the process. Thus, a client who is not responding well to a moderation approach can be switched to an abstinence goal, and vice versa. Likewise, the client who does not attain his or her goal with minimal intervention can be offered more extensive or individualized services. One such model for integrated outpatient services is illustrated in figure 2.1.

Finally, we wish to emphasize the importance of evaluation research within your own treatment setting. This can be as informal as routine follow-up calls to all clients (which, by the way, make for better aftercare and permit early identification of emerging problems) or as formal as the controlled studies we have reviewed earlier. Treatment populations differ. What works for one group, or in one setting, or for one therapist or team may not work elsewhere. As therapists, we all have a built-in tendency to want to believe that what we are doing is most effective. The fact is that that isn't always true. Some treatment methods once thought to be effective are now known to make some people worse. In our own research we have encountered one surprise after another, leading us to conclusions that we would never have drawn from clinical experience alone—and our treatment programs are the better for it. You'll never know (although it may seem that you do) what really works and what doesn't work for you without some commitment to follow-up evaluation. Think of it as "program development" rather than a test of worth, for in fact that's what it is. In return, there is the fascination of finding out, and the knowledge that the fruits of your efforts will be more effective services for those who look to you for help.

References

Adinolfi, A. A., McCourt, W. F., & Geoghegan, S. Group assertiveness training for alcoholics. *Journal of Studies on Alcohol*, 1976, **37**, 311-320.

Akiskal, H. S., Beard, J. D., Fink, R. D., & Knott, D. H. Diuretic-antidepressant combination in alcoholic depressives: Preliminary findings, *Diseases of the Nervous System*, 1974, **35**, 207-211.

The alcoholic felon. *Alcohol Health and Research World*, 1974 (Summer), 17-23.

Alcoholics Anonymous. *Alcoholics Anonymous: The story of how many thousands of men and women have recovered from alcoholism*. New York: A.A. World Services, 1955.

Alden, L. Evaluation of a preventive self-management programme for problem drinkers. *Canadian Journal of Behavioural Science*, 1978, **10**, 258-263.

Alden, L. Personal communication, August 27, 1979.

Alibrandi, L. A. The folk psychotherapy of Alcoholics Anonymous. In S. Zimberg, J. Wallace, & S. B. Blume (Eds.), *Practical approaches to alcoholism psychotherapy*. New York: Plenum, 1978.

Allman, L. R., Taylor, H. A., & Nathan, P. E. Group drinking during stress: Effects on drinking behavior, affect, and psychopathology. *American Journal of Psychiatry*, 1972, **129**, 669-678.

Alterman, A. I., Gottheil, E., & Crawford, H. D. Mood changes in an alcoholism treatment program based on drinking decisions. *American Journal of Psychiatry*, 1975, **132**, 1032-1037.

Alterman, A. I., Gottheil, E., Gellens, H. K., & Thornton, C. C. Relationships between drinking behavior of alcoholics in a drinking-decisions treatment program and treatment outcome. In P. E. Nathan, G. A. Marlatt, & T. Løberg (Eds.), *Alcoholism: New directions in behavioral research and treatment*. New York: Plenum, 1978.

Alterman, A. I., Gottheil, E., Skoloda, T. E., & Grasberger, J. C. Social modification of drinking by alcoholics. *Quarterly Journal of Studies on Alcohol*, 1974, **35**, 917-924.

Alterman, A. I., Gottheil, E., Skoloda, T. E., & Thornton, C. C. Consequences of social modification of drinking behavior. *Journal of Studies on Alcohol*, 1977, **38**, 1032-1035.

Amir, M., & Eldar, P. An experiment in the treatment of alcoholics in Isreal. *Drug Forum*, 1979, **7**, 105-119.

Amit, Z., & Levitan, D. E. Ethanol and morphine self-administration: A possible relationship based on differential involvement of catecholamines. In J. D. Sinclair & K. Kiianmaa (Eds.), *The effects of centrally active drugs on voluntary alcohol consumption. Journal of Studies on Alcohol*, 1977, **38**, 1896-1897. (Abstract)

Amit, Z., Sutherland, E. A., & Weiner, A. *Guide to intelligent drinking*. New York: Walker, 1977.

Anant, S. S. A note on the treatment of alcoholics by a verbal aversion technique. *Canadian Psychologist*, 1967, **1**, 19-22.

Anant, S. S. Alcoholics Anonymous and aversion therapy. *Canada's Mental Health*, 1968, **16**, 23-27. (a)

Anant, S. S. The use of verbal aversion (negative conditioning) with an alcoholic: A case report. *Behaviour Research and Therapy*, 1968, **6**, 395-396, (b)

Anderson, L., Lubetkin, B., Logan, D., & Alpert, M. Comparison of relaxation methods for alcoholics: Differential relaxation versus sensory awareness. *Proceedings of the American Psychological Association*, 1973, **81**, 391-392.

Annis, H. M., & Liban, C. B. A follow-up study of male halfway-house residents and matched nonresident controls. *Journal of Studies on Alcohol*, 1978, **40**, 63-69.

Annis, H. M., & Smart, R. G. Arrests, readmissions and treatment following release from detoxication centers. *Journal of Studies on Alcohol*, 1978, **39**, 1276-1283.

Argeriou, M., & Manohar, V. Relative effectiveness of nonalcoholics and recovered alcoholics as counselors. *Journal of Studies on Alcohol*, 1978, **39**, 793-799.

Arikawa, K., & Inanaga, K. The therapeutic mechanism of the double medication technique with cyanamide for alcoholism. *Folia Psychiatrica Neurologica Japonica*, 1973, **27**, 9-15.

Arikawa, K., Kotorii, M., & Mikasa, H. [The therapeutic effect of cyanamide on the alcoholic addicts in outpatient clinic.] *Clinical Psychiatry* (Japan), 1972, **14**, 219-227.

Arikawa, K., Naganuma, R., & Oshima, M. [The change of behavior pattern of alcohol addicts treated with cyanamide double medication: Observations by their family.] *Clinical Psychiatry* (Japan), 1972, **14**, 447-455.

Armor, D. J., Polich, J. M., & Stambul, H. B. *Alcoholism and treatment*. New York: Wiley, 1978.

Armstrong, J. D., & Kerr, H. T. A new protective drug in the treatment of alcoholism. *Canadian Medical Association Journal*, 1956, **74**, 795-797.

Armstrong, R. C. Playback technique in group psychotherapy. *Psychiatric Quarterly Supplement*, 1964, **38**, 247-252.

Aron, A., & Aron, E. N. The Transcendental Meditation program's effect on addictive behavior. *Addictive Behaviors*, 1980, **5**, 3-12.

Ashem, B., & Donner, L. Covert sensitization with alcoholics: A controlled replication. *Behaviour Research and Therapy*, 1968, **6**, 7-12.

Azrin, N. H. Improvements in the community-reinforcement approach to alcoholism. *Behaviour Research and Therapy*, 1976, **14**, 339-348.

Baekeland, F. Evaluation of treatment methods in chronic alcoholism. In B. Kissin, & H. Begleiter (Eds.), *The biology of alcoholism*. Vol. 5. *Treatment and rehabilitation of the chronic alcoholic*. New York: Plenum, 1977.

Baekeland, F., & Lundwall, L. K. Effects of discontinuity of medication on the results of a double-blind drug study in outpatient alcoholics. *Journal of Studies on Alcohol*, 1975, **36**, 1268-1272.

Baekeland, F., Lundwall, L., Kissin, B., & Shanahan, T. Correlates of outcome in disulfiram treatment of alcoholism. *Journal of Nervous and Mental Disease*, 1971, **153**, 1-9.

Bailey, K. G., & Sowder, W. T. Audiotape and videotape self-confrontation in psychotherapy. *Psychological Bulletin*, 1970, **74**, 127-137.

Bailey, M. B., & Stewart, J. Normal drinking by persons reporting previous problem drinking. *Quarterly Journal of Studies on Alcohol*, 1967, **28**, 305-315.

Baker, S. L., Jr., Lorei, T., McKnight, H. A., Jr., & Duvall, J. L. The Veterans Administration's comparison study: Alcoholism and drug abuse—combined and conventional treatment settings. *Alcoholism: Clinical and Experimental Research*, 1977, **1**, 285-291.

Baker, T. B., & Cannon, D. S. Taste aversion therapy with alcoholics: Techniques and evidence of a conditioned response. *Behaviour Research and Therapy*, 1979, **17**, 229-242.

Baker, T. B., Cannon, D. S., Stephenson, G. M., & Droubay, E. Procedures for taste aversion therapy for alcoholism. *American Journal of Psychiatry*, 1978, **135**, 1439.

Baker, T. B., Sobell, M. B., Sobell, L. C., & Cannon, D. S. Halfway houses for alcoholics: A review, analysis and comparison with other halfway house facilities. *International Journal of Social Psychiatry*, 1976, **22**, 130-139.

Baker, T. B., Udin, H., & Vogler, R. E. The effects of videotaped modeling and self-confrontation on the drinking behavior of alcoholics. *International Journal of the Addictions*, 1975, **10**, 779-793.

Bandura, A. *Principles of behavior modification*. New York: Holt, 1969.

Barber, T. X., Spanos, N. P., & Chaves, J. F. *Hypnosis: Imagination and human potentialities*. New York: Pergamon, 1974.

Bartholomew, A. A., & Guile, L. A. A controlled evaluation of Librium in the treatment of alcoholics. *Medical Journal of Australia*, 1961, **2**, 578-581.

Bassin, A. Psychology in action: Red, white, and blue poker chips; an A. A. behavior modification technique. *American Psychologist,* 1975, **30,** 695-696.

Bateman, N. I., & Petersen, D. M. Variables related to outcome of treatment for hospitalized alcoholics. *International Journal of the Addictions,* 1971, **6,** 215-224.

Battegay, R. The different kinds of group psychotherapy with patients with different diagnoses. *Acta Psychiatrica Scandinavica,* 1977, **55,** 345-354.

Bebbington, P. E. The efficacy of Alcoholics Anonymous: The elusiveness of hard data. *British Journal of Psychiatry,* 1976, **128,** 572-580.

Beck, A. T. *Cognitive therapy and the emotional disorders.* New York: International Universities Press, 1976.

Becker, C. E. Pharmacotherapy in the treatment of alcoholism. In J. H. Mendelson & N. K. Mello (Eds.), *The diagnosis and treatment of alcoholism.* New York: McGraw-Hill, 1979.

Beil, H., & Trojan, A. The use of apomorphine in the treatment of alcoholism and other addictions: Results of a general practitioner. *British Journal of Addiction,* 1977, **72,** 129-134.

Belasco, J. A. The criterion question revisited. *British Journal of Addiction,* 1971, **66,** 39-44.

Belasco, J. A., & Trice, H. M. *The assessment of change in training and therapy.* New York: McGraw-Hill, 1969.

Bell, R. G. Clinical trial of citrated calcium carbimide. *Canadian Medical Association Journal,* 1956, **74,** 797-798.

Bellwood, L. R. Grief work in alcoholism treatment. *Alcohol Health and Research World,* 1975 (Summer), 8-11.

Benson, H. Decreased alcohol intake associated with the practice of meditation: A retrospective investigation. *Annals of the New York Academy of Sciences,* 1974, **233,** 174-177.

Bhakta, M. Clinical application of behaviour therapy in the treatment of alcoholism. *Journal of Alcoholism* (London), 1971, **6,** 75-83.

Bigelow, G., Cohen, M., Liebson, I., & Faillace, L. A. Abstinence or moderation? Choices by alcoholics. *Behaviour Research and Therapy,* 1972, **10,** 209-214.

Bigelow, G., & Liebson, I. Cost factors controlling alcoholic drinking. *Psychological Record,* 1972, **22,** 305-314.

Bigelow, G., Liebson, I. & Griffiths, R. Alcoholic drinking: Suppression by a brief time-out procedure. *Behaviour Research and Therapy,* 1974, **12,** 107-115.

Bigelow, G., Strickler, D., Liebson, I., & Griffiths, R. Maintaining disulfiram ingestion among outpatient alcoholics: A security-deposit contingency contracting procedure. *Behaviour Research and Therapy,* 1976, **14,** 378-381.

Blake, B. G. The application of behaviour therapy to the treatment of alcoholism. *Behaviour Research and Therapy,* 1965, **3,** 75-85.

Blake, B. G. A follow-up of alcoholics treated by behaviour therapy. *Behaviour Research and Therapy,* 1967, **5,** 89-94.

Blane, H. T. Psychotherapeutic approach. In B. Kissin & H. Begleiter (Eds.), *The biology of alcoholism.* Vol. 5. *Treatment and rehabilitation of the chronic alcoholic.* New York: Plenum, 1977.

Block, M. A. Don't place alcohol on a pedestal. *Journal of the American Medical Association,* 1976, **235,** 2103-2104.

Blumberg, L. The ideology of a therapeutic social movement: Alcoholics Anonymous. *Journal of Studies on Alcohol,* 1977, **38,** 2122-2143.

Blume, S. B. Group psychotherapy in the treatment of alcoholism. In S. Zimberg, J. Wallace, & S. B. Blume (Eds.), *Practical approaches to alcoholism psychotherapy.* New York: Plenum, 1978. (a)

Blume, S. B. Psychodrama and the treatment of alcoholism. In S. Zimberg, J. Wallace, & S. B. Blume (Eds.), *Practical approaches to alcoholism psychotherapy.* New York: Plenum, 1978. (b)

Blume, S. B., Robins, J., & Branston, A. Psychodrama techniques in the treatment of alcoholism. *Group Psychotherapy,* 1968, **21,** 241-246.

Bois, C., & Vogel-Sprott, M. Discrimination of low blood alcohol levels and self-titration skills in social drinkers. *Quarterly Journal of Studies on Alcohol,* 1974, **35,** 86-97.

Boland, F. J., Mellor, C. S., & Revusky, S. Chemical aversion treatment of alcoholism: Lithium as the aversive agent. *Behaviour Research and Therapy,* 1978, **16,** 401-409.

Bourne, P. G., Alford, J. A., & Bowcock, J. Z. Treatment of Skid Row alcoholics with disulfiram. *Quarterly Journal of Studies on Alcohol,* 1966, **27,** 42-48.

Bowen, W. T., Soskin, R. A., & Chotlos, J. W. Lysergic acid diethylamide as a variable in the hospital treatment of alcoholism: A follow-up study. *Journal of Nervous and Mental Disease,* 1970, **150,** 111-118.

Bowman, K. M., Simon, A., Hine, C. H., Macklin, E. A., Crook, G. H., Burbridge, N., & Hanson, K. A clinical evaluation of tetraethylthiuramdisulphide (Antabuse) in the treatment of problem drinkers. *American Journal of Psychiatry,* 1951, **107,** 832-838.

Brandsma, J. M., Maultsby, M. C., & Welsh, R. J. *The outpatient treatment of alcoholism: A review and comparative study.* Baltimore, Md.: University Park Press, in press.

Bratter, T. E. Reality therapy: A group psychotherapeutic approach with adolescent alcoholics. *Annals of the New York Academy of Sciences,* 1974, **233,** 104-114.

Brown, S., & Yalom, I. D. Interactional group therapy with alcoholics. *Journal of Studies on Alcohol,* 1977, **38,** 426-456.

Browne-Mayers, A. N., Seelye, E. E., & Brown, D. E. Reorganized alcoholism service: Two years after. *Journal of the American Medical Association,* 1973, **224,** 233-235.

Bruun, K. Outcome of different types of treatment of alcoholics. *Quarterly Journal of Studies on Alcohol,* 1963, **24,** 280-288.

Bryce, J. C. An evaluation of LSD in the treatment of chronic alcoholism. *Canadian Psychiatric Association Journal,* 1970, **15,** 77-78.

Burnett, G. B., & Reading, H. W. The pharmacology of disulfiram in the treatment of alcoholism. *British Journal of Addiction,* 1970, **65,** 281-288.

Burnum, J. F. Outlook for treating patients with self-destructive habits. *Annals of Internal Medicine,* 1974, **81,** 387-393.

Burt, D. W. A behaviorist looks at AA. *Addictions* (Toronto), 1975, **22**(3), 56-69.

Burton, G., & Kaplan, H. M. Marriage counseling with alcoholics and their spouses. II. The correlation of excessive drinking behavior with family pathology and social deterioration. *British Journal of Addiction,* 1968, **63,** 161-170.

Butterworth, A. T. Depression associated with alcohol withdrawal: Imipramine therapy compared with placebo. *Quarterly Journal of Studies on Alcohol,* 1971, **32,** 343-348.

Butterworth, A. T., & Watts, R. D. Double-blind comparison of thiothixene, trifluoperazine, and placebo in chronic alcoholism. *Psychosomatics,* 1974, **15,** 85-87.

Buzzetta, F. A comparative study of the effectiveness of recovered alcoholic and non-alcoholic alcoholism counselors on specific counseling skills and the differential effect of microcounseling training. *Dissertation Abstracts International,* 1976, **36,** 5034A. (Abstract)

C., Bill The Growth and effectiveness of Alcoholics Anonymous in a southwestern city. *Quarterly Journal of Studies on Alcohol,* 1965, **26,** 279-284.

Caddy, G. R. How not to replicate: A commentary on Maxwell et al.'s (1974) replication of Lovibond and Caddy's (1970) "discriminated aversive control" study. *Behavior Therapy,* 1975, **6,** 710-711.

Caddy, G. R. Blood alcohol concentration discrimination training: Development and current status. In G. A. Marlatt & P. E. Nathan (Eds.), *Behavioral approaches to alcoholism.* New Brunswick, N.J.: Rutgers Center of Alcohol Studies, 1978.

Caddy, G. R., Addington, H. J., Jr., & Perkins, D. Individualized behavior therapy for alcoholics: A third-year independent double-blind follow-up. *Behaviour Research and Therapy,* 1978, **16,** 345-362.

Caddy, G. R., & Lovibond, S. H. Self-regulation and discriminated aversive conditioning in the modification of alcoholics' drinking behavior. *Behavior Therapy,* 1976, **7,** 223-230.

Caddy, G. R., Sutton, M., & Lewis, J. The role of feedback and internal cues in blood alcohol concentration estimation. *International Journal of the Addictions,* in press.

Cadogan, D. A. Marital group therapy in the treatment of alcoholism. *Quarterly Journal of Studies on Alcohol,* 1973, **34,** 1187-1194.

Cahalan, D. *Problem drinkers: A national survey.* San Francisco: Jossey-Bass, 1970.

Campbell, D. T., & Stanley, J. C. *Experimental and quasi-experimental designs for research.* Chicago: Rand McNally, 1963.

Canter, F. M. Personality factors related to participation in treatment by hospitalized male alcoholics. *Journal of Clinical Psychology,* 1966, **22,** 114-116.

Canter, F. M. The requirement of abstinence as a problem in institutional treatment of alcoholics. *Psychiatric Quarterly,* 1968, **42,** 217-231.

Carlsson, C., & Fasth, B. G. A comparison of the effects of propranolol and diazepam in alcoholics. *British Journal of Addiction,* 1976, **21,** 321-326.

Carrère, J. La psychochoc cinématographique. Principes et technique. Application au traitement des malades convalescents de delirium tremens. [Cinematographic psychoshock. Principles and technique. Application to the treatment of patients convalescing from delirium tremens.] *Annales Medico-psychologique,* 1954, **112,** 240-244.

Carrère, M. J. Psychogénie de l'alcoholism et attitude psychotherápique. *Annales Medico-psychologique,* 1958, **116,** 481-495.

Casier, H., & Merlevede, E. On the mechanism of the disulfiram-ethanol intoxication symptoms. *Archives Internationales de Pharmacodynamie et al Thérapie,* 1962, **139,** 165-176.

Caudill, B. D., & Marlatt, G. A. Modeling influences in social drinking: An experimental analogue. *Journal of Consulting and Clinical Psychology*, 1975, **43**, 405-415.

Cautela, J. R. Treatment of compulsive behavior by covert sensitization. *Psychological Record*, 1966, **16**, 33-41.

Cautela, J. R. Covert sensitization. *Psychological Reports*, 1967, **20**, 459-468.

Cautela, J. R. The treatment of alcoholism by covert sensitization. *Psychotherapy: Theory, Research and Practice*, 1970, **7**, 86-90.

Chafetz, M. E. Drugs in the treatment of alcoholism. *Medical Clinics of North America*, 1967, **51**, 1249-1259.

Chalfant, H. P., Martinson, L., & Crowe, D. J. Success of recovering alcoholics as counsellors in a professional setting. *British Journal of Alcohol and Alcoholism*, 1978, **13**, 116-121.

Chandler, A., & Hartman, M. Lysergic acid diethylamide (LSD-25) as a facilitating agent in psychotherapy. *AMA Archives of General Psychiatry*, 1960, **2**, 286-299.

Chaney, E. F., O'Leary, M. R., & Marlatt, G. A. Skill training with alcoholics. *Journal of Consulting and Clinical Psychology*, 1978, **46**, 1092-1104.

Charnoff, S. M., Kissin, B., & Reed, J. I. An evaluation of various psychotherapeutic agents in the long-term treatment of chronic alcoholism. Results of a double blind study. *American Journal of the Medical Sciences*, 1963, **246**, 172-179.

Cheek, F. E., Franks, C. M., Laucius, J., & Burtle, V. Behavior modification training for wives of alcoholics. *Quarterly Journal of Studies on Alcohol*, 1971, **32**, 456-461.

Cheek, F. E., & Holstein, C. M. Lysergic acid diethylamine tartrate (LSD-25) dosage levels, group differences, and social interaction. *Journal of Nervous and Mental Disease*, 1971, **153**, 133-147.

Child, G. P., Osinski, W., Bennett, R. E., & Davidoff, E. Therapeutic results and clinical manifestations following the use of tetraethylthiuram disulfide. *American Journal of Psychiatry*, 1951, **107**, 774-780.

Christensen, A., Miller, W. R., & Muñoz, R. F. Paraprofessionals, partners, peers, paraphernalia, and print: Expanding mental health service delivery. *Professional Psychology*, 1978, **9**, 249-270.

Chwelos, N., Blewett, D. B., Smith, C. M., & Hoffer, A. Use of d-lysergic acid diethylamide in the treatment of alcoholism. *Quarterly Journal of Studies on Alcohol*, 1959, **20**, 577-590.

Ciminero, A. R., Doleys, D. M., & Davidson, R. S. Free-operant avoidance of alcohol. *Journal of Behaviour Therapy and Experimental Psychiatry*, 1975, **6**, 242-245.

Claeson, L. E., & Malm, U. Electro-aversion therapy of chronic alcoholism. *Behaviour Research and Therapy*, 1973, **11**, 663-665.

Clancy, J., Vanderhoof, E., & Campbell, P. Evaluation of an aversive technique as a treatment for alcoholism. *Quarterly Journal of Studies on Alcohol*, 1967, **28**, 476-485.

Clancy, J., Vornbrock, R., & Vanderhoof, E. Treatment of alcoholics: A follow-up study. *Diseases of the Nervous System*, 1965, **26**, 555-561.

Cohen, M., Liebson, I., & Faillace, L. A technique for establishing controlled drinking in chronic alcoholics. *Diseases of the Nervous System*, 1972, **33**, 46-49.

Cohen, M., Liebson, I., & Faillace, L. Controlled drinking by chronic alcoholics over extended periods of free access. *Psychological Reports*, 1973, **32**, 1107-1110.

Cohen, M., Liebson, I. A., Faillace, L. A., & Allen, R. P. Moderate drinking by chronic alcoholics. *Journal of Nervous and Mental Disease*, 1971, **153**, 434-444.

Cohen, M., Liebson, I. A., Faillace, L. A., & Speers, W. Alcoholism: Controlled drinking and incentives for abstinence. *Psychological Reports*, 1971, **28**, 575-580.

Compton, J. V., & Vogler, R. E. Validation of the Alco-calculator. *Psychological Reports*, 1975, **36**, 977-978.

Conger, J. J. Reinforcement theory and the dynamics of alcoholism. *Quarterly Journal of Studies on Alcohol*, 1956, **17**, 296-305.

Corder, B. F., Corder, R. F., & Laidlaw, N. D. An intensive treatment program for alcoholics and their wives. *Quarterly Journal of Studies on Alcohol*, 1972, **33**, 1144-1146.

Costello, R. M., Biever, P., & Baillargeon, J. G. Alcoholism treatment programming: Historical trends and modern approaches. *Alcoholism: Clinical and Experimental Research*, 1977, **1**, 311-318.

Costello, R. M., Giffen, M. B., Schneider, S. L., Edgington, P. W., & Manders, K. R. Comprehensive alcohol treatment planning, implementation, and evaluation. *International Journal of the Addictions*, 1976, **11**, 553-570.

Covner, J. J. Screening volunteer alcoholism counselors. *Quarterly Journal of Studies on Alcohol*, 1969, **30**, 420-425.

Crawford, R. J. M. Treatment success in alcoholism. *New Zealand Medical Journal*, 1976, **84**, 93-96.

Crawford, R. J. M. Antabuse implantation. *New Zealand Medical Journal*, 1977, **86**, 41.

Cronkite, R. C., & Moos, R. H. Evaluating alcoholism treatment programs: An integrated approach. *Journal of Consulting and Clinical Psychology*, 1978, **46**, 1105-1119.

Curlee, J. Alcoholic women: Some considerations for further research. *Bulletin of the Menninger Clinic*, 1967, **31**, 154-163.

Curlee, J. Sex differences in patient attitudes toward alcoholism treatment. *Quarterly Journal of Studies on Alcohol*, 1971, **32**, 643-650.

Cutter, H. S. G., Schwaab, E. L., Jr., & Nathan, P. E. Effects of alcohol on its utility for alcoholics and nonalcoholics. *Quarterly Journal of Studies on Alcohol*, 1970, **31**, 369-378.

Danet, B. N. Self-confrontation in psychotherapy reviewed. *American Journal of Psychotherapy*, 1968, **22**, 245-257.

Davidson, A. F. An evaluation of the treatment and after-care of a hundred alcoholics. *British Journal of Addiction*, 1976, **71**, 217-224.

Davis, D. I. Berenson, D., Steinglass, P., & Davis, S. The adaptive consequences of drinking. *Psychiatry*, 1974, **37**, 209-215.

Davis, M. A self-confrontation technique in alcoholism treatment. *Quarterly Journal of Studies on Alcohol*, 1972, **33**, 191-192.

Denson, R., & Sydiaha, D. A controlled study of LSD treatment in alcoholism and neurosis. *British Journal of Psychiatry*, 1970, **116**, 443-445.

Devenyl, P., & Sereny, G. Aversive treatment with electro-conditioning for alcoholism. *British Journal of Addiction*, 1970, **65**, 289-292.

DeVito, R. A., Flaherty, L. A., & Mozdzierz, G. J. Toward a psychodynamic theory of alcoholism. *Diseases of the Nervous System*, 1970, **31**, 43-49.

Dichter, M., Driscoll, G. Z., Ottenberg, D. J., & Rosen, A. Marathon therapy with alcoholics. *Quarterly Journal of Studies on Alcohol*, 1971, **32**, 66-77.

Dimond, R. E., Havens, R. A., & Jones, A. C. A conceptual framework for the practice of prescriptive eclecticism in psychotherapy. *American Psychologist*, 1978, **33**, 239-248.

Ditman, K. S., & Crawford, G. G. The use of court probation in the management of the alcohol addict. *American Journal of Psychiatry*, 1966, **122**, 757-762.

Ditman, K. S., Crawford, G. G., Forgy, E. W., Moskowitz, H., & MacAndrew, C. A controlled experiment on the use of court probation for drunk arrests. *American Journal of Psychiatry*, 1967, **124**, 160-163.

Donahue, J. A halfway-house program for alcoholics. *Quarterly Journal of Studies on Alcohol*, 1971, **32**, 468-472.

Donahue, J., & Donahue, M. Hope House: A halfway facility for alcoholics. *Current Psychiatric Therapy*, 1975, **15**, 259-262.

Doroff, D. R. Group psychotherapy in alcoholism. In B. Kissin & H. Begleiter (Eds.), *The biology of alcoholism*. Vol. 5. *Treatment and rehabilitation of the chronic alcoholic*. New York: Plenum, 1977.

Dubourg, G. O. After-care for alcoholics: A follow-up study. *British Journal of Addiction*, 1969, **64**, 155-163.

Dulfano, C. Family therapy of alcoholism. In S. Zimberg, J. Wallace, & S. B. Blume (Eds.), *Practical approaches to alcoholism psychotherapy*. New York: Plenum, 1978.

Dumont, M. P. Self-help treatment programs. *American Journal of Psychiatry*, 1974, **131**, 631-635.

Eckardt, M. J., Parker, E. S., Noble, E. P., Feldman, D. J., & Gottschalk, L. A. Relationship between neuropsychological performance and alcohol consumption in alcoholics. *Biological Psychiatry*, 1978, **13**, 551-565.

Edwards, D., Bucky, S., Coben, P., Fichman, S., & Berry, N. H. Primary and secondary benefits from treatment for alcoholism. *American Journal of Psychiatry*, 1977, **134**, 682-683.

Edwards, G. Hypnosis in treatment of alcohol addiction. *Quarterly Journal of Studies on Alcohol*, 1966, **27**, 221-241.

Edwards, G., & Guthrie, S. A comparison of inpatient and outpatient treatment of alcohol dependence. *Lancet*, 1966, **1**, 467-468.

Edwards, G., & Guthrie, S. A controlled trial of inpatient and outpatient treatment of alcohol dependency. *Lancet*, 1967, **1**, 555-559.

Edwards, G., Orford, J., Egert, S., Guthrie, S., Hawker, A., Hensman, C., Mitcheson, M., Oppenheimer, E., & Taylor, C. Alcoholism: A controlled trial of "treatment" and "advice." *Journal of Studies on Alcohol*, 1977, **38**, 1004-1031.

Edwards, J. D., Jr., & Dill, J. E. Alcoholism clinic in a military setting: A combined disulfiram and group therapy outpatient program. *Military Medicine*, 1974, **139**, 206-209.

Egan, W. P., & Goetz, R. Effect of metronidazole on drinking by alcoholics. *Quarterly Journal of Studies on Alcohol*, 1968, **29**, 899-902.

Eisner, B., & Cohen, S. Psychotherapy with lysergic acid diethylamide. *Journal of Nervous and Mental Disease*, 1958, **127**, 528-539.

Elkins, R. L. A therapeutic phoenix: Emergent normal drinking by "failures" in an abstinence-oriented program of verbal aversion therapy for alcoholism. *Scandinavian Journal of Behavior Therapy,* 1977, **6** (Supplement No. 4), 55. (Abstract)

Elkins, R. L. Personal communication, June, 1979.

Elkins, R. L. A reconsideration of the relevance of recent animal studies for development of treatment procedures for alcoholics. *Drug and Alcohol Dependence,* in press.

Elkins, R. L., & Murdock, R. P. The contribution of successful conditioning to abstinence maintenance following covert sensitization (verbal aversion) treatment of alcoholism. *IRCS Medical Science: Psychology & Psychiatry; Social & Occupational Medicine,* 1977, **5,** 167.

Emrick, C. D. A review of psychologically oriented treatment of alcoholism. I. The use and interrelationships of outcome criteria and drinking behavior following treatment. *Quarterly Journal of Studies on Alcohol,* 1974, **35,** 523-549.

Emrick, C. D. A review of psychologically oriented treatment of alcoholism. II. The relative effectiveness of different treatment approaches and the effectiveness of treatment versus no treatment. *Journal of Studies on Alcohol,* 1975, **36,** 88-108.

Emrick, C. D., Lassen, C. L., & Edwards, M. T. Nonprofessional peers as therapeutic agents. In A. S. Gurman & A. M. Razrin (Eds.), *Effective psychotherapy: A handbook of research.* Elmsford, N.Y.: Pergamon, 1977.

Ends, E. J., & Page, C. W. A study of three types of group psychotherapy with hospitalized inebriates. *Quarterly Journal of Studies on Alcohol,* 1957, **18,** 263-277.

Epstein, N. B., & Guild, J. Further clinical experience with TEDT in the treatment of alcoholism. *Quarterly Journal of Studies on Alcohol,* 1951, **12,** 366-380.

Ewing, J. A. Behavioral approaches for problems with alcohol. *International Journal of the Addictions,* 1974, **9,** 389-399.

Ewing, J. A., & Rouse, B. A. Failure of an experimental treatment program to inculcate controlled drinking in alcoholics. *British Journal of Addiction,* 1976, **71,** 123-134.

Faia, C., & Shean, G. Using videotapes and group discussion in the treatment of male chronic alcoholics. *Hospital and Community Psychiatry,* 1976, **27,** 847-851.

Faillace, L. A., Flamer, R. N., Imber, S. D., & Ward, R. F. Giving alcohol to alcoholics: An evaluation. *Quarterly Journal of Studies on Alcohol,* 1972, **33,** 85-90.

Faillace, L. A., Vourlekis, A., & Szara, S. Hallucinogenic drugs in the treatment of alcoholism: A two-year follow-up. *Comprehensive Psychiatry,* 1970, **11,** 51-56.

Farrar, C. H., Powell, B. J., & Martin, L. K. Punishment of alcohol consumption by apneic paralysis. *Behaviour Research and Therapy,* 1968, **6,** 13-16.

Father Joseph Martin: Too few counselors effective. *U.S. Journal of Drug and Alcohol Dependence.* January 1980, 3 (12), p. 9.

Feinstein, C., & Tamerin, J. S. Induced intoxication and videotape feedback in alcoholism treatment. *Quarterly Journal of Studies on Alcohol,* 1972, **33,** 408-416.

Feldman, D. J., Pattison, E. M., Sobell, L. C., Graham, T., & Sobell, M. B. Outpatient alcohol detoxification: Initial findings on 564 patients. *American Journal of Psychiatry,* 1975, **132,** 407-412.

Feldmann, H. The ambulatory treatment of alcoholic addiction. A study of 250 cases. *British Journal of Addiction,* 1959, **55,** 121-127.

Fenichel, O. *The psychoanalytic theory of neurosis.* New York: Norton, 1945.

Ferguson, F. N. A treatment program for Navaho alcoholics: Results after four years. *Quarterly Journal of Studies on Alcohol*, 1970, **31**, 898-919.

Ferguson, J. K. W. A new drug for alcoholism treatment. *Canadian Medical Association Journal*, 1956, **74**, 793-795.

Fine, E. W. Treatment of alcoholism. *Journal of the American Medical Association*, 1976, **236**, 1235.

Finlay, D. G. Alcoholism: Illness or problem in interaction? *Social Work*, 1974, **19**, 398-405.

Fitzgerald, B. J., Pasewark, R. A., & Clark, R. Four-year follow-up of alcoholics treated at a rural state hospital. *Quarterly Journal of Studies on Alcohol*, 1971, **32**, 636-642.

Ford, J. L. Labeling the alcoholic: Some predisposing factors and treatment consequences. *Dissertation Abstracts International*, 1976, **37**, 1227A. (Abstract)

Fox, R. Normal drinking in recovered alcohol addicts: Comment on the article by D. L. Davies. *Quarterly Journal of Studies on Alcohol*, 1963, **24**, 117.

Fox, R. A multidisciplinary approach to the treatment of alcoholism. *American Journal of Psychiatry*, 1967, **123**, 769-778.

Fox, V. The controlled drinking controversy. *Journal of the American Medical Association*, 1976, **236**, 863.

Fox, V., & Smith, M. A. Evaluation of a chemopsychotherapeutic program for the rehabilitation of alcoholics: Observations over a two-year period. *Quarterly Journal of Studies on Alcohol*, 1959, **20**, 767-780.

Foy, D. W., Miller, P. M., Eisler, R. M., & O'Toole, D. H. Social-skills training to teach alcoholics to refuse drinks effectively. *Journal of Studies on Alcohol*, 1976, **37**, 1340-1345.

Franks, C. M. Alcoholism. In C. G. Costello (Ed.), *Symptoms of psychopathology*. New York: Wiley, 1970.

Frederiksen, L. W., & Miller, P. M. Peer-determined and self-determined reinforcement in group therapy with alcoholics. *Behaviour Research and Therapy*, 1976, **14**, 385-388.

Freedberg, E. J., & Johnston, W. E. *The effects of relaxation training within the context of a multi-modal alcoholism treatment program for employed alcoholics*. Toronto, Ontario: Alcoholism and Addiction Research Foundation, Substudy No. 988, 1978. (a)

Freedberg, E. J., & Johnston, W. E. *The effects of assertion training within the context of a multi-modal alcoholism treatment program for employed alcoholics*. Toronto, Ontario: Alcoholism and Addiction Research Foundation, Substudy No. 976, 1978. (b)

Gabrynowicz, J. Hypnosis in a treatment programme for alcoholism. *Medical Journal of Australia*, 1977, **64**, 653-656.

Gallant, D. M., Bishop, M. P., Camp, E., & Tisdale. C. A six-month controlled evaluation of metronidazole (Flagyl) in chronic alcoholic patients. *Current Therapeutic Research*, 1968, **10**, 82-87. (a)

Gallant, D. M., Bishop, M. P., Faulkner, M. A., Simpson, L., Cooper, A., Lathrop, D., Brisolara, A. M., & Bossetta, J. R. A comparative evaluation of compulsory (group therapy and/or Antabuse) and voluntary treatment of the chronic alcoholic municipal court offender. *Psychosomatics*, 1968, **9**, 306-310. (b)

Gallant, D. M., Bishop, M. P., Mouledoux, A., Faulkner, M. A., Brisolara, A., & Swanson, W. A. The revolving-door alcoholic: An impasse in the treatment of the chronic alcoholic. *Archives of General Psychiatry,* 1973, **28,** 633-635.

Gallant, D. M., Rich, A., Bey, E., & Terranova, L. Group psychotherapy with married couples: A successful technique in New Orleans alcoholism clinic patients. *Journal of the Louisiana State Medical Society,* 1970, **122,** 41-44.

Gaston, E. T., & Eagle, C. T., Jr. The function of music in LSD therapy for alcoholic patients. *Alcoholism* (Zagreb), 1974, **10,** 98-106.

Gay, A., & Lecours, E. Applications de la musicothérapie aux alcooliques. [Applications of music therapy to alcoholics.] *Vie Médicale au Canada Francais,* 1976, **5,** 1051-1052.

Gerard, D. L., & Saenger, G. *Out-patient treatment of alcoholism: A study of outcome and its determinants.* Toronto: University of Toronto Press, 1966.

Gerard, D. L., Saenger, G., & Wile, R. The abstinent alcoholic. *Archives of General Psychiatry,* 1962, **6,** 83-95.

Gerrein, J. R., Rosenberg, C. M., & Manohar, V. Disulfiram maintenance in outpatient treatment of alcoholism. *Archives of General Psychiatry,* 1973, **28,** 798-802.

Gessner, P. K. Drug therapy of the alcohol withdrawal syndrome. In E. Majchrowicz and E. P. Noble (Eds.) *Biochemistry and pharmacology of ethanol.* (Vol. 2) New York: Plenum, 1979.

Gibbs, L., & Flanagan, J. Prognostic indicators of alcoholism treatment outcome. *International Journal of the Addictions,* 1977, **12,** 1097-1141.

Gitlow, S. E. Alcoholism: A disease. In P. G. Bourne & R. Fox (Eds.), *Alcoholism: Progress in research and treatment.* New York: Academic Press, 1973.

Glasgow, R. E., & Rosen, G. M. Behavioral bibliotherapy: A review of self-help behavior therapy manuals. *Psychological Bulletin,* 1978, **85,** 1-23.

Gliedman, L. H., Rosenthal, D., Frank, J. D., & Nash, H. T. Group therapy of alcoholics with concurrent group meetings of their wives. *Quarterly Journal of Studies on Alcohol,* 1956, **17,** 655-670.

Glover, J. H., & McCue, P. A. Electrical aversion therapy with alcoholics: A comparative follow-up study. *British Journal of Psychiatry,* 1977, **130,** 279-286.

Goldman, M. S., Taylor, H. A., Carruth, M. L., & Nathan, P. E. Effects of group decision-making on group drinking by alcoholics. *Quarterly Journal of Studies on Alcohol,* 1973, **34,** 807-822.

Goldstein, A. P. Heller, K., & Sechrest, L. B. *Psychotherapy and the psychology of behavior change.* New York: Wiley, 1966.

Goldstein, A. P., & Stein, N. *Prescriptive psychotherapies.* New York: Pergamon, 1976.

Gomes-Schwartz, B., Hadley, S. W., & Strupp, H. H. Individual psychotherapy and behavior therapy. *Annual Review of Psychology,* 1978, **29,** 435-471.

Goodwin, D. W. The outpatient management of alcoholism. *Laryngoscope,* 1978, **88** (Supplement No. 8), 84-86.

Goodwin, D. W., Crane, J. B., & Guze, S. B. Felons who drink: An 8-year follow-up. *Quarterly Journal of Studies on Alcohol,* 1971, **32,** 136-147.

Goodwin, D. W., & Reinhard, J. Disulfiramlike effects of trichomonacidal drugs: A review and double-blind study. *Quarterly Journal of Studies on Alcohol,* 1972, **33,** 734-740.

Gottheil, E., Alterman, A. I., Skoloda, T. E., & Murphy, B. F. Alcoholics' patterns of controlled drinking. *American Journal of Psychiatry,* 1973, **130,** 418-422.

Gottheil, E., Corbett, L. O., Grasberger, J. C., & Cornelison, F. S. Treating the alcoholic in the presence of alcohol. *American Journal of Psychiatry,* 1971, **128,** 475-480.

Gottheil, E., Corbett, L. O., Grasberger, J. C., & Cornelison, F. S., Jr. Fixed-interval drinking decisions. I. A research and treatment model. *Quarterly Journal of Studies on Alcohol,* 1972, **33,** 311-324. (a)

Gottheil, E., Murphy, B. F., Skoloda, T. E., & Corbett, L. O. Fixed interval drinking decisions. II. Drinking and discomfort in 25 alcoholics. *Quarterly Journal of Studies on Alcohol,* 1972, **33,** 325-340. (b)

Goyer, P. F., & Major, L. F. Hepatotoxicity in disulfiram-treated patients. *Journal of Studies on Alcohol,* 1979, **40,** 133-137.

Greer, R. M., & Callis, R. The use of videotape models in an alcohol rehabilitation program. *Rehabilitation Counseling Bulletin,* 1975, **18,** 154-159.

Griffiths, R. D. P. Videotape feedback as a therapeutic technique: Retrospect and prospect. *Behaviour Research and Therapy,* 1974, **12,** 1-8.

Gunderson, E. K. E., & Schuckit, M. A. Prognostic indicators in young alcoholics. *Military Medicine,* 1978, **143,** 168-170.

Haberman, P. W. Factors related to increased sobriety in group psychotherapy with alcoholics. *Journal of Clinical Psychology,* 1966, **22,** 229-235.

Hall, S. The abstinence phobia. In N. A. Krasnegor (Ed.), *Behavioral analysis and treatment of substance abuse.* Washington, D.C.: National Institute on Drug Abuse, 1979.

Hallam, R., & Rachman, S. Theoretical problems of aversion therapy. *Behaviour Research and Therapy,* 1972, **10,** 341-353.

Hallam, R., Rachman, S., & Falkowski, W. Subjective, attitudinal, and physiological effects of electrical aversion therapy. *Behaviour Research and Therapy,* 1972, **10,** 1-13.

Halvorsen, K. A. L., & Martensen-Larsen, O. Apomorphine revived: Fortified, prolonged, and improved therapeutical effect. *International Journal of the Addictions,* 1978, **13,** 475-484.

Hamburg, S. Behavior therapy in alcoholism: A critical review of broad-spectrum approaches. *Journal of Studies on Alcohol,* 1975, **36,** 69-87.

Hamburg, S. R., Miller, W. R., & Rozynko, V. *Understanding alcoholism and problem drinking.* Half Moon Bay, Calif.: Social Change Associates, 1977.

Hamilton, F., & Maisto, S. A. Assertive behavior and perceived discomfort of alcoholics in assertion-required situations. *Journal of Consulting and Clinical Psychology,* 1979, 47, 196-197.

Hanna, J. M. Metabolic responses of Chinese, Japanese, and Europeans to alcohol. *Alcoholism: Clinical and Experimental Research,* 1978, **2,** 89-92.

Hartman, C. H. A structured treatment program for alcoholics. *Hospital and Community Psychiatry,* 1971, **22,** 179-182.

Hartman, C. H. Group relaxation training for control of impulsive behavior in alcoholics. *Behavior Therapy,* 1973, **4,** 173-174.

Hartocollis, P., & Sheafor, D. Group psychotherapy with alcoholics: A critical review. *Psychiatry Digest,* 1968, 29(6), 15-22.

Hay, W. M., Hay, L. R., & Nelson, R. O. The adaptation of covert modeling procedures to the treatment of chronic alcoholism and obsessive-compulsive behavior: Two case reports. *Behavior Therapy,* 1977, **8,** 70-76.

Hayman, M. Current attitudes to alcoholism of psychiatrists in Southern California. *American Journal of Psychiatry,* 1956, **112,** 485-493.

Hedberg, A. G., & Campbell, L. M. A comparison of four behavioral treatment approaches to alcoholism. *Journal of Behaviour Therapy and Experimental Psychiatry,* 1974, **5,** 251-256.

Hemmingsen, R., Kramp, P., & Rafaelsen, O. J. Delirium tremens and related clinical states. Aetiology, pathophysiology, and treatment. *Acta Psychiatrica Scandinavica,* 1979, **59,** 337-369.

Henning, J. S. A test of the ability to monitor blood-alcohol concentrations among male heavy drinkers. *Dissertation Abstracts International,* 1974, **35,** 3582B. (Abstract)

Henry, S., & Robinson, D. Understanding Alcoholics Anonymous: Results from a survey in England and Wales. *Lancet,* 1978, **1,** 372-375.

Hersen, M., Eisler, R. M., & Miller, P. M. Development of assertive responses: Clinical, measurement, and research considerations. *Behaviour Research and Therapy,* 1973, **11,** 505-521.

Hester, R. K. *Recovery of cognitive skills in alcoholics.* Unpublished doctoral dissertation, Washington State University, 1979.

Hill, M. J., & Blane, H. T. Evaluation of psychotherapy with alcoholics: A critical review. *Quarterly Journal of Studies on Alcohol,* 1967, **28,** 76-104.

Hingson, R., Scotch, N., & Goldman, E. Impact of the "Rand Report" on alcoholics, treatment personnel, and Boston residents. *Journal of Studies on Alcohol,* 1977, **38,** 2065-2076.

Hirsch, S. M., Von Rosenberg, R., Phelan, C., & Dudley, H. K., Jr. Effectiveness of assertiveness training with alcoholics. *Journal of Studies on Alcohol,* 1978, **39,** 89-97.

Hodgson, R. J., & Rankin, H. J. Modification of excessive drinking by cue exposure. *Behaviour Research and Therapy,* 1976, **14,** 305-307.

Hoff, E. C. The use of pharmacological adjuncts in the psychotherapy of alcoholics. *Quarterly Journal of Studies on Alcohol,* 1961, **22,** (Supplement No. 1), 138-150.

Hoff, E. C., & McKeown, C. E. An evaluation of the use of tetraethylthiuram disulfide in the treatment of 560 cases of alcohol addiction. *American Journal of Psychiatry,* 1953, **109,** 670-673.

Hollister, L. E., Shelton, J., & Krieger, G. A controlled comparison of lysergic acid diethylamide (LSD) and dextroamphetamine in alcoholics. *American Journal of Psychiatry,* 1969, **125,** 1352-1357.

Holmes, E. D. A comparison of three aversive conditioning paradigms in the treatment of alcoholism. *Dissertation Abstracts International,* 1972, **32,** 6049B. (Abstract)

Holzinger, R., Mortimer, R., & Van Dusen, W. Aversion conditioning treatment of alcoholism. *American Journal of Psychiatry,* 1967, **124,** 246-247.

Hsu, J. J. Electroconditioning therapy of alcoholics. A preliminary report. *Quarterly Journal of Studies on Alcohol,* 1965, **26,** 449-459.

Huber, H., Karlin, R., & Nathan, P. E. Blood alcohol level discrimination by nonalcoholics: The role of internal and external cues. *Journal of Studies on Alcohol,* 1976, **37,** 27-39.

Hunt, G. M., & Azrin, N. H. A community-reinforcement approach to alcoholism. *Behaviour Research and Therapy*, 1973, **11**, 91-104.

Hussain, M. Z., & Harinath, M. Helping alcoholics abstain: An implantable substance. *American Journal of Psychiatry*, 1972, **129**, 363.

Imber, S., Schultz, E., Funderburk, F., Allen, R., & Flamer, R. The fate of the untreated alcoholic: Toward a natural history of the disorder. *Journal of Nervous and Mental Disease*, 1976, **162**, 238-247.

Intagliata, J. C. Increasing the interpersonal problem-solving skills of an alcoholic population. *Journal of Consulting and Clinical Psychology*, 1978, **46**, 489-498.

Jackson, T. R., & Smith, J. W. A comparison of two aversion treatment methods for alcoholism. *Journal of Studies on Alcohol*, 1978, **39**, 187-191.

Jacobsen, E. Biochemical methods in the treatment of alcoholism, with special reference to Antabuse. *Proceedings of the Royal Society of Medicine*, 1950, **43**, 519-526.

Jacobson, N. O., & Silfverskiöld, N. P. A controlled study of a hypnotic method in the treatment of alcoholism, with evaluation by objective criteria. *British Journal of Addiction*, 1973, **68**, 25-31.

Jensen, S. E., & Ramsay, R. Treatment of chronic alcoholism with lysergic acid diethylamide. *Canadian Psychiatric Association Journal*, 1963, **8**, 182-188.

Jindra, N. J., & Forslund, M. A. Alcoholics Anonymous in a western U. S. city. *Journal of Studies on Alcohol*, 1978, **39**, 110-120.

Johnson, F. G. LSD in the treatment of alcoholism. *American Journal of Psychiatry*, 1969, **126**, 481-487.

Johnson, F. G. A comparison of short-term treatment effects of intravenous sodium amytal-methedrine and LSD in the alcoholic. *Canadian Psychiatric Association Journal*, 1970, **15**, 493-497.

Kalb, M., & Propper, M. S. The future of alcohology: Craft or science? *American Journal of Psychiatry*, 1976, **133**, 641-645.

Kantorovich, N. An attempt at associative-reflex therapy in alcoholism. *Psychological Abstracts*, 1930, **4**, 493. (Abstract)

Kaplan, R., Blume, S., & Rosenberg, S. Phenytoin, metronidazole, and multivitamins in the treatment of alcoholism. *Quarterly Journal of Studies of Alcohol*, 1972, **33**, 97-104.

Katz, N. W. Comparative efficacy of behavioral training, training plus relaxation, and a sleep/trance hypnotic induction in increasing hypnotic susceptibility. *Journal of Consulting and Clinical Psychology*, 1979, **47**, 119-127.

Kelly, G. R. Behaviorism and psychodrama: Worlds not so far apart. *Group Psychotherapy Psychodrama and Sociometry*, 1978, **31**, 154-162.

Kendall, R. E., & Staton, M. C. The fate of untreated alcoholics. *Quarterly Journal of Studies on Alcohol*, 1966, **27**, 30-41.

Kennedy, R. W., Gilbert, G. S., & Thoreson, R. A self-control program for drinking antecedents: The role of self-monitoring and control orientation. *Journal of Clinical Psychology*, 1978, **34**, 238-243.

Kepner, E. Application of learning theory to the etiology and treatment of alcoholism. *Quarterly Journal of Studies on Alcohol*, 1964, **25**, 279-291.

Kilpatrick, D. G., Roitzsch, J. C., Best, C. L., McAlhany, D. A., Sturgis, E. T., & Miller, W. C. Treatment goal preference and problem perception of chronic alcoholics: Behavioral and personality correlates. *Addictive Behaviors*, 1978, **3**, 107-116.

Kirk, S. A., & Masi, J. Aftercare for alcoholics: Services of community mental health centers. *Journal of Studies on Alcohol*, 1978, **39**, 545-547.

Kirkpatrick, J. *Turnabout: Help for a new life*. Quakertown, Pa.: Women for Sobriety, 1978.

Kish, G. B., & Hermann, H. T. The Fort Meade alcoholism treatment program: A follow-up study. *Quarterly Journal of Studies on Alcohol*, 1971, **32**, 628-635.

Kissin, B., & Gross, M. M. Drug therapy in alcoholism. *American Journal of Psychiatry*, 1968, **125**, 31-41.

Kissin, B., Platz, A., & Su, W. H. Social and psychological factors in the treatment of chronic alcoholism. *Journal of Psychiatric Research*, 1970, **8**, 13-27. (a)

Kissin, B., Platz, A., & Su, W. H. Selective factors in treatment choice and outcome in alcoholics. In N. K. Mello & J. H. Mendelson (Eds.), *Recent advances in studies of alcoholism*. Washington, D.C.: U.S. Government Printing Office, 1970. (b)

Kissin, B., Rosenblatt, S., & Machover, S. Prognostic factors in alcoholics. *Psychiatric Research Report*, 1968, **24**, 22-43.

Kitson, T. M. The disulfiram-ethanol reaction: A review. *Journal of Studies on Alcohol*, 1977, **38**, 96-113.

Kitson, T. M. On the probability of implanted disulfiram's causing a reaction to ethanol. *Journal of Studies on Alcohol*, 1978, **39**, 183-186.

Kline, N. S., Wren, J. C., Cooper, T. B., Varga, E., & Canal, O. Evaluation of lithium therapy in chronic and periodic alcoholism. *American Journal of Medical Science*, 1974, **268**, 15-22.

Kline, S. A., & Kingstone, E. Disulfiram implants: The right treatment but the wrong drug? *Canadian Medical Association Journal*, 1977, **116**, 1382-1383.

Knox, W. J. Four-year follow-up of veterans treated on a small alcoholism treatment ward. *Quarterly Journal of Studies on Alcohol*, 1972, **33**, 105-110.

Kraft, T. Alcoholism treated by systematic desensitization: A follow-up of eight cases. *Journal of the Royal College of General Practice*, 1969, **18**, 336-340.

Kraft, T., & Al-Issa, I. Alcoholism treated by desensitization: A case report. *Behaviour Research and Therapy*, 1967, **5**, 69-70.

Kraft, T., & Al-Issa, I. Desensitization and treatment of alcoholic addiction. *British Journal of Addiction*, 1968, **63**, 19-23.

Krasner, N., Moore, M. R., Goldberg, A., Booth, J. C. D., Frame, A. H., & McLaren, A. D. A trial of fenfluramine in the treatment of the chronic alcoholic patient. *British Journal of Psychiatry*, 1976, **128**, 346-353.

Krystal, H., & Moore, R. A. Who is qualified to treat the alcoholic? A discussion. *Quarterly Journal of Studies on Alcohol*, 1963, **24**, 705-720.

Kwentus, J., & Major, L. F. Disulfiram in the treatment of alcoholism. *Journal of Studies on Alcohol*, 1979, **40**, 428-446.

Lader, M. H. Alcohol reactions after single and multiple doses of calcium cyanamide. *Quarterly Journal of Studies on Alcohol*, 1967, **28**, 468-475.

Lain, M. E., & Schoenfeld, L. S. Effects of three conditioning paradigms on visual attention to alcoholic stimuli. *Perceptual and Motor Skills*, 1974, **38**, 409-410.

Lake, C. R., Major, L. F., Ziegler, M. G., & Kopin, I. J. Increased sympathetic nervous system activity in alcoholic patients treated with disulfiram. *American Journal of Psychiatry*, 1977, **134**, 1411-1414.

Lal, S. Metronidazole in the treatment of alcoholism: A clinical trial and review of the literature. *Quarterly Journal of Studies on Alcohol,* 1969, **30,** 140-151.

Lansky, D., Nathan, P. E., Ersner-Hershfield, S. M., & Lipscomb, T. R. Blood alcohol level discrimination: Pre-training monitoring accuracy of alcoholics and nonalcoholics. *Addictive Behaviors,* 1978, **3,** 209-214.

Lansky, D., Nathan, P. E., & Lawson, D. M. Blood alcohol level discrimination by alcoholics: The role of internal and external cues. *Journal of Consulting and Clinical Psychology,* 1978, **46,** 953-960.

Lanyon, R. I., Primo, R. V., Terrell, F. , & Wener, A. An aversion-desensitization treatment for alcoholism. *Journal of Consulting and Clinical Psychology,* 1972, **38,** 394-398.

Lau, M. P. Acupuncture and addiction: An overview. *Addictive Diseases,* 1976, **2,** 449-463.

Laverty, S. G. Aversion therapies in the treatment of alcoholism. *Psychosomatic Medicine,* 1966, **28,** 651-666.

Lawson, G. W. Selected counselor variables and their relationship to counseling process in alcoholism treatment. *Dissertation Abstracts International,* 1976, **36,** 7869A. (Abstract)

Leach, B. Does Alcoholics Anonymous really work? In P. G. Bourne & R. Fox (Eds.), *Alcoholism: Progress in research and treatment.* New York: Academic, 1973.

Leach, B., & Norris, J. L. Factors in the development of Alcoholics Anonymous (A.A.). In B. Kissin & H. Begleiter (Eds.), *The biology of alcoholism.* Vol. 5. *Treatment and rehabilitation of the chronic alcoholic.* New York: Plenum, 1977.

Lemere, F. Psychological factors in the conditioned-reflex treatment of alcoholism. *Quarterly Journal of Studies on Alcohol,* 1947, **8,** 261-265.

Lemere, F. What happens to alcoholics? *American Journal of Psychiatry,* 1953, **109,** 674-676.

Lemere, F., & Voegtlin, W. L. An evaluation of the aversion treatment of alcoholism. *Quarterly Journal of Studies on Alcohol,* 1950, **11,** 199-204.

Lemere, F., Voegtlin, W. L., Broz, W. R., O'Hollaren, P., & Tupper, W. E. The conditioned reflex treatment of chronic alcoholism. VII. A review of six years' experience with this treatment of 1,526 patients. *Journal of the American Medical Association,* 1942, **120,** 269-270.

Levinson, T. Controlled drinking in the alcoholic — A search for common features. In J. S. Madden, R. Walker, & W. H. Kenyon (Eds.), *Alcoholism and drug dependence: A multidisciplinary approach.* New York: Plenum, 1977.

Levinson, T., & Sereny, G. An experimental evaluation of "insight therapy" for the chronic alcoholic. *Canadian Psychiatric Association Journal,* 1969, **14,** 143-146.

Levitt, R. O., & Weedman, R. D. An alcoholism unit in a general hospital: A multidisciplinary and multidimensional approach. *Proceedings of the Institute of Medicine of Chicago,* 1973, **29,** 427-434.

Levy, M. S., Livingstone, B. L., & Collins, D. M. A clinical comparison of disulfiram and calcium carbimide. *American Journal of Psychiatry,* 1967, **123,** 1018-1022.

Lewis, M. J., Bland, R. C., & Baile, W. Disulfiram implantation for alcoholism. *Canadian Psychiatric Association Journal,* 1975, **20,** 283-286.

Liebson, I. A., Cohen, M., Faillace, L. A., & Ward, R. F. The token economy as a research method in alcoholism. *Psychiatric Quarterly,* 1971, **45,** 574-581.

Lied, E. R., & Marlatt, G. A. Modeling as a determinant of alcohol consumption: Effect of subject sex and prior drinking history. *Addictive Behaviors,* 1979, **4,** 47-54.

Lijinski, W. Personal communication, June 29, 1979. (Research to be described in the *American Chemical Society Monograph Symposium Series,* No. 101, in press)

Linton, P. H., & Hain, J. D. Metronidazole in the treatment of alcoholism. *Quarterly Journal of Studies on Alcohol,* 1967, **28,** 544-546.

Loranger, P. D. An analysis of problem drinkers undergoing treatment through educational therapy, group therapy, and family orientation. *Dissertation Abstracts International,* 1973, **33,** 4350B. (Abstract)

Lovibond, S. H. Use of behavior modification in the reduction of alcohol-related road accidents. In T. Thompson & W. S. Dockens 3rd. (Eds.), *Applications of behavior modification.* New York: Academic, 1975.

Lovibond, S. H., & Caddy, G. Discriminated aversive control in the moderation of alcoholics' drinking behavior. *Behavior Therapy,* 1970, **1,** 437-444.

Lowenstam, I. The effect of mesoridazine, a new thioridazine derivative in alcoholics: A preliminary study. *Journal of Clinical Pharmacology,* 1967, **7,** 111-115.

Lowenstam, I. Metronidazole and placebo in the treatment of chronic alcoholism: A comparative study. *Psychosomatics,* 1969, **10,** (Supplement), 43-45.

Lubetkin, B. S., Rivers, P. C., & Rosenberg, C. M. Difficulties of disulfiram therapy with alcoholics. *Quarterly Journal of Studies on Alcohol,* 1971, **32,** 168-171.

Ludwig, A. M., Levine, J., & Stark, L. H. *LSD and alcoholism.* Springfield, Ill.: C. C. Thomas, 1970.

Ludwig, A., Levine, J., Stark, L., & Lazar, R. A clinical study of LSD treatment in alcoholism. *American Journal of Psychiatry,* 1969, **126,** 59-69.

Lundwall, L., & Baekeland, F. Disulfiram treatment of alcoholism. *Journal of Nervous and Mental Disease,* 1971, **153,** 381-394.

Lynn, E. J. Treatment for alcoholism: Psychotherapy is still alive and well. *Hospital and Community Psychiatry,* 1976, **27,** 282-283.

Lysoff, G. O. Anti-addictive chemotherapy: Metronidazole and alcohol aversion. *British Journal of Addiction,* 1972, **67,** 239-244.

MacCulloch, M. J., Feldman, M. P., Orford, J. F., & MacCulloch, M. L. Anticipatory avoidance learning in the treatment of alcoholism: A record of therapeutic failure. *Behaviour Research and Therapy,* 1966, **4,** 187-196.

MacDonough, T.S. The relative effectiveness of a medical hospitalization program vs. a feedback-behavior modification program in treating alcohol and drug abusers. *International Journal of the Addictions,* 1976, **11,** 269-282.

MacLean, J. R., MacDonald, D. C., Byrne, U. P., & Hubbard, A. M. The use of LSD-25 in the treatment of alcoholism and other psychiatric problems. *Quarterly Journal of Studies on Alcohol,* 1961, **22,** 34-45.

Madden, J. S., & Kenyon, W. H. Group counselling of alcoholics by a voluntary agency. *British Journal of Psychiatry,* 1975, **126,** 289-291.

Madill, M., Campbell, D., Laverty, S. G., Sanderson, R. E., & Vanderwater, S. L. Aversion treatment of alcoholism by succinylcholine-induced apneic paralysis. *Quarterly Journal of Studies on Alcohol,* 1966, **27,** 483-509.

Madsen, W. *The American alcoholic: The nature-nurture controversy in alcoholic research and therapy.* Springfield, Ill.: C. C. Thomas, 1974.

Maisto, S. A., & Adesso, V. J. The effect of instructions and feedback on BAL discrimination training in nonalcoholic social drinkers. *Journal of Consulting and Clinical Psychology,* 1977, **45**, 625-636.

Malcolm, M. T., Madden, J. S., & Williams, A. E. Disulfiram implantation critically evaluated. *British Journal of Psychiatry,* 1974, **125**, 485-489.

Maletzky, B. M. Assisted covert sensitization for drug abuse. *International Journal of the Addictions,* 1974, **9**, 411-429.

Manohar, V. Training volunteers as alcoholism treatment counselors. *Quarterly Journal of Studies on Alcohol,* 1973, **34**, 869-877.

Manos, S. S. The Manhattan Bowery Project. *Alcohol Health and Research World,* 1975, (Winter), 11-15.

Marconi, J., Solari, G., Gaete, S., & Piazza, L. Comparative clinical study of the effects of disulfiram and calcium carbimide. I. Side effects. *Quarterly Journal of Studies on Alcohol,* 1960, **21**, 642-654.

Marconi, J., Solari, G., & Gaete, S. Comparative clinical study of the effects of disulfiram and calcium carbimide. II. Reaction to alcohol. *Quarterly Journal of Studies on Alcohol,* 1961, **22**, 46-51.

Marlatt, G. A. A comparison of aversive conditioning procedures in the treatment of alcoholism. Paper presented at the annual meeting of the Western Psychological Association, Anaheim, California, April 1973.

Martensen-Larsen, O. Five years' experience with disulfiram in the treatment of alcoholics. *Quarterly Journal of Studies on Alcohol,* 1953, **14**, 406-418.

Matthews, D. B., & Miller, W. R. Estimating blood alcohol concentration: Two computer programs and their applications in therapy and research. *Addictive Behaviors,* 1979, **4**, 55-60.

Maxwell, R. *The booze battle.* New York: Ballantine, 1976.

Maxwell, W. A., Baird, R. L., Wezl, T., & Ferguson, L. Discriminated aversion conditioning within an alcoholic treatment program in the training of controlled drinking. *Behavioral Engineering,* 1974, **2**, 17-19.

Mayer, J., & Myerson, D. J. Outpatient treatment of alcoholics: Effects of status, stability, and nature of treatment. *Quarterly Journal of Studies on Alcohol,* 1971, **32**, 620-627.

Mazza, N. Poetry: A therapeutic tool in the early stages of alcoholism treatment. *Journal of Studies on Alcohol,* 1979, **40**, 123-128.

McCance, C., & McCance, P. F. Alcoholism in northeast Scotland: Its treatment and outcome. *British Journal of Psychiatry,* 1969, **115**, 189-198.

McClelland, D. C. Drinking as a response to power needs in man. *Psychopharmacology Bulletin,* 1974, **10**(4), 5-6.

McCrady, B. S., Paolino, T. J., Jr., Longabough, R., & Rossi, J. Effects of joint hospital admission and couples treatment for hospitalized alcoholics: A pilot study. *Addictive Behaviors,* 1979, **4**, 155-165.

McFarlain, R. A., Mielke, D. H., & Gallant, D. M. Comparison of muscle relaxation with placebo medication for anxiety reduction in alcoholic inpatients. *Current Therapeutic Research,* 1976, **20**, 173-176.

McGuire, R. J., & Vallance, M. Aversion therapy by electric shock, a simple technique. *British Medical Journal,* 1964, **1**, 151-153.

McKenzie, R. E., Costello, R. M., & Buck, D. C. Electrosleep (electrical transcranial stimulation) in the treatment of anxiety, depression, and sleep disturbance in chronic alcoholics. *Journal of Altered States of Consciousness*, 1975, **2**, 185-196.

Meichenbaum, D. *Cognitive-behavior modification: An integrative approach*. New York: Plenum, 1977.

Mendelson, J. H., LaDou, J., & Solomon, P. Experimentally induced chronic intoxication and withdrawal in alcoholics. III. Psychiatric findings. *Quarterly Journal of Studies on Alcohol*, 1964, **25**, (Supplement No. 2), 40-52.

Merry, J., Reynolds, C. M., Bailey, J., & Coppen, A. Prophylactic treatment of alcoholism by lithium carbonate: A controlled study. *Lancet*, 1976, **2**, 481-482.

Merry, J., & Whitehead, A. Metronidazole and alcoholism. *British Journal of Psychiatry*, 1968, **114**, 859-861.

Mertens, G. C. *A behavioral approach to self-control*. St. Cloud, Minn.: Wilmar State Hospital, 1972.

Meyer, J. E. Psychochirurgische Behandlung der Sucht? [Psychosurgical treatment of addiction?] *Nervenarzt*, 1974, **45**, 223-224.

Meyers, A., Mercatoris, M., & Artz, L. On the development of a cognitive self-monitoring skill. *Behavior Therapy*, 1976, **7**, 128-129.

Michaelsson, G. Short-term effects of behavior therapy and hospital treatment of chronic alcoholics. *Behaviour Research and Therapy*, 1976, **14**, 69-72.

Miller, E. C., Dvorak, A., & Turner, D. W. A method of creating aversion to alcohol by reflex conditioning in a group setting. *Quarterly Journal of Studies on Alcohol*, 1960, **21**, 424-431.

Miller, M. M. Treatment of chronic alcoholism by hypnotic aversion. *Journal of the American Medical Association*, 1959, **171**, 1492-1495.

Miller, M. M. Hypnoaversion treatment in alcoholism, nicotinism, and weight control. *Journal of the National Medical Association*, 1976, **68**, 129-130.

Miller, P. M. The use of behavioral contracting in the treatment of alcoholism: A case study. *Behavior Therapy*, 1972, **3**, 593-596.

Miller, P. M. A behavioral intervention program for chronic public drunkenness offenders. *Archives of General Psychiatry*, 1975, **32**, 915-918.

Miller, P. M. Behavior modification and Alcoholics Anonymous: An unlikely combination. *Behavior Therapy*, 1978, **9**, 300-301.

Miller, P. M., & Eisler, R. M. Assertive behavior of alcoholics: A descriptive analysis. *Behavior Therapy*, 1977, **8**, 146-149.

Miller, P. M., & Hersen, M. Quantitative changes in alcohol consumption as a function of electrical aversive conditioning. *Journal of Clinical Psychology*, 1972, **28**, 590-593.

Miller, P. M., Hersen, M., Eisler, R. M., & Hemphill, D. P. Electrical aversion therapy with alcoholics: An analogue study. *Behaviour Research and Therapy*, 1973, **11**, 491-497.

Miller, P. M., Hersen, M., Eisler, R. M., & Watts, J. G. Contingent reinforcement of lowered blood/alcohol levels in an outpatient chronic alcoholic. *Behaviour Research and Therapy*, 1974, **12**, 261-263.

Miller, P. M. & Mastria, M. A. *Alternatives to alcohol abuse*. Champaign, Ill.: Research Press, 1977.

Miller, P. M., Stanford, A. G., & Hemphill, D. P. A social-learning approach to alcoholism treatment. *Social Casework*, 1974, **55**, 279-284.

Miller, W. R. Alcoholism scales and objective assessment methods: A review. *Psychological Bulletin*, 1976, **83**, 649-674.

Miller, W. R. Behavioral self-control training in the treatment of problem drinkers. In R. B. Stuart (Ed.), *Behavioral self-management: Strategies, techniques and outcomes.* New York: Brunner/Mazel, 1977.

Miller, W. R. Behavioral treatment of problem drinkers: A comparative outcome study of three controlled drinking therapies. *Journal of Consulting and Clinical Psychology*, 1978, **46**, 74-86. (a)

Miller, W. R. *Effectiveness of nonprescription therapies for problem drinkers.* Paper presented at the annual meeting of the American Psychological Association, Toronto, Ontario, August, 1978. (b)

Miller, W. R. Maintenance of behavior change: A note on experimental design. *Professional Psychology*, in press.

Miller, W. R., & Caddy, G. R. Abstinence and controlled drinking in the treatment of problem drinkers. *Journal of Studies on Alcohol*, 1977, **38**, 986-1003.

Miller, W. R., Gribskov, C. J., & Mortell, R. L. Effectiveness of a self-control manual for problem drinkers with and without therapist contact. *International Journal of the Addictions*, in press.

Miller, W. R., Hedrick, K., & Taylor, C. A. *Relationship between alcohol consumption and related life problems before and after behavioral treatment of problem drinkers.* Paper presented at the annual convention of the Association for Advancement of Behavior Therapy, San Francisco, December, 1979.

Miller, W. R., & Joyce, M. A. Prediction of abstinence, controlled drinking, and heavy drinking outcomes following behavioral self-control training. *Journal of Consulting and Clinical Psychology*, 1979, **47**, 773-775.

Miller, W. R., & Munõz, R. F. *How to control your drinking.* Englewood Cliffs, N.J.: Prentice-Hall, 1976.

Miller, W. R., & Orr, J. Nature and sequence of neuropsychological deficits in alcoholics, *Journal of Studies on Alcohol*, in press.

Miller, W. R., Pechacek, T. F., & Hamburg, S. Group behavior therapy for problem drinkers. *International Journal of the Addictions*, in press.

Miller, W. R., & Taylor, C. A. Relative effectiveness of bibliotherapy, individual and group self-control training in the treatment of problem drinkers. *Addictive Behaviors*, 1980, **5**, 13-24.

Miller, W. R., Taylor, C. A. & West, J. B. Focused versus broad-spectrum behavior therapy for problem drinkers. *Journal of Consulting and Clinical Psychology*, in press.

Mills, K. C., Sobell, M. B., & Schaefer, H. H. Training social drinking as an alternative to abstinence for alcoholics. *Behavior Therapy*, 1971, **2**, 18-27.

Mooney, H. B., Ditman, K. S., & Cohen, S. Chlordiazepoxide in the treatment of alcoholics. *Diseases of the Nervous System*, 1961, **22** (Supplement), 44-51.

Moore, R. A. Who is qualified to treat the alcoholic? *Quarterly Journal of Studies on Alcohol*, 1963, **24**, 712-718.

Moore, R. A., & Buchanan, T. K. State hospitals and alcoholism: A nation-wide survey of treatment techniques and results. *Quarterly Journal of Studies on Alcohol*, 1966, **27**, 459-468.

Moore, R. A., & Ramseur, F. Effects of psychotherapy in an open-ward hospital on patients with alcoholism. *Quarterly Journal of Studies on Alcohol*, 1960, **21**, 233-252.

Moos, R., & Bliss, F. Difficulty of follow-up and outcome of alcoholism treatment. *Journal of Studies on Alcohol*, 1978, **39**, 473-490.

Moos, R. H., Mehren, B., & Moos, B. S. Evaluation of a Salvation Army alcoholism treatment program. *Journal of Studies on Alcohol*, 1978, **39**, 1267-1275.

Morosko, T. E., & Baer, P. E. Avoidance conditioning of alcoholics. In R. Ulrich, T. Stachnik, & J. Mabry (Eds.), *Control of human behavior*. Vol. 2. Glenview, Ill.: Scott, Foresman, 1970.

Mosher, V., Davis, J., Mulligan, D., & Iber, F. L. Comparison of outcome in a 9-day and 30-day alcoholism treatment program. *Journal of Studies on Alcohol*, 1975, **36**, 1277-1281.

Mottin, J. L. Drug-induced attenuation of alcohol consumption: A review and evaluation of claimed, potential or current therapies. *Quarterly Journal of Studies on Alcohol*, 1973, **34**, 444-472.

Mukasa, H., & Arikawa, K. A new double medication method for the treatment of alcoholism using the drug cyanamide. *The Kurume Medical Journal*, 1968, **15**, 137-143.

Mukasa, H., Ichihara, T., & Eto, A. A new treatment of alcoholism with cyanamide (H_2NCN). *The Kurume Medical Journal*, 1964, **11**, 96-101.

Mullan, H., & Sangiuliano, I. *Alcoholism: Group psychotherapy and rehabilitation*. Springfield, Ill.: C. C. Thomas, 1966.

Müller, D., Roeder, F., & Orthner, H. Further results of stereotaxis in the human hypothalamus in sexual deviations: First use of this operation in addiction to drugs. *Neurochirurgia*, 1973, **16**, 113-126.

Nagy, B. Rand Report — Its significance for physicians. *New York State Journal of Medicine*, 1977, **77**, 1495-1496.

Narrol, H. G. Experimental application of reinforcement principles to the analysis and treatment of hospitalized alcoholics. *Quarterly Journal of Studies on Alcohol*, 1967, **28**, 105-115.

Nathan, P. E. Reflections on behavioral efforts to treat chronic alcoholics. *The Psychotherapy Bulletin*, 1976, **9**(3), 21-24.

Nathan, P. E., & O'Brien, J. S. An experimental analysis of the behavior of alcoholics and nonalcoholics during prolonged experimental drinking. *Behavior Therapy*, 1971, **2**, 455-476.

Nathan, P. E., Titler, N. A., Lowenstein, L. M., Solomon, P., & Rossi, A. M. Behavioral analysis of chronic alcoholism. *Archives of General Psychiatry*, 1970, **22**, 419-430.

National Council on Alcoholism, Criteria Committee. Criteria for the diagnosis of alcoholism. *American Journal of Psychiatry*, 1972, **129**, 127-135.

Neubuerger, O. W., Matarazzo, J. D., Schmidt, R. E., & Pratt, H. One year follow-up of total abstinence in chronic alcoholic patients following emetine conditioning. *Journal of Studies on Alcohol*, in press.

Norris, J. L. Prevention of chronicity in alcoholism. *Psychiatric Annals*, 1978, **8**, 48-53.

Nørvig, J., & Nielsen, B. Follow-up study of 221 alcohol addicts in Denmark. *Quarterly Journal of Studies on Alcohol*, 1956, **17**, 633-642.

Obholzer, A. M. A follow-up study of nineteen alcoholic patients treated by means of tetraethyl-thiuram disulfide (Antabuse) implants. *British Journal of Addiction,* 1974, **69,** 19-23.

Obtiz, F. W. Alcoholics' perceptions of selected counseling techniques. *British Journal of Addiction,* 1975, **70,** 187-191.

Obitz, F. W. Control orientation and disulfiram. *Journal of Studies on Alcohol,* 1978, **39,** 1297-1298.

Ogborne, A. C. Recidivism among clients of alcoholism halfway houses. *Drug and Alcohol Dependence,* 1978, **3,** 216-217.

Ogborne, A. C., & Collier, D. F. The drinking habits of residents of a rehabilitation program with a controlled drinking option: A preliminary report. *Drug and Alcohol Dependence,* 1976, **1,** 367-372.

Ogborne, A. C., & Smart, R. G. Halfway houses for Skid Row alcoholics: Are they rehabilitative? *Addictive Behaviors,* 1976, **1,** 305-309.

Ogborne, A. C., & Wilmot, R. Evaluation of an experimental counseling service for male Skid Row alcoholics. *Journal of Studies on Alcohol,* 1979, **40,** 129-132.

O'Leary, M. R., Donovan, D. M., Chaney, E. F., & Walker, R. D. Cognitive impairment and treatment outcome with alcoholics: Preliminary findings. *Journal of Clinical Psychiatry,* in press.

O'Reilly, P. O., & Funk, A. LSD in chronic alcoholism. *Canadian Psychiatric Association Journal,* 1964, **9,** 258-261.

Orford, J. A comparison of alcoholics whose drinking is totally uncontrolled and those whose drinking is mainly controlled. *Behaviour Research and Therapy,* 1973, **11,** 565-576.

Orford, J., Oppenheimer, E., & Edwards, G. Abstinence or control: The outcome for excessive drinkers two years after consultation. *Behaviour Research and Therapy,* 1976, **14,** 409-418.

Ozarin, L. D., & Witkin, W. J. Halfway houses for the mentally ill and alcoholics: A 1973 survey. *Hospital and Community Psychiatry,* 1975, **26,** 101-103.

Pahnke, W. N., Kurland, A. A., Unger, S., Savage, C., & Grof, S. The experimental use of psychedelic (LSD) psychotherapy. *Journal of the American Medical Association,* 1970, **212,** 1856-1863.

Palez, A. Hypnotherapy in the treatment of alcoholism. *Bulletin of the Menninger Clinic,* 1952, **16,** 14-19.

Paolino, T. J., McCrady, B. S., & Kogan, K. B. Alcoholic marriages: A longitudinal empirical assessment of alternative theories. *British Journal of Addiction,* 1978, **73,** 129-138.

Papas, A. N. An Air Force alcoholic rehabilitation program. *Military Medicine,* 1971, **136,** 277-281.

Paredes, A., & Cornelison, F. S., Jr. Development of an audiovisual technique for the rehabilitation of alcoholics. *Quarterly Journal of Studies on Alcohol,* 1968, **29,** 84-92.

Paredes, A., Gregory, D., & Jones, B. M. Induced drinking and social adjustment in alcoholics: Development of a therapeutic model. *Quarterly Journal of Studies on Alcohol,* 1974, **35,** 1279-1293.

Paredes, A., Ludwig, K. D., Hassenfeld, I. N., & Cornelison, F. S., Jr. A clinical study of alcoholics using audiovisual self-image feedback. *Journal of Nervous and Mental Disease,* 1969, **148,** 449-456.

Parker, J. C., Gilbert, G. S., & Thoresen, R. W. Anxiety management in alcoholics: A study of generalized effects of relaxation techniques. *Addictive Behaviors*, 1978, **3**, 123-127. (a)

Parker, J. C., Gilbert, G. S., & Thoreson, R. W. Reduction of autonomic arousal in alcoholics: A comparison of relaxation and meditation techniques. *Journal of Consulting and Clinical Psychology*, 1978, **46**, 879-886. (b)

Parloff, M. B., & Dies, R. R. Group psychotherapy outcome research, 1966-1975. *International Journal of Group Psychotherapy*, 1977, **27**, 281-319.

Passini, F. T., Watson, C. G., Dehnel, L., Herder, J., & Watkins, B. Alpha wave biofeedback training therapy in alcoholics. *Journal of Clinical Psychology*, 1977, **33**, 292-299.

Pattison, E. M. Ten years of change in alcoholism treatment and delivery. *American Journal of Psychiatry*, 1977, **134**, 261-266.

Pattison, E. M., Brissenden, A., & Wohl, T. Assessing specific effects of inpatient group psychotherapy. *International Journal of Group Psychotherapy*, 1967, **17**, 283-297.

Pattison, E. M., Coe, R., & Rhodes, R. J. Evaluation of alcoholism treatment: A comparison of three facilities. *Archives of General Psychiatry*, 1969, **20**, 478-488.

Pattison, E. M., Headley, E. D., Gleser, G. C., & Gottschalk, L. A. Abstinence and normal drinking: An assessment of changes in drinking patterns in alcoholics after treatment. *Quarterly Journal of Studies on Alcohol*, 1968, **29**, 610-633.

Pattison, E. M., Sobell, M. B., & Sobell, L. C. *Emerging concepts of alcohol dependence*. New York: Springer, 1977.

Peele, R. Craft versus profession in alcoholism treatment. *American Journal of Psychiatry*, 1976, **133**, 1345.

Penick, S. B., Carrier, R. N., & Sheldon, J. B. Metronidazole in the treatment of alcoholism. *American Journal of Psychiatry*, 1969, **125**, 1063-1066.

Penick, S. B., Sheldon, J. B., Templer, D. I., & Carrier, R. N. Four year follow-up of metronidazole treatment program for alcoholism. *Industrial Medicine*, 1971, **40**, 30-32.

Penk, W. E., Charles, H. L., & Van-Hoose, T. A. Comparative effectiveness of day hospital and inpatient psychiatric treatment. *Journal of Consulting and Clinical Psychology*. 1978, **46**, 94-101.

Pettersson, H., & Kiessling, K. H. Acetaldehyde occurrence in cerebrospinal fluid during ethanol oxidation in rats and its dependence on the blood level and on dietary factors. *Biochemical Pharmacology*, 1977, **26**, 237-240.

Pfeffer, A. Z., & Berger, S. A follow-up study of treated alcoholics. *Quarterly Journal of Studies on Alcohol*, 1957, **18**, 624-648.

Pickens, R., Bigelow, G., & Griffiths, R. An experimental approach to treating chronic alcoholism: A case study and one-year follow-up. *Behaviour Research and Therapy*, 1973, **11**, 321-325.

Piorkowski, G. K., & Mann, E. T. Issues in treatment efficacy research with alcoholics. *Perceptual and Motor Skills*, 1975, **41**, 695-700.

Pittman, D. J., & Tate, R. L. A comparison of two treatment programs for alcoholics. *International Journal of Social Psychiatry*, 1972, **18**, 183-193.

Platz, A., Panepinto, W. C., Kissin, B., & Charnoff, S. M. Metronidazole and alcoholism: An evaluation of specific and non specific factors in drug treatment. *Diseases of the Nervous System*, 1970, **31**, 631-636.

Pomerleau, O., Pertschuk, M., Adkins, D., & d'Aquili, E. Treatment for middle income problem drinkers. In P. E. Nathan, G. A. Marlatt, & T. Løberg (Eds.), *Alcoholism: New directions in behavioral research and treatment.* New York: Plenum, 1978.

Pomerleau, O., Pertschuk, M., & Stinnett, J. A critical examination of some current assumptions in the treatment of alcoholism. *Journal of Studies on Alcohol*, 1976, **37,** 849-867.

Popham, R. E., & Schmidt, W. Some factors affecting the likelihood of moderate drinking by treated alcoholics. *Journal of Studies on Alcohol*, 1976, **37,** 868-882.

Pursch, J. A. From quonset hut to naval hospital: The story of an alcoholism rehabilitation service. *Journal of Studies on Alcohol*, 1976, **37,** 1655-1665.

Quinn, J. T., & Henbest, R. Partial failure of generalization in alcoholics following aversion therapy. *Quarterly Journal of Studies on Alcohol*, 1967, **28,** 70-75.

Rachman, S. Aversion therapy: Chemical or electrical. *Behaviour Research and Therapy*, 1965, **2,** 289-299.

Rachman, S., & Teasdale, J. *Aversion therapy and behavior disorders: An analysis.* Coral Gables, Fla.: University of Miami Press, 1969.

Rada, R. T., & Kellner, R. Drug treatment in alcoholism. In J. Davis & D. J. Greenblatt (Eds.), *Recent developments in psychopharmacology.* New York: Grune & Stratton, 1979.

Raymond, M. J. The treatment of addiction by aversion conditioning with apomorphine. *Behaviour Research and Therapy*, 1964, **1,** 287-291.

Razran, G. H. S. Conditioned withdrawal responses with shock as the conditioning stimulus in adult human subjects. *Psychological Bulletin*, 1934, **31,** 111-143.

Regester, D. C. Changes in autonomic responsivity and drinking behavior of alcoholics as a function of aversion therapy. *Dissertation Abstracts International*, 1971, **32,** 1225B. (Abstract)

Reid, J. B. Study of drinking in natural settings. In G. A. Marlatt & P. E. Nathan (Eds.), *Behavioral approaches to alcoholism.* New Brunswick, N.J.: Rutgers Center of Alcohol Studies, 1978.

Reilly, T. M. Peripheral neuropathy associated with citrated calcium carbimide. *Lancet*, 1976, **1,** 911-912.

Reinert, R. E., & Bowen, W. T. Social drinking following treatment for alcoholism. *Bulletin of the Menninger Clinic*, 1968, **32,** 280-290.

Revusky, S., Taukulis, H. K., Parker, L. A., & Coombes, S. Chemical aversion therapy: Rat data suggest it may be countertherapeutic to pair an addictive drug state with sickness. *Behaviour Research and Therapy*, 1979, **17,** 177-188.

Ritson, B. The prognosis of alcohol addicts treated by a specialized unit. *British Journal of Psychiatry*, 1968, **114,** 1019-1029.

Ritson, B. Involvement in treatment and its relation to outcome amongst alcoholics. *British Journal of Addiction*, 1969, **64,** 23-29.

Robbins, J., & Fisher, D. Stopping excessive drinking. In J. Robbins & D. Fisher, *How to make and break habits.* New York: Wyden, 1973.

Robson, R. A. H., Paulus, I., & Clarke, G. G. An evaluation of the effect of a clinic treatment program on the rehabilitation of alcoholic patients. *Quarterly Journal of Studies on Alcohol*, 1965, **26,** 264-278.

Rohan, W. P. A follow-up study of hospitalized problem drinkers. *Diseases of the Nervous System*, 1970, **31,** 259-265.

Rohan, W. P. Follow-up study of problem drinkers. *Diseases of the Nervous System*, 1972, **33**, 196-199.

Rosen, G. M. The development and use of nonprescription behavior therapies. *American Psychologist*, 1976, **31**, 139-141.

Rosenberg, C. M. Drug maintenance in the outpatient treatment of chronic alcoholism. *Archives of General Psychiatry*, 1974, **30**, 373-377.

Rosenberg, C. M., Gerrein, J. R., Manohar, V., & Liftik, J. Evaluation of training of alcoholism counselors. *Journal of Studies on Alcohol*, 1976, **37**, 1236-1246.

Rosenfeld, G. Potentiation of the narcotic action and acute toxicity of alcohol by primary aromatic monoamines. *Quarterly Journal of Studies on Alcohol*, 1960, **21**, 584-596.

Rosenthal, S. D. Alterations in serum thyroxine with cerebral electrotherapy (electro-sleep). *Archives of General Psychiatry*, 1973, **28**, 28-29.

Rossi, J. J. A holistic treatment program for alcoholism rehabilitation. *Medical Ecology and Clinical Research*, 1970, **3**, 6-16.

Rossi, J. J., Stach, A., & Bradley, N. J. Effects of treatment of male alcoholics in a mental hospital: A follow-up study. *Quarterly Journal of Studies on Alcohol*, 1963, **24**, 91-108.

Rowan, D. C. The role of blood alcohol level estimation in training alcoholics to become controlled drinkers. *British Journal of Addiction*, 1978, **73**, 316-318.

Rubington, E. The halfway house for the alcoholic. *Mental Hygiene*, 1967, **51**, 552-560.

Rubington, E. The future of the halfway house. *Quarterly Journal of Studies on Alcohol*, 1970, **31**, 167-174.

Rubington, E. The role of the halfway house in the rehabilitation of alcoholics. In B. Kissin & H. Begleiter (Eds.), *The biology of alcoholism*. Vol. 5. *Treatment and rehabilitation of the chronic alcoholic*. New York: Plenum, 1977.

Rubington, E. Halfway houses and treatment outcomes: A relationship between institutional atmosphere and therapeutic effectiveness. *Journal of Studies on Alcohol*, 1979, **40**, 419-427.

Sagan, C. *Broca's brain*. New York: Random House, 1979.

Sanchez-Craig, M. A self-control strategy for drinking tendencies. *The Ontario Psychologist*, 1975, **7**(4), 25-29.

Sanchez-Craig, M. Cognitive and behavioral coping strategies in the reappraisal of stressful social situations. *Journal of Counseling Psychology*, 1976, **23**, 7-12.

Sanchez-Craig, M. Random assignment to abstinence or controlled drinking in a cognitive-behavioral program: short-term effects on drinking behavior. *Addictive Behaviors*, 1980, **5**, 35-39.

Sanchez-Craig, M., & Walker, K. *Teaching alcoholics how to think defensively: A cognitive approach for the treatment of alcohol abuse*. Paper presented at the North American Congress on Alcohol and Drug Problems, San Francisco, 1974.

Sanderson, R. E., Campbell, D., & Laverty, S. G. An investigation of a new aversive conditioning treatment for alcoholism. *Quarterly Journal of Studies on Alcohol*, 1963, **24**, 261-275.

Sands, P. M., & Hanson, P. G. Psychotherapeutic groups for alcoholics and relatives in an outpatient setting. *International Journal of Group Psychotherapy*, 1971, **21**, 23-33.

Schaefer, H. H. Twelve-month follow-up of behaviorally trained ex-alcoholic social drinkers. *Behavior Therapy,* 1972, **3**, 286-289.

Schaefer, H. H., Sobell, M. B., & Miller, K. C. Some sobering data on the use of self-confrontation with alcoholics. *Behavior Therapy,* 1971, **2**, 28-39.

Schaefer, H. H., Sobell, M. B., & Sobell, L. C. Twelve month follow-up of hospitalized alcoholics given self-confrontation experiences by videotape. *Behavior Therapy,* 1972, **3**, 283-285.

Scherer, S. E., & Freedberg, E. J. Effects of group videotape feedback on development of assertiveness skills in alcoholics: A follow-up study. *Psychological Reports,* 1976, **39**, 983-992.

Schlatter, E. K. E., & Lal, S. Treatment of alcoholism with Dent's oral apomorphine method. *Quarterly Journal of Studies on Alcohol,* 1972, **33**, 430-436.

Schual, F., Salter, H., & Paley, M. G. ''Thematic'' group therapy in the treatment of hospitalized alcoholic patients. *International Journal of Group Psychotherapy,* 1971, **21**, 226-233.

Scott, E. M. Group therapy for schizophrenic alcoholics in a state-operated outpatient clinic: With hypnosis as an integrated adjunct. *International Journal of Clinical and Experimental Hypnosis,* 1966, **14**, 232-242.

Scott, E. M. The alcoholic group: Formation and beginnings. *Group Process,* 1976, **7**, 95-116.

Selzer, M. L. The personality of the alcoholic as an impediment to psychotherapy. *Psychiatric Quarterly,* 1967, **41**, 38-45.

Selzer, M. L., & Holloway, W. H. Follow-up of alcoholics committed to state hospital. *Quarterly Journal of Studies on Alcohol,* 1957, **18**, 98-120.

Semer, J. M., Friedland, P., Vaisberg, M., & Greenberg, A. The use of metronidazole in the treatment of alcoholism: A pilot study. *American Journal of Psychiatry,* 1966, **123**, 722-724.

Shaffer, J. W., Freinek, W. R., Wolf, S., Foxwell, N. H., & Kurland, A. A. A controlled evaluation of chlordiazepoxide (Librium) in the treatment of alcoholics. *Journal of Nervous and Mental Disease,* 1963, **137**, 494-507.

Shaffer, J. W., Freinek, W. R., Wolf, S., Foxwell, N. H., & Kurland, A. A. Replication of a study of nialamide in the treatment of convalescing alcoholics with emphasis on prediction of response. *Current Therapeutic Research,* 1964, **6**, 521-531.

Shaw, I. A. The treatment of alcoholism with tetraethylthiuram disulfide in a state mental hospital. *Quarterly Journal of Studies on Alcohol,* 1951, **12**, 576-586.

Shaw, J. A., Donley, P., Morgan, D. W., & Robinson, J. A. Treatment of depression in alcoholics. *American Journal of Psychiatry,* 1975, **132**, 641-644.

Shea, J. E. Psychoanalytic therapy and alcoholism. *Quarterly Journal of Studies on Alcohol,* 1954, **15**, 595-605.

Silber, A. An addendum to the technique of psychotherapy with alcoholics. *Journal of Nervous and Mental Disease,* 1970, **150**, 423-437.

Silverstein, S. J., Nathan, P. E., & Taylor, H. A. Blood alcohol level estimation and controlled drinking by chronic alcoholics. *Behavior Therapy,* 1974, **5**, 1-15.

Simpson, W. S., & Webber, P. W. A field program in the treatment of alcoholism. *Hospital and Community Psychiatry,* 1971, **22**, 170-173.

Skoloda, T. E., Alterman, A. I., Cornelison, F. S., Jr., & Gottheil, E. Treatment outcome in a drinking-decisions program. *Journal of Studies on Alcohol*, 1975, **36**, 365-380.

Smart, R. G. Spontaneous recovery in alcoholics: A review and analysis of the available research. *Drug and Alcohol Dependence*, 1976, **1**, 277-285.

Smart, R. G. Characteristics of alcoholics who drink socially after treatment. *Alcoholism: Clinical and Experimental Research*, 1978, **2**, 49-52. (a)

Smart, R. G. Do some alcoholics do better in some types of treatment than others? *Drug and Alcohol Dependence*, 1978, **3**, 65-75. (b)

Smart, R. G. A comparison of recidivism rates for alcoholic detox residents referred to treatment facilities. *Drug and Alcohol Dependence*, 1978, **3**, 218-220. (c)

Smart, R. G., & Gray, G. Minimal, moderate and long-term treatment for alcoholism. *British Journal of Addiction*, 1978, **73**, 35-38.

Smart, R. G., & Storm, T. The efficacy of LSD in the treatment of alcoholism. *Quarterly Journal of Studies on Alcohol*, 1964, **25**, 333-338.

Smart, R. G., Storm, T., Baker, E. F. W., & Solursh, L. A controlled study of lysergide in the treatment of alcoholism. I. The effects on drinking behavior. *Quarterly Journal of Studies on Alcohol*, 1966, **27**, 469-482.

Smith, C. J. Alcoholics: Their treatment and their wives. *British Journal of Addiction*, 1969, **115**, 1039-1042.

Smith, C. M. A new adjunct to the treatment of alcoholism, the hallucinogenic drugs. *Quarterly Journal of Studies on Alcohol*, 1958, **19**, 406-417.

Smith, J. A., Wolford, J. A., Weber, M., & McLean, D. Use of citrated calcium carbimide (Temposil) in the treatment of chronic alcoholism. *Journal of the American Medical Association*, 1957, **165**, 2181-2183.

Smith, R. B., & O'Neill, L. Electrosleep in the management of alcoholism. *Biological Psychiatry*, 1975, **10**, 675-680.

Smith, R. E., & Gregory, P. B. Covert sensitization by induced anxiety in the treatment of an alcoholic. *Journal of Behaviour Therapy and Experimental Psychiatry*, 1976, **7**, 31-33.

Smith-Moorehouse, P. M. Hypnosis in the treatment of alcoholism. *British Journal of Addiction*, 1969, **64**, 47-55.

Sobell, L. C., & Sobell, M. B. A self-feedback technique to monitor drinking behavior in alcoholics. *Behaviour Research and Therapy*, 1973, **11**, 237-238. (a)

Sobell, M. B., & Sobell, L. C. Individualized behavior therapy for alcoholics. *Behavior Therapy*, 1973, **4**, 49-72. (b)

Sobell, M. B., & Sobell, L. C. Evaluating the external validity of Ewing and Rouse. *British Journal of Addiction*, 1978, **73**, 343-345.

Soskin, R. A., Grof, S., & Richards, W. A. Low doses of dipropyltryptamine in psychotherapy. *Archives of General Psychiatry*, 1973, **28**, 817-821.

Staub, G. E., & Kent, L. M. *The paraprofessional in the treatment of alcoholism*. Springfield, Ill.: C. C. Thomas, 1973.

Steffen, J. J. Electromyographically induced relaxation in the treatment of chronic alcohol abuse. *Journal of Consulting and Clinical Psychology*, 1975, **43**, 275.

Steffen, J. J., Nathan, P. E., & Taylor, H. A. Tension-reducing effects of alcohol: Further evidence and some methodological considerations. *Journal of Abnormal Psychology*, 1974, **83**, 542-547.

Stein, L. I., Newton, J. R., & Bauman, R. S. Duration of hospitalization for alcoholism. *Archives of General Psychiatry,* 1975, **32,** 247-252.

Steiner, C. M. *Games alcoholics play.* New York: Grove Press, 1971.

Steinglass, P. Experimenting with family treatment approaches to alcoholism, 1950-1975: A review. *Family Process,* 1976, **15,** 97-123.

Steinglass, P. Family therapy in alcoholism. In B. Kissin & H. Begleiter (Eds.), *The biology of alcoholism.* Vol. 5. *Treatment and rehabilitation of the chronic alcoholic.* New York: Plenum, 1977.

Steinglass, P. An experimental treatment program for alcoholic couples. *Journal of Studies on Alcohol,* 1979, **40,** 159-182.

Steinglass, P., Davis, D. I., & Berenson, D. Observations of conjointly hospitalized "alcoholic couples" during sobriety and intoxication: Implications for theory and therapy. *Family Process,* 1977, **16,** 1-16.

Steinglass, P., Weiner, S., & Mendelson, J. H. A systems approach to alcoholism: A model and its clinical application. *Archives of General Psychiatry,* 1971, **24,** 401-408.

Stinson, D. J., Smith, W. G., Amidjaya, I., & Kaplan, J. M. Systems of care and treatment outcomes for alcoholic patients. *Archives of General Psychiatry,* 1979, **36,** 535-539.

Stuart, R. B. Self-help group approach to self-management. In R. B. Stuart (Ed.), *Behavioral self-management: Strategies, techniques and outcomes.* New York: Brunner/Mazel, 1977.

Sturgis, E. T., Calhoun, K. S., & Best, C. L. Correlates of assertive behavior in alcoholics. *Addictive Behaviors,* 1979, **4,** 193-197.

Sulzer, E. S. Behavior modification in adult psychiatric patients. In L. P. Ullmann & L. Krasner (Eds.), *Case studies in behavior modification.* New York: Holt, 1965.

Swinson, R. P. Long-term trial of metronidazole in male alcoholics. *British Journal of Psychiatry,* 1971, **119,** 85-89.

Sytinsky, I. A., & Galebskaya, L. V. Physiologo-biochemical bases of drug dependence treatment by electro-acupuncture. *Addictive Behaviors,* 1979, **4,** 97-120.

Tamerin, J. S., & Mendelson, J. H. The psychodynamics of chronic inebriation: Observations of alcoholics during the process of drinking in an experimental group setting. *American Journal of Psychiatry,* 1969, **125,** 886-899.

Taylor, C. A., & Miller, W. R. *Relative effectiveness of bibliotherapy, individual and group self-control training in the treatment of problem drinkers.* Paper presented at the Taos International Conference on Treatment of Addictive Behaviors, Taos, New Mexico, February, 1979.

Taylor, J. A. T. Metronidazole: A new agent for combined somatic and psychic therapy of alcoholism. *Bulletin of the Los Angeles Neurological Society,* 1964, **29,** 158-162.

Tepfer, K. S., & Levine, B. A. Covert sensitization with internal aversive cues in the treatment of chronic alcoholism. *Psychological Reports,* 1977, **41,** 92-94.

Thimann, J. Conditioned reflex treatment of alcoholism. II. The risks of its application, its indications, contraindications, and psychotherapeutic aspects. *New England Journal of Medicine,* 1949, **241,** 406-410.

Thornton, C. C., Gottheil, E., Gellens, H. K., & Alterman, A. I. Voluntary versus involuntary abstinence in the treatment of alcoholics. *Journal of Studies on Alcohol,*

1977, **38**, 1740-1748.

Tomsovic, M. A follow-up study of discharged alcoholics. *Hospital and Community Psychiatry,* 1970, **21**, 94-97.

Tomsovic, M. Group therapy and changes in the self-concept of alcoholics. *Journal of Studies on Alcohol,* 1976, **37**, 53-57.

Tomsovic, M., & Edwards, R. V. Lysergide treatment in schizophrenic and nonschizophrenic alcoholics: A controlled evaluation. *Quarterly Journal of Studies on Alcohol,* 1970, **31**, 932-949.

Tomsovic, M., & Edwards, R. V. Cerebral electrotherapy for tension-related symptoms in alcoholics. *Quarterly Journal of Studies on Alcohol,* 1973, **34**, 1352-1355.

Tournier, R. E. Alcoholics Anonymous as treatment and as ideology. *Journal of Studies on Alcohol,* 1979, **40**, 230-239.

Trice, H. M., & Roman, P. M. Sociopsychological predictors of affiliation with Alcoholics Anonymous: A longitudinal study of "treatment success." *Social Psychiatry,* 1970, **5**, 51-59.

Trudel, R. M. Group therapy with women alcoholics: A perspective for rehabilitation. *Dissertation Abstracts International,* 1978, **38**, 6182B. (Abstract)

Tuchfeld, B. S., Simuel, J. B., Schmitt, M. L., Ries, J. L., Kay, D. L., & Waterhouse, G. J. *Changes in patterns of alcohol use without the aid of formal treatment: An exploratory study of former problem drinkers. Final report.* Research Triangle Park, N.C.: Research Triangle Institute, 1976.

Turek, I. S., Ota, K., Brown, C., Massari, F., & Kurland, A. A. Thiotixene and thioridazine in alcoholism treatment. *Quarterly Journal of Studies on Alcohol,* 1973, **34**, 853-859.

Tyndel, M., Fraser, J. G., & Hartlieb, C. J. Metronidazole as an adjunct in the treatment of alcoholism. *British Journal of Addiction,* 1969, **64**, 57-61.

Vallance, M. Alcoholism: A two-year follow-up of patients admitted to the psychiatric department of a general hospital. *British Journal of Psychiatry,* 1965, **111**, 348-356.

Van-Dijk, W. K., & Van-Dijk-Koffeman, A. A follow-up study of 211 treated male alcoholic addicts. *British Journal of Addiction,* 1973, **68**, 3-24.

Van Hasselt, V. B., Hersen, M., & Milliones, J. Social skills training for alcoholics and drug addicts: A review. *Addictive Behaviors,* 1978, **3**, 221-233.

Van Thiel, D. H., Gavaler, J. S., Paul, G. M., & Smith, W. I. Disulfiram-induced disturbances in hypothalamic-pituitary function. *Alcoholism: Clinical and Experimental Research,* 1979, **3**, 230-234.

Voegtlin, W. L. The treatment of alcoholism by establishing a conditioned reflex. *American Journal of the Medical Sciences,* 1940, **199**, 802-810.

Voegtlin, W. L. Conditioned reflex therapy of chronic alcoholism: Ten years' experience with the method. *Rocky Mountain Medical Journal,* 1947, **44**, 807-812. (a)

Voegtlin, W. L. Limitations and adjunctive therapies in treatment of chronic alcoholism. *Medical World,* 1947, **65**, 165-168. (b)

Voeglin, W. L., & Broz, W. R. The conditioned reflex treatment of chronic alcoholism. X. An analysis of 3125 admissions over a period of ten and a half years. *Annals of Internal Medicine,* 1949, **30**, 580-597.

Voegtlin, W. L., Lemere, F., Broz, W. R., & O'Hollaren, P. Conditioned reflex therapy of chronic alcoholism. IV. A preliminary report on the value of reinforcement. *Quarterly Journal of Studies on Alcohol,* 1941, **2**, 505-511.

Voegtlin, W. L., Lemere, F., Broz, W. R., & O'Hollaren, P. Conditioned reflex therapy of alcoholic addiction. V. Follow-up report of 1042 cases. *American Journal of the Medical Sciences,* 1942, **203,** 525-528.

Vogler, R. E., & Caddy, G. R. Treatment and prevention of alcoholism: The moderation approach. *Proceedings of the American Psychological Association,* 1973, **81,** 927-928.

Vogler, R. E., Compton, J. V., & Weissbach, T. A. Integrated behavior change technique for alcoholism. *Journal of Consulting and Clinical Psychology, 1975,* **43,** 233-243.

Vogler, R. E., Lunde, S. E., Johnson, G. R., & Martin, P. L. Electrical aversion conditioning with chronic alcoholics. *Journal of Consulting and Clinical Psychology,* 1970, **34,** 302-307.

Vogler, R. E., Lunde, S. E., & Martin, P. L. Electrical aversion conditioning with chronic alcoholics: Follow-up and suggestions for research. *Journal of Consulting and Clinical Psychology,* 1971, **36,** 450.

Vogler, R. E., Weissbach, T. A., & Compton, J. V. Learning techniques for alcohol abuse. *Behaviour Research and Therapy,* 1977, **15,** 31-38. (a)

Vogler, R. E., Weissbach, T. A., Compton, J. V., & Martin, G. T. Integrated behavior change techniques for problem drinkers in the community. *Journal of Consulting and Clinical Psychology,* 1977, **45,** 267-279. (b)

Walker, K., Sanchez-Craig, M., & MacDonald, K. *Teaching coping strategies for interpersonal problems.* Paper presented at the North American Congress on Alcohol and Drug Problems, San Francisco, 1974.

Wallace, J. A. A comparison of disulfiram therapy and routine therapy in alcoholism. *Quarterly Journal of Studies on Alcohol,* 1952, **13,** 397-398.

Wallerstein, R. S. Comparative study of treatment methods for chronic alcoholism: The alcoholism research at Winter V. A. Hospital. *American Journal of Psychiatry,* 1956, **113,** 228-233.

Wallerstein, R. S., Chotlos, J. W., Friend, M. B., Hammersley, D. W., Perlswig, E. A., & Winship, G. M. *Hospital treatment of alcoholism: A comparative experimental study.* New York: Basic Books, 1957.

Wallerstein, R. S. Psychologic factors in chronic alcoholism. *Annals of Internal Medicine,* 1958, **48,** 114-122.

Weiner, H. B. Psychodramatic treatment for the alcoholic. In R. Fox (Ed.), *Alcoholism: Behavioral research, therapeutic approaches.* New York: Springer, 1967.

Weston, D. *Guidebook for alcoholics: How to succeed without drinking.* New York: Exposition Press, 1964.

Wexberg, L. E. The outpatient treatment of alcoholism in the District of Columbia. *Quarterly Journal of Studies on Alcohol,* 1953, **14,** 514-524.

Whyte, C. R., & O'Brien, P. M. J. Disulfiram implant: A controlled trial. *British Journal of Psychiatry,* 1974, **124,** 42-44.

Wiens, A. N., Montague, J. R., Manaugh, T. S., & English, C. J. Pharmacological aversive counterconditioning to alcohol in a private hospital: One-year follow-up. *Journal of Studies on Alcohol,* 1976, **37,** 1320-1324.

Willems, P. J. A., Letemendia, F. J. J., & Arroyave, F. A two-year follow-up study comparing short with long stay in-patient treatment of alcoholics. *British Journal of Psychiatry,* 1973, **122,** 637-648.

Wilson, A. Disulfiram implantation in alcoholism treatment: A review. *Journal of Studies on Alcohol,* 1975, **36,** 555-565.

Wilson, A., Davidson, W. J., Blanchard, R., & White, J. Disulfiram implantation: A placebo-controlled trial with two-year follow-up. *Journal of Studies on Alcohol,* 1978, **39,** 809-819.

Wilson, A., Davidson, W. J., & White, J. Disulfiram implantation: Placebo, psychological deterrent, and pharmacological deterrent effects. *British Journal of Psychiatry,* 1976, **129,** 277-280.

Wilson, G. T. Booze, beliefs, and behavior: Cognitive processes in alcohol use and abuse. In P. E. Nathan, G. A. Marlatt, & T. Løberg (Eds.), *Alcoholism: New directions in behavioral research and treatment.* New York: Plenum, 1978.

Wilson, G. T., Leaf, R. C., & Nathan, P. E. The aversive control of excessive alcohol consumption by chronic alcoholics in the laboratory setting. *Journal of Applied Behavior Analysis,* 1975, **8,** 13-26.

Wilson, G. T., & Tracey, D. A. An experimental analysis of aversive imagery versus electrical aversive conditioning in the treatment of chronic alcoholics. *Behaviour Research and Therapy,* 1976, **14,** 41-51.

Wilson, I. C., Lacoe, B. A., & Riley, L. Tofranil in the treatment of post alcoholic depressions. *Psychosomatics,* 1970, **11,** 488-494.

Winokur, G., Reich, T., Rimmer, J., & Pitts, F. N., Jr. Alcoholism. III. Diagnosis and familial psychiatric illness in 259 alcoholic probands. *Archives of General Psychiatry,* 1970, **23,** 104-111.

Winokur, G., Rimmer, J., & Reich, T. Alcoholism. IV. Is there more than one type of alcoholism? *British Journal of Psychiatry,* 1971, **118,** 525-531.

Winters, A. *Drinkwatchers.* Haverstraw, New York: Gullistan Press, 1977.

Wolfe, S., & Holland, L. A questionnaire follow-up of alcoholic patients. *Quarterly Journal of Studies on Alcohol,* 1964, **25,** 108-118.

Wolff, K. Hospitalized alcoholic patients. III. Motivating alcoholics through group psychotherapy. *Hospital and Community Psychiatry,* 1968, **19,** 206-209.

Wolpe, J. *The practice of behavior therapy.* 2nd ed. New York: Pergamon, 1973.

Wood, D., Del Nuevo, A., Michalik, M., Schein, S., & Bucky, S. Psychodrama with an alcohol abuse population. *Group Psychotherapy Psychodrama and Sociometry,* in press.

Yalom, I. D. Group therapy and alcoholism. *Annals of the New York Academy of Sciences,* 1974, **233,** 85-103.

Young, L. D., & Keeler, M. H. Sobering data on lithium in alcoholism. *Lancet,* 1977, **1,** 144.

Zimberg, S. Evaluation of alcoholism treatment in Harlem. *Quarterly Journal of Studies on Alcohol,* 1974, **35,** 550-557.

Zimberg, S. Psychiatric office treatment of alcoholism. In S. Zimberg, J. Wallace, & S. B. Blume (Eds.), *Practical approaches to alcoholism psychotherapy.* New York: Plenum, 1978.

Zimberg, S., Wallace, J., & Blume, S. B. (Eds.) *Practical approaches to alcoholism psychotherapy.* New York: Plenum, 1978.

3

Alternative Strategies in the Treatment of Narcotic Addiction: A Review*

Edward J. Callahan

Department of Psychology
West Virginia University
Morgantown, West Virginia 26506

*The opinions expressed in this chapter do not necessarily represent the views of the Regents of West Virginia University.

The fact that men live in groups necessitates agreement on acceptable lifestyles and mechanisms to control behavior which deviates from group norms. It seems probable that acceptable behaviors evolve naturalistically within most living environments. It is also apparent that these behavior patterns vary greatly from group to group and from issue to issue. One important cultural norm is the amount and variety of substances used for recreation and other purposes.

Narcotics are one of a variety of chemically active substances which are used by members of the American society. As a class of drugs, narcotics produce euphoric effects and alleviate pain very effectively. Indeed, narcotics are the most effective medication in existence for alleviating pain (Brecher et al., 1972). These positive aspects of narcotics are counterbalanced by their pharmacological properties of tolerance and physical dependence; that is, over a period of time a person who is taking narcotics will require larger and larger quantities of the drug in order to experience euphoria (tolerance) and, if the drug supply is stopped, strong physiological disturbance will ensue (physical dependence). Physiological disturbances include runny nose, watering eyes, diarrhea, vomiting, fever, and a variety of psychological cravings. The occurrence of tolerance and withdrawal are usually seen as equivalent to addiction (e.g. Wikler, 1953) although the World Health Organization's definition of addiction (WHO, 1964) allows for physical *or* psychological dependence. Regardless of definition, narcotic addiction is seen as a major health problem in the U.S. (Glasscote et al., 1972).

Interestingly, narcotic addiction was fairly common in the United States in the late 1800s (Brecher et al., 1972). The typical addict at that time was a middle-aged woman going through menopause who may have bought the narcotics in elixirs, in over-the-counter drugs or in prescription drugs. Narcotics were easy to find and quite inexpensive. To understand the current status of narcotics, let us look briefly at the issue of substance abuse historically, the issue of substance use and abuse in the United States, the legal changes which have resulted in the narcotic problem in the United States, and finally consider both therapy for the narcotic addict and prevention of narcotic addiction.

Substance Abuse Historically

No doubt, early men explored their environment and discovered many potential sources of food. In the course of exploration, it is likely that they discovered that some of the things that they ate had psycho-active effects; that is, while pursuing mushrooms they might discover that some mushrooms were good nutrients, that other mushrooms made individuals nauseous, that still other mushrooms killed, and finally that some mushrooms had the effect of producing pleasant sensory enhancement to the point of hallucinations. Since pursuing only trial-and-error exploration of environment would have proven very costly to early man, it is likely indeed that they observed what the animals in the region safely consumed.

In this way, it seems likely that men sampled most of the chemically active substances in their own particular region. Further use of those substances was no doubt controlled by the effect they had on the organism; that is, if a substance had pleasant effects, it would be likely to be used again. If the effects were toxic or lethal, it was unlikely that the society would allow its further use. Such information would be transmitted from father to son, mother to daughter, friend to friend. When substances were not lethal or toxic, however, their effects could sometimes be perceived as reinforcing and, under other circumstances, as not reinforcing. For example, alcohol taken in small quantities produces pleasant feelings and repeated use. Alcohol taken in larger quantities can produce drunkenness and reduce inhibition of agression or sexual assault, and alcohol taken in massive quantities can lead to death. Therefore, societies have developed particular control mechanisms for alcohol and other substances like it.

Sulkunen (1976) has pointed out that the particular substances used in a region are those which are endogenous to that region; that is, in areas which grow wine grapes naturally, there is a long history of drinking wine. In regions such as Israel, long traditions of the use of wine have evolved naturalistically. In such cases where cultural expectations are very strong, legal restrictions over the use of a substance are not necessary. In fact, it is possible that legal restrictions over use of a substance prevent a culture from gradually developing its own norms for the use of the substance. Trial-and-error use of the substance may be necessary for the development of effective cultural control of the use of that substance.

For example, coca leaves are chewed by native South Americans off the bush during the day. There appears to be no concern with overuse of coca leaves. On the other hand, in the United States, where there has been no cultural history of the use of cocaine (a derivative of coca leaves), the drug is feared and prohibited by law. In the early 1900s the effect of cocaine was seen as the release of the black man's inhibitions against violence against whites (Musto, 1973). Thus, strong controlling legislation was passed. The actual behavioral effects of the drugs were not considered. As a result, cultural norms for the use of cocaine are evolving only in sub-cultures using the substance outside the law. Ironically, coffee may have had a parallel history. When coffee was first introduced to medieval Europe, coffee houses sprang up in which abusers would gather late at night and drink massive amounts of coffee until they hallucinated. Now that a long history of coffee use has occurred, more naturalistic control of coffee drinking has evolved. Thus, the novelty of a substance in a culture probably facilitates its abuse.

Opiate use without addiction had been fairly common in China for centuries. Only when tobacco was introduced in the 1600s and opiate smoking occurred did addiction become a problem. At one point, the Chinese government outlawed opiate use with severe penalties. After the 19th-century Imperial Edict which required the beheading of any Chinese smoking opium, opium use began to decline. Fearing economic loss, the British began the Opium Wars to reverse that particular ruling and keep the opium trade running smoothly (Platt and Labate, 1976). Later, when Chinese laborers were brought to the United States in the 1800s to build the great western railroads, they brought with them a tradition of smoking opium. This tradition continued in the Chinese ghetto in San Francisco. As an economically indigent area, the Chinese ghetto was close to the high crime areas in San Francisco. Thus, a combination of racial fear and fear of an unknown substance led the city of San Francisco in 1855 to pass the first United States ordinance against the use of opium.

This trend was furthered when, for economic purposes, the United States urged the banning of international trade in opiates at the first of several international conventions at Hague in 1904 (Platt and Labate, 1976). Caught in the embarrassing position of having no internal laws against the manufacture and sale of opiates, the United States began such legislation and, by 1914, the Harrison act was passed. The Harrison act prohibited both the production and sale of opiates except through prescription. Later Supreme Court rulings severely restricted the freedom of a physician to prescribe opiates. It became necessary that a physician prescribing opiates prove that he or she was prescribing the opiates only to withdraw the person from their addiction. Opiate maintenance was no longer allowed. Further Supreme Court rulings restricted physicians even further and put opiate prescription into clinics. Finally, legislation was passed and these clinics were closed, gradually moving opiate sales from across-the-counter home remedies into the hands of organized crime. At the same time, a change in scientific explanation of addiction was occurring: the addict was described as a psychopath (Kolb, 1925), rather than as a person whose metabolism had been changed by the introduction of opiates to his or her system. A normal individual would not feel any pleasure from opiates; it took the personality distortion of psychopathy to feel pleasure from opiates. The perceived user of opiates had thus gradually changed from the middle-aged housewife in the late 1800s to the underworld criminal addict "psychopath" of the 1930s. This underworld addict was usually a member of a racial minority (Maurer and Vogel, 1974). It is possible that the increase in the number of white addicts in the 1960s was responsible for the increased treatment funding for narcotic addiction in the 1970s, furthering the contribution of racism to the story of heroin addiction in the U.S.

During World War II, the availability of heroin decreased and addiction became almost non-existent. Thus, many people became impressed by the potential of dealing with heroin addiction by restricting the flow of heroin into the country, an alternative discussed extensively by Phares (1973). Unfortunately, peacetime control of drug flow is much more difficult than the natural drying-up which occurred during the Second World War. The implementation of drug curtailment by the Nixon administration in the early 1970s led, ironically, to raising the price of heroin while the number of addicts still increased. It is important to note that legal changes are still an alternative to dealing with the heroin addiction problem. Several people, including Szasz (1973), advocate the legalization of heroin and the establishment of heroin maintenance clinics as a way of dealing with the current bind of the United States. However, two other alternatives appear to be more likely courses of action. The first of these is the treatment of heroin addiction. The second is the prevention of heroin addiction. Let us now consider each of these alternatives in order.

Treatment of Heroin Addiction

Traditionally, the treatment of heroin addiction has been singularly unsuccessful. It has been handled in three distinctive fashions, depending upon how heroin addiction is conceptualized by those providing treatment. The first tradition of treatment is medical-pharmacological. Here, heroin addiction is seen as a pharmacological adaptation to a chemical which can be changed by removing the availability of that substance (Bishop, 1920). The second tradition of treatment is that the heroin addict is a particular personality type who must undergo an extensive personality change in order to overcome his or her dependence upon the substance (Kolb, 1925). The third alternative is behavioral; that is, the heroin addict is conceptualized as a person who has learned cravings to a substance through classical conditioning (Wikler, 1965), and operant conditioning (Cahoon & Crosby, 1972) and who has a particular set of skills and deficits (Callahan, Dalkoetter, & Price, 1980). These skills are then seen as a key to training the person in a new life-style which will lead him or her away from the use of narcotics. Let us review each of these forms of treatment in turn. The first that we will consider is the medical tradition.

Medical Treatment of Heroin Addiction

Dole and Nyswander (1965) make clear their conceptualization of heroin addiction as a metabolic disease, a stance proposed earlier by Bishop (1920). They feel that through a single administration of a narcotic, and more potently, through multiple administrations of the narcotic, a person's metabolism changes; that is, the nervous system is altered by the presence of the narcotic and after that point, that person's nervous system is "normal" only when a narcotic is present. Recent speculation on the possible existence of endorphins (Goldstein & Cox, 1977) follows similar logic: the presence of narcotics suppresses an hypothesized endogenous chemical (endorphins) which makes the individual feel "high." While many of the earlier advocates of medical treatment of heroin addiction did not subscribe to Dole and Nyswander's view or the endorphin theory, they do share the idea that since narcotic addiction involves addiction to a chemical substance, medical treatment is indeed the appropriate course of action.

Most early treatment of narcotic addiction in this country took place either in hospitals or in jails. In both instances, the problem was equated with pharmacological aspects of the addiction; that is, once the person was weaned off the narcotic and physiological disturbance subsided, it was assumed that he or she would not return to the use of the narcotic. Most treatment consisted of gradually reducing the person's doses of the narcotic, or else cutting off the availability of the narcotic completely. The results of this form of early treatment were disastrous. Most addicts returned to heroin use within hours or days of release from these restricted environments, even after five years or more away from the drug. (Ball, Thompson, & Allen, 1970; Vaillant, 1966; and Winick, 1962).

The second medical treatment also stems from this idea of narcotic addiction as a disease. Again, in Dole and Nyswander's theory, people's metabolism changes with the introduction of narcotics to the system. They are "normal" only with a narcotic in their system. Thus, the treatment of choice would be maintenance on a long-acting narcotic such as methadone or levo-alpha acetyl methadyl (LAAM) (Trueblood, Judson, & Goldstein, 1978). Dole and Nyswander's (1965) initial evaluation of methadone effects was quite positive. They found reduced crime, increased education, increased employment, and improved social adjustment in a group of narcotic addicts who were treated in their methadone maintenance clinic. Later evaluations of methadone treatment programs have not been so positive, however. Bowden and Maddox (1972) and Desmond and Maddox (1975) have pointed out several of the shortcomings of the traditional methadone maintenance clinics. The ideal clinic as developed by Dole and Nyswander had a good staff-patient ratio and involved intensive job placement help and personal counseling. Later methadone maintenance clinics were based on the same model, with the exception that intensive counseling was not available. Clinics instead became large warehouses in which methadone could be doled out to a great number of people each day. The vast numbers of clients attending the clinic obviated any possibility of intensive counseling for most clients. Other problems existed beyond the failure of counseling in these clinics, however.

Methadone maintenance clinics have become focal points for narcotic addict communities. Thus, a good deal of "dealing" of other drugs occurs around the methadone clinics. Take-home doses of methadone are often stolen or sold illegally on the streets (Desmond & Maddox, 1975), and methadone doses are often supplemented with other illegal drugs. Many methadone clinics have severe problems with client use of other illegal drugs as shown in the urine screens of addicts in treatment. Interestingly, a behavior-modification technique, contingency management, has been successful in dealing with dirty urines in these programs.

Nightingale, Michaux, and Platt (1973) have shown that the implementation of contingencies for dirty urines could indeed limit illegal drug use in the methadone clinic. In the first phase of their study, they counted the number of dirty urines given by clients in a methadone clinic. In the next phase, they told clients that they would be suspended if they produced more than three dirty urines. In the third phase, they implemented this contingency and began to suspend violators from treatment. The clinic showed a slight decrease in dirty urines after the warning and a statistically significant decline in dirty urines after the contingency was put into effect. Although some of this decline was due to clientele change during the study, the authors report that those clients who started the study and were not suspended showed a marked decrease in their rate of dirty urines. Thus, punishment has effected a reduction in the illegal use of drugs; positive reinforcement has been effective as well.

Stitzer, Biglow, Lawrence, Cohen, O'Lugoff, and Hawthorne (1977) used take-home doses of methadone as a reinforcer for providing clean urines (urine showing no drugs other than methadone). In a reversal design, they were able to demonstrate that addicts showed lower rates of dirty urines when clean urines were required for take-home methadone than when the contingency was not in effect. In these instances, one of the most serious criticisms against methadone clinics has been overcome. A second criticism has been that giving out methadone does not improve a person's employment situation.

Hall, Loeb, and Yang (1977) have demonstrated a second way in which behavioral technology has been useful in a methadone maintenance program. They randomly divided a group of clients into one group receiving a job interviewing training program and a control group. The experimental group went through a behavioral skills shaping program, parallel to that used in assertion training. Significantly more clients in this group found and maintained employment after training than did the clients in the control group. Thus, a behavioral program was utilized to help overcome a major deficit in a methadone program: poor job acquisition and maintenance.

While a medical conceptualization of narcotic addiction as a disease cannot easily be proved or disproved, one resulting treatment, methadone maintenance, has been improved by the addition of behavioral technology to pre-existing medical conceptualizations. While there is a dynamic tension involved in the use of methadone as a disease-curing chemical and the behavioral philosophy of narcotic addiction as a problem behavior, such a tension may produce more creative treatment than may be available in either methodology expressed in pure form. We will explore another amalgam of behavioral and medical treatment—narcotic antagonists—in a later section of this chapter. First, let us examine another approach to the analysis and treatment of narcotic addiction which is one orthgonal to both medical and behavioral approaches. It replaced the original domination of the medical model for heroin addiction in the 1920s. It can sometimes be compatible with either of those alternate approaches, but is indeed an independent approach to the analysis of narcotic addiction. This is the analysis and treatment of narcotic addiction as a personality dysfunction.

Narcotic Addiction Personality Model

Probably no single topic has generated more pages on narcotic addiction than the issue of what is the personality of the narcotic addict. While there are those who would contend that this plethora of research data is more a function of the ease with which publications can be generated than a function of the existence of an "addictive personality," personality research has been the most prominent focus of researchers in the area of narcotic addiction. Since the present author has a bias which must be stated as pro-therapeutic intervention, as opposed to pro-static study of a problem, we will put less emphasis on this particular section than on other sections of the chapter. There are, however, several interesting statements which have been made about the personality of the narcotic addict.

One of the few consistent findings in the past has been that the narcotic addict has been much less assertive than any control group studied (Ausubel, 1961; Kraft, 1969, 1970). Recently, Platt and Lank studied young narcotic addicts versus a control group of other inmates at county jails. Their surprising discovery was that the narcotic addict had better social skills than the control population within the jail which had not used narcotics. Thus, the single most consistent finding of personality research no longer appears valid. It may be premature to arrive at the conclusion that no personality factors are related to narcotic addiction, however.

One interesting new twist in the study of narcotic addiction is provided by Charles Wallace at Camarillo State Hospital. Wallace (1979) has reported his work in studying personality attributes of narcotic addicts through behavioral tasks. He targeted the ability to delay gratification, susceptibility to peer pressure and expression of aggression through operant tasks.

Wallace worked with 45 males and 30 females: 15 addicts and 15 non-addicts for both sexes with an additional 15 non-addict delinquent males. Each subject provided data for each study: (1) a delay of gratification task; (2) an Asch-type test for conformity to social pressure; and (3) an aggression response.

Addicts showed different personality attributes according to the MMPI and a variety of other paper and pencil tests used. On the delay of gratification task (a choice between lever pulls producing a nickel immediately or a dime ten days later), addicts chose the immediate reward significantly more often. On the second task, subjects had to determine which of two lines was longer. On each trial they had "information" on the choices supposedly made by either a peer group or a non-peer group. In actuality, the "peer" or "non-peer" group which the subjects watched briefly making decisions had made no decision;

instead, choices were weighted to reflect varying amounts of conformity among the "model group" choices. All subjects showed increased agreement as the amount of confederate agreement increased. The interesting result found on this task was that addicts agreed with the "straight" group significantly more often than with the addict-peer group. Non-addict males showed significantly less conformity with the "straight" peers than the addicts.

On the third task, subjects had the opportunity to pull a lever to earn money. This task was randomly interrupted on an average of every 12 seconds by a 86-decibel, 400-Hz noise. This noise could be terminated by a "punching" or aggression response against a padded manipulandum. However, many of the subjects never terminated the tone, thus failing to provide an agression response. None of the hypothesized excess aggression was found. Thus, on two of the three hypothesized personality characteristics, Wallace found behavioral differences in his observed populations. Wallace's work may mark the start of more carefully operationalized studies in addiction. But what of treatment for disordered personality?

Personality-Based Treatment

Two major strategies have been used under the umbrella of personality modification as treatment for heroin addiction: psychotherapy and therapeutic community. Psychotherapy is reported only sparsely in the literature, possibly because it requires substantial motivation on the part of the participant.

The goals of psychotherapy with the drug user are based on the idea that the addict seeks drugs to assuage an early childhood trauma or, more often, consistent lack of security from caring parents. Switzer (1974) claims that therapy then involves abreaction of old trauma, counteraction in abandoning drug use behavior, and proaction in opening up to new behavior options. However, psychotherapy usually involves long-term commitment. For this reason, Platt and Labate (1973) suggest that psychotherapy has been quite unsuccessful. Some better success has been found with therapeutic communities.

Therapeutic communities are based on the idea that an addict's personality is significantly distorted and must be broken down to allow a new personality to emerge (e.g., the theme of Phoenix House). Charles Dederich founded Synanon in 1958 on that basis (Yablonsky, 1965). The addict is required to make an intensive commitment to the program, resulting in a high "splittee" rate, especially among racial minorities (Aaron and Dailey, 1975).

Therapeutic interaction is often defined as punishment for stated or implied non-compliance with the program and rewards are provided for adoption of group values.

Results are mixed. Those who stay appear to make positive adjustments. However, over 50% of clients terminate prematurely (Scott & Foldberg, 1973) and those who leave the program relapse significantly: only 25% are still clean two years later (Switzer, 1974). In fact, Synanon now holds that addicts must commit themselves to the program for life.

Therapeutic communities do appear to be an effective treatment modality, but for only a small percentage of addicts. Before examining behavioral treatment of addiction, let us first examine direct observations made on narcotic addicts to determine if they can aid in understanding addiction.

Direct Observation Studies

Very little direct observation has been done, but a few fairly creative studies are available at this point. Wikler (1952) presented the first direct observation of the narcotic addiction process. In this psychoanalytically-oriented study, Wikler made narcotics available to a young addict at the Lexington treatment facility. This inpatient then gradually began to self-addict within the treatment environment. Unfortunately, Wikler did much of his observation through a psychoanalytic perspective and thus does not report simple direct observations very often. What he does report, though, is that over the first few days of using the narcotic, the client gradually became more withdrawn. Over a period of time, he told the staff that he would cut back his usage of narcotics on his own. When the staff went along with this, the client instead continued to use narcotics. Finally, he became angry, upset, and manipulative as the staff began to gradually withdraw narcotics.

In the years which followed, a great deal of direct observation of alcohol use has been accomplished (e.g., Mello & Mendelsohn, 1965; Nathan & O'Brien, 1971; Schaefer, Sobell, & Mills, 1971; see Bridell & Nathan, 1976 & Sobell, 1978 for reviews). Much less has been accomplished in narcotic addiction.

Griffith, Fann, and Tapp (1968) allowed their subjects access to narcotics through an operant response. They reported few physical symptoms or complaints in the early stages of access to the drug. Over a period of time, subjects reported increasing amounts of anger and withdrawal symptoms, despite ready access to large amounts of morphine. In two other observation studies (Haertzen & Hook, 1969; and Martin, Jasinski, & Haertzen, 1973), similar results were reported: physical complaints increased with addiction along with irritability while the pleasure of "shooting up" decreased by subjective rating. All of this paints a portrait of narcotic use as an increasingly unpleasant yet undeniably compelling behavior with the onset of addiction. It is unclear at present whether these responses to narcotic use are conditioned responses trained during prior experiences with addiction in a "street" environment or whether they are pharmacological effects of the drug.

Further observation studies have been reported by Meyer and his colleagues at McLean Hospital in Boston (Altman, Meyer, Nivins et al., 1976; Babor,

Meyer, Mirin, McNamee, & Davies, 1976; Meyer, Mirin, Altman, & McNamee, 1976; and Mirin, Meyer, & McNamee, 1976). They concerned themselves with physiological measures of heroin use, subjects' self-reports, clinical ratings by staff members, and behavioral observations. These observations took place as street addicts underwent successive phases of withdrawal, readdiction, drug free status, use of narcotic antagonists, and shooting heroin while on narcotic antagonists.

The immediate effects of shooting heroin were to produce a calm and relaxed state, but addiction (eight to ten days of use) brought increasing agitation and anger. These changes were accompanied by sleep disruption, social withdrawal, anxiety, and depression. These same problems—somatic concerns, anxiety, and depression—had all decreased in early heroin use. Thus, the reinforcers for early heroin use appear paradoxically to plague the user as tolerance increases and withdrawal becomes an issue. These direct observation studies point out the importance of social withdrawal as an indicator of potential readdiction. This sign is no doubt salient enough to alert heroin programs that they may be losing a client to readdiction, and deserves close attention. Hopefully, further direct observation studies will prove useful in developing successful treatment of narcotic addiction. Let us now turn our attention from laboratory analysis of narcotic addiction to its treatment using behavioral strategies.

Behavioral Treatment of Narcotic Addiction

Behavioral treatment of narcotic addiction has evolved in parallel with the evolution of behavioral approaches to human disorders. First, it has moved from the case-study analysis to the controlled outcome design. Second, it has moved from the controlled inpatient setting to the community. Third, there has been an evolution in the model of behavioral pathology from a fairly simplistic statement of a single problem to a listing of behavioral assets and deficits. Through this listing of assets and deficits, the behavioral clinician has the option of developing the person's assets as opposed to merely attacking deficits. Early behavioral work had conceptualized narcotic addiction as an excessive behavior which must be eliminated. By focusing so strongly on the elimination of the injection of narcotics into the veins, early researchers and clinicians failed to recognize the behavioral deficits of many of their clients. For reviews of early treatment of narcotic addiction, the reader is referred to Callner (1973), Callahan & Rawson (1980), and Callahan, Dahlkoetter, & Price (1980).

Early treatment for narcotic addiction focused on the act of ingesting the narcotic almost as though it were the entire problem in addiction. By oversimplifying the problem, researchers were able to present simplistic solutions: classical conditioning, with an aversive event, covert sensitization, electrical

aversion therapy, systematic desensitization, operant conditioning and extinction were among the treatments for narcotic addiction put forth in early
behavioral interventions. Let us consider each of these areas briefly.

Chemical Aversion

Narcotics are powerful agents in classical conditioning. O'Brien (1974) has
shown clearly that addicts show conditioned physiological responses to a
variety of stimuli paired with use of narcotics. Wikler (1965) has theorized
these classical conditioning events maintain narcotic use and facilitate relapse.
One way to change the valence of narcotic-related stimuli would be to pair
these stimuli with aversive events; the optimal aversive event for narcotic
addiction would be an event operating on the same physiological system as the
narcotic. Thus, pairing a narcotic with a chemical aversive event would seem
the optimal strategy.

Such a strategy was pursued in several small studies. Burroughs (1952)
reports devising such a strategy in his autobiographical reports of kicking
morphine addiction. He timed his own injection of apomorphine to take effect
soon after feeling the effects of the self-injected morphine. Raymond (1964)
also used apomorphine with an addicted client. The client in this case, however, did not have all of Burrough's skills. During treatment, the client became
suicidal and ECT was used to break her depression. Further treatment was
complicated by marital distress. Thus, the straight-forward classical conditioning treatment became very complicated.

Thomson and Rathod (1964) used a straightforward chemical aversion
model. In this work, succinylcholine chloride or scoline was used to suppress
the desire of the addict to abuse a narcotic. In this short report, however, they
also reported that this treatment was used in a social milieu context in which
extensive social retraining was done. Extensive follow-up was planned and
intensive individual counseling occurred. Treatment often took place for a full
six months. Later uses of scoline, reported by Campbell et al., (1967) for
alcoholism and in unpublished papers in the United States, used scoline
without this intensive supportive counseling. Thus, while Thomson and
Rathod showed impressive early results with this method, later replications
were far less successful and serious ethical issues arose as some saw chemical
aversion as an easy alternative with poorly motivated clients.

Blanchard, Libet, and Young (1973) listed the effects of both apneic
aversion and covert sensitization in a within-subject design. In the first phase
of the study, covert sensitization was used. Covert sensitization involves the
verbal description of aversive scenes following verbal descriptions of the
unwanted behavior. Thus, in the case of a paint-sniffer, the subject would be
asked to imagine sniffing paint and then to feel very aversive effects such as
nausea, vomiting, etc. The second phase of the study was apneic aversion

using succinylcholine. Throughout the study, the client was observed to determine how much he would sniff during free access to paint. In this study, the first 16 sessions were covert sensitization. There was no significant reduction in paint-sniffing during this time. The second phase consisted of apneic aversion, which produced suppression of paint-sniffing behavior. In the third phase, they returned to the use of covert sensitization. During this time, the sniffing of paint remained suppressed. In this study, it appears that covert sensitization was not effective initially in suppressing paint-sniffing. It appears to have gained some effects in that it maintained the suppression of paint-sniffing produced by apneic aversion. On its own, however, covert sensitization was not very impressive. Let us now look at other instances of the use of covert sensitization in the literature to determine whether or not they seem likely to have effects useful in the treatment of narcotic addiction.

Covert Sensitization

Covert sensitization is a verbal aversion technique which is usually attributed to Joseph Cautela (1966). In this procedure, the subject usually first relaxes and then listens to scenes which describe the behavior which he or she wants to suppress, followed by verbal description of intense noxious stimuli. These noxious stimuli have ranged from nausea and vomiting to wasp stings to socially aversive events, and are sometimes supplemented with nauseous odors (Maletzky, 1975). In this latter usage, the covert sensitization is known as "assisted covert sensitization."

Covert sensitization has been reported to be successful in the treatment of a variety of unwanted behaviors, including gasoline-sniffing (Kolvin, 1967), alcoholism (Amant, 1967), and sexual deviation (Barlow, Agras, & Leitenberg, 1969; Callahan & Leitenberg, 1973). Two early single-case studies reported the use of covert sensitization with narcotic addicts. Wisocki (1973) and Boudin (1972) used covert sensitization as part of the treatment in their single-case studies. Wisocki used wasp stings as the imagined aversive events in her application of this technique. She reported that she found it more difficult to increase the client's prosocial behavior than to reduce his drug urges in this study. Boudin, on the other hand, mainly used contingency contracting in his treatment of a young amphetamine user. In both cases, it is impossible to determine what the critical therapeutic factors were.

In a later study, Maletzky used his version of assisted covert sensitization in a comparison to one-to-one drug counseling. He found that the covert sensitization was significantly more effective in reducing self-reported instances of substance abuse. He also reported that significant others validated these results. Thus, while covert sensitization has some interesting applications, the literature on its use is fairly sparse and it is still not clear whether the technique would be acceptable to minority addict populations. It is entirely possible that such a population would find this sophisticated technique to be aversive in itself. Let us now look at electrical aversion therapy.

Electrical Aversion Therapy

Wolpe (1965) presents the first case of electrical aversion therapy for drug dependence. His client in this case was a physician who was addicted to Demerol. Wolpe supplemented his office sessions of punishment for drug thoughts and drug urges to community application. He gave the physician a portable shocker to use in his home environment. Unfortunately, the client moved away to another city and treatment was not completed in this case study. There was no follow-up presented. Wolpe's study, however, is an interesting example of the major flaw which exists in the early behavior modification research. His client was definitely not the usual heroin addict. As a physician, it is obvious that he had no problem with employment. It is not clear whether his social functioning was adequate or whether this was an additional problem. His problems, however, were probably significantly less than those of most minority drug addicts.

Later, the Lubetkin and Fishman (1974) study reported on a graduate student with a fairly long history of "chipping" or the infrequent use of heroin. They treated this client with a series of electrical aversion therapy. They reported good follow-up after 20 sessions of treatment using electrical shock. In other early work, John O'Brien and his colleagues (O'Brien & Raynes, 1970; O'Brien, Raynes, & Patch, 1972) reported on the use of electrical aversion therapy as one treatment that they used in combination with covert sensitization. They reported a successful outcome in a series of five single-case studies of heroin addiction. Their follow-up ranged up to 14 months. There are no longer-range follow-up studies available on electrical aversion with heroin addicts. It seems that the predominant use of electric shock is being replaced by more systematic applications of cognitive therapies and of behavior management procedures such as contingency contracting. Before moving to these other forms of intervention, let us review two final early treatment strategies for narcotic addiction: systematic desensitization, and extinction.

Systematic Desensitization

The early use of systematic desensitization as a treatment for narcotic addiction is best exemplified in the work of Kraft (1969, 1970). In his work, Kraft speculated that narcotic addiction and other forms of drug abuse were due to social anxiety. He felt that the addict used the drugs merely to overcome feelings of social inadequacy. In a series of cases, Kraft treated individuals for drinamyl and physeptome abuse, using systematic desensitization around social interaction themes. He reported success in this intervention. His work, however, did not appear to inspire a great deal of other work and the more recent conceptualizations of narcotic addiction have been far less simplistic than a simple social anxiety model. Since Kraft is a practitioner, his clients had to be able to afford his treatment. Thus, his work can be criticized (as can most early single-case studies in narcotic addiction) as having used clients who are not representative of the overall narcotic addiction population.

It should be noted that many of the successful single-case studies focus on well-educated, middle-class, white males or females. Questions arise as to whether these methodologies can be applied directly to narcotic addiction as found in minority populations with few social, educational, and vocational skills. It seems apparent that ancillary treatment for these deficits is necessary. Rather than berating the literature for a void which is acknowledged as existing, let us instead see these early single-case studies as providing hope that a behavioral methology could be used successfully to treat narcotic addiction, even in those clients with fewer skills than the clientele ordinarily described in early reports. For a complete methodological critique of these early studies, see Callner (1973), Callner & Ross (in press), and Callahan, Dahlkoetter, & Price (1980). Frankly, however, the methodological inadequacy of the early literature is no surprise. One has to develop successful treatment procedures before one can be concerned with fine methodological analysis of treatment operation. Current and future literature will not be spared such methodological scrutiny, however, even as more effective clinical methodology is developing.

Before turning to complex behavioral programs, let us look briefly at a technology developed from the extinction process.

Extinction

An alternative to direct suppression of a behavior through aversive events is the omission of rewards for those behaviors: extinction. Such a strategy in narcotic addiction would be based on the idea that narcotic injection is supported by the positive effects which ensue.

An early example of this was Rubenstein's (1931) work with tuberculoid addicts. He gradually increased the saline to narcotic ratio in the injections of a group of subjects. In this way, he eliminated the narcotic they were receiving. However, Rubenstein reports only on a three-month follow-up for one addict. Long-term results were not reported.

Gotestam and Melin (1972) have extended extinction work in another direction: they have dealt with extinction of narcotic cravings through imagination. In their work, they asked clients to imagine their fixing ritual but not to imagine any rush or euphoria resulting. They recorded clients' pulse, respiration, and galvanic skin response. Each of these physiological measures de-

clined with repeated non-rewarded exposure in imagination. At four-month
follow-up, three of four clients were clean but no long-term follow-up was
reported.

Extinction seems to be a viable methodology to pursue in the treatment of
narcotic addiction. One means of pursuing extinction in narcotic addiction is
through a chemical blockade of the receptor sites. Let us now look at narcotic
antagonists—a class of drugs which accomplish just such a blockade.

Narcotic Antagonists: A Special Form of Extinction

Narcotic antagonists are a class of drugs which block the euphoric effects of
heroin, apparently by occupying the narcotic receptor sites in the brain.
Because the addict can inject narcotics and feel no euphoria, it was originally
hoped that narcotic antagonists would offer a naturalistic extinction of heroin
cravings; that is, cravings would occur and result in narcotic injection, but no
euphoria would ensue. By repeated, non-rewarded self-injections, it was
assumed that heroin would gradually lose its stimulus control (Wikler, 1976).

However, it has become apparent that few addicts experience cravings or
inject narcotics even once after beginning to take a narcotic antagonist (Altman, Meyer, Nivins et al., 1976; Callahan, Rawson, Glazer, McCleave, &
Arias, 1976; Hurzeler, Gewirtz, & Kleber, 1976; Greenstein, O'Brien,
Mintz, Woody, & Hanna, 1976). Instead, it appears that clients feel no urge to
use narcotics while on an antagonist blockade. While clients report that this is a
welcome experience, it means that no extinction of narcotic cravings can
occur. Just as Leitenberg, Rawson, and Bath (1969) discovered that a previously rewarded response must occur without reward for extinction to occur
(merely not engaging in a response does not diminish its strength), so must
heroin cravings occur and go unrewarded in order to decrease in strength.

In addition, a major clinical problem has existed with naltrexone: most
investigators (e.g., Hurzeler et al., 1976; Renault et al., 1976) have had
trouble persuading clients to try the drug and continue taking it. Since the drug
is non-addicting, some have despaired about its potential. While some dis-
couragement has been voiced, it may be that narcotic antagonists can find their
best efficacy in community-based programs using behavior modification. Let
us look now at behavior modification programs which have operated in the
natural environment.

Community Applications of Behavioral Engineering

Tharp and Wetzel (1969) unleashed a potent community force through their
work with juvenile delinquents in the community. In this work, the clinical

researchers focused on training mediators in the natural environment to bring about behavior change with the adolescents. By doing so, they avoided the problem of how to generalize treatment gains across environments (Stokes & Baer, 1976). Henry Boudin and his colleagues (Boudin, 1972; Boudin, Valentine, Ingraham, Brantley, Ruiz, Smith, Catlin, & Regan, 1977) followed a similar strategy in treating heroin addiction in the natural environment.

Working at the Drug Project in Gainesville, Florida, Boudin and his co-workers developed an effective treatment methodology using intensive behavioral analysis, self-observation, self-reporting, and behavior change principles. Their main clinical tool was a contigency contract; dependent measures for each individual were developed in an intensive, operant conditioning framework. It will be worthwhile to first look intensively at Boudin's model and then discuss its application to minority populations (Callahan et al., 1976; Rawson, Glazer, Callahan, & Liberman, 1979).

It appears that two clinical elements were most critical in the success of Boudin's project. First was his use of ideas of generating self-control. Kanfer (1973) describes the training of self-control as a three-stage process: first, accurate self-observation; second, self-evaluation; and third, programming behavior change. In this process, a person is asked to observe his or her own behavior to note the occurrence of functional patterns: target behaviors, antecedents, and consequences.

In the Boudin project, target behaviors were called "pin-points." Pinpoints included any covert or overt behavior which might be thought to trigger the use of heroin. For example, a person might be asked to observe his or her drinking pattern, to observe the number of "tokes" of marijuana taken, to observe arguments with a spouse, etc. Any of these pinpoints which might lead to the use of narcotics were targeted for self-observation. The self-control model is structured to allow a person to discover what antecedents reliably trigger heroin use and what consequences maintain it. This knowledge can be used clinically by an individual to change his or her own behavior. The next phase in self-control training, according to Kanfer, is self-evaluation.

In Boudin's work, self-evaluation was not used initially. Instead, the therapist took control of the evaluation process and determined which behavior should change. This was especially true for court referrals, with whom Boudin reported his greatest success (Boudin et al, 1977), and was most true for all clients in their earliest stages of treatment. Over a period of time, Boudin's clients earned more and more control of their therapeutic program. Gradually, they moved from total project-manager control to negotiated control to self-control along the lines of Homme's (1969) conceptualization of varying stages of contingency contracts: the first contingency contract signed involves total manager control; after success with these early contracts, negotiated contracts are developed between the therapist and the client; finally, self-control contracts are the ultimate therapeutic goal. The third stage of Kanfer's self-controlled treatment occurred only in the final stages of client involvement with the drug project. In this third and final stage of both programs, self-programming occurs. Ideally, at this end of the program the client should have the skills of behavior analyst. He or she ought to be able then to look at his or her own behavior, to understand what controls that behavior, to evaluate whether or not he or she wants to continue or to decrease the behavior, and finally to have tools to bring about such a change in the behavior successfully.

Over the course of this project, counselors moved away from the traditional one-to-one behavior therapies to the use of behavioral analysis and engineering. While this conceptual adjustment sounds fairly straightforward, the mechanism to administer the program was complex.

Each client was seen by a team of therapists, one of whom acted as client manager. All or all but one of the treatment team were volunteer paraprofessionals under the supervision of project staff. Pinpoints were reported to the staff through several phone calls a day at the start of treatment; the frequency of phone calls was gradually reduced with client compliance.

Phone calls, therapy, appointments, urine tests, and daily social structure training were covered in client contracts. In addition, it was emphasized to clients and staff that each urge to use heroin was a crisis and needed to be treated as such. The goal of the crisis intervention was not merely to avoid using heroin, but also to discover more about what triggers urges and what can be done to solve problems without using heroin.

In creating a project capable of teaching and applying behavior analysis this intensively in the natural environment, Boudin developed a complex and well-organized structure. The results of treatment probably have as much to do with that organization as they do with the contingency principles used in treatment. Both factors are further enhanced by the social relationship of clients to staff, but both the organizational structure and the interpersonal ambience of the project are more difficult to define and will not be dealt with further here.

Boudin et al., (1977) reported on four levels of adjustment post-treatment: (1) work/school performance; (2) personal/social adjustment; (3) incidence of drug intake; and (4) the frequency of arrests or convictions. These were measured by: (1) days worked or in school; (2) staff evaluation of client skill in dealing with crises; (3) urinalysis; and (4) agency records. They found positive adjustment in terms of work and school for 16 of 19 clients, positive social adjustment for 13 of 19, drug-free status for 12 of 19, and freedom from arrest or conviction for 15 of 19. Interestingly, 11 of the 19 clients terminated before the staff wanted them to; of these clients two had known negative outcomes and two were lost to follow-up. Seven of the 11 had positive outcome on adjustment variables.

Overall, then, the results from Boudin and his colleagues are very encouraging. The one criticism which might be made is that the clients were not representative of the usual addict population; despite the fact that most Gainesville addicts are black, the clients at the Drug Project were almost exclusively white. Can such a model work with minority addicts? Such a question was at hand as the Heroin Antagonist and Learning Therapy Project began in 1974 in Ventura County, California.

The HALT Project

Fueled by the practical success of the Drug Project's behavioral engineering and the theoretical promise of the narcotic antagonists, the Heroin Antagonist and Learning Therapy (HALT) Project was designed to compare the effectiveness of behavior therapy and narcotic antagonists alone and in combination. The target population was an addict community of Chicanos, blacks, and whites living in Ventura County, California. The county is a formerly agricultural, now industrialized area along the Pacific coast about 50 miles outside Los Angeles. It is known for the availability of smuggled brown (Mexican) heroin.

Each addict had to earn full client status (and services) at the project by fulfilling a probationary contract. This was done to provide a behavioral index of motivation instead of relying on verbal behavior. Over a two-year period, 181 potential clients came to the project to discuss entering treatment, 132 actually wrote a probation contract, and 58 succeeded in that contract. Clients entering the naltrexone alone treatment group were more successful in earning full client status (53%) than were the combined treatment clients (44%) or the behavior therapy clients (34%). This indicated a significant difference between success of entry rates for the naltrexone-only condition and the behavior therapy alone condition (Rawson et al., 1979).

Once in treatment, clients receiving naltrexone remained in treatment nearly twice as long as did clients in the behavior therapy alone group. Naltrexone clients stayed a mean of 29.6 weeks, combined treatment clients stayed 29.1 weeks, and behavior therapy clients remained in treatment 16.1 weeks. This meant that there was a significantly better treatment maintenance record for those receiving naltrexone. On the other process measures, naltrexone-taking clients also outperformed the behavior therapy alone clients. For example, they completed a higher percentage of assignments and provided fewer dirty urines. Thus naltrexone appeared more effective on process measures than behavior therapy.

Interestingly, at first evaluation, the combined treatment was more effective in maintaining clients in the program than the naltrexone alone condition. Eighteen months after the project's beginning, combined clients were taking naltrexone for an average of 88 days versus 43 days for naltrexone alone clients (Callahan et al., 1976). By the close of the project, naltrexone clients stayed on the drug an average of 165 days versus 184 days for combined clients. Thus, the data show less measurable effect due to behavior therapy across time. The comparative data across clinics (e.g., Greenstein et al., 1976; Kleber et al., 1976) showed that the combined treatment was successful in keeping clients in treatment longer than naltrexone treatment at other clinics. Perhaps the crucial factor was establishing credibility for naltrexone: in early client interactions, the increased contact time between staff and client may have helped maintain client participation. Over a period of time, the drug's history became better known on the "street" and less feared. Ironically, this rise in the popularity of naltrexone may have contributed to the demise of behavior therapy at the Project. Clients expressed the desire to take naltrexone on entering the Project and were often disappointed when randomly assigned to the behavior therapy alone condition. Behavior therapy maintenance was best for women clients who were not allowed to receive naltrexone by federal regulations.

Urine data show another problem with the behavior therapy condition: slipping back into use and readdiction is probable during behavior therapy treatment but not in naltrexone treatment. Seventy-two percent of the urines given during behavior therapy treatment were clean versus 94% of urines given by the naltrexone groups. At one-year follow-up, four of 14 behavior therapy clients were opiate-free, as were ten of 20 naltrexone clients and eight of 15 combined clients. Thus naltrexone proved to be a useful tool in treatment of addiction, while behavior tharapy alone proved to be disappointing.

It should be pointed out, however, that the naltrexone alone group had access to an employment interviewing training program contingent upon providing clean urines and taking naltrexone. While this is not "therapy," it may be the most critical life skill any addict needs: the single best predictor of therapeutic success in treatment of narcotic addiction is work history (Kramer, 1965). Since the number of addicts is so great and treatment seems still fairly ineffective, it may be worthwhile to consider alternatives such as prevention.

Prevention

One of the more interesting laboratory behaviors studied in the past 20 years has been adjunctive behaviors (Falk, 1961). These are high-frequency behaviors which an animal will engage in despite the fact that they are toxic to the animal. In this sense, adjunctive behaviors may be a laboratory model of addictive behaviors. It may be possible to use an adjunctive behavior model to prevent addiction.

There appear to be four requirements for the occurrence of adjunctive behaviors (Callahan, Cross, & Schmid, n.p.): (1) deprivation of a significant reinforcer; (2) a demanding schedule for obtaining reward; (3) a restricted environment; and (4) access to materials for the adjunctive behavior. In the case of addiction, monetary and job availability appear to be common reinforcers to which addicts have little access. Minority wage levels and unemployment make the attainment of those rewards difficult (Callahan & Rawson, 1980); the addicts tend to live in ghetto environments, close to large cities with easily available narcotics.

While attempts to restrict drug availability (4) have failed badly (e.g., Operation Intercept, 1972), relocating (3) has helped individuals kick addictions. The most critical factors may be deprivation (1) and reward schedule (2). For these issues, minorities need better education and job training. High-risk areas for addiction might well use federal programs more profitably for job training than treatment programs for addiction. This is, however, one area in which treatment and prevention go closely together. Access to job training and educational opportunities can serve the purposes of (1) shaping pro-social behavior and (2) facilitating the creation of a new peer group.

Conclusion

Treatment of narcotic addiction in the U.S. has undergone rapid change in mood and content over the past 100 years. In mood, the addict has been seen as benign (e.g., 1800s grandmother), alien (Chinese laborers in San Francisco), medically ill, mentally ill, and/or dangerous. Content of treatment has ranged from drying out to chemical substitution to radical personality change to working with client assets and deficits. The single consistency perhaps is the usual persistence of the desire to use narcotics.

While medical treatments alone appear ineffective, behavior management strategies appear to have improved the efficacy of some medical techniques. Behavior strategies administered purely and intensively have been successful in working on a single-case basis with addicts with few other deficits. They have even worked quite well in creative application in a large-scale study targeting white middle class addicts. They have yet to be shown useful alone with minority populations. In conjunction with narcotic antagonists, behavioral techniques have worked in minority populations, however.

Substantial work remains to be done in developing adequate treatment programming for culturally deprived addict populations. Well-controlled research needs are as great as the continuing need for well-defined and effective treatment programming.

References

Altman, J. L., Meyer, R. E., & Nivins, S. M. Opiate antagonists and the modification of heroin self-administration in man. *International Journal of the Addictions*, 1976, **11**, 485-500.

Anant, S. S. Treatment of alcoholics and drug addicts by verbal aversion techniques. *The International Journal of Addictions*, 1968, **3**, 381-388.

Ausubel, D. P. Causes and types of narcotic addiction: A psychosocial view. *Psychiatric Quarterly*, 1961, **35**, 523-531.

Babor , T. F., Meyer, R. E., Mirin, S. M., McNamee, H. B., & Davies, M. Behavioral and social effects of heroin self-administration and withdrawal. *Archives of General Psychiatry*, 1976, **33**, 363-367.

Ball, J. C., Thompson, W. O., & Allen, D. M. Readmission rates at Lexington Hospital for 43,215 narcotic drug addicts. *Public Health Reports*, 1970, **85**, 610-616.

Boudin, H. M. Contingency contracting as a therapeutic tool in the deceleration of amphetamine use. *Behavior Therapy*, 1972, **3**, 604-605.

Boudin, H. M., Valentine, V. E., Ingraham, R. D., Brantley, J. M., Ruiz, M. R., Smith, G. G., Catlin, R. P., & Regan, E. J. Contingency contracting with drug abusers in the natural environment. *The International Journal of the Addictions*, 1977, **12**, 1-16.

Bowden, C. L. & Maddox, J. F. Methadone maintenance: Myth and reality. *American Journal of Psychiatry*, 1972, **128**, 853-856.

Brecher, E. M., *et al.* (Ed.), *Licit and illicit drugs*, Toronto: Little, Brown and Company, 1972.

Bridell, D. W. & Nathan, P. E. Behavioral assessment and modification with alcoholics: Current status and future trends. In M. Hersen, P. Miller, & R. Eisler (Eds.), *Progress in Behavior Modification, Vol. 2.* New York: Academic Press, 1976.

Cahoon, D. D. & Crosby, C. C. A learning approach to chronic drug use: Sources of reinforcement. *Behavior Therapy*, 1972, **3**, 64-71.

Callahan, E. J., Cross, J. & Schmid, T. Adjunctive behaviors and addictions: Parallels and applications to prevention. Manuscript under editorial consideration.

Callahan, E. J., Dahlkoetter, J., & Price, K. A. Drug Abuse. In R. Daitzman (Ed.), *Clinical behavior therapy and behavior modification.* Vol. 1. 1980.

Callahan, E. J. & Rawson, R. A. Behavioral assessment of narcotic addiction and treatment outcome. In L. C. Sobell & M. B. Sobell (Eds.), *Treatment outcome evaluation in alcohol and drug abuse.* New York: Plenum Press, 1980.

Callahan, E. J., Rawson, R. A. Arias, R. J., Glazer, M. A., Liberman, R. P., & McCleave, B. A. Treatment of heroin addiction: Naltrexone alone and with behavior therapy. *International Journal of the Addictions*, in press.

Callahan, E. J., Rawson, R. A., Glazer, M., McCleaver, B. A., & Arias, R. Comparison to two naltrexone treatment programs: Naltrexone alone versus naltrexone plus behavior therapy. In D. Julius & P. Renault (Eds.), *Narcotic antagonists: Naltrexone.* Washington, D. C.: NIDA Research Monograph, 1976, 150-157.

Dole, V. P. & Nyswander, M. A. Medical treatment for diacetyl morphine (heroin) addiction. *Journal of the American Medical Association*, 1965, **193**, 645-656.

Falk, J. L. The nature and determinants of adjunctive behavior. In R. M. Gilbert & J. D. Keehn (Eds.), *Schedule effects: Drugs, drinking and aggression.* Toronto: University of Toronto Press, 1972.

Falk, J. L. & Samson, H. H. Schedule-induced physical dependence on ethanol. *Psychoparmacological Reviews*, 1976, **27**, 449-464.

Glasscote, R. M. *The treatment of drug abuse: Programs, problems and prospects.* Washington, D.C.: NIMH, 1972.

Glasscote, R. M., et al. *The treatment of drug abuse: Programs, problems, prospects.* Washington: Joint Information Services of the American Psychiatric Association and the National Association for Mental Health, 1972.

Goldstein, A. & Cox, B. M. Opioid peptides (endorphins) in pituitary and brain. *Psychoneroendocrinology*, 1977, **2**, 11-16.

Gooberman, L. A. *Operation intercept.* Elmsford, New York: Pergamon Press, 1974.

Gotestam, K. G. & Melin, L. Covert extinction of amphetamine addiction. *Behavior Therapy*, 1974, **5** (1), 90-92.

Griffith, J. D. Fann, E. W., & Tapp, J. Drug-seeking behavior of hospitalized drug addicts. Cited in S. M. Mirin, R. E. Meyer, & H. B. McNamee. Psychopathology and mood during heroin use. *Archives of General Psychiatry*, 1976, **33**, 1503-1508.

Haertzen, C. A. & Hooks, N. T. Changes in personality and subjective experience associated with the chronic administration and withdrawal of opiates. *Journal of Mental Disease*, 1969, **148**, 606-613.

Jasinski, D. R., Martin, W. R., & Haertzen, C. A. The human pharmacology and abuse potential of n-ally inoroxymorphone (naltrexone). *Journal of Pharmacology and Therapy*, 1967, **157**, 420-426.

Kanfer, F. H. & Saslow, G. Behavioral diagnosis. In C. Frank (Ed.), *Assessment and status of the behavior therapies.* New York: McGraw-Hill, 1969.

Kolvin, I. 'Aversive imagery' treatment in adolescents. *Behavior Research and Therapy*, 1967, **5**, 245-248.

Kraft, T. Successful treatment of a case of chronic barbituate addiction. *British Journal of Addictions.* 1969, **64**, 115-120.

Kraft, T. Treatment of drinamyl addiction. *The International Journal of the Addictions*, 1969, **4**, 59-64.

Liberman, R. Aversive conditioning of drug addicts: A pilot study. *Behavior Research and Therapy*, 1968, **6**, 229-231.

MacDonough, T. S. The relative effectiveness of a medical hospitalization program versus a feedback behavior modification program in treating alcohol and drug abusers. *International Journal of the Addictions*, 1976, **11**, 269-282.

Maddox, J. F. & Desmond, D. P. Reliability and validity of information from chronic heroin users. *Journal of Psychiatric Research*, 1975, **12**, 95-97.

Martin, W. R. & Jasinski, D. R. Physiological parameters of morphine dependence in man: Tolerance, early abstinence, protracted abstinence. *Journal of Psychiatric Research*, 1969, **7**, 9-17.

Maurer, D. W. & Vogel, V. H. *Narcotics and narcotic addiction.* Springfield, Ill.: C. C. Thomas, 1974.

McNamee, H. B., Mirin, S. M., Kuehnie, J. C., & Meyer, R. E. Effective changes in chronic opiate use. *British Journal of Addiction*, 1976, **3**, 275-280.

Mello, N. K. & Mendelson, J. H. Operant analysis of drinking patterns in chronic alcoholics. *Nature*, 1965, **206**, 43-46.

Meyer, R. E., Mirin, S. M., Altman, J. L., & McNamee, B. A behavioral paradigm for the evaluation of narcotic antagonists. *Archives of General Psychiatry*, 1976, **3**, 371-377.

Mirin, S. M., Meyer, R. E. & McNamee, B. Psychopathology and mood during heroin use: Acute chronic effects. *Archives of General Psychiatry*, 1976, **33**, 1503-1508.

Nightingale, S., Michaux, W. W., & Platt, P. C. Clinical implications of urine surveillance in a methadone maintenance program. *International Journal of the Addictions*, 1972, **7**, 403-414.

Nurnberger, J. I. & Zimmerman, J. Applied analysis of human behavior: An alternative to conventional motivational inferences and unconscious determination in therapeutic programming. *Behavior Therapy*, 1907, **1**, 59-60.

O'Brien, C. P. "Needle Freaks"—psychological dependence on shooting up. *Medical World News Review*, 1974, **1**, 35-36.

Platt, J. J., & Labate, C. *Heroin addiction: Theory research and treatment*. New York: Wiley, 1976.

Schaefer, H. H., Sobell, M. B., & Mills, K. C. Baseline drinking behaviors in alcoholics and social drinkers: Kinds of sips and sip magnitude. *Behavior Research and Therapy*, 1971, **9**, 23-27.

Scott, D. & Goldberg, H. L. The phenomenon of self-perpetuation in Synanon-type drug treatment programs. *Hospital and Community Psychiatry*, 1973, **24**, 231-233.

Sobell, L. C. Critique of alcoholism treatment evaluation, In G. A. Marlatt & P. E. Nathan (Eds.), *Behavioral approaches to alcoholism*. New Brunswick, N.J.: Rutgers Press, 1978.

Stachnik, T. J. The case against criminal penalties for illicit drug use. *American Psychologist*, 1972, **27**, 637-642.

Stanton, M. D. Family treatment approaches to drug abuse problems: A review. *Family Processes*, 1979, **18**, 252-280.

Stitzer, M., Bigelow, G., Lawrence, L., Cohen, J., D'Lugoff, B., & Hawthorne, J. Medication take home as a reinforcer. *Addictive Behaviors*, 1977, **2**, 9-14.

Sulkunen, P. Production, consumption, and recent changes of consumption of alcoholic beverages. *British Journal of the Addictions*. 1976, **71**, 3-11.

Switzer, A. *Drug abuse and drug treatment*. Sacramento, California Youth Authority, 1974.

Szasz, T. The ethics of addictions. In W. White and R. F. Albano (Eds.), *North American Symposium on Drug Abuse*. Philadelphia: North American Publishing, 1975, 105-111.

Tharp, R. G., & Wetzel, R. J. *Behavior modification in the natural environment*. New York: Academic Press, 1969.

Thomson, I. G. & Rathod, N. H. Aversion therapy for heroin dependence. *The Lancet*, 1968, **2**, 382-384.

Trueblood, B., Judson, B., & Goldstein, A. Acceptability of levo-alpha-acetylmethadyl acetate (LAAM) as compared with methadone in a treatment program for heroin addicts. *Drug and Alcohol Dependence*, 1978, **3**, 125-132.

Vaillant, G. E. A twelve-year follow-up of New York narcotic addicts: I. The relation of treatment to outcome. *American Journal of Psychiatry*, 1966, **122**, 717-737.

Wallace, C. The effects of delayed rewards, social pressure, and frustration on the responses of opiate addicts. In N. Krasnegor (Ed.), Behavioral analysis and treatment of substance abuse. NIDA Research Monograph #25. Washington, D.C.: U.S. Government Printing Office, 1979, pp. 6-25.

Wikler, A. A psychodynamic study of a patient during experimental self-regulated readdiction to morphine. *Psychiatric Quarterly*, 1952, **26**, 270-293.

Wikler, A. Conditioning factors in opiate addiction. In L. Wilner & W. Kasselbaum (Eds.), *Narcotics*. New York: McGraw-Hill, 1965.

Wikler, A. *Opiate addiction and neurophysical aspects.* Springfield, Illinois: Thomas, 1953.

Wikler, A. Dynamics of drug dependence: Implications of a conditioning theory for research and treatment. In S. Fischer & A. M. Freedman (Eds.), *Opiate addiction: Origins and treatment.* New York: Wiley, 1973, 7-22.

Winick, C. Maturing out of narcotic addiction. *Bulletin on Narcotics,* 1962, **14,** 1-7.

World Health Organization. Expert Committee on Addiction-Producing Drugs. Geneva: W.H.O. Technical Report Series # 273, 1964.

Yablonsky, L. *The tunnel back.* New York: Macmillan, 1965.

4

Smoking Cessation Methods: Review and Recommendations

Edward Lichtenstein and Richard A. Brown

Department of Psychology
University of Oregon
Eugene, Oregon 97403

Cigarette smoking is the largest preventable cause of death in America. Each year, there are 80,000 deaths from lung cancer, 22,000 deaths from other cancers, up to 225,000 deaths from cardiovascular disease, and more than 19,000 deaths from pulmonary disease, all related to cigarette smoking. The annual cost of health damage resulting from smoking is estimated to be $27 billion in medical care, absenteeism, decreased work productivity, and accidents. Compared to nonsmokers, smokers compile 81 million excess days of lost work each year and 145 million excess days of disability. A 30- to 35-year-old two-pack-a-day smoker has a mortality rate twice that of a nonsmoker. These facts compiled in the most recent report of the Surgeon General

(USDHEW, 1979) provide powerful reasons for the development and delivery of effective and economical smoking control programs to citizens.

The information on the health consequences of smoking has had some notable effects upon the public. It is estimated that about 30 million people have quit smoking since 1964 when the first Surgeon General's report was published. Approximately 33% of the adult population in the United States now smokes and this is the lowest figure in recent years. On the other hand, this 33% represents about 54 million adult smokers, and the incidence of smoking among teenage women is on the rise as women achieve equality in the smoking realm (USDHEW, 1979).

There is also evidence that the data on health consequences of smoking have affected the attitudes of those who continue to smoke. Survey data indicate that about half of the current smokers want to quit and have tried to do so without success (Gallup Opinion Index, 1974). In a more recent survey, 61% of current smokers report making at least one serious attempt to quit, and this survey estimated that 90% of current smokers have either made an effort to stop smoking or would do so were an easy method available (USPHS, 1976). In summary, smoking is demonstrably a very serious health risk. Most people who smoke are aware of the dangers and would be disposed to try to stop if effective and efficient help were available. This situation presents a great opportunity and challenge for health and mental health professionals.

This chapter presents an overview of research on cessation with specific recommendations for practice based on favorable research and clinical experience. The chapter begins with an analysis of why it is so difficult for so many people to stop smoking. A "state-of-the-art" overview of various smoking control methods is then presented, followed by a brief description of the various levels of intervention available to the health professional. The bulk of the chapter centers around selecting the basic components of a treatment program. Three interrelated stages—preparation, quitting, and maintenance—are discussed and specific recommendations for practice are offered. The chapter concludes with a discussion of evaluation and some miscellaneous practical matters.

Why Is It So Difficult for So Many To Stop?

It is useful to consider the natural history of cigarette smoking. Table 4.1 is adapted from Danaher and Lichtenstein (1978). There are four stages in the course of a smoker's career. Initiation, maintenance, and cessation are the standard three and resumption or relapse has been added because it is such a frequent occurrence. Listed are the main factors thought to be involved in each of the stages. Some factors are more strongly supported by data, others are more speculative; some are inferred from correlational data, some from experimental manipulations. It can be seen that psychosocial factors are the determinants of starting to smoke. The pharmachological effects of nicotine,

Table 4.1.   The Natural History of Smoking

Starting →	Continuing →	Stopping →	Resuming
Availability	Nicotine	Health	Stress
Curiosity	Immediate positive consequences	Expense	Social pressure
Rebelliousness	Signals (cues) in environs	Social pressure	Abstinence violation effect
Anticipation of adulthood	Avoiding negative effects (withdrawal)	Self-mastery	Alcohol consumption
Social confidence		Aesthetics	
Modeling: peers, siblings, parents		Example to others	
Psychosocial	Physiological + psychosocial	Psychosocial	Psychosocial

however, are crucial in the continuation of smoking, along with learned psychosocial factors. The decision to quit and success in so doing is again largely a psychosocial matter. The resumption of smoking, or relapse, is a phenomenon about which we know relatively little, but it appears that stress, social pressure, and the abstinence violation effect (discussed below and in the chapter by Cummings, Gordon, and Marlatt) are key factors.

It is very difficult to quit smoking, but just how difficult cannot be precisely stated. British data indicate that only one in four smokers succeeds in stopping permanently before the age of 60 (Lee, 1976). United States data indicate that the majority of smokers wish that they could quit (USPHS, 1976). More information is available on cessation rates for persons seeking help from smoking control programs. It is likely that program participants are the more "difficult" cases. Most help-seekers at smoking clinics have made one or more serious efforts to stop smoking on their own or with the help of other programs.

The figure shown here (from Hunt and Bespalec, 1974) summarizes results from 89 varied smoking control studies. Although now somewhat dated, this figure is still representative. It should be emphasized that the abstinence figure and the percent of baseline figure shown are based only on participants who were abstinent at termination. Since many participants either drop out of programs or complete them but remain smoking at reduced levels, and since relapse is highly probable for these individuals, this figure is a very conservative estimate of relapse. More realistically, it appears that at six months or one

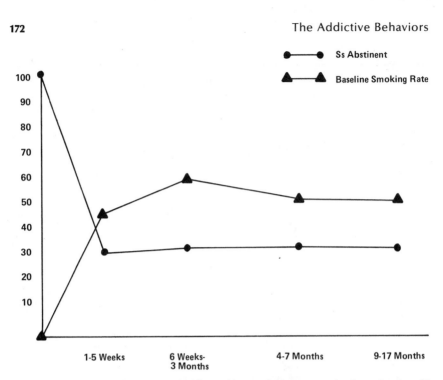

Fig. 4.1. Followup smoking status of subjects who were abstinent at termination, taken from 89 studies (adapted and reprinted from Hunt and Bespalec, 1974).

year after followup, the average participant in the average smoking control program has a 15 to 20% chance of being abstinent. More successful programs report abstinence rates of 30 to 40%. Anything better than that is very good indeed.

A more detailed description of the factors maintaining smoking can deepen one's appreciation of the tenacity of the behavior. Such an appreciation is critical for the design of effective programs, and can suggest realistic expectations for program outcomes.

1. Smoking delivers nicotine to the brain very quickly, in about seven seconds. Much convergent evidence indicates that nicotine is a powerful primary reinforcer (Russell, 1976). Many smokers, especially heavy smokers, appear to smoke in such a way as to regulate their dosage of nicotine (Schachter, 1977, 1978). While the data do not yet show that nicotine is the necessary and sufficient factor in accounting for smoking behavior, there is no doubt that it is a strong factor for many persons.

2. A second consideration is that smoking is possible under a wide variety of circumstances and settings. These numerous settings become signals to smoke, and often later come to serve as learned rewards for smoking. Situations in which smoking occurs repeatedly, such as when drinking coffee or beer, or conversing with another smoker, come to serve as

signals to smoke. An urge is subjectively experienced when these situations are encountered. Smoking then comes to be rewarded by the enjoyment of oral, manual, and respiratory manipulations involved in the process of lighting, puffing, and handling cigarettes, the pleasure and relaxation associated with using alcohol, finishing a good meal, or having a cup of coffee, and the perceived diminution of unpleasant affective states of anxiety, tension, boredom, or fatigue. For some smokers, the combination of nicotine and psychosocial learning produces a dependency such that going without a cigarette is highly unpleasant. Smoking is then further rewarded by the reduction of withdrawal or anticipated withdrawal reactions. Learning of this sort makes it possible for the same smoker to reach for a cigarette when relaxed and enjoying himself, bored, tense, upset, tired, or in need of a lift. No other substance can provide so many kinds of rewards, is so readily and cheaply available, and can be used in so many settings and situations.

3. While there are numerous immediate positive rewards, the negative consequences are delayed and probabilistic.
4. Another significant factor in the tenacity of the smoking habit is sheer number of trials, or practice. Twenty cigarettes a day adds up to about 7,300 cigarettes a year. Each trial, in fact, each puff, is an occasion for experiencing one or more of the rewards just noted.
5. A fifth factor is the encouragement and modeling of smoking provided by the environment in the form of other smokers as well as cigarette advertising.

In sum, cigarette smoking is a highly practiced, overlearned behavior rewarded by both physiological events and a wide variety of psychosocial events. It is cued by a large array of environmental and internal stimuli, is socially and legally acceptable in most settings, has immediate positive effects, and few if any immediate negative consequences.

The preceding discussion is not meant to be discouraging, but instead to provide realistic expectations for cessation programs. There is not yet a ''strong'' technology for smoking intervention, but we believe that we have not applied what we do know in the most effective and efficient manner.

Levels of Intervention

Smoking cessation programs can be mounted at various levels of intensity and cost. These levels include: (a) community wide approaches—low cost efforts such as media campaigns to stop smoking, materials such as I-Quit-Kits, self-help books (e.g. Danaher & Lichtenstein, 1978; Pomerleau & Pomerleau, 1977), or tapes; (b) standardized group approaches for those needing a structured program—these include time-limited group programs, often operated by volunteers, such as the Five Day Plan, or Cancer Society programs; and (c) intensive programs—individual counseling or ongoing group programs for those not profiting from the others or in need of extended treatment because of smoking related illness. Programs with high fees or requiring much professional time to implement would be considered intensive. Interventions at each level should be coordinated to minimize costs and competition, and evaluation should be an integral component.

Besides these levels of intervention, smoking cessation workers should give particular attention to three settings: schools, the work place, and health care settings. School settings are appropriate for primary and secondary prevention efforts. Because our focus is on cessation, we will not pursue this topic. Both work and health care settings have features which may maximize the impact of cessation programs. The work setting affords opportunities for group support or social pressure, for integrating educational and motivational components, and for utilizing economic incentives. For example, small bonuses could be offered for smoking reduction or cessation (Rosen & Lichtenstein, 1977). Health care settings arouse the smoker's concern about health consequences, and health care personnel, such as physicians and nurses, are prestigious influence sources.

State-Of-The-Art of Current Cessation Methods

Many different methods have been used to help people stop smoking. Below we offer evaluative overviews of the major approaches. Our review is brief because more detailed and analytic reviews are available elsewhere (e.g. Lichtenstein & Danaher, 1976; Bernstein & McAlister, 1976; Bernstein & Glasgow, 1979; Pechacek, 1979) and because we focus on practical recommendations. The smoking control methods that are described fall along different points of the levels-of-intervention continuum. Our recommendations for practice, however, are mostly aimed at level (b), more-or-less standardized programs for groups.

Hypnosis

Many persons perceive hypnosis as an effortless way to change behavior. The literature on hypnosis in smoking contains case reports and uncontrolled studies, some of them reporting to be quite successful, but there is no controlled research on effectiveness, especially comparing hypnosis with other alternative interventions (Danaher & Lichtenstein, 1978). The procedures used in hypnosis intervention for smoking—for example, linking unpleasant images with the smoking chain, relaxation and self-instruction—are similar to those used in many behavioral interventions. Katz (in press) has recently reviewed applications of hypnosis in smoking cessation.

Hypnosis is best viewed as a clinical tool and may be useful with smoking if used by a skilled practitioner. Since it requires both individual attention and a skilled practitioner, hypnotic treatment is likely to be expensive and unsuitable for large-scale dissemination.

Drugs

Like hypnosis, drugs are often also viewed as a surrogate for motivation and effort. Tranquilizing drugs are sometimes used to ease withdrawal difficulties, but no evidence is available on their effectiveness in so doing. Nicotine mimetics (e.g., lobeline) purport to mimic the effects of nicotine, thereby reducing the need for it. Products containing such drugs have been sold ''over the counter'' for years and have been found to be no more effective than placebo (Davison & Rosen, 1972). A new and possibly promising development—but one thus far confined to Europe—involves directly replacing nicotine either by means of nicotine aerosol sprays or more commonly by means of nicotine chewing gum. The use of nicotine chewing gum seems quite consistent with accounts of smoking that emphasize the regulation of nicotine dosage by smokers. Several studies have been reported evaluating nicotine chewing gum and the results seem promising, though equivocal (Bernstein & Glasgow, 1979). There are side effects and there is also concern about a person's overdosing with nicotine, which is, of course, a poison. Caution over these matters has restricted the use of nicotine chewing gum and it is still currently illegal in the United States. The possibility remains for the future that nicotine chewing gum might be marketed either by prescription or over the counter. It could permit some people to at least control or reduce their habit. For smokers at high risk or already symptomatic with smoking-related illness, but who are unable to stop, this could be an important benefit.

Commercial Programs

As the tobacco companies have known for years, there's money in cigarette smoking and perhaps in smoking cessation as well. The two most widely known commercial programs are SmokEnders and the Schick Centers. SmokEnders appears to have been the more open of the two to assessment and evaluation. One study found that 39% of those contacted four years after treatment, and who had been abstinent at termination, were not smoking (Kanzler, Jaffe, & Zeidenberg, 1976). The Schick program emphasizes aversion—primarily electric shock but also, at times, rapid smoking—together with a mix of reasonable suggestions and advice. Individual attention and support from a counselor is also a feature of the Schick program, whereas SmokEnders operates in groups. The high fees (as much as $250 for SmokEnders, $495 for Schick) which must engender a lot of motivation are undoubtedly an important factor in the commercial programs. They seem best viewed as providing intensive, but expensive help for those who can afford them.

Clinics

Smoking clinics provide some combination of health information, encouragement, group therapy, moral support, social pressure, and suggestions for resisting temptations to smoke. Specific treatment techniques and number and length of meetings vary considerably across clinics. Most involve groups of smokers coming together to receive help and to help each other.

Clinics generally have a service mission and have not been subjected to careful evaluation. Most clinics find it easy to educate and persuade smokers into quitting by the end of the clinic program. But follow-up success rates—counting *all* those who started out—though varying widely, tend to be in the 20% range (Schwartz, 1979). Clinics, however, are efficient because they treat groups of smokers and are often available at nominal cost to participants. The best known and most widely available clinic is the "Five Day Plan" program sponsored by the Seventh Day Adventist Church. Clinics remain an attractive medium for disseminating new knowledge about smoking control. Their efficiency might be improved by incorporating recent developments in smoking cessation research.

Physicians' Influences (Health Care Settings)

Effectiveness of physicians' influences has been studied both with symptomatic patients, especially myocardial infarction, and patients with no presenting complaints. Lichtenstein and Danaher (1978) have recently reviewed this literature. The success rates for physicians appear to be related to the patients' perceived level of personal risk as determined by the severity of the physical symptoms produced by smoking (e.g., a heart attack) and the intensiveness of the intervention. It is not possible to draw any clear conclusions about the clinical utility of physician admonition because of the methodology and the inadequate number of available reports cited. Tentatively, it appears that, compared to other methods reviewed, physician influence attempts have been economical and relatively effective. This conclusion is supported by the findings of a recent British study which showed that brief, simple advice to quit by a physician was significantly effective compared to a non-advised control group (Russell, 1979).

Communitywide Approaches

Only a few such efforts have been evaluated in any systematic way. In the Stanford Heart Disease Prevention Project, face-to-face counseling was needed to augment mass media presentations in order to attain smoking reduction (Farquar, Maccoby, Wood, Alexander, Breitrose, Brown, Haskell, McAlister, Meyer, Nash, & Stern, 1977). Although the data are equivocal, mass media interventions represent an attractive and economical component of a smoking control intervention. By itself, media presented information is probably of little value, but it may be an important backdrop or adjunct to other interventions (McAlister, 1979).

The Social Learning Approach

The final smoking cessation approach, social learning, is the one we think is most promising and applicable. It provides the framework for recommendations on implementing smoking cessation programs and so is reviewed in much more detail than the others.

Social learning theory can be viewed as a broadening of behavior modification to include modeling and other cognitive processes (Bandura, 1977). From the social learning perspective, smoking is a learned behavior maintained by observable environmental events, including those within the body, which elicit it and by those which it produces. It is the focus on observable antecedents and consequences of smoking and explicit attempts to manipulate these in order to control the behavior that characterize the social learning approach.

Covert events—thoughts, feelings, mood states—are readily incorporated within this framework, providing that they can be reliably self-monitored by the smoker. The modeling of smoking provided by other smokers (Antonuccio & Lichtenstein, in press), as well as by media advertising by cigarette companies, is also subsumed within the social learning model.

The view of smoking proposed here emphasizes the environmental conditions which maintain the smoking habit. Smoking does not occur in isolation, but is typically one component in a "behavioral chain"—antecedent-behavior-consequence. Antecedents, both external and internal cues, precede the behavior of smoking, and serve as "signals" leading to the smoking act. Consequences which follow or accompany smoking are also of both the external and internal variety, and serve to either reward or punish the act of smoking. Unfortunately, the rewards which reinforce the smoking act tend to be the more immediate consequences (i.e., feelings of pleasure, tension reduction), whereas the negative consequences, most notably the serious hazards to one's health, tend to be delayed. One particularly salient reinforcer is the drug nicotine, whose important role was noted above.

As can be seen in table 4.2, cigarette smoking behavior is surrounded by a multiplicity of environmental events. The wide variety of antecedents and consequences, both internal and external, serve to maintain the habit. Treatment involves the systematic identification and manipulation of these antecedents and consequences. Since the variables that originally "caused" smoking are probably not the ones now maintaining it, a focus on the current maintaining factors is best.

A variety of strategies and tactics have been derived from the social learning perspective. Social learning based programs have been investigated more

Table 4.2. Some Environmental Factors Involved in Cigarette Smoking

	Antecedents	Consequences	
		Positive	Negative
Internal Events	feeling tense, anxious being bored experiencing an urge to smoke thinking about smoking trying to concentrate feeling happy, cheerful feeling hungry feeling tired feeling angry, irritable	pleasure tension reduction increased sense of comfort stimulation—getting a "lift" relaxation increased feeling of being able to "cope" reduction or elimination of withdrawal symptoms	guilt negative attributions- ("I'm weak, lacking in willpower")
External Events	drinking coffee finishing a meal driving in a car watching TV seeing others smoking drinking a beer or cocktail talking on the phone reading a book waiting for a person or an appointment waking up in the morning	social approval handling of cigarette	health hazards cough dry throat social disapproval less money (cost of cigarettes) burn marks in clothing, furniture stained fingers

extensively than any other approach to smoking control. The outcome data on many of these programs have been equivocal, but two kinds of programs have yielded good outcomes on sufficient occasions and in various settings so as to warrant both optimism and practical application. One is an aversion strategy—rapid smoking—discussed below. The second is the multicomponent program emphasizing application of self-management strategies in the natural environment (Bernstein & Glasgow, 1979: Danaher & Lichtenstein, 1978).

Both the research literature and our own experience leads us to recommend the multicomponent approach. Aversion strategies are usually more costly and cumbersome to implement and they may have undesirable side effects. Some aversive methods can still be useful in promoting quitting within the frame of multicomponent programs.

Research on multicomponent treatment programs has proliferated in the hope that individual procedures will combine to form a more powerful and comprehensive program. Some multicomponent programs have focused entirely upon self-management strategies. Of these, a few have met with success (e.g. Brengelmann & Sedlmayr, 1977), while others have failed to demon-strate long-term treatment effects (Brockway, Kleinmann, Edleson, & Gruenewald, 1977; Pechacek, 1976). Other programs have combined ele-ments of aversion therapy and self-management. These programs have been more notable in their successes (Best, Owen, & Trentadue, 1978; Delahunt & Curran, 1976; Lando, 1977), although this has not always been the case (Danaher, 1977a; Flaxman, 1978; Glasgow, 1978).

Putting Together a Multicomponent Program

It is useful to think of multicomponent cessation programs as comprised of three interrelated phases: preparing to quit, quitting, and maintenance. They are interrelated in the sense that they overlap in time; maintenance strategies may be presented prior to quitting, and some principles and methods are useful in more than one phase. The discussion of each phase will include a summary of the research literature on various strategies and methods as well as our own recommendations for clinical application.

Preparing to Quit

Some programs (e.g., the Five Day Plan) urge participants to quit im-mediately. We recommend, however, that there be a "preparation" period to quitting, the length of which can vary according to program needs. There are three key objectives for the preparation period. First, there should be a clearly established target quit date that allows participants to "mentally prepare" to quit smoking. Second, participants should self-monitor their smoking in order to establish baseline levels and to begin to learn about smoking signals and consequences. Third, the participants' motivation to quit and commitment to the program must be reviewed and strengthened.

The Importance of a Target Quit Date

We strongly recommend the establishment of a target quit date at the very beginning of a program. Just when this quit date is to occur will vary according to the schedule of meetings and the nature of the program. The critical issue is that there be a clearly established quit time which the participants can work toward. The target quit date should allow time for clients to be prepared to cope with quitting. That is, there should be sufficient time to provide some mainte-nance skills prior to the target quit date. It is possible to build in some degree of reduction of smoking prior to the quit date, but this reduction should generally not be lower than 50% of baseline or about 12 cigarettes a day, whichever is lower. Reductions below this point are likely to be counterproductive (Levin-son, Shapiro, Schwartz & Tursky, 1971).

Self-Monitoring

Self-monitoring is a standard procedure in social learning oriented treatment programs for addictive behaviors. In order to obtain baseline data, clients continue their usual smoking habits and tally each cigarette smoked for a minimum of three days and preferably a week. Self-monitoring should then continue throughout the treatment program as a way of tracking progress. The use of a simple sheet or card which can be attached to the cigarette pack will facilitate the recording. Each cigarette can also be tallied according to the time of day during which it is smoked. By noting the time of day during which the smoking occurs, it may be possible to detect certain patterns useful in treatment.

It is also desirable to obtain data about the situations in which smoking occurs. We strongly recommend including a place on the self-monitoring sheet or card for the client to note succinctly the situation in which the cigarette is smoked. The situational notations might be such as "while studying," "after a meal, " "with coffee," "talking with friends who smoked," "waiting for someone," and so on. Situational information paves the way for a functional analysis of smoking episodes and frequently illuminates those events or signals that are associated with smoking.

Self-monitoring does influence smoking and there is evidence to indicate that this self-monitored smoking rate will be at least several cigarettes per day less than the "real" baseline (McFall & Hammen, 1971; Rozensky, 1974). The target behavior being self-monitored may also influence the amount of reduction in smoking. Abrams and Wilson (1979) found that during pretreatment, smokers who self-monitored nicotine intake reduced their smoking rate more than smokers who self-monitored cigarettes smoked. Thus, self-monitoring can act in the service of the treatment program by helping to reduce smoking.

Motivation-Commitment Training

Most smokers who come to a program for assistance are likely to be ambivalent about the prospect of quitting smoking. They undoubtedly have some very sound reasons for wishing to give up cigarettes, yet they are likely to dread the prospect of quitting—many ex-smokers liken quitting to "losing an old friend." Motivation is a critical factor which determines whether or not a person will be successful in the effort to quit smoking.

Health Information. The challenge for the smoking program is to increase the client's motivation or commitment so he or she will carry out program activities in a meaningful way. One alternative is to present the client with information about the health hazards of smoking. Local units of the American Cancer Society, American Heart Association, and American Lung Association generally offer pamphlets containing such information, free of charge. If this information is given in the preparation stage of the program (i.e., prior to the quit date), it should be coupled with specific directives as to what the client can do to begin to eliminate his or her smoking behavior. Informing smokers about the health consequences of smoking without providing information about how they can change is unlikely to be productive (Leventhal, 1968).

Mausner (1973) found that successful abstainers decided to quit because of perceived positive benefits they would derive from quitting, rather than because of fear of the health consequences of continued smoking. Since most people are well aware of the hazards of cigarette smoking, the use of scare tactics such as showing gory films of diseased lungs or of laryngectomy patients who can speak only through the use of a mechanical device, is not recommended. A better approach is to focus on the health *benefits* that would be derived from quitting. We recommend also providing health-related information to clients during the maintenance phase of treatment, after they have successfully quit smoking, when the information is likely to positively reinforce their recent self-change efforts.

Reasons for Quitting and for Smoking. Another approach to enhance motivation is an exercise wherein clients write down their specific reasons for wanting to stop smoking and their specific reasons for wanting to continue smoking. A listing of specific changes that are expected to occur after quitting may also be included. For this exercise to be effective, items must be expressed concretely and idiosyncratically. For example, "I won't notice myself getting winded when I get to the third floor of my office building," will help strengthen the resolve to quit and remain abstinent. Asking clients to list reasons for continuing to smoke may seem contrary to program objectives. However, it may be best to make explicit the likely "resistances" at the outset. The group then has the opportunity to discuss and combat each participant's "resistances."

We have found that clients tend to be motivated more by the immediate consequences of quitting than by the long-term consequences. The threat of lung cancer or heart disease is well-known to the client and is a probabilistic consequence which may not come to pass for years. Immediate consequences can provide direct reinforcement of efforts toward cessation. We suggest that the smoking counselor assist the client by helping him or her to get in touch with the more immediate benefits to be derived from quitting.

Contingency Deposits. The simplest and most powerful way to enhance cooperation with the treatment program is by means of some contingency deposit. This can be accomplished whether treatment is taking place in a private or public context. After the details of the program have been explained, the smoker is asked to agree to put up a certain amount of money—we usually specify $15, but it can be scaled according to financial status—which is returned contingent upon satisfactory compliance. This typically involves attendance, record keeping, and homework assignments. The deposit is *not* contingent on quitting smoking, but on carrying out program activities that are believed relevant for a successful outcome. Details of how much money is forfeited for which kinds of transgressions can be worked out according to program structure.

A written contract, signed by both client and counselor, can be used to augment the use of a contingency deposit. Even when money deposits are not possible or desirable, we recommend a written contract spelling out the responsibilities of client and program.

Quitting

Most smoking control programs have the goal of abstinence or no smoking for their participants. It is therefore critical that smokers achieve abstinence no later than the end of the program and preferably much before. Reaching abstinence before the end of the program provides an opportunity to deal explicitly with maintenance of non-smoking.

One issue concerning quitting is whether it is better to use a gradual reduction approach or a cold turkey approach. Modest research evidence (Flaxman, 1978) and clinical experience lead us to recommend a combination of the two, wherein smokers gradually reduce their smoking within limits, prior to quitting cold turkey. As previously noted, these reductions should generally not be lower than 50% of baseline or about 12 cigarettes a day, whichever is lower (Levinson et al., 1971). This may be the level of smoking at which nicotine becomes of paramount importance. There is also evidence that withdrawal symptoms disappear more quickly following complete cessation than when participants continue to linger at low levels of smoking (Shiffman, 1979). Those few remaining cigarettes attain additional reward value and become especially hard to give up.

What is the best way to go about helping smokers become abstinent? There is no single best answer since different approaches are likely to work best for different kinds of smokers. Quitting methods should be sought that are relatively economical or as simple as possible and that will also serve to enhance confidence in smokers' ability to control their smoking.

We will describe and evaluate four different approaches ranging in cost or intensity. We suggest using the simplest method or combination of methods for achieving cessation that seems likely to work for a given program. The four approaches are: a simple contracting method wherein a target quit date is set and the participant simply agrees to stop at that date; self-management skills that can first lead to reduction of smoking and then help to cope with quitting; a nicotine fading approach wherein the client switches to ever decreasing tar/nicotine level cigarettes, working toward a target quit date; and two different aversion methods for people who may find it particularly difficult to quit.

Contracting

Contingency contracting has occasionally been employed as the major treatment procedure in smoking cessation programs. The smoker deposits a sum of money (e.g. $100) at the outset and then portions of this money are refunded contingent upon meeting previously stipulated abstinence goals, often extending into a follow-up period. In the few systematic evaluations of this method, reasonably good results have been obtained (Elliott & Tighe, 1968; Winett, 1973; Spring, Sipich, Trimble, & Goeckner, 1978).

Contingency contracting involving sizeable sums may be impractical in private or public settings and does not address the problem of maintenance. Nevertheless, "contingency contracting appears to offer a simple and economical method of producing cessation and may be grafted onto other methods" (Danaher & Lichtenstein, 1978, p. 198). A written contract should be constructed, specifying time and date and signed by both the smoker and at least one of the smoking counselors. If possible, a sum of money or something valuable to the smoker should be deposited contingent upon compliance with the contract. (Sample contracts are displayed in Danaher & Lichtenstein, 1978). Meeting time prior to the quit date can be devoted to presentation of other program components, especially self-management principles and skills.

Self-Management

A major class of smoking control procedures are those which involve self-management. For purposes of this discussion, self-management refers to those tactics intended to rearrange environmental cues that trigger smoking, or alter the consequences of smoking. In contrast to aversion, self-management procedures tend to be more explicitly the product of the smoker's own efforts and they are generally administered in the smoker's natural environment rather than in a treatment clinic. The focus of self-management on the individual-as-change-agent and on the application of the intervention tactics at home, often by means of homework assignments, hopefully ensures that treatment will have some significant impact on the client's real world. For a more detailed review of self-management strategies (alternatively termed self-control), see Lichtenstein and Danaher (1976).

For purposes of this discussion, we have categorized self-management strategies into three somewhat overlapping groups: (a) those involving rearranging environmental cues; (b) those involving rearranging consequences —self-reward and self-punishment; and (c) those aimed at cognitions or internal events.

Rearranging Environmental Cues. These strategies are based on the assumption that smoking is a learned behavior or habit which develops through its reported association with certain environmental events which come to serve as signals or cues for the act of smoking. Self-management focuses on teaching clients to first identify many of the signals which elicit their smoking and then to intervene actively to reduce the number and range of these environmental cues which prompt their own smoking behavior. The identification of smoking cues is usually tied into the client's self-monitoring of smoking rate, since this generally includes the recording of smoking situations as well. Once salient smoking cues have been identified, the client needs to develop an intervention strategy to break the connections between these cues and the smoking act. We attempt to simplify this task for our clients by offering them two general intervention strategies: (a) alter or totally avoid the controlling signals whenever possible; and (b) substitute an alternative behavior to replace smoking cigarettes when it isn't possible to alter or avoid the relevant signal.

Several specific self-management techniques may be useful in disrupting the associations between smoking and the particular situations which prompt the smoking response. Techniques used to disrupt the smoking-to-situation associations include: (a) increasing the time interval between cigarettes; (b) arranging smoking in a hierarchy of situations and then progressively reducing or eliminating its occurrence; and (c) smoking only in "deprived" situations.

Increasing the time interval between cigarettes is a strategy which allows for continued smoking, but limits its performance to particular times which are signaled by some cueing device such as an automatic timer (Levinson et al., 1971). Treatment consists of lengthening the interval, using the timer so that smoking is reduced and eventually eliminated. The notion here is that the signal itself assumes the role of cueing smoking and thus previous associations between situations and smoking are effectively severed.

In hierarchial reduction, clients identify situations in which smoking is more or less probable, more or less desired, or more or less difficult to give up (Marston & McFall, 1971). A hierarchy would then be developed which ranked these situations so that the bottom steps were the least valued and the top steps were the most valued smoking situations. Treatment would proceed by reducing or eliminating smoking in progressive fashion from the easiest to the hardest situations.

By smoking only in "deprived" situations, clients narrow the range of discriminative stimuli for smoking by curtailing the circumstances in which smoking is allowed (Nolan, 1968; Roberts, 1969). For example, smoking would only be allowed in designated smoking areas 'which lacked stimulation, reinforcement, or other possible sources of enjoyment (e.g., in a "smoking chair," in the basement, or the garage). In theory, smoking under these deprived circumstances breaks up the pleasurable associations between situations and smoking, thus reducing its attraction or reward value.

Relaxation Training. Since tension or stress often acts as a cue for smoking, some clients can benefit from training in the use of relaxation procedures. Within the context of self-management treatment, relaxation is considered one of the possible alternative behaviors which can be employed as a substitute for smoking. The use of relaxation procedures may also serve to reduce stress that leads to smoking and that which accompanies the process of quitting. We prefer the use of the Benson relaxation technique (Benson, 1975) to that of the progressive muscular relaxation procedure (Jacobsen, 1938), because it is easier to teach to clients, and also more portable (i.e. easier to use in potential smoking situations).

While relaxation procedures probably serve as a useful adjunct in treatment, there is no evidence to date that these procedures, in and of themselves, constitute an effective treatment for smoking control. The use of relaxation procedures has failed to produce incremental treatment effects when combined with other self-management procedures (Pechacek, 1976), with a nicotine fading procedure (Beaver, Brown, & Lichtenstein, 1979), and with rapid smoking (Danaher, 1977a; Glasgow, 1978). However, relaxation training has been incorporated into at least one successful multicomponent treatment (Best, Owen, & Trentadue, 1978). Relaxation remains a plausible treatment component though it takes time to implement and has little empirical support. We suggest its inclusion as an ''optional'' procedure for participants who may wish to use it as a substitute for smoking.

Self-Reward and Self-Punishment. In self-reward, the smoker assigns self-rewards for successfully attaining a goal. The goal may be defined in any number of ways: successfully resisting an urge to smoke; a day or week of abstinence; or practicing some self-control technique. Rewards could be used in conjunction with any of the environmental planning procedures just described. The research evidence on self-reward is meager. It appears to be an important component of smoking control programs, but it has rarely been used as the sole active agent.

In contrast, self-punishment has been used as a treatment procedure entirely by itself. One successful case had a smoker tear up a dollar bill every time he smoked (Axelrod, Hall, Weis, & Rohrer, 1974). A variety of other punishers have been used, including holding one's breath until it becomes unpleasant, self-administering electric shock, and so on. The results of these procedures have been mixed. Case reports seem to show that aversive consequences will reduce smoking, but there has not been any controlled investigation to date. To the extent that individuals will avoid applying strong negative consequences to themselves (Powell & Azrin, 1968), self-punishment of smoking would appear to have limited potential. More research is clearly needed to establish the utility of self-reward and self-punishment. Contingencies appear to be more effective when they are arranged prior to smoking and when their administration is in the hands of others, as in the case of deposit systems.

Cognitions and Internal Cues. One cognitive approach is to eliminate smoking by strengthening self-statements that are incompatible with its performance. This approach can be tailored to the individual thoughts, beliefs, and feelings of the smoker. To a large extent, all of the procedures used to control smoking behavior include significant cognitive elements. Whether it is vividly imaging an aversion therapy experience or telling oneself not to smoke for fear of losing a deposit, thoughts and other within-the-head behaviors always occur in smoking treatment. While there is quite a bit of evidence that inappropriate thinking or rationalization can reduce the probability of quitting, it may also be possible to systematically program thoughts so that they contribute to a successful outcome. However, to date, the clinical effectiveness of cognitive control techniques alone in producing significant smoking reduction and cessation appears to be minimal.

In contrast to reported success with other addictive behavior problems such as obesity, self-management approaches to smoking reduction have not been impressive. Clients appear to find the procedures burdensome and often terminate prematurely. Rearranging environmental cues has not been very effective (Marston & McFall, 1971; Levinson et al., 1971). Procedures aimed at modifying self-statements related to smoking have yielded weak effects (Lichtenstein & Danaher, 1976), but because a number of multicomponent programs which include self-management methods have been successful, we remain cautiously optimistic.

In our own work, we often use self-management procedures to produce some initial reduction leading up to a target quit date via "cold turkey." The emphasis is on helping clients to learn about their own smoking antecedents or cues, and helping them to cope with the resulting urges to smoke. This focus also ties in nicely with the relapse prevention strategy (described below), where clients learn to identify high risk situations which would put them in jeopardy of relapsing. In fact, it was a somewhat arbitrary decision to place the discussion of self-management principles in our quitting section. We believe that these principles and methods are equally applicable and important to maintenance.

Nicotine Fading

Evidence strongly suggests that nicotine plays a central role in the widespread phenomenon of cigarette smoking (Russell, 1976; Schachter, Silverstein, Kozlowski, Perlick, Herman, & Liebling, 1977). Social learning treatment strategies have emphasized psychological and/or environmental factors that maintain cigarette smoking, while tending to neglect the pharmacological factors involved. Nicotine fading/self-monitoring (shortened to nicotine fading) is a treatment strategy which addresses both pharmacological and psychological factors.

In the nicotine fading procedure, clients are informed that cigarette smoking is physically addicting for many smokers, and that reducing this addiction to a minimum will make quitting cigarettes less difficult. Clients work toward a quit date four weeks hence, by switching brands each week to progressively lower nicotine and tar content cigarettes. After a baseline week of smoking their regular cigarette, there are weekly switches to brands containing 30%, 60%, and 90% less nicotine than their original brand. Tar reductions are roughly equivalent, given the high correlation ($r = 0.96$) between nicotine and tar contents of commercially available cigarettes (Russell, Wilson, Patel, Feyerabend, & Cole, 1975).

Throughout the program, clients self-monitor both smoking rate (as in most smoking cessation programs) and nicotine and tar intake levels by calculating and plotting their estimated intake of nicotine and tar each day. The self-monitoring of nicotine and tar provides clients with positive feedback regarding their efforts, since these levels inevitably go down if clients follow the basic brand-changing instructions. Clients are told their quit date at the first session. The procedure includes having clients sign a contract stipulating that they will: (a) self-monitor smoking rate each day; (b) smoke only the cigarette brand designated by the counselor; and (c) calculate and plot nicotine and tar levels each day.

Foxx and Brown (1979) first evaluated the combined nicotine fading/self-monitoring procedure by comparing it to its two component procedures—nicotine fading alone and self-monitoring (of nicotine and tar intake) alone—and to an American Cancer Society Stop Smoking Program. All treatments were conducted in groups. In combination, the nicotine fading and self-monitoring procedures produced effects that surpassed those of the other procedures in isolation. Of the ten nicotine fading/self-monitoring clients studied, four were completely abstinent after 18 months, while the other six were smoking cigarettes lower in nicotine and tar content than their baseline brands. Overall, the nicotine fading/self-monitoring group maintained nicotine and tar reductions from baseline of 61% and 70% respectively, after 18 months. Although preliminary results with nicotine fading look promising, more definitive conclusions must await further research.

Our own clinical work with nicotine fading leads us to hypothesize that cognitive and aversive factors may be operating along with nicotine reduction to facilitate client success. Brand switching serves to minimize withdrawal effects experienced at quitting time. When smokers quit cold turkey (from their regular brand), there is a definite withdrawal syndrome which accompanies the effort (Shiffman, 1979), making it more difficult for the client. Nicotine-fading clients report that they experience mild withdrawal symptoms throughout the brand-switching stages of the program, suggesting that withdrawal effects are diffused and thus experienced to a lesser degree at quitting time than would be the case for the person quitting directly from his or her original brand.

At a cognitive level, nicotine fading has two compelling features: its underlying rationale appears to be particularly persuasive and face valid; and compliance with the procedure seems to increase clients' feelings of self-confidence in their ability to quit. Many clients believe that there is an addictive component to their smoking and this belief often serves as a convenient rationalization for their inability to quit. The nicotine fading rationale acknowledges the addictive aspects of cigarette smoking, thus joining the client's belief system and potentially mobilizing these beliefs toward an active and positive self-change effort.

Bandura (1977) has hypothesized that the mediating mechanism for all successful therapies is that they enhance efficacy expectations—persons' subjective feelings of confidence that they can perform appropriate coping behaviors in specific situations. Nicotine-fading clients invariably reduce their nicotine and tar intake by changing brands and receive positive feedback regarding their efforts by plotting nicotine and tar levels. Thus, the procedure has a built-in success mechanism. Clients should be encouraged to attribute these gains to their own efforts and our experience suggests that clients will so attribute if encouraged to do so. The result is that clients who enter treatment initially doubting their ability to quit (i.e., with lower self-efficacy), come to gain confidence to their ability to be successful.

Finally, there are likely to be some aversive factors which come into play during nicotine fading. Smokers often do not enjoy the taste of the lowered nicotine and tar cigarettes which are assigned to them during the program. The result may be fortuitous in that clients' final experiences with cigarettes are likely to be unpleasant, which may make quitting easier. This fact should be pointed out to the client who complains about the taste of his or her new brand, although one might wish to temper such statements with a certain, albeit minimal, degree of sympathy/empathy.

One limitation of the nicotine fading procedure is that it cannot be used, without modification, with persons smoking brands below 0.6 mg. nicotine. The possibility of modifying the procedure for such smokers does exist however, either by reducing the number of sequential brand reductions, or by employing commercially available cigarette filters which reduce intake level by a known percentage.

In addition to its primary goal of cigarette abstinence, nicotine fading offers a secondary goal for those unable to quit: that of controlled or moderate smoking. Clients can achieve considerable reductions in nicotine and tar levels by continuing to smoke the lowest nicotine and tar cigarettes commercially available. Teaching non-abstinent clients to control their smoking in this manner appears to be a reasonable goal in light of a 12-year longitudinal study which found that smokers of low nicotine and tar cigarettes were less likely to die of lung cancer and coronary heart disease than smokers of high nicotine and tar brands (Hammond, Garfinkel, Seidman, & Lew, 1976).

Jaffe, Kanzler, Cohen, and Kaplan (1978) attempted to achieve controlled smoking by providing women with economic incentives for purchasing low nicotine and tar cigarettes. Although not required to change brands, these smokers showed significant reductions in tar and nicotine intake at six-month follow-up. A somewhat different approach to controlled smoking was used with some success by Frederiksen, Peterson, and Murphy (1976), who sought to reduce the number of cigarettes their clients smoked.

One concern about nicotine fading's secondary goal of controlled smoking is that those non-abstaining clients who change to a low nicotine cigarette may compensate by increasing rate, inhaling more deeply, or puffing more frequently. Any of these topographical changes could result in an increased intake of toxic gases (Schachter, 1978). Data from Foxx & Brown (1979) and Jaffe et al, (1978) indicate that such compensatory smoking does not occur to any significant degree. For smokers who do compensate, it appears feasible to provide them with training in modifying the manner in which they smoke (Frederiksen & Simon, 1978), so that they may truly become moderate or controlled smokers.

Aversion Strategies

Contracting and self-management may not be a strong enough procedure for some smokers, and nicotine fading may be impractical, perhaps because smokers are already smoking low tar and nicotine cigarettes. In these circumstances, we suggest use of an aversion strategy. As with other intrinsically rewarding behavior problems, especially alcoholism, aversive strategies have been frequently used with cigarette smoking and indeed are perhaps the single most widely used technique. Three major kinds of aversive stimuli have been used; electric shock, imaginal stimuli (covert sensitization), and cigarette smoke itself.

Electrical Aversion. The research literature on the use of contingent electric shock paired with various components of the smoking chain has been consistently negative. Studies of laboratory shock yield weak results in either an absolute or a relative sense. Comprehensive reviews of the smoking research literature all concur on the consistently negative results of laboratory contingent shock (Lichtenstein & Danaher, 1976; Pechacek, 1979).

Transfer to the natural environment is a problem for office-bound treatment methods, especially aversion. Smokers are well aware of the fact that while they may be shocked contingent upon smoking in a clinic or laboratory, no such aversive event will occur at home or at work. One means of overcoming this difficulty is to pair shock with thoughts, images, or covert verbalizations that smokers are assumed to emit prior to or during the smoking chain. While the research is far from conclusive, it appears that this may be a more promising use of shock (e.g. Berecz, 1972, 1976). If electric shock is to be used, it would seem best to pair it with covert or imaginal smoking behavior. We also suggest having smokers self-administer the shock in order to promote self-attribution of treatment gains.

Covert Sensitization (Imaginal Aversion). In covert sensitization, the target behavior and the aversive stimulus are presented imaginally by asking the smoker to visualize getting ready to smoke and then to imagine the experience of nausea and vomiting. An escape or relief dimension is introduced by instructing the smoker to imagine feeling better as he or she turns away and rejects the available cigarette. In covert sensitization, smokers are typically given training and practice in the clinic or laboratory and then encouraged to practice the procedure at home. The procedure is safe and convenient in the sense that it can be self-administered, but the research literature indicates that it is not especially effective (Danaher & Lichtenstein, 1978). We do not recommend programmatic use of covert sensitization, but suggest that counselors who are familiar and skillful in its use may still wish to apply it selectively for certain kinds of clients, especially those who appear to have good imagery skills.

Cigarette Smoke Aversion. The choice of cigarette smoke as the aversive stimulus in smoking treatment may be especially appropriate because excessive smoke affects many of the endogenous cues that characterize smoking and this may increase treatment impact. Cigarette smoke aversion has been delivered in two major ways. In satiation, the smoker is instructed to greatly increase the usual daily consumption of cigarettes, sometimes doubling or even tripling consumption for a specified number of days just prior to quitting. In rapid smoking, the client smokes continuously and rapidly until he or she is unable to continue. Recently, a third method is gaining recognition—focused smoking, wherein the client smokes normally, but concentrates on the negative sensations experienced.

Satiation. Satiation is convenient in that it requires no apparatus and is carried out by smokers in their own environment. Earlier reports on the technique were promising (Resnick, 1968a, 1968b), but subsequent research on satiation as a primary treatment method has been consistently negative (e.g. Sushinsky, 1972; Claiborn, Lewis, & Humble, 1972). More recent studies of satiation in combination with extensive self-control procedures have been more positive (Lando, 1977; Best, Owen, & Trentadue, 1978). If satiation is to be used at all, it would seem best to use it only in the context of a self-management program, where satiation is presented as primarily in the service of cessation and other strategies and techniques are emphasized for maintenance. It must be emphasized, however, that satiation involves many of the same risks to the smoker—because it puts stress on the cardiovascular system—as does the rapid smoking procedure that is discussed below.

Rapid Smoking. In rapid smoking, the participant is instructed to puff rapidly—a puff every six to eight seconds—and to continue puffing until it is no longer bearable. The smoker is told to focus only on smoking and is positioned so as to avoid distracting cues. Programs usually administer two or three trials at six to eight treatment sessions. A series of studies by Lichtenstein and his associates showed consistently strong results with three-and six-month abstinence rates at 50% or better (Schmahl, Lichtenstein, & Harris, 1972; Lichtenstein, Harris, Birchler, Wahl, & Schmahl, 1973; Harris & Lichtenstein, 1971). Later work has been more equivocal, but the overall trend appears to be positive. Danaher (1977b) reviewed nearly 30 studies and concluded that rapid smoking appeared to be the most effective single treatment option available. Danaher's review also noted that it appeared to be important for there to be active cognitive rehearsing of the unpleasant experience between trials, as well as a supportive interpersonal context.

There is, however, an important practical drawback to the use of rapid smoking which leads us to recommend its use only under fairly limited circumstances. The procedure greatly intensifies the naturally harmful effects of smoking by significantly increasing the level of nicotine and carbon monoxide in the blood, thereby putting stress on the cardiovascular system. Lichtenstein and Glasgow (1977) summarized much of the data on the risk of rapid smoking. More recent research (e.g. Russell, Raw, Taylor, Feyerabend, & Saloojee, 1978; Hall, Sachs, & Hall, 1979) indicates that effects of rapid smoking on healthy subjects are not serious, but it is necessary to screen smokers carefully. If rapid smoking is to be used, we suggest that it be used only for healthy individuals under the age of 40, that pregnant women or individuals with a history of cardiovascular or pulmonary disease or diabetes be excluded, that careful informed consent be obtained, and that as a final precaution written physician's approval also be sought. Procedural details for the administration of rapid smoking and for screening and safeguarding participants are presented in Danaher and Lichtenstein (1978).

Focused Smoking. Focused smoking is a safe alternative, either for persons who are unsuitable for rapid smoking or for programs which do not wish to involve participants in the screening procedure that rapid smoking requires (Danaher & Lichtenstein, 1978; Hackett & Horan, 1978). In this procedure, the participants are simply instructed to smoke in their usual way while focusing intently on the negative aspects of smoking. The rationale emphasizes the idea that smoking is usually enjoyable because of pleasant accompanying activity, while focused smoking emphasizes the experience of smoking per se. There are usually two or three five-minute trials per session and scheduling is similar to that employed in rapid smoking. Procedural details are also presented in Danaher and Lichtenstein (1978). As yet, normal-paced aversive smoking has not been extensively evaluated and the outcome results are admittedly modest (Danaher, 1977a; Glasgow, 1978; Hackett & Horan, 1978). The procedure does not have the subjective "clout" of the other two smoke aversion methods. It is, however, a simple, apparatus-free procedure with a credible rationale, which has shown some promising results.

In sum, we recommend aversion strategies essentially as a "last resort" when simple contracting or nicotine fading are inappropriate. Rapid smoking and satiation are powerful and fairly effective aversion strategies but involve physical risk, and thereby require extensive screening procedures. Focused smoking is a safe, convenient alternative and we recommend its use in many situations. If aversion is used, it is useful to instruct clients to recall vividly the aversive stimuli whenever they have an urge to smoke. Such revivification can serve as a cognitive maintenance procedure.

Maintenance

Smoking control programs are able to induce most smokers to quit during treatment, yet most of these smokers will relapse within the next few months (Hunt & Bespalec, 1974). We believe that maintenance of behavior change is the critical issue in smoking cessation; yet, to date, work in this area has yielded relatively disappointing results (Bernstein & Glasgow, 1979). Smoking treatment programs have focused primarily on the preabstinence period and have relatively ignored the postabstinence period. Hopefully, this pattern is beginning to change. As Bernstein and Glasgow (1979) point out: "Researchers are at last recognizing that, if they are to reach the goal of long-term maintenance of nonsmoking behavior, that point at which a person stops smoking must mark the beginning of a new intervention phase, not the onset of follow-up" (p. 245).

As yet, there are no empirically validated principles for enhancing maintenance. Some multicomponent treatment programs which included a maintenance focus have met with success (Chapman, Smith, & Layden, 1971; Lando, 1977); however the incremental effects of the maintenance procedures have not been assessed. Other attempts at enhancing treatment effects via continued contact have not been successful. These include the use of self-management skills in the service of maintenance (Pechacek, 1976), booster sessions for aversive smoking (Kopel, 1974; Relinger, Bornstein, Bugge, Carmody, & Zohn, 1977), and continued telephone contact with therapists (Danaher, 1977a; Relinger et al, 1977; Schmahl et al, 1972). One innovative approach to maintenance which demonstrated promising results (at one month follow-up) is the use of a recorded telephone message service which provides a series of daily tips, encouragement, and reinforcement for nonsmoking (Dubren, 1977). Further work with this approach appears warranted.

Given the lack of proven maintenance procedures, we have chosen to focus on some promising leads based upon recent developments in cognitive behavior therapy. Several other maintenance approaches are also discussed.

Relapse Prevention

We utilize a cognitive-behavioral relapse prevention procedure which is derived largely from the work of Alan Marlatt and Judith Gordon at the University of Washington (Marlatt, 1979; Marlatt & Gordon, 1978; cf. chapter by Cummings, Gordon, and Marlatt in this volume). The approach attempts to increase clients' feelings of perceived control over their smoking behavior by teaching them to cope more effectively with specific problem situations and associated cognitions. The relapse prevention program consists of five component parts: (a) lifestyle balancing; (b) identification of high-risk situations; (c) relapse rehearsal; (d) abstinence violation effect (AVE); and (e) self-rewards.

Lifestyle balancing. It is assumed that smoking is most likely to occur when a person feels stressed, overworked, pressured, or generally "out of control." These feelings can result in an increased need for self-indulgence or gratification, which may result in the resumption of smoking. Treatment focuses on helping clients to achieve a degree of balance in their lifestyles between "shoulds" and "wants." Shoulds are activities that are either neutral or unpleasant, and which we feel obligated to perform; wants are activities which are pleasurable. Life-style imbalance occurs when one's daily activities consist of a preponderance of shoulds, as opposed to wants.

Lifestyle balancing is based on the notion that smoking, a negative addiction, can be replaced by some positive addiction such as meditation, jogging, yoga, relaxation training, or walking. Clients are asked to schedule a minimum of one-half hour per day for engaging in a positively addicting activity, and we supply a weekly schedule and ask them to indicate the exact time each day which they will devote to this "self-time." It is not critical that they decide beforehand exactly what that activity will be, as long as the time is blocked off and devoted to some type of "positively addicting" activity.

Identification of high-risk situations for relapse. Coping with a potential relapse will be easier if clients can anticipate the circumstances under which that relapse might occur and if they can plan some specific strategies to help deal with those situations. The underlying assumption is that it is difficult to deal with relapse at the last moment. Treatment focuses on helping clients to foresee situations that might lead to relapse. These high-risk situations are likely to be the very same smoking signals which the client was working with in the self-management unit.

To assist clients in identifying their own potential relapse situations, we inform them of the two most common relapse situations for smokers (Lichtenstein, Antonuccio, & Rainwater, 1977): (a) situations associated with negative emotional states such as anger, frustration, or stress; and (b) situations associated with positive emotional states—being relaxed, in a good mood—and very possibly involving the consumption of alcoholic beverages. Clients are then asked to reflect on their own smoking behavior and to try and predict specific situations that might cause them difficulty.

Relapse rehearsal. Once the client has identified a potential relapse situation, we ask him or her to imagine the situation in vivid detail. Clients may actually dream of relapsing, or may entertain fantasies in which they find themselves smoking again. Such experiences may serve as cues which are helpful in constructing the relapse scene.

When the relapse scene has been described in sufficient detail, the client is asked to specify exactly what he or she would do to cope with the events associated with the potential relapse. The counselor's task is to help the client to identify the situational determinants of relapse and to develop alternative coping strategies. These strategies would involve the use of specific coping skills (e.g., self-management, relaxation, appropriate self-statements) to prevent or to intervene early in a potential (high-risk) relapse situation. Group members can help one another with problem-solving ideas.

In treatment, clients are instructed to vividly imagine their highest-risk situation, and extensively practice and rehearse coping responses (both behavioral and cognitive). As a homework assignment, they are instructed to go through the same procedure with their second and third high-risk situations. Clients invariably report that these exercises are quite helpful and give them an added sense of confidence in dealing with the post-abstinence period.

Abstinence violation effect (AVE). Despite the client's efforts to anticipate high-risk situations and to develop coping strategies, he or she is unlikely to cope successfully every time. Should a failure to cope result in the smoking of a cigarette, the individual will likely experience a powerful cognitive-affective reaction termed the Abstinence Violation Effect or AVE (Marlatt, 1979). The AVE has two key cognitive elements: (a) a cognitive dissonance effect—the smoking episode is dissonant with the person's self-image as a non-smoker—which is experienced as guilt or conflict; and (b) a personal attribution effect—that the "slip" or relapse was due to personal weakness or lack of willpower. These result in the person experiencing a sense of helplessness, victimization, or loss of personal control. In the face of this new stress, the individual is likely to resort to an old and familiar coping response—smoking—which both serves to reduce the dissonance and may relieve negative affect. Although this process analysis is conjectural, the phenomenon of a return to baseline smoking following an abstinence violation is a frequent occurrence (Lichtenstein, Antonuccio & Rainwater, 1977).

In treatment, we inform clients about the abstinence violation effect in an attempt to prepare them for it, should they smoke. We encourage clients to view the first cigarette as a discrete behavior, a ''slip'' rather than a relapse. A ''slip'' is nothing more than an error or mistake—everyone makes mistakes—and smoking one cigarette need not imply personal weakness or lack of willpower. We urge clients to view the ''slip'' as a learning experience and to retrace their steps to determine what they might do differently next time to avoid another ''slip.''

In addition, we give each client a copy of a script containing the message outlined above. We urge clients to carry this script with them at all times and to read it immediately in the event that they smoke a cigarette. Finally, we stress to clients that no matter what happens, their goal remains the same—not to smoke the *next* cigarette.

Self-rewards. Self-rewards are an important part of any self-change program. Smoking clients are often too hard on themselves—they need to be able to recognize their accomplishments and to reward themselves appropriately. Clients are urged to plan specific rewards, which they can realistically deliver, for increasing periods of cigarette abstinence. The magnitude of the rewards should get larger as the time of abstinence increases. While the research evidence on self-rewards is meager—it has rarely been used as the sole active agent—self-reward appears to be an important component of smoking programs. We recommend the addition of self-reward component in any smoking treatment program.

Social Support

Central to the social support approach is the notion that the support and/or influence of a group (two or more persons) can help a person sustain the necessary motivation in order to maintain some standard of behavior such as not smoking or not drinking. In the area of addictive behaviors, social support strategies have a long clinical history as exemplified by such programs as Alcoholics Anonymous, Synanon, and Weight Watchers (Christensen, Miller, & Muñoz, 1978). Systematic evaluation and implementation of social support strategies are relatively few and with respect to smoking, almost nonexistent. This is surprising given the frequent use of buddy systems in such programs as the Five Day Plan.

Buddy systems are a relatively easy component to introduce into treatment programs. Clients can be paired up during sessions, and instructed or requested to call one another between sessions or after the program has ended. In one study (Janis & Hoffman, 1970), subjects who were paired with a buddy maintained greater smoking reduction than control subjects not so paired. In our own laboratory, we were unable to replicate this effect. A buddy system did not increase the effectiveness of rapid smoking treatment (Rodrigues & Lichtenstein, unpublished). Although the data are equivocal, we continue to recommend the use of buddy systems because of their convenience.

Continued Contact

A straightforward approach to improving maintenance is to provide continued contact with clients after treatment has formally ended. This can be accomplished by scheduled meetings or even by telephone contact. Although it might seem obvious that more contact should be better than less contact, the controlled studies reviewed by Bernstein & Glasgow (1979) indicate that more frequent contact does not improve long-term success rates. Indeed, there are some findings where subjects who are seen or contacted more frequently do less well (Schmahl et al, 1972). It may well be that continued contact is useful for some participants and not for others, who may view it as evidence of distrust of their ability to make it and/or which may lead them to rely on the program rather than their own resources. Given the evidence, however, we do not recommend the routine use of extended contact. As noted previously, we do recommend that programs be scheduled so that there are several meetings after abstinence has been attained to systematically teach maintenance skills.

Data Collection and Evaluation

Data collection and evaluation are often viewed as a nuisance, but they are sometimes necessary to satisfy administrators or budget committees. We view evaluation both as an important responsibility and a necessary and useful part of service delivery. Monitoring the progress of individual smoking clients permits one to evaluate the impact of interventions and to modify interventions where appropriate. Evaluating overall programs or particular treatment strategies permits one to make necessary changes or revisions based on the information obtained. Smoking is a measurable behavior and one can evaluate treatment effectiveness much more readily than is the case with many problems. It just takes a bit of time and preparation.

The basic information required for both program evaluation and treatment monitoring is not difficult or expensive to obtain. Demographic data and information about the participant's smoking history can be gotten from a simple questionnaire. It is critical to measure pretreatment smoking rates and to obtain follow-up data well after the completion of the program. Nearly all participants stop or greatly reduce smoking during the program, but many or most will relapse. Therefore follow-up becomes critical. A minimum follow-up period is three months, and a six-month or one-year evaluation is strongly recommended.

Information on smoking rate is typically obtained by means of self-report. We are probably more optimistic than many about the validity of self-reports, since the rates of false reports in programs where there is some reasonable degree of rapport established between counselor and participants is likely to be low (Lichtenstein et al, 1973; Glasgow, 1978). For many programs, self-report will have to do since it is too expensive and cumbersome to do anything else. It is recommended that participants self-monitor smoking rates for at least five days, rather than just providing global estimates of smoking. These self-monitored smoking rates will tend to be lower than self-report, but thereby provide a more conservative estimate of pretreatment smoking status. Telephone interviews are probably the most efficient way to secure follow-up data. Mailed questionnaires frequently are not returned, and it is critical to follow as many participants from the original sample as possible in order to estimate program effectiveness.

There are ways that self-report can be augmented by other measurement procedures and some of these are relatively inexpensive and well within the reach of many service clinics. One possibility is the use of "significant others"—persons designated by the participant who can be contacted for information about smoking status. Informed consent can be obtained for this procedure and significant others can be contacted either by mail, or preferably by telephone. They can be probed by phone at follow-up, especially to check on whether the subject is smoking or not; significant others cannot provide good data on smoking rates (Lichtenstein & Danaher, 1976). The use of significant others can also enhance treatment by requesting that they support the client's efforts to give up cigarettes.

There are now a number of possible physiological measures of smoking that vary in precision and cost; blood or urinary nicotine analyses (Russell & Feyerabend, 1975), or thiocyanate (Brockway, 1978). The simplest, least expensive, and at the same time most useful for treatment purposes, is carbon monoxide measurement (Hughes, Frederiksen, & Frazier, 1978). Smoking any substance introduces carbon monoxide (CO) into the blood. CO can be estimated from breath samples by means of apparatus analogous to the breath test for blood alcohol. Feedback to clients about pre- and post-treatment CO levels may have useful treatment impact since CO levels change quickly in response to smoking cessation.

Some Practical Matters

This final section considers several practical issues that arise when implementing smoking cessation programs. The suggestions that follow are based almost entirely on clinical experience rather than empirical research.

Paraprofessional Smoking Counselors

Voluminous literature attests to the ability of selected and trained nonprofessionals to carry out various kinds of helping activities as effectively as professionals (Social Action Research Center, 1978). If professional time is a problem, therefore, paraprofessionals can serve as counselors or co-counselors. Two kinds of paraprofessionals might be utilized: college students and indigenous community persons—both are prototypical in the paraprofessional literature (Christensen, Miller, & Muñoz, 1978; Heller & Monahan, 1977). College students will generally work to earn college credit and/or supervised practicum experience, while community persons will often work as volunteers, or perhaps for minimal renumeration. In our past research, we found that selected undergraduates without professional training performed as well as advanced graduate students with several years of professional training (Danaher, 1977a; Glasgow, 1979). In our current work, both types of paraprofessionals function well as counselors. College students bring youth and enthusiasm, the community person, experience and stability.

Helping people stop smoking involves more than just the routine administration of technical procedures. A training program might include: considerable reading in the area of smoking; smoking modification and principles of behavior change; both didactic and experiential exposure to basic helping skills and to specific techniques to be used with smokers (including modeling and role-playing, with feedback); observation of counseling activities performed by others; co-counseling experience; and, finally, supervision of counseling work. Experience indicates that such training is readily accomplished in ten to fifteen hours of actual training, supplemented by five to ten hours of related reading. Once training has been completed, paraprofessional counselors can be provided with ongoing case supervision in a group setting. This type of group supervision provides counselors with opportunities both for direct and for vicarious learning, via the experiences of peers.

Use of Manuals and Self-Administered Materials

Client manuals and other written materials can be used to supplement counselor contact in smoking cessation programs. While no systematic data exist comparing the use of such materials with their nonuse (in counselor-administered programs), we offer this recommendation largely on intuitive grounds. A clear and concise client manual can serve as a useful adjunct to explanations of treatment procedures offered by the counselor. It is easier to explain a treatment program to clients, knowing that the explanation is supplemented by a written version which clients can later review at their leisure. It is also more efficient to have clients digest some of the material in written form, rather than having to explain every detail in session. The client may feel more secure and may ultimately gain greater mastery over the material if it can be referred to at some later date, in the event that this becomes necessary.

We employ a client manual containing descriptions of our various treatment components or "modules." Treatment components can be added or deleted depending on the specific nature of the multicomponent program. The component modules include: a basic introduction to our treatment program, self-monitoring, nicotine fading, normal-paced aversive smoking, self-management, relaxation training, cognitive ecology, and relapse prevention. One word of caution, though: more is not always better when it comes to client materials. All materials should be concisely written and directly relevant to the treatment program. Otherwise, the likelihood that clients will utilize the materials may be greatly reduced.

Collaboration with Physicians

In a recent paper on the role of the physician in smoking cessation Lichtenstein and Danaher (1978) suggested five distinct roles which a smoker's personal physician might play in helping to encourage cessation activities: (a) act as a model of a healthy lifestyle by not smoking; (b) provide information clarifying the risk associated with smoking and the risk reduction if the patient stops; (c) encourage abstinence by direct advice and suggestions; (d) refer the patient to a smoking cessation program; and (e) prescribe and follow up the use of specific cessation and maintenance strategies under his or her own office management. While any efforts by the physician are likely to be useful, it was suggested that a cooperative effort between physician and smoking control clinic would likely be the optimal intervention. The clinic could provide the support and skills training; the physician could contribute support, the prestige and influence inherent in the doctor-patient relationship, and occasionally, appropriate medication (e.g., tranquilizers).

We recommend that the smoking counselor or smoking treatment program pursue the development of such cooperative arrangements, particularly in light of the fact that physician-referred smokers are likely to have some smoking-related illness and so to be the most needful of assistance. This can be done by finding out if participants are under regular physician care. Basic components of such a cooperative arrangement would include feedback to the physician (with the client's consent) of client progress, continued participation of the physician via inclusion of the smoking clinic referral in the client/patient's chart, and checking up on treatment progress and/or smoking status at subsequent office visits. Such a collaborative venture would allow the client to see his or her personal physician as concerned and involved in the cessation effort.

Group or Individual Counseling

Harris and Lichtenstein (1971) found no significant differences between smokers treated individually and those treated in three-person groups. Beyond these findings, there are essentially no data systematically comparing group and individual treatment programs. Individual treatment offers the client the undivided attention of the counselor; group treatment dictates that the client must "share" the counselor's time and attention with other group members. Individual treatment permits tailoring the treatment program more closely to the specific needs, concerns, and problems of the client; group treatment must, of necessity, maintain a certain degree of standard structure.

Group treatment does offer several advantages over individual treatment. A group offers the client the support and encouragement of peers who are sharing a similar experience, as well as the sharing of suggestions and tips on "how to do it." Being part of a group may engender a certain amount of motivation to comply with treatment procedures, if not the motivation to actually maintain nonsmoking status. Furthermore, since a group does *not* offer the individual attention of a counselor, the client may need to rely more upon his or her own intellectual and psychological resources and problem-solving skills. Thus, a potential disadvantage of group treatment may ultimately operate to the client's advantage. Finally, and perhaps most importantly, groups are vastly more cost effective than individual treatment. Our own view is that individual treatment would have to be shown to be clearly superior to group treatment to justify its greater expense. Given that this has not been shown to be the case (and barring a situation wherein a client expresses a strong preference for individual treatment), we recommend the use of group treatment whenever possible. A group size of eight to ten clients seems optimal and can be reasonably conducted by either one counselor or by two co-counselors.

Concluding Remarks

We hope that this chapter will prompt readers to initiate smoking control programs, or perhaps to modify existing ones. Several of the key social learning strategies are applicable to all the addictive behavior problems. Counselors who work primarily with one problem can extrapolate their skills and experience to the other addictions. Smoking has been relatively neglected by mental health professionals, a state of affairs we hope will change as a function of the emerging realization of the intimate connection between health and behavioral life-styles.

Like the other addictions, smoking is both critically important for health and difficult to treat. Perhaps because addictive behaviors are easier to measure as compared to many mental health problems, we know more about treatment outcomes and must be cautious in our therapeutic claims. But this should not deter us from implementing programs based on available knowledge. We remain optimistic that cost-effective programs are within our grasp and that new knowledge will be forthcoming to aid the practitioner. The practitioner's experience and data can, in turn, be useful to the research community. Smoking cessation programs provide an opportunity to combine the delivery of important services and the collection of useful data.

Summary

Cigarette smoking is very difficult to give up. It is the interaction of pharmacological and psychosocial variables that makes smoking so tenacious. Effective treatment programs should address both sets of variables.

There are many extant smoking cessation methods. Nicotine mimetic drugs have not been effective. Nicotine chewing gum is a promising approach, but its use is currently very restricted because of possible side effects. Commercial cessation programs tend to be expensive and their effectiveness has not been carefully researched. Smoking cessation clinics generally have a service mission and have not been carefully evaluated. Their long-term success rates tend to be in the 20% range, but they are efficient and their effectiveness might be improved by incorporating recent developments in cessation research. Physician advice can be helpful, especially if the patient has severe smoking related symptoms.

A social learning perspective is believed to be the most promising and applicable because of its emphasis on observable events (including nicotine effects) that maintain smoking. Two social learning based programs have been modestly successful. One emphasizes an aversion strategy, rapid smoking, which has potential side effects and thus limited applicability. The second is a multicomponent approach that typically involves three interrelated phases; preparing to quit, quitting, and maintenance.

Preparing to quit includes setting a specific target quit date, increasing awareness of the smoking chain by self-monitoring, and reviewing and strengthening motivation to quit. Contracts and/or contingency deposits are especially useful in strengthening motivation and committment.

Quitting can be accomplished by means of simple contracts, use of self-management skills, nicotine fading, or aversion methods. Self-management refers to a variety of tactics for rearranging environmental cues that trigger smoking, or altering the consequences of smoking. Nicotine fading involves brand switching to progressively lower nicotine content cigarettes (and self-monitoring nicotine and tar intake) in order to make quitting easier. Aversion strategies such as rapid smoking are viewed as a last resort. Contracts, self-management, and/or nicotine fading are preferred quitting strategies, either singly or in combination.

Maintenance strategies have not been systematically evaluated. A suggested program emphasizing identification of high risk situations, imaginal coping practice, and the cognitive reframing of abstinence violations was described. Providing social support for the new ex-smoker—via buddy system, for example—can also be helpful. Continued contact, a plausible maintenance approach, has not been effective.

Data collection and program evaluation were viewed as integral components of smoking cessation work and some economical procedures were described. The use of paraprofessional counselors, client manuals, enlisting the support of the client's physician where possible, and group treatment were described and recommended as ways of bolstering program effectiveness and efficiency.

References

Abrams, D. B., & Wilson, G. T. Self-monitoring and reactivity in the modification of cigarette smoking. *Journal of Consulting and Clinical Psychology*, 1979, **47**(2), 243-251.

Antonuccio, D. O., & Lichtenstein, E. Peer modeling influences on smoking behavior of heavy and light smokers. *Addictive Behaviors*, in press.

Axelrod, S., Hall, R. V., Weis, L., & Rohrer, S. Use of self-imposed contingencies to reduce the frequency of smoking behavior. In M. J. Mahoney & C. E. Thoresen (Eds.), *Self-control: Power to the person*. Monterey: Brooks/Cole, 1974.

Bandura, A. Self-efficacy: Toward a unifying theory of behavioral change. *Psychological Review*, 1977, **84**(2), 191-215.

Beaver, C., Brown, R. A., & Lichtenstein, E. Effects of nicotine fading and anxiety management training in high and low anxious smokers. Unpublished manuscript, University of Oregon, 1979.

Benson, H. *The relaxation response*. New York: William Morrow & Co., Inc., 1975.

Best, J. A., Owen, L. E., & Trentadue, L. Comparison of satiation and rapid smoking in self-managed smoking cessation. *Addictive Behaviors*, 1978, **3**, 71-78.

Berecz, J. M. Reduction of cigarette smoking through self-administered aversion conditioning: A new treatment model with implications for public health. *Social Science and Medicine*, 1972, **6**(1), 57-66.

Berecz, J. M. Treatment of smoking with cognitive conditioning therapy: A self-administered aversion technique. *Behavior Therapy*, 1976, **7**, 641-648.

Bernstein, D. A. & Glasgow, R. The modification of smoking behavior. In O. F. Pomerleau & J. P. Brady (Eds.), *Behavioral medicine: Theory and practice*. Baltimore: Williams and Wilkins, 1979.

Bernstein, D. A., & McAlister, A. The modification of smoking behavior: Progress and problems. *Addictive Behaviors*, 1976, **1**(2), 89-102.

Brengelmann, J. C., & Sedlmayr, E. Experiments in the reduction of smoking behavior. In *Proceedings of the 3rd World Conference on Smoking and Health* (Vol. II), DHEW publication No. (NIH) 77-1413, 1977.

Brockway, B. S. Chemical validation of self-reported smoking rates. *Behavior Therapy*, 1978, **9**, 685-686.

Brockway, B. S., Kleinmann, G., Edleson, J., & Gruenewald, K. Non-aversive procedures and their effect on cigarette smoking. *Addictive Behaviors*, 1977, **2**(2), 121-128.

Chapman, R. F., Smith, J. W., & Layden, T. A. Elimination of cigarette smoking by punishment and self-management training. *Behavior Research and Therapy*, 1971, **9**(3), 255-264.

Christensen, A., Miller, W. R., & Muñoz, R. F. Paraprofessionals, partners, peers, paraphernalia, and print: Expanding mental health service delivery. *Professional Psychology*, 1978, **9**, 249-270.

Claiborn, W. L., Lewis, P., & Humble, S. Stimulus satiation and smoking: A revisit. *Journal of Clinical Psychology*, 1972, **28**(7), 416-419.

Danaher, B. G. Rapid smoking and self-control in the modification of smoking behavior. *Journal of Consulting and Clinical Psychology*, 1977, **45**(6), 1068-1075. (a)

Danaher, B. G. Research on rapid smoking: Interim summary and recommendations. *Addictive Behaviors*, 1977, **2**(2), 151-166. (b)

Danaher, B. G., & Lichtenstein, E. *Become an ex-smoker.* Englewood Cliffs, N. J.: Prentice-Hall, 1978.

Davison, G. C., & Rosen, R. C. Lobeline and reduction of cigarette smoking. *Psychological Reports*, 1972, **31**(2), 443-456.

Delahunt, J., & Curran, J. P. Effectiveness of negative practice and self-control techniques in the reduction of smoking behavior. *Journal of Consulting and Clinical Psychology*, 1976, **44**(6), 1002-1007.

Dubren, R. Self-reinforcement by recorded telephone messages to maintain nonsmoking behavior. *Journal of Consulting and Clinical Psychology*, 1977, **45**(3), 358-360.

Elliott, R., & Tighe, T. Effects of a technique involving threatened loss of money. *Psychological Record*, 1968, **18**, 503-513.

Farquhar, J. W., Maccoby, N., Wood, P. D. Alexander, J. K., Breitrose, H., Brown, B. W., Haskell, W. L., McAlister, A. L., Meyer, A. J., Nash, J. D., & Stern, M. P. Community education for cardiovascular health. *The Lancet*, 1977, **1**(8023), 1192-1195.

Flaxman, J. Quitting smoking now or later: Gradual, abrupt, immediate, and delayed quitting. *Behavior Therapy*, 1978, **9**(2), 260-270.

Foxx, R. M., & Brown, R. A. Nicotine fading and self-monitoring for cigarette abstinence or controlled smoking. *Journal of Applied Behavior Analysis*, 1979, **12**(1), 111-125.

Frederiksen, L. W., Peterson, G. L., & Murphy, W. D. Controlled smoking: Development and maintenance. *Addictive Behaviors*, 1976, **1**(3), 193-196.

Frederiksen, L. W., & Simon, S. J. Modifying how people smoke: Instructional control and generalization. *Journal of Applied Behavior Analysis*, 1978, **11**, 431-432.

Gallup Opinion Index. Public puffs on after ten years of warnings. *Gallup Opinion Index* (Report No. 108), 1974, 20-21.

Glasgow, R. E. Effects of a self-control manual, rapid smoking, and amount of therapist contact on smoking reduction. *Journal of Consulting and Clinical Psychology*, 1978, **46**(6), 1439-1447.

Hackett, G., & Horan, J. J. Focused smoking: An unequivocably safe alternative to rapid smoking. *Journal of Drug Education*, 1978, **8**(3), 261-265.

Hall, R. G., Sachs, D. P. L., & Hall, S. M. Medical risk and therapeutic effectiveness of rapid smoking. *Behavior Therapy*, 1979, **10**(2), 249-259.

Hammond, E. C., Garfinkel, L., Siedman, H., & Lew, E. A. "Tar" and nicotine content of cigarette smoke in relation to death rates. *Environmental Research*, 1976, **12**(3), 263-274.

Harris, D. E., & Lichtenstein, E. Contribution of nonspecific social variables to a successful, behavioral treatment of smoking. Paper presented at the meeting of the Western Psychological Association, San Francisco, April, 1971.

Heller, K., & Monahan, J. *Psychology and community change.* Homewood, Ill.: The Dorsey Press, 1977.

Hughes, J. R., Frederiksen, L. W., & Frazier, M. A carbon monoxide analyzer for measurement of smoking behavior. *Behavior Therapy*, 1978, **9**, 293-296.

Hunt, W. A., & Bespalec, D. A. An evaluation of current methods of modifying smoking behavior. *Journal of Clinical Psychology,* 1974, **30**(4), 431-438.

Jacobsen, E. *Progressive relaxation.* Chicago: University of Chicago Press, 1938.

Jaffe, J. H., Kanzler, M., Cohen, M., & Kaplan, T. Inducing low tar/nicotine cigarette smoking in women. *British Journal of Addiction,* 1978, **73,** 271-281.

Janis, I. L., & Hoffman, D. Facilitating effects of daily contact between partners who make a decision to cut down on smoking. *Journal of Personality and Social Psychology,* 1970, **17**(1), 25-35.

Kanzler, M., Jaffe, J. H., & Zeidenberg, P. Long- and short-term effectiveness of a large-scale proprietary smoking cessation program—a four-year follow-up of SmokEnders participants. *Journal of Clinical Psychology,* 1976, **32**(3), 661-669.

Katz, N. W. Hypnosis and the addictions: A critical review. *Addictive Behaviors,* in press.

Kopel, S. A. The effects of self-control, booster sessions, and cognitive factors on the maintenance of smoking reduction. Doctoral Dissertation, University of Oregon, 1974.

Lando, H. A. Successful treatment of smokers with a broad-spectrum behavioral approach. *Journal of Consulting and Clinical Psychology,* 1977, **45**(3), 361-366.

Lee, P. N. (Ed.) Statistics of smoking in the United Kingdom. *Research paper 1* (7th ed.), London: Tobacco Research Council, 1976.

Leventhal, H. Experimental studies of anti-smoking communications. In E. F. Borgatta & R. R. Evans (Eds.) *Smoking, health, and behavior.* Chicago: Aldine Publishing Co., 1968.

Levinson, B. L., Shapiro, D., Schwartz, G. E., & Tursky, B. Smoking elimination by gradual reduction. *Behavior Therapy,* 1971, **2**(4), 477-487.

Lichtenstein, E., Antonuccio, D. O., & Rainwater, G. Unkicking the habit: The resumption of cigarette smoking. Paper presented at the annual meeting of the Western Psychological Association, Seattle, 1977.

Lichtenstein, E., & Danaher, B. G. Modification of smoking behavior: A critical analysis of theory, research, and practice. In M. Hersen, R. M. Eisler & P. M. Miller (Eds.), *Progress in behavior modification* (Vol. 3). New York: Academic press, 1976.

Lichtenstein, E., & Danaher, B. G. What can the physician do to assist the patient to stop smoking? In R. E. Brashear & M. L. Rhodes, (Eds.), *Chronic obstructive lung disease: Clinical treatment and management.* St. Louis: C. V. Mosby Co., 1978.

Lichtenstein, E., & Glasgow, R. E. Rapid smoking: Side effects and safeguards. *Journal of Consulting and Clinical Psychology,* 1977, **45**(5), 815-821.

Lichtenstein, E., Harris, D. E., Birchler, G. R., Wahl, J. M., & Schmahl, D. P. Comparison of rapid smoking, warm, smoky air, and attention placebo in the modification of smoking behavior. *Journal of Consulting and Clinical Psychology,* 1973, **40**(1), 92-98.

Marlatt, G. A. Alcohol use and problem drinking: A cognitive-behavioral analysis. In P. C. Kendall & S. P. Hollon (Eds.), *Cognitive-behavioral interventions: Theory, research, and procedures.* New York: Academic Press, 1979.

Marlatt, G. A., & Gordon, J. R. Determinants of relapse: Implications for the maintenance of behavior change. Paper presented at the Tenth International Conference on Behavior Modification, Banff, Alberta, Canada, March 1978.

Marston, A. R., & McFall, R. M. Comparison of behavior modification approaches to smoking reduction. *Journal of Consulting and Clinical Psychology,* 1971, **36**(2), 153-162.

Mausner, B. An ecological view of cigarette smoking behavior. *Journal of Abnormal Psychology,* 1973, **81**, 115-126.

McFall, R. M., & Hammen, C. L. Motivation, structure, and self-monitoring: Role of nonspecific factors in smoking reduction. *Journal of Consulting and Clinical Psychology,* 1971, **37**(1), 80-86.

McAlister, A. L. Mass communication of cessation counseling: Combining television and self-help groups. In J. L. Schwartz (Ed.) *Progress in smoking cessation: Proceedings of International Conference on Smoking Cessation 1978.* New York: American Cancer Society, 1979.

Nolan, J. D. Self-control procedures in the modification of smoking behavior. *Journal of Consulting and Clinical Psychology,* 1968, **32**, 92-93.

Pechacek, T. F. Specialized treatments for high anxious smokers. Paper presented at the annual meeting of the Association for the Advancement of Behavior Therapy, New York, 1976.

Pechacek, T. F. Modification of smoking behavior (chap. 19). In *Smoking and health: A report of the Surgeon General.* Washington D. C.: U. S. Department of Health, Education, and Welfare, DHEW Publication No. (PHS) 79-50066, 1979.

Powell, J., & Azrin, N. The effects of shock as a punisher for cigarette smoking. *Journal of Applied Behavior Analysis,* 1968, **1**(1), 63-71.

Pomerleau, O. F., & Pomerleau, C. S. *Break the smoking habit: A behavioral program for giving up cigarettes.* Champaign, Ill.: Research Press, 1977.

Relinger, H., Bornstein, P. H., Bugge, I. D., Carmody, T. P., & Zohn, C. J. Utilization of adverse rapid smoking in groups: Efficacy of treatment and maintenance procedures. *Journal of Consulting and Clinical Psychology,* 1977, **45**(2), 245-249.

Resnick, J. H. The control of smoking behavior by stimulus satiation. *Behavior Research and Therapy,* 1968, **6**(1), 113-114. (a)

Resnick, J. H. Effects of stimulus satiation on the overlearned maladaptive response of cigarette smoking. *Journal of Consulting and Clinical Psychology,* 1968, **32**(5-1), 501-505. (b)

Roberts, A. H. Self-control procedures in modification of smoking behavior. Replication. *Psychological Reports,* 1969, **24**, 675-676.

Rodrigues, M. R. P., & Lichtenstein, E. Dyadic interaction for the control of smoking. Unpublished manuscript, University of Oregon, 1977.

Rosen, G. M., & Lichtenstein, E. An employee incentive program to reduce cigarette smoking. *Journal of Consulting and Clinical Psychology,* 1977, **45**(5), 957.

Rozensky, R. H. The effect of timing of self-monitoring on reducing cigarette consumption. *Journal of Behavior Therapy and Experimental Psychiatry,* 1974, **5**, 301-303.

Russell, M. A. H. Tobacco smoking and nicotine dependence. In R. J. Gibbins, Y. Israel, H. Kalant, R. E. Popham, W. Schmidt & R. G. Smart (Eds.), *Research advances in alcohol and drug problems* (Vol. 3). New York: Wiley, 1976.

Russell, M. A. H. Smoking addiction: Some implications for cessation. In J. L. Schwartz (Ed.), *Progress in smoking cessation: Proceedings of International Conference on Smoking Cessation 1978.* New York: American Cancer Society, 1979.

Russell, M. A. H., & Feyerabend, C. Blood and urinary nicotine in nonsmokers. *The Lancet*, 1975, 179-181.

Russell, M. A. H., Raw, M., Taylor, C., Feyerabend, C., & Saloojee, Y. Blood nicotine and carboxyhemoglobin levels after rapid-smoking aversion therapy. *Journal of Consulting and Clinical Psychology*, 1978, **46**(6), 1423-1431.

Russell, M. A. H., Wilson, C., Patel, U. A., Feyerabend, C., & Cole, P. V. Plasma nicotine levels after smoking cigarettes with high, medium, and low nicotine yields. *British Medical Journal*, 1975, **2**, 414-416.

Schachter, S. Nicotine regulation in heavy and light smokers. *Journal of Experimental Psychology: General*, 1977, **106**(1), 5-12.

Schachter, S. Pharmacological and psychological determinants of smoking. *Annals of Internal Medicine*, 1978, **88**(1), 104-114.

Schachter, S., Silverstein, B., Kozlowski, L. T., Perlick, D., Herman, C. P., & Liebling, B. Studies of interaction of psychological and pharmacological determinants of smoking. *Journal of Experimental Psychology: General*, 1977, **106**(1), 3-40.

Schmahl, D. P., Lichtenstein, E., & Harris, D. E. Successful treatment of habitual smokers with warm, smoky air and rapid smoking. *Journal of Consulting and Clinical Psychology*, 1972, **38**(1), 105-111.

Schwartz, J. L. Helping smokers quit: State of the art. In J. L. Schwartz (Ed.), *Progress in smoking cessation: Proceedings of International Conference on Smoking Cessation 1978*. New York: American Cancer Society, 1979.

Shiffman, S. M. The tobacco withdrawal syndrome. In N. A. Krasnegor (Ed.), *Cigarette smoking as a dependence process* (NIDA Research Monograph 23). Washington D. C.: U. S. Department of Health, Education, and Welfare, DHEW Publication No. (ADM) 79-800, 1979.

Social Action Research Center. *Paraprofessionals in mental health: An annotated bibliography from 1966 to 1977*. Berkeley: Author, 1978.

Spring, F. L., Sipich, J. F., Trimble, R. W., & Goeckner, D. J. Effects of contingency and non-contingency contracts in the context of a self-control-oriented smoking modification program. *Behavior Therapy*, 1978, **9**(5), 967-968.

Sushinsky, L. W. Expectation of future treatment, stimulus satiation, and smoking. *Journal of Consulting and Clinical Psychology*, 1972, **39**(2), 343.

U. S. Department of Health, Education, and Welfare. *Smoking and health: A report of the Surgeon General*. Washington D. C.: Author, DHEW Publication No. (PHS) 79-50066, 1979.

U. S. Public Health Service. *Adult use of tobacco, 1975*. Atlanta: Center for Disease Control, 1976.

Winett, R. A. Parameters of deposit contracts in the modification of smoking. *The Psychological Record*, 1973, **23**(1), 49-60.

5

Behavior Therapy and the Treatment of Obesity

G. Terence Wilson

Department of Clinical Psychology
Rutgers University
P.O. Box 819
Piscataway, New Jersey 08854

Obesity has proved uncommonly resistant to lasting modification. A major nutritional problem in the United States, obesity is on the increase despite the negative social consequences the obese person often experiences, the repeated warnings that obesity is hazardous to our health, and diverse attempts to develop effective treatment methods for weight reduction. Treatments for obesity seem to have run the gamut of possible interventions. Beyond the ever-present entreaties of the proponents of the latest "miracle diet," psychotherapy, hypnosis, drugs, wiring people's jaws shut, and even sophisticated surgery that bypasses the small intestine or stomach have all been put forward at one time or another as means for weight reduction. Unfortunately, none of this array of diverse treatment methods has yielded consistent or long-term success, although bypass surgery for the massively obese (over 300 pounds or more) may be recommended (Bray, 1976; Leon, 1976; Stunkard, 1978).

The publication in 1967 of Stuart's landmark paper reporting unprecedented therapeutic success heralded the systematic application of behavioral methods to the treatment of obesity. Based on the earlier proposals of Ferster,

Nurnberger, and Levitt (1962), the impact of this approach was dramatic. The burgeoning research in this area recently led Jeffery, Wing, and Stunkard (1978) to reflect a growing concern that "research on the behavioral treatment of obesity has achieved a popularity verging on faddism" (p. 189). Practitioners too, have eagerly embraced behavioral procedures for the management of obesity. Major behavioral treatment centers have sprung up around the United States, behavioral self-help programs in the form of cassette tapes and books have become widely available, and Weight Watchers, the biggest and most widely accepted commercial weight control program, has modified its basic program to incorporate behavioral self-control procedures (Stuart & Mitchell, 1978; Stunkard & Brownell, 1979). Ideally, this enthusiastic acceptance and widespread implementation of behavioral methods in the treatment of obesity would be firmly based upon unequivocal demonstration of the efficacy of these procedures in scientifically controlled outcome research. Not surprisingly, however, the empirical status of behavior therapy in the treatment of obesity is less clearcut than we would wish.

An evaluation of the evidence for the efficacy of behavior therapy is beyond the scope of the present chapter and the interested reader is instead referred to other sources (Franks & Wilson, 1976-79; Stuart, 1979; Stunkard & Penick, in press; Wilson, 1978 b; Wilson & Brownell, 1980). Suffice it to summarize the available evidence in the following five points: (a) behavior therapy has proved to be more effective than alternative approaches in producing weight loss, at least in the short-term; (b) long-term evaluations of the behavioral treatment of obesity have been relatively rare, while the results of those long-term studies that have been completed are mixed; (c) with few exceptions, weight losses have fallen short of clinical significance even if they are statistically significant within individual studies; (d) behavioral treatment programs have been consistently characterized by marked inter-individual variability in outcome; and (e) reliable predictors of successful treatment outcome have yet to be identified. This pattern of evidence has led some commentators to conclude that behavior therapy is no more effective than previous forms of treatment in the management of obesity (e.g. Yates, 1975). However, despite the obvious limitations of the supporting evidence, it is my contention that behavior therapy is nonetheless the best available alternative for producing weight loss in cases of mild to moderate obesity, a verdict that is shared by Stuart (1979) and Stunkard and Mahoney (1976). Moreover, as I have argued elsewhere (Wilson, in press, b), it is entirely plausible that we have not obtained better results, particularly maintenance of treatment-produced weight loss, because the behavioral treatment programs that have been put to the test in the various outcome studies summarized above have been too limited and thus less powerful than they might have been. In short, I have suggested that we have generally failed to implement treatment programs that are consistent with what is currently known about the optimal methods for initiating and then maintaining long-term changes in chronic and refractory disorders such as obesity. Stuart (1979) has voiced a similar opinion, stating that the failure of some behavioral programs to produce long-term success is attributable "to poorly conceived and executed interventions," and that "when properly administered, behavioral techniques also yield highly acceptable long-term results." The purpose of the present paper is to discuss briefly the nature of a comprehensive behavioral treatment approach to obesity that reflects current understanding not only of the mechanisms of behavior change and maintenance, but also of obesity itself.

The Behavioral Model of Weight Control

The behavioral treatment of obesity departs drastically from alternative forms of treatment such as special diets, drugs, or surgery in that the goal is to alter the obese person's eating and activity habits. The emphasis is on changing behavior, or more broadly conceived, the obese person's *life-style*. No particular diet is prescribed beyond recommending a balanced and nutritionally sound diet. Put bluntly, it is emphasized that a calorie is a calorie is a calorie—and they all count! There is no convincing evidence that the composition of the food one eats will differentially affect weight control, provided that the total number of calories is kept consistent. When diets such as the Atkins (1977) low-carbohydrate diet, in which unlimited amounts of protein and fats are allowed, do produce weight loss, it is because the dutiful dieter's total caloric intake is reduced and not because of any metabolic magic. Excluding other categories of food, like protein or fat, as some of the other diets do, is likely to have a similar effect. In short, diets often appear to work because they indirectly bring about a temporary change in eating habits and overall food intake. The problem with these diets, of course, is that inevitably, dieters go off their diets and rapidly regain the weight they lost. This cyclical pattern of rapid weight loss followed by weight gain is the typical experience of the obese person who has fought the battle of the bulge. It has been referred to somewhat sardonically as the "rhythm method of girth control."

In contrast to the illusory promise of a "quick fix" that is offered by most miracle diets, the behavioral approach is geared to slow but sure weight loss of roughly one to two pounds per week as a direct result of fundamental changes in eating and activity patterns. It is emphasized that there are no quick and simple solutions to permanent weight loss and that success in controlling weight involves a major, long-term commitment on the part of the person in which his or her active cooperation is a must. Without this motivation and commitment, there can be little realistic hope of lasting weight loss.

In terms of the behavioral approach to weight control, whatever its root causes, obesity is viewed as ultimately a function of number of calories consumed and expended. The overall goal is to restrict caloric consumption and to increase the expenditure of calories through physical activity, thereby producing a negative energy balance and weight loss. There are marked individual differences in how much and how fast different obese people will lose weight under these conditions, because of the important influence of genetic and biological factors in the regulation of body weight (Wooley, Wooley, & Dyrenforth, 1979). It may be that in certain cases of obesity, particularly extreme obesity, biological determinants are such that they cannot (or should not) be modified along typical behavioral lines. In general, however, the emphasis on behavioral change need not be incompatible with biological considerations, although as I indicate below, the therapist should be alert at all times to the potential limiting influence of biological factors on behavioral weight control programs.

Behavioral Assessment of Obesity

A cardinal tenet of behavior therapy is that treatment is specifically tailored to the particular, often unique needs of each individual client on the basis of a full functional analysis of the presenting problem (Goldfried & Davison, 1976; Lazarus, 1971; Mischel, 1968). The emphasis is on fitting the treatment to the disorder in a flexible, problem-solving manner rather than on routinely applying a standard technique to a variety of problems, as has often been the practice in traditional psychotherapy. Within the applied behavior analysis approach to behavior therapy, this emphasis on the individual has always been paramount, accounting in large part for the importance attached to single-case experimental designs in the evaluation of treatment effects (e.g., Hersen, & Barlow, 1976). The irony is that this distinguishing characteristic of behavioral assessment has been widely ignored in the behavioral treatment of obesity. Almost without exception, the behavioral treatment programs that have been evaluated in controlled outcome studies have been limited adaptations of the basic program originally used by Stuart (1967) and described more fully by Stuart and Davis (1972). As such, the principal treatment techniques have consisted mainly of behavioral self-control methods such as self-monitoring, stimulus control, contingency management, and procedures designed to control the act of eating directly. The impressive consistency with which essentially the same treatment program has been adopted from study to study indicates that a premature formalization and standardization of behavioral treatment for obesity has occurred (Mahoney, 1975; Wilson, in press, a). This developed despite the caveat expressed by Stuart and Davis (1972) themselves that one of the myths in the treatment of obesity is that any program is useful for everyone.

Contrast this premature standardization of *the* behavioral treatment program for obesity in much of the available outcome research with the clinical practice of behavior therapy with individuals. Completing behavioral assessments of individual obese clients readily reveals the range of psychological and environmental variables that contribute to the problem. It is certainly not uncommon to find the client who is overweight because of overeating primarily as a result of snacking and an apparent inability to limit what and when to eat. In a case like this, a basic program that focuses on establishing stimulus control of eating, together with direct modification of the specific eating pattern and some contingency management in order to slow eating rate and control the amount consumed, is probably an effective and efficient intervention. However, as therapists have repeatedly discovered, diverse other influences are often identifiable in the maintenance of obesity. A few examples will illustrate this basic point. One of our clients, for instance, initially responded well to a basic behavioral self-control program until we noticed periodic, but consistent lapses in self-regulation of food intake that reliably resulted in weight gain. Further investigation showed that these lapses were associated with serious conflicts with her husband. Unable to assert herself effectively with her husband when she felt demeaned or badly treated, she would deliberately overeat in the sure knowledge that this behavior angered her husband. Overeating not only served the purpose of "getting back" at her husband, but also provided her with temporary relief from her own unexpressed frustration and the resentment that she experienced as a result of her marital dissatisfaction. Circumstances such as these require a multifaceted treatment intervention in which behavioral marital therapy, involving problem-solving and communication training, would be an important strategy.

In other cases, clinical assessment indicates that strong emotional states, usually featuring anxiety or depression, are critical precursors of overeating and weight gain. Accordingly, these emotional antecedants would require specific therapeutic attention in a comprehensive behavioral treatment program. Finally, there are a relatively small number of "binge eaters" (Stunkard, 1959) whose compulsive overeating patterns appear to be governed by factors other than those usually associated with more commonplace problems of overeating and weight gain, particularly a sense of loss of personal control. I have suggested that binge eaters differ sharply from other obese persons in that they do not seem to be especially vulnerable to food stimuli, do not necessarily snack unnecessarily under inappropriate conditions, and have little difficulty in maintaining normal dietary and caloric requirements between binges (Wilson, 1976). They do not respond well to the standardized behavioral self-control program adapted from Stuart and Davis (1972), probably because this sort of program does not address the deep emotional conflicts and lack of self-efficacy that seem to be so much a part of this severe form of eating disorder.

The behavioral assessment of a case of obesity proceeds along lines similar to the assessment of any other clinical disorder (Goldfried & Davison, 1976). In addition to detailed interviews, the client is asked to keep a daily diary in which he or she self-monitors specific thoughts, feelings, and activities that are related to the problem. The goal of obtaining this information is to identify the particular antecedants, concurrent events, and consequences that are associated with eating and physical activity. Typically, the client is instructed to monitor what is eaten, when, with whom, and with what effect. There is no more important or vital an element of behavior therapy for obesity than consistent and conscientious self-monitoring of food-related behavior by the client, and specific steps must be taken to try to ensure optimal client cooperation in this respect, as I indicate below. Adjunctive questionnaires that variously provide family and life history data relevant to eating behavior and current patterns of food intake are often useful. Examples include the Stanford Eating Disorders Questionnaire (Agras, Ferguson, Greaves, Qualls, Rand, Ruby, Stunkard, Taylor, Werne, & Wright, 1976), the Eating Behavior Inventory (O'Neil, Currey, Hirsch, Malcolm, Riddle, & Sexauer, 1979), the Eating Patterns Questionnaire (Wollersheim, 1970), and the Mahoney Master Questionnaire (Mahoney, Rogers, Straw, & Mahoney, in press). These and other methods of assessment in the treatment of obesity are more fully discussed by Brownell (in press) in his comprehensive review of this important topic.

As Brownell points out, several metabolic and physiological processes are often related to obesity, either as causes or consequences of the disorder. Accordingly, it behooves the behavior therapist to be alert to the possibility of the biological origins of overweight, associated medical complications, and contraindications for weight reduction. Bray, Jordan and Sims (1976) have developed a flow chart for evaluating these medical considerations in obesity. Behavior therapists typically obtain a physician's consent prior to implementing a behavioral weight control program and Brownell suggests that the Bray et al. (1976) guidelines be used as a basis upon which the physician might make an informed determination about suitability for treatment.

Behavioral investigators have increasingly emphasized the importance of biological factors in the regulation of weight and have underscored the need to take account of these influences in treatment programs (Brownell, in press; Stunkard & Mahoney, 1976; Wooley et al., 1979). How does the behavior therapist assess the potential impact of biological factors in a weight reduction program? Unfortunately, there is no easy answer to this question, in large part because the biology of obesity is as yet far from clearly understood. The set-point theory of obesity holds that different people have different set-points for body weight and that in response to weight changes, metabolic or physiological reactions occur in order to defend that body weight (Nisbett, 1972). While there does appear to be evidence that supports the notion of a regulatory set-point for weight (Keesey, 1978), its relevance for weight reduction programs is unclear. It has been argued that obesity in some individuals is their biologically normal state and that successful weight reduction programs predicated on societal judgements of what is obese might produce a biologically unnatural state in which the person is energy depleted. If this were the case, as Nisbett (1972) originally predicted, the person should show physiological or psychological signs of distress such as heightened irritability, emotionality, and so on. For this and other reasons, it is important for the therapist to assess the psychological side-effects of behavioral treatment programs (Wilson, 1978b). Happily, the evidence has consistently shown that behavioral programs have produced a few if any adverse side-effects such as depression or irritability (Mahoney et al., in press; Öst & Götestam, 1977; Taylor, Ferguson & Reading, 1978; Wollersheim, 1970). Indeed, overwhelmingly, weight reduction has produced strikingly positive generalized effects on psychological functioning. Again, it must be remembered that these data are drawn from studies of the treatment of the mild to moderately obese. It is still an open question whether or not similar benefits will accrue to the massively obese to the extent that such persons are successful in losing weight.

The fat cell theory of obesity has attracted considerable attention and some solid experimental support. Briefly, this theory posits that adipose tissue or fat cells can affect body weight either by cellular multiplication (hyperplasia) or cellular enlargement (hypertrophy) (Sjostrom, 1978). It was initially thought that in juvenile-onset obesity, it was the greater number of fat cells that was the villain, as opposed to adult-onset obesity in which fat cell size was the culprit. The implications of this adipose cellularity theory were that juvenile-onset obesity would be more recalcitrant to weight reduction programs because only the size and not the number of fat cells can be reduced. Moreover, it is hypothesized that the body will draw upon lean tissue mass to replenish fat cells that are depleted as a result of caloric restriction. However, there is firm evidence that age of onset does not predict weight loss or response to treatment (Brownell, Heckerman, Westlake, Hayes, & Monti, 1978; Ferguson, 1976; Jeffery, Wing, & Stunkard, 1978, Mahoney et al., in press). It may be that age of onset of obesity correlates imperfectly with cellularity and there is evidence from other sources that cellularity is related to weight loss (Bjorntorp, Carlgren, Isaksson, Krotkiewski, Larsson, & Sjostrom, 1975). At present the precise nature of this relationship is uncertain and fat cell theory provides no guidelines for the behavior therapist in embarking upon a weight reduction program. The simple pragmatic rule that behavioral treatment is indicated, provided that continual assessment provides no sign of adverse physiological or psychological side-effects, must suffice until future research provides more specific guidance.

Behavioral Treatments

Basic Assumptions of Behavioral Treatment of Obesity

In setting out to modify obesity, behavioral researchers and therapists acted upon a number of far-reaching assumptions about the nature of this disorder.

As summarized by Mahoney (1978), the more important of these assumptions included the following:

1. Obesity is a learning disorder, created by and amenable to principles of conditioning.
2. Obesity is a simple disorder resulting from excess calorie intake.
3. The obese individual is an overeater.
4. Obese persons are more sensitive to food stimuli than are non-obese individuals.
5. There are important differences in the "eating style" of obese and non-obese persons.
6. Training an obese person to behave like a non-obese one will result in weight loss.

With the belated benefit of hindsight, we have come to realize that many of these assumptions were uncritically and prematurely accepted (Mahoney, 1975). The evidence disputing these assumptions derives from a number of important sources and is comprehensively reviewed by Bray (1976), Stunkard (1978), and Wooley et al. (1979). Thus, the data increasingly indicate that a variety of genetic, metabolic, and physiological factors contribute to weight regulation aside from individual learning and socioculture influences. Far from being simple, obesity is a complex disorder that may well comprise different "obesities" that have different etiologies and will respond differentially to alternative treatments. It is not clear that the obese person does eat more than his or her lean counterpart. Much of the impetus for the early behavioral treatment of obesity was provided by Schachter's (1971) highly influential theory that the obese were significantly more responsive to external food cues (e.g., time of day, the sight of tempting foods), but less responsive to internal stimuli (e.g., gastric contractions) than normal weight individuals. The apparent vulnerability of the obese to external food cues lent great plausibility to behavioral interventions that sought to alter eating habits by environmental changes (Ferster et al., 1962). However, Rodin (1978b) has concluded that "the internal versus external concept is far too simple a description of, or explanation for, differences between obese and normal-weight individuals." (p. 587). It appears that most people are responsive to some external food cues and that there are people in all weight categories who are exceptionally responsive to environmental stimuli that are related to food. Similarly, a relative lack of responsiveness to internal-physiological cues in guiding eating behavior appears to be distributed across weight categories. The manner in which external (environmental) and internal (physiological) cues interact to regulate food intake is both complex and important, and for further detail and understanding of its implications for weight loss the interested reader is referred to Rodin's (1978 a & b) critical analysis of this subject.

It was Ferster et al. (1962) who described an "obese eating style" in terms of which the obese were said to eat more rapidly than normal weight individuals by taking larger and more frequent bites. Although they did not document the existence of a distinctive eating style in the obese, the report of Ferster et al. fostered attempts to modify the topography of eating patterns in the obese (e.g., teaching them to eat more slowly). Only recently have observational studies been conducted to assess the presence of any distinctive differences in eating behavior between obese and normal weight persons. Although some of the research findings are mixed, all in all it seems safe to conclude that attempts to demonstrate consistent differences in eating topography between obese and normal weight samples have not succeeded (Adams, Ferguson, Stunkard, & Agras, 1978; Stunkard & Kaplan, 1977). Of course, it is possible that the behavioral techniques that Stuart and others have devised to limit the obese person's exposure to tempting environmental food cues (e.g., stimulus control) and to modify eating style directly (e.g., putting the fork down between bites) might still be effective irrespective of the lack of differences between obese and normal weight people in external responsiveness or eating style. Indeed, the continued use of several of these techniques are strongly recommended as indicated below.

To summarize, some of the fundamental assumptions on which behavioral treatment of obesity has been based have been shown to be questionable. It is not that our recognition of what seem to have been faulty assumptions should lead to the abandonment of behavioral treatment of obesity. On the contrary, our greater knowledge provides us with new insights and a more effective base from which to operate. Our better understanding of the nature of obesity can help in designing not only more effective treatment programs, but also in contributing to the more humane management of obese people in general. No one has made this last point better than Wooley et al. (1979) in their thoughtful criticism of behavior modification treatments that are narrowly predicated on the rigid assumptions that obesity is the result of too much overeating and too much slothfulness:

Instead, it would seem to be consistent with the philosophy and tradition of behavior therapies to acquaint patients with the facts about obesity, including the lack of evidence that the obese eat more than others, the effects of dieting on metabolism, and the modest outcomes of most treatment, and to engage them in a process of goal-setting based on these facts. Although therapists tend to be reluctant to discourage patients, the facts of their own experience will have discouraged them or given them hope. If the experience of dieting has been one of constant failure, despite enormous effort, they will be relieved to have their experience confirmed and understood, and some may be better able to withstand the difficulties knowing that they are not exclusively attributable to their own failings. Some may choose to give up dieting and work on minimizing the negative consequences of being obese. Others will recognize that weight loss is, in fact, relatively easy for them and worth the effort. It has been our experience that few patients embrace these pieces of information as "rationalizations"; the concept of rationalization, of course, implies a self-serving denial of the "truth," which in the case of obesity is not known [p. 20].

Specific Behavioral Treatment Methods

As I have already mentioned, the behavioral treatment of obesity has relied primarily if not exclusively on the various self-control techniques described by Stuart (1967) and Stuart and Davis (1972). These methods are well-known and need not be discussed in detail here. Suffice it for me to comment briefly on some important aspects of their clinical use. Self-monitoring forms the basis for most behavioral self-control methods and has been carefully studied. As a result, we have identified some of the specific parameters of self-monitoring and its effects. For example, self-monitoring has been shown to be reactive in the sense that it can result in significant weight loss (Romanczyk, Tracey, Wilson, & Thorpe, 1973). The specific nature of *what* is monitored is important. Thus, Green (1978) has shown that self-monitoring of daily caloric intake is significantly more reactive in producing weight loss than is monitoring of other food-related events. Significantly, Green's findings also suggest that whether or not the obese person does this monitoring before or after eating makes little difference. However, rate of compliance with the therapist's instructions to self-monitor caloric intake before eating was significantly less worse than that with post-prandial monitoring. Accordingly, unless subsequent research shows otherwise, it makes sound clinical sense not to insist on clients self-monitoring before eating, an assignment with a relatively low probability of compliance. While I am unaware of hard data on this vital matter, my clinical experience tells me that non-compliance begets non-compliance. Compliance is all-important in the treatment of obesity.

People do not react passively to external events—they actively perceive and process them. Self-monitoring will be reactive only to the extent that performance is subjectively evaluated in terms of self-selected standards (Bandura, 1977). In social learning theory it is assumed that it is the discrepancy between self-monitored performance and personal goals that will motivate corrective actions. Bandura and Simon (1977) have demonstrated that simple, short-term (proximal) sub-goals are significantly more effective in producing behavioral change and weight loss than more long-term (distal) goals. Chapman and Jeffrey (1978) have also shown the importance of clients' specific self-selected performance goals in self-evaluation and weight loss. Specific research findings like those of Green (1978) and Bandura and Simon (1977) indicate how even an ostensibly straightforward technique such as self-monitoring can result in varying effects, depending on the skill and expertise with which it is implemented in the applied arena.

The behavioral self-control techniques that have become so much a part of the treatment of obesity fall roughly into three categories: stimulus control, or those that attempt to regulate the antecedants of eating; contingency control, or those that alter the reinforcing consequences of eating; and techniques that are designed to modify the topography of eating patterns themselves. As Brownell (in press) points out, there is no direct evidence that restricting food cues or decreasing their salience, as is attempted in stimulus control procedures (e.g., eat only in one place, do nothing else like reading or watching T.V. while eating), actually result in weight change. In fact, the only studies to assess the role of these techniques directly have not revealed a systematic relation between cue control and weight reduction (Brownell et al., 1978; Stalonas, Johnson, & Christ, 1978). Toro, Fisher, and Levenkron (1979) found that a treatment method consisting solely of stimulus control procedures was relatively ineffective. These authors state that whether or not stimulus control procedures are useful in combination with other methods, as in the Stuart and Davis (1972) program, remains to be determined. Toro et al.'s data are important since there appears to be a consensus among behavioral investigators that stimulus control methods are useful and programs that are broadly based on their application have shown impressive weight loss (e.g., McReynolds & Paulsen, 1976) despite the previously mentioned failure to demonstrate the direct causal influence of restricting food cues.

Despite their widespread use, there is no direct evidence reliably linking change in eating topography to weight loss. As Mahoney (1975) and others have observed, the efficacy of these and other treatment methods have usually been inferred from program-produced weight loss in post hoc fashion. However, Brownell and Stunkard (1978) have recently questioned whether or not the weight loss achieved in behavioral programs is the result of changes in behavior effected by compliance to therapeutic instructions to alter eating topography (e.g., eat more slowly, place eating utensils down between bites, and so on). Wollersheim (1970) and Hagen (1974) reported significant correlations between weight loss and behavior change as measured by the Eating Patterns Questionnaire, as did Mahoney (1974) and Öst and Götestam (1976) using self-report and independent assessment of habit change. Yet other studies that analyzed detailed eating behavior records of obese clients have failed to show correlations between habit change and weight loss (Bellack, Rozensky, & Schwartz, 1974; Brownell et al., 1978; Jeffery et al., 1978; Stalonas et al., 1978). These inconsistencies might simply reflect the difficulty in accurately and reliably assessing eating patterns. Wooley et al. (1979) have speculated that these inconsistencies may be attributable to the fact that habit change is related to weight loss directly. They argue that it would make more sense to relate behavioral changes to alterations in overall food intake, which in their analysis is only one of the factors that determine weight. At the very least, however, these data call for careful assessment of compliance to therapeutic instructions and its direct relation to weight control to future outcome studies.

Several forms of reinforcement procedures have been used to regulate eating habits. A particularly promising variation that has not been employed as broadly as it might be is self-reinforcement. Mahoney (1974), for example, showed that self-reinforcement produced significantly greater weight losses than did control methods, both shortly after treatment and even at a one-year follow-up. Mahoney also found that self-reinforcement for changes in eating habits was more effective than self-reinforcement for weight loss per se. More traditional reinforcement methods have entailed more externally controlled contingency management than self-administered consequences. In contingency contracting, for instance, the therapist typically arranges a contract in which a specified outcome such as habit change or a designated amount of weight loss is rewarded by the return to the client of portions of a refundable money deposit. Alternatively, failure to meet predetermined goals may result in the client forfeiting a sum of money to his or her most disliked organization or political group.

One potential problem with contingency contracting for weight loss is that it may engender unhealthy dietary practices. Thus, Mann (1972) obtained significant weight loss with contingency contracting, but only at the unacceptable cost of subjects resorting to a variety of hazardous procedures such as the use of diuretics, vomiting, starvation, and steam baths in order to meet the weight loss quotas they had committed themselves to. This method has also led to increased absences from therapy sessions (Jeffrey, 1974). My personal clinical experience with this method is that most clients are reluctant to enter into externally controlled contracts that they variously describe as a merely temporary crutch ("what happens when the contract ends?"), or a mechanistic and manipulative method that is unwarranted and unduly coercieve. Or they may simply decide that they want out of the contract when compliance becomes too demanding. Furthermore, even if a client enters into a contract, there is no guarantee that the contingency will always have the desired effect. The client of a colleague of mine agreed to get rid of a valued possession, an expensive music-box, if she failed to lose what seemed like a reasonable amount of weight. She failed to lose the weight, followed through on the contract, and became doubly upset over what was still further proof to her that she was unable to control herself! This might be an exceptional case, but there are additional reasons to recommend against contingency contracting for weight loss. Most importantly, it does not develop the necessary robust self-regulatory abilities in clients to maintain their weight control after the end of treatment. Indeed, as I have indicated, externally administered controls like this may even serve to undermine whatever self-control the client has or believes he or she possesses.

Having expressed my reservations about contingency contracting, I must note a recent study by Jeffery, Thompson, and Wing (1978) that yielded favorable results. Contracts in which large sums of money ($20 per session) were contingent upon either a prescribed weight loss or changes in eating habits estimated to result in a comparable weight loss produced significantly greater weight losses (approximately 20 pounds) over a ten-week period than did a treatment in which attendance at treatment sessions only was contracted for. The negative side-effects reported by Mann (1972) were not observed and apparently no subject voiced any displeasure with the method.

Finally, various aversion conditioning methods have been used to control overeating and obesity. The most commonly applied technique has been covert sensitization, in which the client imagines experiencing profound nausea or other aversive consequences contingent upon eating a particular food(s). Contrary to claims for its efficacy (e.g., Cautela, 1967), a number of well-controlled studies have shown that covert sensitization is no more effective than a placebo treatment and does not reduce consumption of specific foods through any conditioning mechanism (Diament & Wilson, 1975; Foreyt & Hagen, 1973). Nor is there any justification for requiring obese clients to rehearse images of their fatness as repugnant compared to attractive images of themselves as slimmer. Wooley et al. (1979) state the case against such procedures as follows: "It seems doubtful that lack of shame over eating or appearance can be a cause of obesity; on the contrary, shame frequently leads to perpetuation of such self-destructive attempts at self-help as solitary eating, avoidance of public gatherings, and intermittent self-starvation. There is no evidence that the techniques that foster shame show any advantage over other techniques and even if weight losses were found to be greater, it could still be argued that the overall benefit to the patient is diminished" (p. 20).

Treatment Format: Problems and Possibilities

It is not only the content of behavioral treatment programs that has tended to become too standardized and too routine. The format in which treatment is delivered has been inflexible and unimaginative. In the first place, given the complex and refractory nature of obesity as a clinical disorder, the majority of treatment programs that have been evaluated in controlled studies have been relatively brief—typically lasting from eight to twelve weeks. The rationale for this time schedule has never been made clear, although elsewhere I have suggested that since much of the treatment outcome research has been conducted within university departments, the length of treatment has been determined in large part by the length of the semester. Many university activities, including university clinic-based treatment programs come to a conclusion at the end of a semester! The fact that programs have been invariably time-limited is attributable to research designs that require uniform treatment across conditions. This is a common constraint that is imposed in controlled therapy outcome studies across different problems. More protracted interventions appear warranted. Jeffery et al. (1978) found that the longer the duration of treatment the greater the weight loss at the end of treatment. However, their own findings at the Stanford Eating Disorders Clinic indicated that increasing treatment length did not facilitate long-term success.

A second problem relates to the time-limited nature of treatment programs. It makes better behavioral sense to decide to continue or terminate treatment as a function of change in the behavior in question than to impose treatment limits arbitrarily on the basis of some factor that is unrelated to the person's behavioral performance. Given the assumptions underlying the behavioral approach to weight reduction, treatment decisions of this sort would presumably be based on changes in eating habits rather than weight loss per se. However, recent research has indicated that in addition to actual behavior change, the person's expectations of self-efficacy that derive from such change might be a more powerful predictor of future performance (Bandura, 1977; Wilson, 1979).

Finally, the scheduling of treatment sessions may not have been as effective as it could be. For example, Jeffery et al. (1978) reported that greater weight losses tended to be associated with a higher frequency of treatment sessions. Stuart's (1967) original study combined frequent sessions of intensive treatment over a full year of treatment. The usual practice of scheduling treatment sessions on a fixed weekly basis is an arbitrary one that undoubtedly is based more on the convenience it affords the investigators than on any advantage it may offer the subjects. Fixed, weekly treatment sessions may do for some obese clients, but prove a less satisfactory arrangement for others. Especially difficult cases may require more frequent, intensive treatment sessions several times a week, at least at the start of therapy. Thereafter, treatment sessions may be distributed over longer time intervals.

Standardized treatment programs have, as I mentioned in the earlier discussion of behavioral assessment in obesity, limited the degree to which therapeutic interventions have been tailored to individual needs. In his original study, Stuart (1967) treated his clients on an individual basis and emphasized the importance of individualizing treatment. Yet, subsequent treatment studies have overwhelmingly used a group setting. Lacking empirical justification, this trend is probably attributable to the fact that group treatment is more efficient and to the apparently widespread perception that the treatment techniques could be implemented on a standardized, group basis. In the only study of its kind, Kingsley and Wilson (1977) directly compared the effects of individual versus group behavioral treatment of obesity. The results showed that at the end of an eight-week treatment phase, individual treatment had an edge over group treatment, although this difference did not even approach statistical significance. However, subjects treated on an individual basis showed significant relapse over the one-year follow-up period, whereas group behavioral treatment resulted in successful maintenance of weight loss. At the one-year follow-up assessment, the group treatment was significantly superior to the individual treatment in terms of weight lost. These results indicate that a group setting might be especially useful for maintaining weight loss. This is an area that requires continued investigation.

An optimal treatment approach might consist of varying combinations of individual and group treatment. A flexible, joint approach of this nature would ensure the detailed and individualized assessment of each individual's particular problem, in addition to taking advantage of the motivational benefits afforded by the group context.

An unfortunate characteristic of the clinical behavior therapy literature has been the de-emphasis or even total neglect of the therapist's contribution to behavior change (Wilson & Evans, 1976). Obesity is not exception to this trend, with the qualifications of therapists in outcome studies described only sketchily, if at all (Stuart, 1979; Wilson, 1978b). Yet the role of the therapeutic relationship in the behavioral treatment of complex clinical disorders is important and can be usefully analyzed in terms of social learning theory (Wilson & Evans, 1976). It is not without interest therefore, that Jeffery et al. (1978) reported that experienced therapists produced greater weight loss in their behavioral treatment program and that Levitz and Stunkard (1974) found that professional behavior therapists obtained significantly better results than lay therapists in their successful outcome study. Although the results obtained with a relatively impersonal self-prescription treatment manual have been comparable to those obtained with a therapist-administered program in some studies (e.g., Hagen, 1974; Hanson et al., 1976), Brownell, Heckerman, and Westlake (1978) have reported the superiority of therapist-administered treatment over bibliotherapy. Moreover, Stunkard and Brownell (1979) have reported that a replication and extension of Hagen's (1974) study by Fernan (1973) revealed that an uncontrolled degree of therapist contact with clients in Hagen's bibliotherapy treatment may have been responsible for the good results obtained with this condition. When minimal therapist contact was ensured in Fernan's replication, the outcome was far less favorable. A skilled and experienced therapist can enhance the efficacy of behavioral methods in many ways. Not the least important of these many contributions of the therapist may be his or her role in improving compliance to therapeutic assignments (Wilson, 1979; Wilson & Evans, 1976).

Broadening the Base of Behavior Therapy in the Treatment of Obesity

The usual behavioral treatment program thus far has been unnecessarily limited in nature. Deriving from too simple an operant conditioning model, the exclusive focus was on environmental cues that were assumed to govern overeating. Although described as behavioral self-control, the methods used actually amounted to external situational control of behavior. The behavioral treatment literature on obesity shows surprisingly little evidence of the systematic use of additional behavioral procedures that have been found to be of value in the treatment of other clinical disorders. Some examples may be mentioned.

Social Skills Training. Social skills training that would enable obese individuals to cope more constructively with problem situations has been demonstrated to produce impressive improvement among diverse patient populations, including alcoholics. For example, Chaney, O'Leary, and Marlatt

(1978) have shown that training alcoholics in critical social skills required to resist interpersonal pressure to drink and to cope with untoward emotional reactions like frustration and anger resulted in significantly greater improvement than appropriate control groups. Many of the social or interpersonal difficulties faced by the problem drinker are shared by the obese. Declining a cocktail when dining out with friends or acquaintances at a restuarant is not terribly different from refusing dessert. The obese person has to have the assertive skills to be able to say "no" without becoming a killjoy and without suffering feelings of guilt, shame, or rejection. The obesity treatment literature contains only scattered references to explicit assertion or social skills training (e.g., Musante, 1976).

In our obesity treatment program at Rutgers University, we have adapted the specific social situations used by Chaney et al. (1978) to teach assertive skills competence in coping with emotional upset to overweight college students. An example of the situations that we employ in role-play interactions is the following:

You are eating with friends in a good restaurant on a special occasion. The waitress comes over and asks, "dessert orders?" Everyone else orders a dessert and now all eyes seem to be turned toward you.

Although the laboratory-based research findings are mixed (Ruderman, 1980), few therapists would dispute the contention that emotional factors are often (albeit not always) critical antecedants of overeating and obesity. Thorough behavioral assessment frequently reveals that obese individuals overeat in response to anxiety, anger, or depression. Once again, the parallel to alcohol abuse can be drawn where the clinical evidence strongly implicates the role of emotional distress among the important precipitants of excessive drinking (e.g., Hodgson, Stockwell, & Rankin, 1978). It follows that a comprehensive treatment program would include techniques designed to neutralize the situations that elicit anxiety, anger, or depression and to equip these individuals with effective alternative coping skills. Behavior therapy is demonstrably successful in reducing stress or anxiety (e.g., Goldfried & Davison, 1976) and, more recently, effective treatment programs for coping with anger (Novaco, 1977) and depression (Rush, Beck, Kovacs, & Hollon, 1977) have been developed. It is time that these treatment methods are incorporated into more intensive weight reduction programs that are based more closely on adequate behavioral assessment.

Cognitive Processes in Weight Control. The role of cognitive processes in the regulation and modification of weight has been overlooked in the behavioral treatment literature. This neglect of the role of cognitive processes in the maintenance and modification of obesity is directly traceable to the hard-line operant conditioning model from which the behavioral treatment of obesity was originally derived. Stuart and Davis (1972) characterized this position well in their influential text by emphasizing that "the environment rather than the man is the agent of control in human behavior, so that efforts to modify behavior should be addressed to changing the environment rather than the man" (p. 62). However, not all behavior therapists hold such an extreme view of environmental influence on behavior. The alternative social learning veiwpoint recognizes the importance of environmental influences on behavior but emphasizes that the impact of these influences is, to a large extent, cognitively mediated. In terms of this social learning view, the person is both the object as well as the agent of behavior change (Bandura, 1977; Wilson & O'Leary, 1980). It follows directly from this view that cognitive processes will feature prominently in an effective treatment program. Suffice it to note here the current enthusiasm for "cognitive-behavior therapy" and the mounting evidence of its therapeutic efficacy (cf. Beck, 1976; Mahoney & Arnkoff, 1978; Meichenbaum, 1977; Rachman & Wilson, in press).

The importance of these relatively recent therapeutic developments is underscored by the fact that there is good evidence that cognitive factors influence the obese person's eating behavior (e.g., Rodin, 1978a). A recent self-help book by Mahoney and Mahoney (1976) has emphasized the importance of cognitive factors and includes several cognitive treatment methods. Controlled outcome studies are needed to evaluate the effects of cognitive-behavioral interventions and some initial investigations have begun to appear. Dunkel and Glaros (1978) compared a cognitive treatment based on Meichenbaum's (1977) self-instructional training approach to a stimulus control treatment, a combined self-instructional and stimulus control treatment, and a placebo treatment, and showed that the self-instructional and combined treatments were superior at a seven-week follow-up. Particularly promising results have been reported by Rodin (1978a). She has found that a thoughtfully developed multifaceted treatment program combining behavioral and cognitive reappraisal and coping strategies produces significantly greater weight loss than either the conventional behavioral program alone or an educational approach. Among the several cognitive strategies employed by Rodin are self-instructional training and stress-innoculation training (Meichenbaum, 1977), relabeling of hunger and other internal sensations, cognitive transformations and attentional shifts, reanalysis of attributional processes, and guided imagery. The fact that Rodin reports substantial weight losses that are maintained over an 18-month follow-up for roughly 60% of the people who receive the multifaceted cognitive-behavioral program is especially noteworthy. On a less positive note, Collins (1980) found that while a combined cognitive-behavioral treatment program produced slightly greater weight loss than either a behavioral, a cognitive, or a placebo control treatment alone, the differences were not statistically significant due to the familiar finding of marked inter-individual variability in outcome.

The Importance of Physical Exercise. A most important component of a comprehensive treatment program for obesity that is frequently omitted or underemphasized is an explicit emphasis on physical exercise. The role of physical exercise in the development, maintenance, and modification of obesity is receiving increasing attention, detailed analyses being provided by Bjorntorp (1978) and Mahoney et al. (in press).

There is hard evidence of the beneficial effect of including an exercise component in a behavioral weight control program. Harris and Hallbauer (1973) found no difference between behavioral treatment focusing on changing eating habits and an expanded treatment program that was designed to increase exercise in addition to decreasing food intake at the end of a 12-week treatment period. At a four-month follow-up, however, the treatment that included an emphasis on exercise produced significantly more weight loss. In a well-controlled outcome study, Stalonas, Johnson, and Christ (1978) found that a structured exercise component contributed importantly to the maintenance of weight loss in their behavioral treatment program at a one-year follow-up. More recently, Zegman, Wilson, and Dubbert (1979) demonstrated that adding a systematic exercise component to a multifaceted cognitive-behavioral program produced greater weight loss at the end of three months of treatment than the behavioral program that focused on eating habits with simple advice about the benefits of exercise.

Maintenance of Treatment-Produced Weight Loss

Evaluation of treatment outcome must distinguish among the initial induction of behavioral change, its generalization across people and settings, and its maintenance over time (Bandura, 1969). Different variables may govern each of these separate but related processes, and maintenance of treatment effects can be ensured only to the extent that strategies explicitly designed to accomplish this objective are part and parcel of the overall intervention. Despite the recognition of this important conceptual distinction by behavioral investigators, long-term follow-up studies have been lacking and research on the development of effective maintenance strategies slow in coming (Kazdin & Wilson, 1978). This lack is particularly significant in the treatment of obesity, a disorder that has been indelibly characterized by a notoriously high relapse rate following initial weight loss in treatment. How to maintain weight loss is *the* problem in the treatment of obesity. Of course, as the other chapters in this volume make clear, there is a pressing need to develop maintenance strategies in the treatment of all addictive disorders. This is clearly one area in which there is a very real commonality in substance abuse and specific maintenance strategies are likely to prove broadly effective across disorders (see chapter by Cummings, Gordon, and Marlatt in this volume). Consequently, the recent interest on the part of behavioral researchers in maintenance strategies is a most welcome development.

The emerging literature on maintenance strategies is summarized elsewhere (e.g., Franks & Wilson, 1978). Suffice it here to indicate briefly the strategies that have been applied in the treatment of obesity.

Booster Sessions

Historically in behavior therapy, booster sessions have long been advanced as a major means of maintaining behavior change (Eysenck & Rachman, 1965). Several studies have now been completed with obese populations and the results are not encouraging. In contrast to the favorable findings of Hall, Bass, and Monroe (1978) and Kingsley and Wilson (1977), Ashby and Wilson (1977), Hall, Hall, Borden, and Hanson (1975) and Wilson and Brownell (1978) all failed to show that booster sessions promoted lasting weight losses. Negative results using booster sessions have also been reported in the treatment of cigarette smoking (Elliot & Denney, 1978; Relinger, Bornstein, Bugge, Carmody, & Zohn, 1977).

The inconsistent results obtained with booster sessions call for a reconceptualization of the nature and purpose of booster sessions as a maintenance strategy. The use of booster sessions derives from the conditioning model in which they are designed to strengthen conditioned responses that were established in treatment. These conditioned responses are considered to be the result of an automatic conditioning process which is subsequently weakened by the natural course of extinction. However, in terms of a social learning analysis, conditioned reactions are self-activated rather than automatically elicited (Bandura, 1977). This latter framework emphasizes self-regulatory strategies, rather than stimulus-response bonds, and the person assumes greater responsibility for self-directed behavior change. Booster sessions that are pre-arranged to occur at fixed time intervals following treatment may be insufficient to ensure implementation of the self-regulatory strategies the individual acquires during therapy. According to the social learning approach, clients have to learn to monitor their problem behaviors and to reinstate self-corrective procedures at the first signs of the erosion of treatment-produced improvement. An example of this sort of maintenance strategy is described by Bandura and Simon (1977). In this procedure, clients monitored their weight and used a specific weight level as a cue to reinstate self-regulatory strategies for controlling weight gain. It should also be noted that one of the main correlates of the maintenance of weight lost through the behavioral program offered by Weight Watchers was the perception by people of themselves as ''overweight'' when they were only a few pounds above their goal weight (Stuart & Guire, 1978). Although caution must be exercised in drawing conclusions from this correlational study of Stuart and Guire's, this interesting finding is consistent with the view proposed here that successful maintenance of weight loss requires constant vigilance and the willingness to nip problems in the bud as it were by the timely reinstatement of self-regulatory procedures.

In addition to the availability of the necessary self-regulatory strategies—which have been reasonably well delineated in behavior therapy and self-monitoring of progress and the provision of well-defined early warning systems that will trigger a self-regulatory alarm before individuals lose behavioral control—successful maintenance of therapeutic change involves arranging the incentives that sustain the reinstatement of self-regulatory measures. Booster sessions may be effective on occasion because they happen to occur at the appropriate time and serve as incentives for reinstating waning self-control activities. In other cases, booster sessions determined by the therapist may be too little and too late to check deteriorating self-regulatory capacities. In these instances, sources of external support probably need to be tailored to the individual client's particular needs.

Social Support Systems

One obvious but as yet largely untapped source of external support is the obese person's immediate family, particularly his or her spouse. Stuart and Davis (1972) emphasized the potentially important contribution of family members to weight loss but systematic investigation of this possibility is a very recent development. The initial results are extremely encouraging. Brownell et al. (1978) found that including the obese person's spouse in a fairly conventional behavioral self-control treatment program modeled after Stuart and Davis (1972) produced significantly greater weight loss at three- and six-month follow-ups than groups in which spouses did not participate. Another important finding of this study was that subjects in the couples training (spouse present) treatment showed an average weight loss of nearly 30 pounds eight and a half-months after the beginning of treatment. This clinically significant result ranks with the most impressive weight losses reported thus far in a controlled outcome study. In a field where inconsistent results and variability in outcome have been commonplace, it is gratifying to note that other investigators have replicated the superiority of couples training in a similar program (Pearce, LeBow, & Orchard, 1979).

Beyond the family, other social support systems that look like good candidates for promoting maintenance of weight loss include the person's natural work environment and community-sponsored interventions. In industry, management and trade unions alike have expressed considerable interest in developing cost-effective behavioral health programs that include weight control components. We can anticipate increased research in these areas, together with innovative uses of the media to promote better dietary practices and weight control.

Cognitive Maintenance Strategies

Cognitive maintenance strategies have begun to assume considerable importance in recent psychological explanations of the phenomena of relapse and how to forestall relapse (Marlatt & Gordon, 1979; Rodin, 1978a; Wilson, 1978a). Cummings, Gordon, and Marlatt (in this volume) present a detailed cognitive-behavioral formulation of the process of relapse in the addictive disorders and suggest what steps might be taken to facilitate maintenance of therapeutic improvement. Although as yet untested, this cognitive-behavioral analysis promises to improve our treatment of many obese clients and can be summarized in the following manner.

Consider the case of an obese individual who has been treated successfully and has lost a substantial amount of weight. At some point after the termination of treatment, the person starts slipping and begins to deviate from the strictures of the behavioral self-control program. At this point, whether the person reverts to previous patterns of overeating (and failure to exercise sufficiently), or re-establishes control by himself or herself, or re-enters treatment for this purpose, will be influenced in part by the way in which this person construes the violation of postreatment adherence to a program for control of weight gain. In other words, it may not be the slips per se that will determine subsequent behavior but the meaning that the person attaches to them. Marlatt and Gordon (in press) point out that a typical negative reaction is for the person to attribute the transgressions to what in the terminology of attribution theory would be an internal-stable cause. In short, the person sees in his or her failure to adhere to the requirements of the weight control program an affirmation of his or her personal inability to regulate weight. Previous treatment success, albeit short-term, is dismissed or discounted as insignificant. Among the adverse sequelae of such an attribution is a sense of helplessness. Other self-defeating cognitions involve extensive rationalization. For example, the obese person who eats too much on occasion might decide that since he or she has "blown" the treatment program for that day, why not go ahead and overindulge for the remainder of the day and return to the treatment program tomorrow—and tomorrow, and tomorrow.

In a closely related vein, I have suggested that the degree to which the client will be able to resist these negative cognitive reactions to post-treatment setbacks in adhering to a controlled behavioral routine will depend on treatment-induced expectations of self-efficacy. As proposed by Bandura (1977), efficacy expectations are the conviction that one can cope successfully with a given situation. Self-efficacy theory holds that efficacy expectations will determine whether coping behavior will be initiated, with what effort, and how resolute one will be in continuing to cope in the face of the inevitable pressures and problems that are encountered by the individual struggling to control weight. The client who, as a result of treatment, has strong efficacy expectations about coping with high risk situations is more likely to overcome the potentially destructive consequences of a posttreatment transgression.

A number of specific treatment and maintenance strategies derive from these cognitive-behavioral formulations of the maintenance of treatment effects. It is important to anticipate possible or probable setbacks or transgressions during treatment, and to equip the client with cognitive and behavioral

coping strategies for negotiating such setbacks. Teaching the client the appropriate cognitive reappraisal and coping strategies involves role-playing and
imaginal rehearsal of high-risk situations. Specific difficulties are confronted
and the client's self-statements, self-evaluation, and labeling of the situation
carefully monitored. In our treatment program at Rutgers University, borrow-
ing from Marlatt and Gordon (1979), we rehearse the following ''Emergency
Drill Information'' with clients and provide them with a copy of these instructions that they are asked to keep with them at all times:

Your treatment success will depend on the preseverance you show in following program instructions now that formal treatment sessions have ended. However, you are fallible, and it is highly
probable that you will overeat at a particular meal or on a specific day. When you do, it is
IMPORTANT that you take ten minutes out and remind yourself of the following facts:

1. To err is human. A deviation from the program is not unusual. It does *not* mean that you are a
treatment failure. It does *not* mean that you have lost control or that you have no will-power.
It does *not* mean that all previous weight loss was in vain. It does *not* mean that further weight
gain is inevitable. Do not catastrophize.

2. It *does* mean that you have to watch carefully the thoughts and feelings you experience
immediately after overeating. It *does* mean that you have to take some helpful actions right
now.

3. Be honest and acknowledge that you have made a mistake. But use this mistake to your
advantage. Make a commitment to learn from your mistake so that you can avoid it in the
future. For example, if the same situation occurred in the future, think how you would cope
better with the situation without overeating. *Imagine* yourself succeeding in this coping
response in the future. Think of the *future;* do not dwell on the past.

4. Try not to feel guilty, frustrated, or discouraged. If you do, remind yourself that these
feelings will pass. Keep telling yourself that your deviation from the program does *not* mean
that you have to continue overeating. Do not use the mistake to punish yourself.

5. Get back to the program NOW. Not tomorrow, not next week but right NOW. Avoid the
''cop-out'' response, i.e., ''since I have blown the program today I might as well go ahead
and eat as much as I want and go back to the program tomorrow or next week.''

Compliance with Therapeutic Instructions

No treatment strategy will be successful in the long run unless clients comply
with therapeutic instructions. More than any other form of psychological
intervention, behavior therapy involves asking the person to *do*
something—self-monitor daily caloric intake, place the fork down on the table
between bites, identify maladaptive cognitions and replace them with more
constructive self-statements, act assertively, and so on. Much of the success of
behavior therapy has been in the development and refinement of a wide range
of different techniques for the modification of psychological functioning.
However, there has been less emphasis on, and hence less progress in, the
clinical realities of maximizing clients' compliance with these technical advances. To some extent, non-compliance with therapeutic instructions often

resembles the well-known phenomenon of *resistance* in traditional psychotherapy. More often than not, the outcome of behavioral interventions will hinge on the degree to which clients' resistance or non-compliance with therapeutic instructions is successfully negotiated.

As Brownell and Stunkard (1978) and Mahoney (1975) have pointed out, there has been little direct assessment of compliance with therapeutic instructions in behavioral treatment programs for obesity. The handful of studies that has related self-reported habit change to weight loss has yielded mixed results. It is difficult to derive an estimate of compliance itself from most of these investigations. Epstein and Martin (1977) conducted a study in which they assessed subjects' compliance to treatment instructions to self-monitor daily food intake and exercise activities. They found that training subjects in the skill of self-monitoring prior to actual treatment increased compliance over simply instructing clients to self-monitor. Compliance was estimated by associates of the subjects with whom they often ate and was derived from subjects' behavior while eating two meals a week. It remains to be shown whether compliance measures based on limited sampling of this nature are generally representative of subjects' behavior. Not surprisingly, compliance under both conditions was variable and ''probably not uniformly high enough to insure adequate learning of new responses'' (p. 556). Stalonas et al. (1978) reported that given the limitations of self-reports of compliance, the subjects stuck to program instructions ''at or near optimal level'' (p. 466).

Few serious behavioral formulations of the phenomena encompassed by the concept of resistance or non-compliance have been attempted. Davison (1973) and Mahoney (1974a) have discussed some of the key issues in resistance in terms of the client's counter-control against the therapist's influence, and a preliminary outline of a behavioral analysis of compliance has been put forward by Zifferblatt (1975). Among the various strategies for improving compliance with therapeutic regimens are the following.

One of the problems with the traditional psychodynamic concept of resistance is that it is inevitably assumed to be purposive or unconsciously motivated. However, resistance or non-compliance is not necessarily volitional. A more parsimonious explanation in many instances is that the client is unable rather than unwilling to respond in the manner desired by the therapist. For example, the task demands may be impractical given the current situation and mood of the client, or instructing an obese client to count calories consistently might be too demanding because of interfering anxieties and depression. Alternatively, the person may not possess the necessary behavioral repertoire to comply with particular assignments. In this case, direct training and rehearsal of specific assignments during therapy is indicated.

In developing alternative behavioral patterns, it is important to adopt a carefully graded approach (the operant conditioning notion of shaping). Take physical exercise as an example. Attempting to move too fast may not only pose a physical hazard to the overweight and out-of-shape person, but also result in premature drop-outs due to the generally negative consequences most people initially experience as they embark upon structured exercise programs. In our clinical research we have found that it may take varying amounts of time, ranging from weeks to months, before the benefits of systematic exercise begin to outweigh the initial negative effects. Of course, not everyone reaches this point where physical exercise seems to become intrinsically reinforcing, but many do on the basis of a sensibly regulated one-step-at-a-time program.

A consistent finding from the literature on compliance with medical regimens is that as the complexity of treatment increases, compliance decreases (Blackwell, 1976; Dunbar & Stunkard, 1979). In this regard, it is important to bear in mind that most behavioral treatment programs have been multifaceted interventions that have required far-ranging changes in lifestyle over the course of a relatively short time span (e.g., eight to twelve weeks). It is quite likely that these complex programs have amounted to asking the obese person to do too much too soon, with spotty compliance and perhaps variable treatment effecting the net result (Wilson, 1979a). If clients are presented with a smorgasbord of different techniques—as is usually the case in the behavioral treatment of obesity—they might easily infer that compliance to at least one or two is sufficient. Their choice might not always be the desirable one, especially since they are likely to forego time-consuming and effortful but effective methods (e.g., self-monitoring of daily caloric intake). The therapist might inadvertently contribute to this client behavior. There is evidence that the therapist's attitudes towards treatment procedures influence client compliance. For example, clients prescribed anti-psychotic drugs by a physician who did not believe fully in drug treatment showed lower compliance rates than patients treated by a physician who subscribed to their efficacy (Blackwell, 1976). It may be that, in instructing a client to engage in a number of different homework assignments, the therapist conveys the attitude that he or she does not expect 100% compliance to all tasks. However, if the therapist is intervening with a single technique, he or she is likely to be more decisive in conveying to the client the necessity of adhering to the assignment. For one thing, the therapist is obviously committed to that technique at that time and is likely to communicate enthusiasm and a belief in its efficacy. These ''nonspecifics'' are an important part of all successful treatments, including behavior therapy (Wilson, 1979b). Required to carry out a single task (or at least limited assignments), clients know that they are more easily accountable to the therapist the following session when homework assignments are reviewed. This analysis might account for McReynolds and Paulsen's (1976) finding that a component of the total treatment program (stimulus control) was significantly more effective than the full program itself in producing weight loss at three-, six-, and nine-month follow-ups. The implication of this is to add further weight to one of the recommendations proposed earlier in this chapter, namely, that programs should be tailored to each individual and multiple techniques introduced contingent upon the person's actual progress and response to previous methods.

Behavior change will be facilitated to the extent that it is made as easy as possible and can be integrated into the person's natural life-style without undue disruption. Again, increasing physical exercise serves to illustrate this point. A certain proportion of people who participate in weight reduction programs will take avidly to structured exercise programs such as jogging. Others will find such activities artificial and intrusive, and are likely drop-outs if they ever agree to try the program in the first place. For these many individuals, it is recommended that naturally available exercise options are utilized. Modest but consistent changes in activity such as taking the stairs rather than the elevator, parking reasonable distances from one's destination rather than risking a ticket for illegal parking close to the supermarket entrance, disembarking from a bus at an earlier stop, and simply walking or bicycling where once the automobile was used should be encouraged (Brownell, in press; Mahoney & Mahoney, 1976).

Therapeutic assignments should be specific and well-defined, and clients should be encouraged to make a public comittment to completing them. The therapist or group leader should provide a clear rationale for the use of different treatment methods and outline what effects he or she expects them to produce. The overall tone of the presentation is preferably one of balanced optimism, pointing out the probable positive consequences without overlooking the realistic and inevitable difficulties associated with weight control. As discussed in the section on cognitive control as a maintenance strategy, realistic expectations and the anticipation of possible pitfalls will help to buffer the shocks of minor setbacks along the rocky road to durable weight loss.

The manner in which therapeutic assignments are prescribed can be crucial. It is vital that the therapist or person conducting the weight reduction program communicate to clients that homework assignments are an integral part of the treatment and that full compliance is expected. Most importantly, all homework assignments must be diligently checked first thing at the following session. Any difficulties the clients encountered should be analyzed fully and alternative strategies suggested or the nature of the assignments appropriately modified. Clients are quick to sense that a therapist or group leader is not fully committed to regular compliance with assignments and it should come as no surprise therefore if, in fact, that therapist or group leader finds declining or inconsistent compliance.

Another behavioral strategy for obtaining compliance has been the use of externally imposed incentive systems or contingency contracting. An example of this strategy would be entering into a contract with the client that specifies the return of portions of a refundable deposit contingent upon completion of prescribed program activities. The pros and cons of this use of external incentives have been discussed earlier in this chapter. Although it might prove useful in certain limited situations, contingency contracting of this sort is unlikely to have wide applicability in combating non-compliance. Indeed, as I have cautioned, it might under some circumstances elicit non-compliance.

In the treatment of any clinical disorder, obesity included, non-compliance should lead the therapist to evaluate the nature of his or her therapeutic relationship with the client. To check that the client is not distrustful or lacking confidence in the treatment program embarked upon, it is recommended that the therapist encourage subjective feedback about the client's feelings and expectations. The evidence from compliance with medical regimens shows that elements of the therapeutic relationship such as the person's trust in the physician (therapist) can significantly influence compliance (Dunbar & Stunkard, in press). Similarly, the data indicate that patients' expectations of treatment outcome will affect compliance (Becker & Maiman, 1975; Blackwell, 1976; Dunbar & Stunkard, 1980).

References

Adams, N., Ferguson, J., Stunkard, A. J., & Agras, W. S. The eating behavior of obsese and nonobese women. *Behaviour Research and Therapy*, 1978, **16**, 225-232.

Agras, W. S., Ferguson, J. M., Greaves, C., Qualls, B., Rand, C. S. W., Ruby, J., Stunkard, A. J., Taylor, C. B., Werne, J., & Wright, C. A clinical and research questionnaire for obese patients. In B. J. Williams, S. Martin, & J. P. Foreyt (Eds.) *Obesity: Behavioral approaches to dietary management*. New York: Brunner/Mazel, 1976.

Ashby, W. A., & Wilson, G. T. Behavior Therapy for obesity: Booster sessions and long-term maintenance of weight loss. *Behaviour Research and Therapy*, 1977, **15**, 451-466.

Atkins, R. C. *Dr. Atkins super energy diet,* New York: Crown, 1977.

Bandura, A. *Principles of behavior modification*. New York: Holt, 1969.

Bandura, A. *Social learning theory,* Englewood Cliffs, N.J.: Prentice-Hall, 1977.

Banduara, A. & Simon, K. M. The role of proximal intentions in self-regulation of refractory behavior. *Cognitive Therapy and Research*, 1977, **1**, 177-193.

Bellack, A. S., Rozensky, R. H., & Schwartz, J. A comparison of two forms of self-monitoring in a behavioral weight reduction program. *Behavior Therapy*, 1974, **5**, 523-530.

Bjorntorp, P., Carlgren, G., Isaksson, B., Krotkiewski, M., Larsson, & Sjostrom, L. Effects of an energy-reduced dietary regimen in relation to adipose tissue cellularity in obese women. *American Journal of Clinical Nutrition*, 1975, **28**, 445-452.

Bray, G. A. *The obese patient*. Philadelphia: Saunders, 1976.

Bray, G. A., Jordan, H. A., & Sims, E. A. H. Evaluation of the obese patient. *Journal of the American Medical Association*, 1976, **235**, 1487-1491.

Brownell, K. D. Assessment in the treatment of eating disorders. In D. H. Barlow (Ed.), *Behavioral assessment of adult disorders*. New York: Guilford, in press.

Brownell, K. D., Heckerman, C. L. & Westlake, R. T. Therapist and group contact as variables in the behavioral treatment of obesity. *Journal of Consulting and Clinical Psychology*, 1978, **46**, 593-596.

Brownell, K. D., Heckerman, C., Westlake, R. J., Hayes, S. C., & Monti, P. The effect of couples training and partner cooperativeness in the behavioral treatment of obesity. *Behaviour Research and Therapy,* 1978, **16,** 323-333.

Brownell, K. D. & Stunkard, A. J. Behavior therapy and behavior change: Uncertainties in programs for weight control. *Behaviour Research and Therapy,* 1978, **16,** 301.

Cautela, J. Covert sensitization. *Psychological Reports,* 1967, **20,** 459-468.

Chaney, E. F., O'Leary, M. R., & Marlatt, G. A. Skill training with alcoholics. *Journal of Consulting and Clinical Psychology,* 1978, **46,** 1092-1104.

Chapman, S. L. & Jeffrey, B. Situational management, standard setting and self-reward in a behavior modification weight loss program. *Journal of Consulting and Clinical Psychology,* 1978, **46,** 1588-1589.

Collins, L. A cognitive-behavioral approach in the treatment of obesity. Unpublished doctoral dissertation, Rutgers University, 1980.

Diament, C., & Wilson, G. T. An experimental investigation of the effects of covert sensitization in an analogue eating situation. *Behavior Therapy,* 1975, **6,** 499-509.

Dunbar, J. & Stunkard, A. J. Adherence to diet and drug regimen. In R. Levy, B. Rifkind, B. Dennis & N. Ernst (Eds.), *Nutrition, lipids, and coronary heart disease.* New York: Raven Press, 1979.

Dunkel, L. D. & Glaros, A. Comparison of self-instructional and stimulus control treatments for obesity. *Cognitive Therapy and Research,* 1978, **2,** 75-78.

Elliott, C. H. & Denney, D. R. A multiple-component treatment approach to smoking reduction. *Journal of Consulting and Clinical Psychology,* 1978, **46,** 1330-1339.

Eysenck, H. J. & Rachman, S. *Causes and cures of neuroses.* London: Routledge and Kegan Paul, 1965.

Ferguson, J. M. *Learning to eat: Behavior modification for weight control.* Palo Alto, Ca: Bull, 1975.

Fernan, W. S. The role of experimenter contact in behavioral bibliotherapy of obesity. Unpublished manuscript, The Pennsylvania State University, 1973.

Ferster, C. B., Nurnberger, J. I., & Levitt, E. B. The control of eating. *Journal of Mathetics,* 1962, **1,** 87-109.

Foreyt, J. P. & Hagen, R. L. Covert sensitization: Conditioning or suggestion? *Journal of Abnormal Psychology,* 1973, **82,** 17-23.

Franks, C. M. & Wilson, G. T. *Annual review of behavior therapy: Theory and practice,* Vol. IV. New York: Brunner/Mazel, 1976.

Franks, C. M., & Wilson, G. T. *Annual Review of behavior therapy: Theory and practice,* Vol. V. New York: Brunner/Mazel, 1977.

Franks, C. M., & Wilson, G. T. *Annual review of behavior therapy: Theory and practice,* Vol. VI New York: Brunner/Mazel, 1978.

Goldfried, M. R., & Davison, G. C. *Clinical behavior therapy.* New York: Holt, Rinehart & Winston, 1976.

Green, L. The temporal and stimulus dimensions of self-monitoring in the behavioral treatment of obesity. *Behavior Therapy,* 1978, **9,** 328-341.

Hagen, R. L. Group therapy versus bibliotherapy in weight reduction. *Behavior Therapy,* 1974, **5,** 222-234.

Hagen, R. L., Foreyt, J. P., & Durham, I. W. The dropout problem: Reducing attrition in obesity research. *Behavior Therapy,* 1976, **7,** 463-471.

Hall, S. M., Bass, A. & Monroe, J. Continued contact and monitoring as follow-up strategies: A long-term study of obesity treatment, *Addictive Behaviors,* 1978, **3,** 139-147.

Hall, S. M., Hall, R. G., Borden, B. L., & Hanson, R. W. Follow-up strategies in the behavioral treatment of overweight. *Behaviour Research and Therapy,* 1975, **13**, 167-172.

Hanson, R. W., Borden, B. L., Hall, S. M., & Hall, R. G. Use of programmed instruction in teaching self-management skills to overweight adults. *Behavior Therapy,* 1976, **7**, 366-373.

Hersen, M. & Barlow, D. H. *Single use experimental designs: Strategies for studying behavior change.* New York: Pergamon Press, 1976.

Hodgson, R., Rankin, H., & Stockwell, T. Craving and loss of control. In P. E. Nathan, G. A. Marlatt & T. Loberg (Eds.), *Alcoholism: New directions in behavioral research and treatment.* New York: Plenum, 1978.

Jeffery, R. W., Thompson, P. D., & Wing, R. R. Effects on weight reduction of string monetary contracts for calorie restriction of weight loss. *Behaviour Research and Therapy,* 1978, **16**, 363-370.

Jeffery, R. W., Wing, R. R., & Stunkard, A. J. Behavioral treatment of obesity: The state of the art. *Behavior Therapy,* 1978, **9**, 189-199.

Jeffrey, D. B. A comparison of the effects of external control and self-control on the modification and maintenance of weight. *Journal of Abnormal Psychology,* 1974, **83**, 404-410.

Kazdin, A. E. & Wilson, G. T. *Evaluation of behavior therapy: Issues, evidence and research strategies.* Cambridge, Mass: Ballinger, 1978.

Keesey, R. E. Set-points and body-weight revaluation. *Psychiatric Clinics of North America,* 1978, **1**, 5230544.

Kingsley, R. G. & Wilson, G. T. Behavior therapy for obesity: A comparative investigation of long-term efficacy. *Journal of Consulting and Clinical Psychology,* 1977, **45**, 288-298.

Lazarus, A. A. *Behavior therapy and beyond,* New York: McGraw-Hill, 1971.

Leon, G. R. Current directions in the treatment of obesity. *Psychological Bulletin,* 1976, **83**, 557-578.

Loro, A. D., Jr., Fisher, E. B., Jr., & Levekron, J. C. Comparison of established and innovative weight-reduction treatment procedures. *Journal of Applied Behavior Analysis,* 1979, **12**, 141-155.

Mahoney, M. J. Self-reward and self-monitoring techniques for weight control. *Behavior Therapy,* 1974, **5**, 48-57.

Mahoney, M. J. Fat fiction. *Behavior Therapy,* 1975, **6**, 416-418.

Mahoney, M. J. Behavior modification in the treatment of obesity. *Psychiatric Clinics of North America,* 1978, **1**, 651-660.

Mahoney, M. J. & Arnkoff, D. Cognitive and self-control therapies. In S. L. Garfield & A. E. Bergin (Eds.), *Handbook of psychotherapy and behavior change,* 2nd Ed. New York: Wiley, 1978.

Mahoney, M. J. & Mahoney, K. *Permanent weight control.* New York: W. W. Norton, 1976.

Mahoney, B. K., Rogers, T., Straw, M. K., & Mahoney, M. J. *Human obesity: Assessment and treatment,* Englewood Cliffs, N. J.: Prentice-Hall, in press.

Mann, R. A. The behavior-therapeutic use of contingency contracting to control an adult behavior problem: weight control. *Journal of Applied Behavior Analysis,* 1972, **5**, 99-109.

Marlatt, G. A. & Gordon, J. R. Determinants of relapse: Implications for the maintenance of behavior change. In P. Davidson & S. Davidson (Eds.), *Behavioral medicine: Changing health life styles,* New York: Brunner/Mazel, 1971.

McReynolds, W. T. & Paulsen, B. K. Stimulus control in the behavioral basis of weight loss procedures. In B. J. Williams, S. Martin, & J. Foreyt, (Eds.), *Obesity: Behavioral approaches to dietary management.* New York: Brunner/Mazel, 1976, Pp. 43-64.

Meichenbaum, D. *Cognitive behavior modification.* New York: Plenum, 1977b.

Mischel, W. *Personality and assessment.* New York: Wiley, 1968.

Musante, G. J. The dietary rehabilitation clinic: Evaluative report of a behavioral and dietary treatment of obesity. *Behavior Therapy,* 1976, **7,** 198-204.

Nisbett, R. Hunger, obesity, and the ventromedial hypothalamus. *Psychological Review,* 1972, **79,** 433-470.

Novaco, R. W. Stress inoculation: A cognitive therapy for anger and its application in a case of depression. *Journal of Consulting and Clinical Psychology,* 1977, **45,** 600-605.

O'Neil, P. M., Currey, H. S., Hirsch, A. A., Malcolm, R. J., Riddle, E., & Sexauer, J. D. *Eating behavior inventory.* Paper presented at the Taos International Conference on Addictive Disorders. Taos, New Mexico, February, 1979.

Öst, L. & Götestam, K. Behavioral and pharmacological treatments for obesity: An experimental comparison. *Addictive Behaviors,* 1976, **1,** 331-338.

Pearce, J. W., LeBow, M. D., & Orchard, J. The role of spouse involvement in the behavioral treatment of obese women. Paper presented at the Canadian Psychological Association, Quebec City, Quebec, June 15, 1979.

Ruderman, A. Social anxiety and over-eating: An experimental analysis of tension reduction in the maintenance of obesity. Unpublished doctoral dissertation, Rutgers University, 1980.

Relinger, H., Bornstein, P. H., Bugge, I. D., Carmody, T. P., & Zohn, C. J. Utilization of adverse rapid smoking in groups: Efficacy of treatment and maintenance procedures. *Journal of Consulting and Clinical Psychology,* 1977, **45,** 245-249.

Rodin, J. Cognitive-behavioral strategies for the control of obesity. New York: In D. Meichenbaum (Ed.) *Cognitive behavior therapy.* BMA Audio Cassette Publications, 1978 (a).

Rodin, J. Environmental factors in obesity. *Psychiatric Clinics of North America,* 1978, **1,** 581-592 (b).

Romanczyk, R. G., Tracey, D. A., Wilson, G. T., & Thorpe, G. L. Behavioral techniques in the treatment of obesity: A comparative analysis. *Behaviour Research and Therapy,* 1973, **11,** 629-640.

Rush, A. J., Beck, A. T. Kovacs, M., & Hollon, S. Comparative efficacy of cognitive therapy and pharmacotherapy in the treatment of depressed out-patients. *Cognitive Therapy and Research,* 1977, **1,** 17-37.

Schachter, S. Some extraordinary facts about obese humans and rats. *American Psychologist,* 1971, **25,** 129-144.

Sjostrom, L. The Contribution of fat cells to the determination of body weight. *Psychiatric Clinics of North America,* 1978, **1,** 493-522.

Stalonas, P. M., Johnson, W. G., & Christ, M. Behavior modification for obesity: The evaluation of exercise, contingency management and program adherence. *Journal of Consulting and Clinical Psychology*, 1978, **46**, 463-469.

Stuart, R. B. Behavioral control of overeating. *Behaviour Research and Therapy*, 1967, **5**, 357-365.

Stuart, R. B. Weight loss and beyond: Are they taking it off and keeping it off? In P. O. Davidson & S. Davidson (Eds.) *Behavioral medicine: Techniques for promoting life style change*. New York: Brunner/Mazel, 1979.

Stuart, R. B., & Davis, B. *Slim chance in a fat world*. Champaign, Ill.: Research Press, 1972.

Stuart, R. B. & Guire, K. Some correlates of the maintenance of weight loss through behavior modification. *International Journal of Obesity*, 1978, **2**, 225-235.

Stuart, R. B. & Mitchell, C. A professional and a consumer perspective on self-help weight control programs. In A. J. Stunkard (Ed.), *The Psychiatric Clinics of North America: Symposium on Obesity*. Philadelphia, Pa: W. B. Saunders, 1978.

Stunkard, A. J. Eating patterns and obesity. *Psychiatric Quarterly*, 1959, **33**, 284-297.

Stunkard, A. J. (Ed.) Symposium on obesity. *Psychiatric Clinics of North America*, 1978, **1**.

Stunkard, A. J. & Brownell, K. D. Behaviour therapy and self-help programmes for obesity. In J. F. Munro (Ed.), *Treatment of obesity*. Lancaster, England: MTP Press, 1979.

Stunkard, A. J., Coll, M. & Lundquist, S. Obesity and eating style. *Archives of General Psychiatry*, in press.

Stunkard, A. J. & Kaplan, D. Eating in public places: A review of reports of the direct observation of eating behavior. *International Journal of Obesity*, 1977, **1**, 89-101.

Stunkard, A. J. & Mahoney, M. J. Behavioral treatment of the eating disorders. In H. Leitenberg (Ed.), *Handbook of behavior modification and behavior therapy*. New York: Appleton Century Crofts, 1976.

Stunkard, A. J. & Penick, S. Behavior modification in the treatment of obesity. The problem of maintaining weight loss. *Archives of General Psychology*, in press.

Taylor, C. B., Ferguson, J. M., R. Reading, J. C. Gradual weight loss and depression. *Behavior Therapy*, 1978, **9**, 622-625.

Wilson, G. T. Obesity, binge eating, and behavior therapy: Some clinical observations. *Behavior Therapy*, 1976, **7**, 700-701.

Wilson, G. T. Booze, beliefs, and behavior: Cognitive processes in alcohol use and abuse. In P. E. Nathan, G. A. Marlatt & T. Loberg (Eds.) *Alcoholism: New directions in behavioral research and treatment*. New York: Plenum Press, 1978a.

Wilson, G. T. Methodological considerations in treatment outcome research on obesity. *Journal of Consulting and Clinical Psychology*, 1978b, **46**, 687-702.

Wilson, G. T. Cognitive factors in life-style changes: A Social learning perspective. In P. Davidson (Ed) *Behavioral medicine*. New York: Brunner/Mazel, 1979.

Wilson, G. T. The behavioral treatment of obesity: Current status and future direction. In *Proceedings of the Conference on Commonalities in Substance Abuse*. Washington, D.C.: National Institute of Drug Abuse, in press (a).

Wilson, G. T. Toward specifying the "nonspecifics" in behavior therapy: A social learning analysis. In M. J. Mahoney (Ed.), *Cognition and clinical science*. New York: Plenum, in press (b).

Wilson, G. T. & Brownell, K. D. Behavior therapy for obesity: Including family members in the treatment process. *Behavior Therapy,* 1978, **9,** 943-945.

Wilson, G. T. & Brownell, K. D. The efficacy of the behavioral treatment of obesity. Unpublished manuscript, 1980.

Wilson, G. T. & Evans, I. M. Adult behavior therapy and the therapist-client relationship. In C. M. Franks & G. T. Wilson, *Annual review of behavior therapy: Theory and Practice,* Vol. IV, New York: Brunner/Mazel, 1976.

Wilson, G. T. & O'Leary, K. D. *Principles of behavior therapy.* Englewood Cliffs, N. J.: Prentice-Hall, 1980.

Wollersheim, J. P. Effectiveness of group therapy based upon learning principles in the treatment of overweight women. *Journal of Abnormal Psychology,* 1970, **76,** 462-472.

Wooley, S. C., Wooley, O. W., & Dyrenforth, S. R. Theoretical, practical, and social issues in behavioral treatments of obesity. *Journal of Applied Behavior Analysis,* 1979, **12,** 3-25.

Yates, A. *Theory and practice in behavior therapy.* New York: Wiley, 1975.

Zegman, M., Wilson, G. T., & Dubbert, P. The role of exercise in the behavior treatment of obesity. Paper presented at the Society for Behavioral Medicine, San Francisco, December 1978.

Zitter, R. E., & Fremouw, W. J. Individual versus partner consequation for weight loss. *Behavior Therapy,* 1978, **9,** 808-813.

III
COMMONALITIES IN SUBSTANCE ABUSE

6
Etiology and Process in the Addictive Behaviors*
Peter E. Nathan

Department of Clinical Psychology
Rutgers University
P.O. Box 819
Piscataway, New Jersey 08854

*Preparation of this chapter was facilitated by NIAAA Grant AA00259-10; this also provided financial support for the research reviewed in this paper which took place at the Alcohol Behavior Research Laboratory, Rutgers University.

This review of views on the etiology and process of alcoholism and the drug dependencies will consider the state of theory and knowledge on both behavioral and nonbehavioral factors in these disorders. Although our special interest and experience is in looking at these processes and factors from the social learning perspective, a more broadly-based perspective is necessary to obtain the clearest view of these disorders. More than most behavioral disorders, the substance use disorders require a multifaceted stance on etiology. This requirement derives, in part, from our admittedly primitive state of knowledge, which nonetheless informs us that no single etiologic equation will be all-encompassing, in part, from the fact that every substance abuser presents us with an array of behavioral dysfunctions that accompany the physical or psychological dependence. No alcoholic or drug abuser does not also have a host of associated behavioral, familial, and vocational problems, some clearly related to excessive consumption of alcohol or drugs, others not.

What follows, then, is a brief review of certain factors (biophysiological and genetic, sociocultural and psychodynamic) and a more detailed review of others (social learning and behavioral) which together comprise what is known and thought about why human beings come to abuse themselves by abusing drugs and alcohol. Separately, each view explains a part of every abuser's problem; together they provide a comprehensive etiologic perspective.

Most of the research reviewed in this chapter, especially that guided by social learning theory, centers on the etiology of alcoholism. The reason for this disproportion is the inability of researchers to justify administration of drugs other than alcohol to experimental subjects on ethical and legal grounds. It is one thing to give alcohol to an alcoholic in order to observe his or her behavior; it is quite another to provide a heroin or barbiturate addict with his or her drug of abuse. The former can easily be justified; the latter cannot. Hence, the overwhelming number of studies on alcohol's effects on behavior, the few on drug effects.

Biophysiological and Genetic Studies

One of the most persistent of the biophysiological theories of alcoholism is that alcoholics and nonalcoholics differ in the rate at which they metabolize alcohol. If such a difference could be found, it would suggest that an etiological factor—perhaps *the* etiological factor—lies in the rate-limiting mechanisms involved in the metabolism of ethanol. However, no metabolic studies of alcoholism indicate the existence of such a rate difference, at least when amount of alcohol consumed is kept constant (Mello & Mendelson, 1978). Another possible biophysiological model of alcoholism sees the disorder as the product of the route of alcohol metabolism; according to this theory, alcoholics metabolize alcohol differently from nonalcoholics, in that way gaining the capacity to consume larger amounts of alcohol for longer periods of time than nonalcoholics. Here, the data are more equivocal. Though many investigators question the finding, one leading metabolic researcher, Charles Lieber, claims that alcoholics have two metabolic routes by which they break down alcohol while nonalcoholics have but one (Korsten & Lieber, 1979). If replicated, this finding could represent the definitive proof necessary for a biophysiological explanation of alcoholism. At the same time, it should be noted that, even if such proof were forthcoming, it would not rule out the necessary role of environmental, behavioral, and sociocultural factors in alcoholism; metabolic differences between individuals become relevant to alcoholism only when some of them drink enough alcohol for long enough periods of time to develop the disorder.

If metabolic or other biophysiological differences between alcoholics and nonalcoholics do exist, some of them are probably transmitted genetically. For this reason, intensive exploration of genetic determinants of alcoholism has begun; these research efforts have started to bear fruit. A research team led by Donald Goodwin, a University of Kansas psychiatrist, has reported that sons of Danish alcoholics are four times more likely to be alcoholic than are sons of nonalcoholics, whether they are raised by alcoholic parents or not (Goodwin, 1979). By contrast, daughters of Danish alcoholics, adopted and nonadopted, do not have a higher rate of alcoholism than adopted controls (Goodwin, Schulsinger, Knop, Mednick, & Guze, 1977). These data, taken together, suggest that there may well be a genetic component to alcoholism, though its extent and influence within and between the sexes remains to be determined more precisely.

The pharmacology and physiology of physical dependence and tolerance to the drugs of abuse continue to be explored, but so far no one has developed an adequate etiological theory of drug dependence based on biophysiological factors. This is so for largely the same reasons that alcoholism has not been identified as primarily a biophysiological entity: no differences have been found in rate of metabolism, route of metabolism, site of metabolism, or susceptibility to the effects of drugs between people who become addicts and those who do not. The history of medicine suggests that such differences are crucial to the ultimate discovery of biophysiological etiologic factors.

However, one important step forward in the search for biophysiological factors in drug addiction has recently been taken by Snyder (1978). His discovery of sites of action of the opiate drugs in the brain and identification of naturally occurring substances (''endorphins'') similar to the opiate drugs that bind at these sites offer researchers the opportunity both to develop drugs that inhibit binding at these sites (in order to eliminate the powerful reinforcement addicts experience from their drugs) and to determine whether there is any difference between addicts and nonaddicts in the distribution or action of these opiate receptors (in order to explore etiologic factors in the opiate addictions).

Sociocultural Perspectives

Many investigators have pointed to the profound impact that cultural patterns of drinking have on rates of alcoholism. First-generation Italian-Americans and Jewish-Americans, both from cultures in which drinking takes place in a family or religious context, are likely to drink but unlikely to become alcoholic (Cahalan, 1978a). The Irish, who drink in pubs, have lower consumption rates but higher rates of alcoholism than the other cultural groups. As all these groups become acculturated within the American "melting pot," their rates of alcoholism become more similar. Recent data indicate that second- and third-generation American Jews have a significantly higher rate of alcoholism than first-generation Jews; the reverse is true of Irish-American (Cahalan, 1978b).

Though cultural influences can predispose a person to alcoholism, social variables play a major role in translating that predisposition to actual addiction. They can also operate to keep the alcoholic drinking. Peer pressure, for example, has a powerful influence on the development of deviant drinking patterns among adolescents (Jessor & Jessor, 1975). As well, social historians have recently pointed to the pervasiveness of social setting-related influences on persons to drink heavily (Zinberg & Fraser, 1979). Some of these discrete influences have also been examined by behavioral researchers in their quest for empirically-based social learning explanations for alcoholism. These studies are reviewed later in this chapter.

There are few other psychopathological disorders in which the influence of sociocultural factors is as striking as in the drug dependencies. Sociocultural variables play two key roles in drug addiction: they differentiate drug users from nonusers and they determine the kind of drug a user selects. By now, everyone knows that heroin addiction is endemic to the ghetto. Unlike so many other items of "common knowledge," this one seems to be true. The now-classic Chein study, which evaluated the social and economic characteristics of 15 high-drug-use areas of New York City, found significant relationships between juvenile delinquency and drug (largely heroin) addiction, between delinquency and poverty, between poverty and drug addiction, and between the proportion of blacks in an area and the rate of drug use there (Chein, Gerard, Lee, & Rosenfeld, 1964). In 12 of the 14 areas studied, blacks and Puerto Ricans made up more than 70% of the population. But Chein also observed that while "the highest-drug-rate areas are all high-delinquency areas, delinquency is not [caused by drugs], except in the sense that the varieties of delinquency tend to change to those most functional for drug use; the total amount of delinquency is independent of the drug use" (pp. 64-65).

In other words, these data do not justify the conclusions, drawn by some authorities, that drug addiction "causes" juvenile delinquency, that blacks and Puerto Ricans are more commonly drug addicts because they are black or Hispanic, and that poverty and drug use are invariably linked. Significant correlations like those reported by Chein are deceptive because they imply causality without in any way proving it. Two facts are clear, however, from such studies: (1) Heroin is a poor person's drug, at least in the United States; (2) Its use is intimately associated with high crime rates.

Psychoanalytic Theories

Psychoanalysts explain alcoholism in several ways. Some see alcoholics as fundamentally suicidal, trying to destroy "bad, depriving mothers" with whom they have identified. Others claim that alcoholics are "defending" themselves against underlying depression by drinking to oblivion. Still others say that alcoholics drink in defense against overwhelming anxiety (Williams, 1976). Critics of the psychoanalytic approach to alcoholism point out that there are no empirical data to support these hypotheses and that psychoanalysis does not help most alcoholics who seek treatment (Schuckit & Haglund, 1977).

Dynamic theories of drug addiction, like dynamic theories of alcohol addiction, describe the addict as a person whose habit represents a return to the oral stage of psychosexual development. As a result, dependency needs are paramount, but the addict is frustrated by his or her inability to derive satisfaction of these needs. Since they cannot satisfy their "oral dependency needs" in more appropriate ways, addicts use drugs and alcohol to obtain this gratification.

This brief summary vastly oversimplifies the complex psychoanalytic formulation of drug addiction. Despite its complexity, however, it has had relatively little impact on prevailing views of etiology and treatment, largely because efforts to validate it (e.g., Freudenberger, 1973) have been anecdotal rather than empirical.

Behavioral Theories of Drug Dependence

Psychiatrist Abraham Wikler was the first to offer a behavioral theory of drug addiction. He views drug addiction as a product of instrumental conditioning (1965), assuming that each injection or ingestion of a drug reinforces drug-seeking behavior by providing immediate, powerful positive reinforcement. Hustling for drugs becomes a secondary reinforcer because of its relation to the primary reinforcement furnished by injection and the resultant "drive reduction." Wikler explains the extremely high rate of return to drug addiction by detoxified addicts as "due simply to incomplete extinction of reinforced drug-seeking behavior."

Richard Solomon, a motivational-learning theorist, more recently proposed an alternative behavioral model of drug dependence that he calls the "opponent-process theory of acquired motivation" (1977). Derived primarily from laboratory research with animals, the opponent-process theory assumes, first, that the brains of all mammals, including human beings, are organized to oppose and suppress strong affect and feeling, whether it is positive or negative. This process, presumably, serves to moderate behavior so that it is not so intense as to cause behavioral disruption. Solomon terms the primary affective processes elicited by strong unconditioned stimuli or emitted following operant reinforcement "*a* processes." He calls the opponent process aroused by an *a* process the "*b* process." The *b* process opposes and suppresses the affective strength of the *a* process in order to moderate it. Because the *b* process is an opponent process, it has an affective quality *opposite* to that of the *a* process. If the *a* process is pleasant and reinforcing, the *b* process will be unpleasant and punishing (and vice versa.) The overall affective condition of the organism, then, will depend on whether the *a* or *b* process is stronger; whenever *a* is greater than *b*, the organism is in state A; if being in state A is positively reinforcing, being in state B will be aversive.

The other feature of the opponent processes necessary for understanding drug dependence is that the *a* process follows the initial stimulus closely and lasts a relatively short time; the *b* process, by contrast, develops more slowly and lasts longer.

According to the opponent-process model, the addict derives immediate, intense reinforcement from the drug and its acquired properties through the *a* process. After a brief period in reinforcing state A, the *b* process begins to eat away at that pleasure until state A has been replaced by state B, an unpleasant state. In order to replace state B with state A, then, the addict ingests more of the drug so as to reexperience the *a* process and, if possible, state A. Compounding this learned sequence is behavior designed to reduce the psychological and physical pains of physical withdrawal from an addicting drug; like state B, the sensations of withdrawal motivate the addict to return to the drug.

An unproved but intriguing theory, Solomon's opponent-process model of addiction remains to be investigated in humans. It must also be integrated better with physiological processes. Where does *b* process end and withdrawal begin, for example?

Social Learning Perspectives on Alcoholism

Empirical Research on Personality Factors

The earliest psychological efforts to discover the etiology of alcoholism were guided by psychodynamic theory. Consequently, they emphasized study of relationships between dynamic traits and types and developmental milestones on the way to disordered behavior. Resultant data, however, revealed no specific personality trait or type as a consistent predictor of alcoholism (Miller, 1976; Sutherland, Schroeder, & Tordella, 1950; Syme, 1957). More recently, non-dynamic researchers (e.g., Cahalan & Room, 1972) reached similar conclusions, while others have investigated the role of newly-defined personality traits less closely tied to dynamic theory in this continuing quest. For example, McClelland (McClelland, David, Kalin, & Wanner, 1972) has suggested that individuals with power needs are particularly vulnerable to alcohol excess because alcohol can provide temporary satisfaction for such needs. Methodological deficiencies (for example, reliance on projective personality tests, shown to have limited reliability and validity) weaken these claims, however. More promising are studies using sophisticated factor analytic techniques to identify a number of personality types associated with alcoholism (Nerviano, 1976; Skinner, Jackson & Hoffman, 1974). Another interesting current effort to identify alcoholic personality types with etiologic significance involves development of the Drinking Related Locus of Control Scale (DRIE: Donovan & O'Leary, 1979; O'Leary & Donovan, 1979). Creation of the DRIE stems from research suggesting that alcoholics may differ from nonalcoholics in the degree to which they attribute their behavior to self or other (environmental) influences (O'Leary et al., 1974; O'Leary et al., 1976).

Tension Reduction Hypothesis: The First Behavioral Explanation

The first behavioral explanation of alcoholism, still an influential one, is the "tension-reduction" hypothesis (TRH). The TRH is based upon the observation that alcohol often appears to reduce anxiety. For this reason, alcohol is presumed to reinforce drinking by alcoholics, many of whom seem to experience high levels of anxiety. Formal, empirical support for the TRH derived from early (Conger, 1951, 1956; Masserman & Yum, 1946) and more recent (Freed, 1967; Smart, 1965) studies of experimentally-induced conflict in animals. The tension-reduction hypothesis has not, however, received universal support. Cappell and Herman (1972), for example, extensively reviewed the animal tests of the tension-reduction hypothesis from the vantage points of avoidance and escape learning, conflict and experimental neurosis, conditioned suppression, extinction and partial reinforcement, stress and behavioral disruption, psychophysiological studies, and human self-report and risk-taking. Despite the magnitude of the effort to confirm the TRH, Cappell and Herman concluded that the only studies providing consistent empirical support for it were those exploring conflict situations. Brown and Crowell (1974), in a subsequent analysis of the conflict studies, concluded that even they do not support a tension-reduction hypothesis, since closer approach to a bivalent goal after alcohol administration may actually increase conflict (because of increased strength of both approach and avoidance tendencies closer to the goal). Reviews of tension reduction research with human subjects also suggest the inadequacy of the simple tension-reduction view of alcohol effects (Cappell, 1974; Marlatt, 1975; Mello, 1972).

Following a period of quiescence extending until very recently, a group of researchers from the Addiction Research Unit, Institute of Psychiatry, University of London, have again raised the question of the viability of the tension-reduction model as an explanation for excess alcohol consumption. One focus of interest by this group, led by psychologist R. J. Hodgson, is the animal research literature, which Cappell and Herman (1972) and other influential researchers concluded disproves a tension-reduction model. However, Hodgson, Rankin, and Stockwell (in press) question Cappell and Herman's conclusions on methodologic grounds. They point out that these reviewers fail to distinguish between active and passive avoidance and between one-and two-way avoidance. If they had made these distinctions, Hodgson and his colleagues aver, Cappell and Herman would have concluded that passive avoidance is reduced by alcohol consumption but that well-learned active avoidance is not. Hence, Hodgson and his coworkers suggest that the tension-reduction model of alcohol consumption by animals may be viable after all, given that appropriate experimental design factors are arranged.

In a companion paper, Stockwell, Hodgson, and Rankin (in press) review prior research with humans questioning the tension-reduction hypothesis because alcoholics appear to become more rather than less tense as they drink (e.g., Nathan et al., 1970). Confirming these earlier observations in their own alcoholic subjects, Stockwell and his colleagues also confirm, as did earlier researchers, that alcohol induces small, short-term reductions in tension. Stockwell and his colleagues do not find either consequence of drinking to be seriously at variance with the TRH. They explain their subjects' subsequent increase in tension levels following short-term reduction in tension as the result of "minimal withdrawal symptoms" or "rebound" from the first day of drinking; they see the decision of alcoholics to continue to drink in the face of increased tension as a function of "relativity of reinforcement—it is far worse to stop drinking than to continue." These explanations harken back to the effort by Nathan and his colleagues (1970) to explain the alcoholic's decision to continue to drink in the face of increased tension: the short-term decrease in tension is remembered when drinking is over, while the long-term increase is forgotten; the pains of withdrawal outweigh the pains of increased tension during continued drinking.

Stockwell and his colleagues also point to the role of expectancy in maintaining tension-reduction in humans, concluding that many or most alcoholics *expect* alcohol to reduce tension, at least for a time. The expanding research on alcohol and expectancy, reviewed below, would certainly suggest that *believing* that alcohol performs a tension-reduction function, even if it does not do so consistently, may be as influential in the decision to drink as alcohol's pharmacologic effects on tension. Interestingly, a recent study of motivational determinants of alcohol use in college students (Schwarz, Burkhart, & Green, 1978) reveals that more students drink as a "sensation seeking" device than to reduce tension. College students, however, are not necessarily like alcoholics in their reasons for drinking; they may very well have lower prevailing tension levels and greater need for enhanced stimulation.

The failure of the "simple" tension-reduction hypothesis to achieve consistent empirical support leads us to conclude that no unimodal behavioral mechanism suffices to explain the development and maintenance of excessive drinking. Both the pharmacologic effects of alcohol, including its short-term tension-reducing effects, and numerous intero- and exteroceptive cues and reinforcers not directly a function of these effects must also be considered in this context. The task that remains is explication of these mechanisms.

Expectancy and Alcohol Effects: Cognitive Processes in Alcohol Use

Marlatt, Demming, and Reid (1973), building on work by Engle and Williams (1972), were the first to show clearly the potency of alcohol expectancy—as against its pharmacologic effects—by demonstrating that alcoholic subjects' drinking was determined by the *belief* that they were drinking alcohol rather than by the pharmacologic effects of that consumption. First "priming" alcoholics with a single dose of beverage and then, under the guise of a "taste-testing" experiment, allowing subjects to regulate their own beverage consumption for 15 minutes, Marlatt and his colleagues manipulated the actual beverage consumed (alcohol or tonic-placebo) and what subjects were told they were drinking (alcohol or plain tonic) in a two-by-two ("balanced placebo") design. Results were striking: actual consumption was determined by subjects' expectations, not by actual alcohol content. At about the same time, Ludwig, Wikler, and Stark (1974) reported that craving by alcoholics may be as sensitive to expectancy effects as is consumption itself, in that way adding fuel to the fire of expectancy research.

Mood. As instrumental in promoting interest in this research area was Pliner and Cappell's (1974) demonstration that the belief that alcohol will serve as a euphoriant is determined in part by situational cues. Consuming alcohol (to a blood alcohol level of 50 mg/%) or placebo, non-alcoholic subjects were then required to complete a "creativity" task either in small groups or alone. Subjects in groups reported more positive affect on both self-report and observational measures when they had consumed alcohol. By contrast, subjects who completed the task alone revealed no differences in self-reported affect between alcohol and placebo conditions. For self-reported physical symptoms, the effect was reversed; solitary subjects reported more such symptoms while drinking alcohol, whereas subjects in groups reported no differences in symptoms between alcohol and placebo conditions. Referring to

Schachter's (1964) two-factor model of drug effects, Pliner and Cappell (1974) concluded that alcohol induces behavioral ''plasticity'' such that actual behavioral effects depend on situational and cognitive—rather than strictly pharmacologic—factors.

Tension-Reduction. Recent empirical findings from research employing the balanced placebo design developed by Marlatt suggest that alcohol's pharmacologic and attitudinal effects on anxiety and tension are complex indeed. This research speaks both to the important role cognitions play in alcohol's effects and to the viability of the tension-reduction hypothesis; these are separate but clearly overlapping issues.

In a recent study by Polivy and her colleagues (Polivy, Schueneman, & Carlson, 1976), groups of nonalcoholic subjects were divided randomly into four subgroups by the two-by-two design. One group was told it would consume alcohol and did, another that it would consume alcohol while it actually consumed a placebo, a third that it would consume vitamin C while it actually consumed a placebo, and the fourth that it would consume vitamin C while it actually consumed alcohol. Subjects were then made anxious by threatening them with the possibility of electric shock. Subjects who actually consumed alcohol reported and experienced less anxiety shortly after alcohol administration than did those who had not consumed alcohol; by contrast, subjects who believed they had consumed alcohol were actually more anxious than were those who believed they had consumed vitamin C. These results suggested to Polivy and her colleagues that, independent of the influence of expectancy, alcohol acts as a sedative; with expectancy effects allowed to operate, however, presumed consumption of the substance may actually induce heightened rather than lessened tension and anxiety.

This conclusion is consistent with the findings of Steffen, Nathan, and Taylor (1974), who monitored both self-ratings and electromyographs of four alcoholics every two hours over 12 days of laboratory drinking. Although muscle tension level decreased as blood alcohol level (BAL) increased, subjective distress and BAL were directly related. In other words, even though alcohol predictably acted as a physiological tension-reducer, its subjective effects reflected tension increase.

Another empirical approach to this question was recently made by Wilson and Abrams (1977) and Abrams and Wilson (1979). Thirty-two male social drinkers (1977) and 32 female social drinkers (1979) were divided into the four cells of the two-by-two expectancy design. After consuming their drinks, subjects' heart rates were monitored during a brief social interaction with a confederate of the opposite sex. (The interaction was designed to induce brief but intense social anxiety.) Self-report and questionnaire measures of social anxiety and physiologic measures of arousal were taken before and after the interaction. Men who believed they had consumed alcohol showed less of an increase in heart rate than those who believed that they consumed tonic only, regardless of the actual content of their drinks. By contrast, women who believed they had consumed alcohol showed an increase in heart rate greater than women who believed they had only consumed tonic.

The results of the studies reviewed in this section are in such conflict that they prevent a coherent view of the respective contributions of expectancy and pharmacology to alcohol's effects on anxiety and tension. What seems most likely, though, is that alcohol's sedative properties do reduce tension and anxiety on a short-term basis *unless* the individual's attitudes towards drinking are so conflicted that he or she experiences anxiety as a consequence of those conflicts. By the same token, the increase in anxiety and tension that typically accompanies long-term alcohol ingestion appears to be a dual function of the negative physiologic consequences of prolonged drinking and the guilt, ambivalence, and interpersonal discomfort that typically accompany alcoholic drinking.

Does tension-relief, real or imagined, play an etiologic role in alcoholism? For the troubled adolescent, the harried housewife, or the pressured executive, whether tension-relief stems from the sedative effects of alcohol or the belief that those effects are real, the consequences appear to be much the same. So, we conclude, the etiologic role is a real one—even if the basis of the effect is not wholly drug-related.

Aggression. The effects of alcohol on aggressive behavior may also be subject to expectancy phenomena. Marlatt and his colleagues conducted a study of the role of expectancy in alcohol's effect on aggression (Lang, Goeckner, Adesso, & Marlatt, 1975). It employed the balanced placebo design. Aggressive behavior was found to be largely a function of expectancy, even at the substantial 100 mg/% BAL used in this study. Subjects who thought they had consumed alcohol were more aggressive regardless of whether or not they had actually done so than were those who thought they had consumed tonic water, even though half of them had actually consumed alcohol.

Sexual Arousal. Expectancy factors greatly determine alcohol's impact on both subjective and objective measures of sexual arousal. In one of the earliest studies of this effect, Wilson and Lawson (1976a) reported that nonalcoholic men experienced higher levels of sexual arousal when they believed they had consumed alcohol (whether or not they had actually done so) than when they thought they had consumed tonic water; at the same time, Wilson and Lawson (1976b) and Briddell and Wilson (1976) observed that alcohol actually decreases penile and vaginal responses to erotic stimuli. More recent research by Wilson and Lawson (1978), with another group of nonalcoholic women, confirmed that alcohol as a drug does decrease sexual arousal in women but failed to confirm prior findings by Wilson and Lawson with males (1976a) that those who believe they have consumed alcohol, whether they have or not, most often show increases in sexual arousal. Wilson explains this disparity by suggesting that men may hold stronger expectances concerning alcohol's facilitative impact on sexual arousal and that they may have better cognitive control over sexual arousal than do women.

Wilson, Lawson, and Abrams (1978) also explored the effects of alcohol on sexual arousal in male alcoholics, in order to contrast their behavior to that of nonalcoholic males studied earlier (Wilson & Lawson, 1976a). The alcoholic males, like the nonalcoholic males studied earlier, experienced an actual decrease in sexual arousal when they consumed alcohol, regardless of whether or not they believed they were consuming alcohol. As before, however, all subjects reported that consuming alcohol either had no effect on sexual arousal or increased it, views quite at variance with objective physiologic measures.

In a final study in this area, Briddell, Rimm, Caddy, Krawitz, Sholis, and Wunderlin (1978) tested sexual arousal in 48 male social drinkers in the two-by-two expectancy design. The expectancy effect was observed (sexual arousal increased when subjects thought they were consuming alcohol whether or not they really were), but the usual alcohol effects was not (that is, alcohol as a drug did not influence levels of sexual arousal). Interestingly, subjects who believed they had consumed alcohol showed more arousal to auditory stimuli associated with deviant sexual acts, suggesting another dimension—that of disinhibition—to the expectancy/sexual arousal interaction.

The extent to which the drug and expectancy effects of alcohol ingestion impact differentially on behavior remains uncertain, largely because of dosage level differences and differences in the kind and temporal sequencing of sexual stimuli and instructions offered subjects. Nonetheless, the data do suggest that alcohol's drug and expectancy effects often work at variance to each other when intoxication and sexual arousal coincide.

Pain Perception. Expectancies also influence alcohol's impact on pain perception. In one of the most telling of the studies in this area, Cutter, Maloof, Kurtz, and Jones (1976) subjected both alcoholics and non-alcoholics to cold-pressor (pain-inducing) tests before and after administration of moderate doses of alcohol. Alcoholic subjects reported a decrease in pain that accelerated with an increased dosage of alcohol while nonalcoholics reported no such effect. Since the groups did not differ in basic physiologic responsivity to pain, the subjective pain reduction the alcoholics experienced must have been a function of expectancy factors interacting with the interoceptive cues of the increased dosage. Brown and Cutter (1977) then went on to test nonalcoholics' pain responses to finger pressure and cold pressor tests before and after administration of a low or high alcohol dose or a placebo. Subjects also completed a questionnaire asking about their customary drinking habits. Results showed that alcohol effects were strongly influenced by prior drinking habits. For example, while superior pain reduction was generally associated with the higher alcohol dose in solitary drinkers, that dose actually increased the pain experienced by subjects who drank at home with family or friends. In other words, alcohol expectancies were mediated by prior drinking patterns, as well as by interoceptive cues associated with differing dosages.

That interoceptive cues produced by different dosages influence expectancies has been confirmed more recently by Williams and Goldman (1978). These two researchers reported that subjects showed fewer signs of intoxication on a variety of self-report and psychomotor tests at BAL's of 60 mg/% when they thought they had ingested alcohol than when they were led to believe they had consumed only tonic. This effect was not present at BAL's of 30 mg/%, at which alcohol expectancies impaired performance.

Summary: Expectancy and Drug Effects of Alcohol. The behavioral effects of alcohol involve a complex interaction of factors. Important among these are the expectancies one holds about alcohol's effects on behavior. Although we know now that expectancies influence alcohol's behavioral effects, there remains the question of whether expectancies only produce effects when they interact with alcohol (e.g., Pliner & Cappell, 1974) or whether they can also produce effects in the absence of alcohol (e.g., Lang, Goeckner, Adesso, & Marlatt, 1975). Expectancies themselves are complex; they are related to belief systems; prior drinking experience, the immediate physical and social setting of drinking, dosage levels, and the rise and fall of the BAL curve. Such complexity suggests that the potential reinforcing capabilities of alcohol central to a search for the etiologies of alcoholism still remain to be clarified.

Our review of empirical research on the role of expectancies of the effects of alcohol on behavior suggests that what people think alcohol does to and for them may be as important in determining their behavior as its pharmacologic effects, at least at the moderate dosage levels employed in the research. Hence, we conclude that expectancies play an important role in the behavior of those who drink as well as in their decision to drink. If one believes alcohol will enhance sexual arousal, reduce tension and pain, and heighten mood, one is more likely to choose to drink, regardless of whether or not alcohol as a drug actually has this effect on us. Alan Marlatt, whose own research launched this line of inquiry, draws the same conclusion in a recent comprehensive review (Marlatt & Rohsenow, 1980). In that review, Marlatt also considers the impact of expectancies about alcohol's capacity to induce craving and to lead to loss of control on treatment goals and methods. Believing that alcohol has such malignant behavioral effects creates the *abstinence violation effect,* the conviction that as little as a single drink by a person who wishes to achieve abstinence means that he or she has broken the abstinence pledge and forfeited the abstinence goal. Instead, Marlatt suggests, altering expectancies about one's ability to modulate or stop drinking even after an occasional "slip" is an important therapeutic step forward.

The abstinence violation effect, of course, is a characteristic of all of the disorders considered in this volume. Whether one is obese and attempting to maintain a strict diet, a smoker attempting to stop smoking, or a drug user or alcoholic trying to maintain abstinence, a "slip" usually spells treatment failure. Hence, it would seem useful to extend Marlatt's behavioral prescriptions—to consider with every patient the likelihood that a "slip" might occur during the course of treatment and to agree that such a transgression from treatment does not mean that treatment has failed—from alcoholism alone to the substance use disorders, obesity, and smoking.

What role do expectancy effects play in the etiology of alcoholism and problem drinking? A recent survey of attitudes about alcohol's effects on behavior (Brown, Goldman, Inn, and Anderson, in press) suggests that large numbers of people expect alcohol effects that empirical research now strongly suggests are not physiologic. Among the expectancies identified in a large group of male and female social drinkers were that alcohol positively transforms experiences, enhances social and physical pleasure and sexual performance and experience, increases power and aggression, alters personal characteristics and improves social skills, and reduces tension. Most of these expectancies, tested with Marlatt's balanced placebo design, have turned out to be a function of expectation and attitude and not drug effect. In fact, alcohol's pharmacologic effects are at direct variance with expectations concerning tension reduction, mood, sexual performance, and social skills.

We conclude, then, that while the precise role that expectancies about alcohol's effects play in the etiology of alcoholism remains uncertain, those attitudes must play important roles in leading young people to try alcohol and then to sustain their commitment to it in the hopes that it will magically "transform" them into persons who are sexually competent, interpersonally skilled, and emotionally serene. As long as consumption of alcohol remains at moderate levels, these effects can actually be achieved, if not by alcohol as a drug, then because of the beliefs many of us have in its power to transform.

We also conclude that expectancies about the effects of the drugs of abuse, of nicotine, and of certain foods in conjunction with the transcendent effects of a full stomach are fully as influential in determining overconsumption of these substances as are expectancies about the effects of alcohol. What drug addict has not striven to achieve the feelings of power and fulfillment cocaine is said to permit or the peace and tranquility heroin is to bring on? By the same token, how few addicts have achieved these expectations, in part because of environmental interference, in part because of drug adulteration, in part because of the effects of tolerance? Yet the pursuit of the ideal drug state continues. For that matter, what cigarette smoker does not know the "best" time to smoke, for the "best" effect from smoking—and what overeater does not have his or her favorite time, site, and style of overconsumption? Yet objective data in support of the direct effects of these ingestions remain to be gathered!

Comprehensive Social Learning Conceptions: Social and Modeling Influences

There is considerable evidence that alcohol use is both cued and reinforced by factors other than the real or anticipated effects of alcohol itself. To this end, the work of Jessor and his associates (Jessor, Collins & Jessor, 1972; Jessor & Jessor, 1975) confirms that introduction to alcohol use is an integral and important part of adolescent peer-group interactions. O'Leary, O'Leary, and Donovan (1976) have even suggested, for that matter, that pre-alcoholics can be identified by their deficits in social skills during adolescence. A number of laboratory studies of drinking alcoholics have also implicated a wide range of social stimuli as both cues and reinforcers for drinking (cf., Nathan, 1976; Nathan & Briddell, 1977) while, in the natural environment, Miller, Hersen, Eisler, and Hilsman (1974) have shown that when alcoholics are subjected to the interpersonal stress of having to make assertive responses, they are more likely to turn to alcohol than are social drinkers.

Imitation of a role model has also been shown recently to increase drinking in male social drinkers (Caudill & Marlatt, 1975). Following on this initial demonstration of the power of a companion to "model" drinking behavior for another, researchers have reported that couples tend to "synchronize" their drinking, with nonalcoholic couples more synchronous than couples with one alcoholic member (Billings, Gomberg, Nash, Kessler, & Weiner, 1978) and that modeling of alcohol consumption is also influenced by the sex of the model and the prior drinking history of the subject (Hendricks, Sobell, & Cooper, 1978; Lied & Marlatt, 1979). This research lends empirical support and a research strategy to efforts to define more clearly the role of peer-group interactions around alcohol on the subsequent development of alcoholism.

Research on peer group mechanisms involved in substance use and abuse, of more recent vintage, is also in an ascending phase (e.g., Freudenberger, 1975; Nathan & Harris, 1980). Perhaps to an even greater extent than the alcoholic, the drug abuser depends on peers for social and emotional support and as drug use models. Whether peer group interaction and modeling also influence smoking behavior and obesity remains unreported, though our eyes would suggest that these behaviors, too, are influenced by others and their use patterns.

Internality-Externality

Research at the Alcohol Behavior Research Laboratory, Rutgers University, into the processes by which alcoholics and nonalcoholics inform themselves of their level of intoxication suggests differences between alcoholics and nonalcoholics in this capacity; these differences may have etiologic significance and may represent one behavioral mode by which genetic predisposition to alcoholism is transmitted.

In the first study in this series, Silverstein, Nathan and Taylor (1974) explored alcoholics' ability to acquire and maintain blood alcohol level (BAL) discrimination accuracy. An initial baseline period revealed alcoholic subjects to be extremely inaccurate in their untrained BAL estimations. Subjects sharpened their discrimination accuracy dramatically when external feedback on BAL was provided during a subsequent discrimination training period. When feedback was again withdrawn during a second baseline period, however, accuracy deteriorated markedly. Subjects were required to drink *ad lib* to a target BAL of 80 mg/% during the second phase of this study. However, subjects could not moderate their drinking, although all had received extensive BAL discrimination training for this purpose, until feedback on BAL was again provided. When this was done, subjects monitored BAL well enough to moderate their drinking as requested. These results suggested to Nathan and his colleagues that alcoholics may only be able to maintain BAL discrimination skills when they receive some form of occasional external feedback on BAL. Accordingly, these researchers then asked whether anyone, alcoholic or not, can be trained to discriminate BAL on the basis on internal cues alone.

Huber, Karlin and Nathan (1976) directly addressed this issue by comparing the effectiveness of internal and external BAL discrimination training provided to a group of 36 male social drinkers. All subjects were first required to give estimates of BAL at several intervals during an initial programmed drinking sequence. They were then matched for discrimination accuracy and assigned to one of three training groups. Subjects receiving internal training completed body-function checklists and self-report instruments designed to teach them to associate a variety of internal sensations and feelings with a range of BALs. Externally-trained subjects were trained to calculate BALs from a programmed booklet which taught dose-strength-time-metabolism relationships. Subjects receiving internal plus external training were given both kinds of training. All subjects were then retested for BAL estimation accuracy during a final test session. Unlike the alcoholic subjects studied previously by Silverstein and his coworkers, the nonalcoholic subjects did learn to estimate BAL on the basis of both internal and external cues.

Lansky, Nathan, and Lawson (1977) then undertook a direct test of this apparent difference between alcoholics and nonalcoholics by comparing the results of external and internal training provided matched groups of alcoholics. As expected, all subjects made highly inaccurate pre-training BAL estimates. But when they were retested for estimation accuracy following training, the alcoholic subjects who had received external cue training estimated BALs significantly more accurately than they had before training, while subjects trained to use internal cues did not change in accuracy. These findings supported the hypothesis first put forth by Silverstein, Nathan and Taylor (1974) and subsequently refined by Huber, Karlin and Nathan (1976)—that alcoholics may have a fundamental deficit in the ability to discriminate blood alcohol levels on the basis of internal cues. To explain this deficit, Nathan and his colleagues proposed a variety of hypotheses. Alcoholics cannot utilize internal cues to BAL, he and his coworkers speculated in these early papers, because of inherited dysfunction of internal receptors, damage to them from the toxic effects of circulating ethanol, or the impact of tolerance on the receptors' sensitivity to changing levels of alcohol in the blood.

These hypotheses were tested for the first time in a recent study by Lipscomb and Nathan (in press). Twenty-four nonalcoholic subjects selected to fall into four experimental groups on the basis of usual drinking pattern (heavy versus light) and familial alcoholism (present versus absent) received internal-cue training. Following initial assessment of discrimination ability, subjects were then grouped according to differences in body sway when sober and intoxicated. Recognized as an extremely sensitive measure of intoxication, body sway has also been proposed recently as an accurate and reliable measure of tolerance to ethanol (Moskowitz, Daily, & Henderson, 1974). Persons who show substantial differences in body sway during sobriety and intoxication have likely acquired little or no tolerance to the effects of ethanol while those who show little or no such differences have acquired at least moderate tolerance to ethanol. Results of the study by Lipscomb and Nathan were that groups differing in drinking pattern or familial alcoholism did not differ in the ability to utilize internal cues to BAL. By contrast, when subjects were grouped according to performance on the body sway tolerance measure, "low tolerance" subjects were significantly better able to employ internal cues to BAL than were "high tolerance" subjects. In other words, these results supported the hypothesis that the alcoholic's shifting tolerance levels pervent him from using internal cues to BAL which nonalcoholics can use to good effect.

Research is currently underway at the Alcohol Behavior Research Laboratory to determine whether individuals who experience few or no adverse consequences of drinking when they first begin to drink during adolescence also rapidly develop high tolerance to the effects of alcohol. According to this line of reasoning, the inborn tendency to develop tolerance to alcohol's effects quickly leads, in turn, to the ability to consume large quantities of alcohol without unpleasant consequences since feedback on level of intoxication is impaired by tolerance.

The amalgam of behavioral and genetic research on the etiology of alcoholism represented by this research effort bespeaks a somewhat less compartmentalized approach to understanding of etiology than has previously characterized the field. It also foreshadows other efforts to bring together disparate data from domains of knowledge which have previously been isolated from one another. Finally, it suggests the wisdom of the search for commonalities among the substance use disorders and alcoholism to which this book addresses itself. Our research finding that alcoholics appear much less able than nonalcoholics to utilize internal cues to intoxication for the purposes of blood alcohol estimation suggests an interesting parallel linking alcoholism and obesity. Recent evidence suggests that the obese may be more dependent on external cues, such as time of day or physical presence of food, than they are on internal hunger cues to determine quantity and frequency of food consumed. The non-obese, on the other hand, are said to rely on internal cues to regulate eating (Nisbett & Storms, 1974; Schachter, 1971). This distinction between the obese and non-obese applies, then, to alcoholics and nonalcoholics as well. Taken together, these data suggest that alcoholism and obesity — both characterized by compulsive, self-destructive behavior — may have a basic, underlying process in common, the inability to monitor bodily reaction to the abused substance.

A Comprehensive Social Learning Model

One of the most articulate recent explications of a contemporary social learning view of alcoholism is summarized in the following excerpt from a longer position paper:

Within a social-learning framework alcohol and drug abuse are viewed as socially acquired, learned behavior patterns maintained by numerous antecedent cues (classical conditioning) and consequent reinforcers (operant conditioning) that may be of a psychological, sociological, or physiological nature. Such factors as reduction in anxiety, increased social recognition and peer approval, enhanced ability to exhibit more varied, spontaneous social behavior, or the avoidance of physiological withdrawal symptoms may maintain substance abuse (Miller & Eisler, 1975, p. 5).

If one adds to this model empirical insights gained in the five years separating publication of this statement in 1975 and publication of the book in which this chapter appears, one would urge inclusion of the following in a comprehensive model: recognition of modeling influences on consumptive behavior; awareness of the power of cognitive factors, including cognitions about the effects of alcohol on behavior (whether accurate or not); and recognition of the interplay of behavioral and genetic mechanisms (including the apparent inability of alcoholics, possibly on a genetic basis, to discriminate intoxication levels). Adding these findings to the 1975 model yields a comprehensive, contemporary social learning view of the etiology of alcoholism. According to this 1980 view, the operation of classical and operant modes of learning and modeling, modulated by cognitions about alcohol's reinforcing and publishing effects, together impact on inborn physiological mechanisms to yield problem drinking and alcoholism.

The advantage of this conception of etiology lies in its relevance to treatment. Learning-based treatment methods have been developed to deal with many of the stimuli to and consequences of abusive alcohol consumption.

Detailed in a prior chapter (Miller & Hester), these methods, with the social learning insights into etiology reviewed in this chapter, provide a comprehensive, learning-based system for understanding alcoholism and problem drinking from a systematic, consistent perspective.

References

Abrams, D. B., & Wilson, G. T. Effects of alcohol on social anxiety in women: Cognitive versus physiological processes. *Journal of Abnormal Psychology,* 1979, **88,** 161-173.

Armstrong, J. D. The search for the alcoholic personality. *Annals of the American Academy of Political and Social Sciences,* 1958, **315,** 40-47.

Billings, A. G., Gomberg, C. A., Nash, B.H., Kessler, M., & Weiner, S. Synchronized sipping in alcoholics and social drinkers: A preliminary investigation. *Journal of Studies on Alcohol,* 1978, **39,** 554-559.

Briddell, D. W., Rimm, D. C., Caddy, G. R., Krawitz, G., Sholis, D., & Wunderlin, R. J. Effects of alcohol and cognitive set on sexual arousal to deviant stimuli. *Journal of Abnormal Psychology,* 1978, **87,** 418-430.

Briddell, D. W., & Wilson, G. T. The effects of alcohol and expectancy set on male sexual arousal. *Journal of Abnormal Psychology,* 1976, **85,** 225-234.

Brown, J. S., & Crowell, C. R. Alcohol and conflict resolution, a theoretical analysis. *Quarterly Journal of Studies on Alcohol,* 1974, **35,** 66-85.

Brown, R., & Cutter, H. Alcohol, customary drinking behavior and pain. *Journal of Abnormal Psychology,* 1977, **86,** 179-188.

Brown, S. A., Goldman, M. S., Inn, A., & Anderson, L. R. Expectations of reinforcement from alcohol: Their domain and relation to drinking patterns. *Journal of Consulting and Clinical Psychology,* in press.

Cahalan, D. Implications of American drinking practices and attitudes for prevention and treatment of alcoholism. In G. A. Marlatt & P. E. Nathan (Eds.), *Behavioral approaches to alcoholism.* New Brunswick, NJ. Rutgers Center of Alcohol Studies, 1978 (a).

Cahalan, D. Subcultural differences in drinking behavior in U.S. national surveys and selected European studies. In P. E. Nathan & G. A. Marlatt (Eds.), *Alcoholism: New directions in behavioral research and treatment.* New York: Plenum Press, 1978 (b).

Cahalan, D., & Room, R. Problem drinking among American men aged 21-59. *American Journal of Public Health,* 1972, **62,** 1473-1482.

Cappell, H. An evaluation of tension models of alcoholic consumption. In Y. Israel et al. (Ed.), *Research advances in alcohol and drug problems.* New York: John Wiley & Sons, Inc., 1974.

Cappell, H., & Herman, C. P. Alcohol and tension reduction — a review. *Quarterly Journal of Studies on Alcohol,* 1972, **33,** 33-64.

Caudill, B. D., & Marlatt, G. A. Modelling influences in social drinking: An experimental analogue. *Journal of Consulting and Clinical Psychology,* 1975, **43,** 405-415.

Chein, L., Gerard, D., Lee, R., & Rosenfeld, E. *The road to H.* New York: Basic Books, 1964.

Conger, J. J. The effects of alcohol on conflict behavior in the albino rat. *Quarterly Journal of Studies on Alcohol*, 1951, **12**, 1-29.

Conger, J. J. Alcoholism; Theory, problem and challenge. II. Reinforcement theory and the dynamics of alcoholism. *Quarterly Journal of Studies on Alcohol*, 1956, **14**, 291-324.

Cutter, H. S. G., Maloof, B., Kurtz, N. R., & Jones, W. C. "Feeling no pain." Differential responses to pain by alcoholics and nonalcoholics before and after drinking. *Journal of Studies on Alcohol*, 1976, **37**, 273-277.

Donovan, D. M., & O'Leary, M. R. The Drinking Related Locus of Control Scale (DRIE): I. Reliability and factor structure. Unpublished manuscript, Veterans Administration Hospital, Seattle, 1979.

Engle, K. B., & Williams, T. K. Effect of an ounce of vodka on alcoholics' desire for alcohol. *Quarterly Journal of Studies on Alcohol*, 1972, **33**, 1099-1105.

Freed, E. The effect of alcohol upon approach-avoidance conflict in the white rat. *Quarterly Journal of Studies on Alcohol*, 1967, **28**, 236-254.

Freudenberger, H. J. A patient in need of mothering. *The Psychoanalytic Review*, 1973, **60**, 7-14.

Freudenberger, H. J. The dynamics and treatment of the young drug abuser in an Hispanic therapeutic community. *Journal of Psychedelic Drugs*, 1975, **7**, 273-280.

Goodwin, D. W. Genetic determinants of alcoholism. In J. H. Mendelson & N. K. Mello, (Eds.) *The diagnosis and treatment of alcoholism* New York: McGraw-Hill, 1979.

Goodwin, D. W., Schulsinger, F., Knop, J., Mednick, S., & Guze, S. B. Psychopathology in adopted and nonadopted daughters of alcoholics. *Archives of General Psychiatry*, 1977, **34**, 1005-1009.

Hendricks, R. D., Sobell, M. B., & Cooper, A. M. Social influences on human ethanol consumption in an analogue situation. *Addictive Behaviors*, 1978, **3**, 253-259.

Hodgson, R. J., Stockwell, T. R., & Rankin, H. J. Can alcohol reduce tension? *Behaviour Research and Therapy*, in press.

Huber, H., Karlin, R., & Nathan, P. E. Blood alcohol level discrimination by non-alcoholics: The role of internal and external cues. *Journal of Studies on Alcohol*, 1976, **37**, 27-39.

Jessor, R., Collins, M. I., & Jessor, S. L. On becoming a drinker: Social-psychological aspects of an adolescent transition. *Annals of the New York Academy of Sciences*, 1972, **197**, 199-213.

Jessor, R., & Jessor, S. L. Adolescent development and the onset of drinking: A longitudinal study. *Journal of Studies on Alcohol*, 1975, **36**, 27-51.

Korsten, M. A., & Lieber, C. S. Hepatic and gastrointestinal complications of alcoholism. In J. H. Mendelson & N. K. Mello (Eds.), *The diagnosis and treatment of alcoholism*. New York: McGraw-Hill, 1979.

Lang, A. R., Goeckner, D. J., Adesso, V. T., & Marlatt, G. A. The effects of alcohol on aggression in male social drinkers. *Journal of Abnormal Psychology*, 1975, **84**, 508-518.

Lansky, D., Nathan, P. E., & Lawson, D. M. Blood alcohol level discrimination by alcoholics: The role of internal and external cues. *Journal of Consulting and Clinical Psychology*, 1978, **46**, 953-960.

Lied, E. R., & Marlatt, G. A. Modelling as a determinant of alcohol consumption: Effect of subject sex and prior drinking history. *Addictive Behaviors,* 1979, **4,** 47-54.

Lipscomb, T. H., & Nathan, P. E. Effect of family history of alcoholism, drinking pattern, and tolerance on blood alcohol level discrimination. *Archives of General Psychiatry,* in press.

Ludwig, A. M., Wikler, A., & Stark, L. H. The first drink: Psychobiological aspects of craving. *Archives of General Psychiatry,* 1974, **30,** 539-547.

Marlatt, G. A. Alcohol, stress, and cognitive control. Paper at NATO-sponsored International Conference on Dimensions of Stress and Anxiety, 1975.

Marlatt, G. A., Demming, B., & Reid, J. B. Loss of control drinking in alcoholics: An experimental analogue. *Journal of Abnormal Psychology,* 1973, **81,** 233-241.

Marlatt, G. A., & Rohsenow, D. J. Cognitive processes in alcohol use: Expectancy and the balanced placebo design. In N. K. Mello (Ed.), *Advances in substance abuse: Behavioral and biological research.* Greenwich, Conn.: JAI Press, 1980.

Masserman, J. H., & Yum, K. S. An analysis of the influence of alcohol and experimental neurosis in cats. *Psychosomatic Medicine,* 1946, **8,** 36-52.

McClelland, D. C., Davis, W. N., Kalin, R., & Wanner, E. *The drinking man: Alcohol and human motivation.* New York: Free Press, 1972.

Mello, N. K. Behavioral studies of alcoholism. In B. Kissen & H. Begleiter (Eds.), *The biology of alcoholism,* Volume II. New York: Plenum Press, 1972.

Mello, N. K., & Mendelson, J. H. Alcohol and human behavior. In L. L. Iversen, S. D. Iversen, & S. H. Snyder (Eds.), *Handbook of psychopharmacology.* New York: Plenum Press, 1978.

Miller, P. M., & Eisler, R. M. Alcohol and drug abuse. In W. E. Craighead, A. E. Kazdin, & M. J. Mahoney (Eds.), *Behavior modification principles, issues, and applications.* Boston, Massachusetts: Houghton Mifflin, 1975.

Miller, P. M., Hersen, M., Eisler, R. M., & Hilsman, G. Effects of social stress on operant drinking of alcoholics and social drinkers. *Behaviour Research and Therapy,* 1974, **12,** 67-72.

Miller, W. R. Alcoholism scales and objective assessment methods: A review. *Psychological Bulletin,* 1976, **83,** 649-674.

Moscowitz, H., Daily, J., & Henderson, R. Acute tolerance to behavioral impairment of alcohol in moderate and heavy drinkers. Report to the Highway Research Institute, National Highway Traffic Safety Administration, Department of Transportation, Washington, D.C., 1974.

Nathan, P. E. Alcoholism. In H. Leitenberg (Ed.), *Handbook of behavior modification.* New York: Appleton-Century-Crofts, 1976.

Nathan, P. E., & Briddell, D. W. Behavior assessment and treatment of alcoholism. In B. Kissin & H. Begleiter (Eds.), *The biology of alcoholism,* Volume 5. New York: Plenum Press, 1977.

Nathan, P. E., & Harris, S. L. *Psychopathology and society* (2nd edition). New York: McGraw-Hill, 1980.

Nathan, P. E., Titler, N. A., Lowenstein, L. M., Solomon, P., & Rossi, A. M. Behavioral analysis of chronic alcoholism. *Archives of General Psychiatry,* 1970, **22,** 419-430.

Nerviano, V. J. Common personality patterns among alcoholic males: A multivariate study. *Journal of Consulting and Clinical Psychology,* 1976, **44,** 104-110.

Nisbett, R. E., & Storms, M. D. Cognitive and social determinants of food intake. In H. London & R. E. Nisbett (Eds.), *Thought and feeling: Cognitive alteration of feeling states.* Chicago: Aldine, 1974.

O'Leary, M. R., & Donovan, D. M. The Drinking Related Locus of Control Scale (DRIE): II. Concurrent validation against personality measures. Unpublished manuscript, Veterans Administration Hospital, Seattle, 1979.

O'Leary, M. R., Donovan, D. M., & Hague, W. H. Relationships between locus of control and MMPI scales among alcoholics: A replication and extension. *Journal of Clinical Psychology*, 1974, **30**, 312-314.

O'Leary, D. E., O'Leary, M. R., & Donovan, D. M. Social skill acquisition and psychosocial development of alcoholics: A review. *Addictive Behaviors*, 1976, **1**, 111-120.

O'Leary, M. R., Rohsenow, D. J., & Donovan, D. M. Locus of control and patient attrition from an alcoholism treatment program. *Journal of Consulting and Clinical Psychology*, 1976, **44**, 686-687.

Pliner, P., & Cappell, H. Modification of affective consequences of alcohol: A comparison of social and solitary drinking. *Journal of Abnormal Psychology*, 1974, **83**, 418-425.

Polivy, J., Schueneman, A. L., & Carlson, K. Alcohol and tension reduction: Cognitive and physiological effects. *Journal of Abnormal Psychology*, 1976, **85**, 595-606.

Schachter, S. The interaction of cognitive and physiological determinants of emotional state. In L. Berkowitz (Ed.), *Advances in experimental social psychology.* New York: Academic Press, 1964.

Schachter, S. Some extraordinary facts about obese humans and rats. *American Psychologist*, 1971, **26**, 129-144.

Schuckit, M. A., & Haglund, R. M. J. An overview of the etiological theories on alcoholism. In N. J. Estes & M. E. Heinemann (Eds.), *Alcoholism: Development, consequences, and interventions.* Saint Louis: Mosby, 1977.

Schwarz, R. M., Burkhart, B. R., & Green, S. B. Turning on or turning off: Sensation seeking or tension reduction as motivational determinants of alcohol use. *Journal of Consulting and Clinical Psychology*, 1978, **46**, 1144-1145.

Silverstein, S. J., Nathan, P. E., & Taylor, H. A. Blood alcohol level estimation and controlled drinking by chronic alcoholics. *Behavior Therapy*, 1974, **5**, 1-15.

Skinner, H. A., Jackson, D. N., & Hoffman, H. Alcoholic personality types: Identification and correlates. *Journal of Abnormal Psychology*, 1974, **83**, 658-666.

Smart, R. G. Effects of alcohol on conflict and avoidance behavior. *Quarterly Journal of Studies on Alcohol*, 1965, **26**, 187-205.

Snyder, S. H. The opiate receptor and morphine-like peptides in the brain. *American Journal of Psychiatry*, 1978, **135**, 645-652.

Solomon, R. L. An opponent-process theory of acquired motivation: The affective dynamics of addiction. In J. D. Maser & M. E. P. Seligman (Eds.), *Psychopathology: Experimental models.* San Francisco: Freeman, 1977.

Steffen, J. J., Nathan, P. E., & Taylor, H. A. Tension-reducing effects of alcohol: Further evidence and some methodological considerations. *Journal of Abnormal Psychology*, 1974, **83**, 542-547.

Stockwell, T. R., Hodgson, R. J., & Rankin, H. J. An experimental look at the use of alcohol for tension-reduction and tension-avoidance by alcoholics. *British Journal of Addictions*, in press.

Sutherland, E. H., Schroeder, H. G., & Tordella, C. L. Personality traits and the alcoholic. *Quarterly Journal of Studies on Alcohol,* 1950, **11,** 547-561.

Syme, L. Personality characteristics of the alcoholic. *Quarterly Journal of Studies on Alcohol,* 1957, **18,** 288-301.

Wikler, A. Conditioning factors in opiate addiction and relapse. In D. M. Wilner & G. G. Kassebaum (Eds.), *Narcotics.* New York: McGraw-Hill, 1965.

Williams, A. F. The alcoholic personality. In B. Kissin & H. Begleiter (Eds.), *The biology of alcoholism,* Volume 4. New York: Plenum Press, 1976.

Williams, R., & Goldman, M. S. The parameters of the alcohol expectancy effect. Unpublished manuscript, Wayne State University, 1978.

Wilson, G. T., & Abrams, D. Effects of alcohol on social anxiety and physiological arousal: Cognitive versus pharmacological processes. *Cognitive Therapy and Research,* 1977, **1,** 195-210.

Wilson, G. T., & Lawson, D. M. Expectancies, alcohol, and sexual arousal in male social drinkers. *Journal of Abnormal Psychology,* 1976, **85,** 587-594 (a).

Wilson, G. T., & Lawson, D. M. Effects of alcohol on sexual arousal in women. *Journal of Abnormal Psychology,* 1976, **85,** 489-497 (b).

Wilson, G. T., & Lawson, D. M. Expectancies, alcohol, and sexual arousal in women. *Journal of Abnormal Psychology,* 1978, **87,** 358-367.

Wilson, G. T., Lawson, D. M., & Abrams, D. B. Effects of alcohol on sexual arousal in male alcoholics. *Journal of Abnormal Psychology,* 1978, **87,** 609-616.

Zinberg, N. E., & Fraser, K. M. The role of the social setting in the prevention and treatment of alcoholism. In J. H. Mendelson & N. K. Mellow (Eds.), *The diagnosis and treatment of alcoholism.* New York: McGraw-Hill, 1979.

7

Theoretical and Practical Issues in Substance Abuse Assessment and Treatment

Peter M. Miller

Sea Pines Behavioral Institute
Hilton Head Island, South Carolina 29928

Historically, behavioral studies of substance use and abuse have targeted *individual* addictions. The four major addictive behaviors—problem drinking, drug abuse, obesity, and cigarette smoking—have been studied as separate entities with little attempt to compile and share knowledge or to formulate general theories of addiction. Clinical researchers, particularly in drug and alcohol fields, have isolated themselves not only from one another, but from the more general field of addictions as a whole.

Currently, a recent and growing trend is appearing in which addictive behaviors are seen as a single area of study. In addition, relationships *among* addictions are considered important to the understanding and treatment of each addiction separately.

At first glance, there appear to be three major ways in which addiction are related. *First,* substance abuses are not only linked but also interrelated in terms of the health hazards they represent. The abuse and sometimes merely the use of drugs, alcohol, food, and cigarettes can result in serious physical and psychological health problems. The combined abuse of two or more substances simultaneously can add significantly to these health risks. For example, the combination of smoking and obesity is particularly detrimental to health. The overweight smoker triples his risk of heart attack compared to the slim non-smoker (Heyden, Cassel, Bartel, Tywler, & Hames, 1971). Chronic alcohol consumption in combination with smoking is implicated in the development of mouth and throat cancer (Hirayama, 1970).

These higher multiple risks are especially crucial when one considers the rather high correspondence between the use of one substance and the use of another. For example, health surveys indicate that a strong positive correlation exists between heavy drinking and heavy smoking (Brown & Campbell, 1961; Walton, 1972). This correlation is even evident in teenage years. Brunswick (1973) found smoking to be the *single* most important predictor of drinking in boys 12 to 17 years of age. In addition, regular drinkers are especially likely to use psychoactive substances non-medically. The minor tranquilizers are the drugs most frequently combined with alcohol.

In addition, there seems to be a significant correlation among unhealthy habits in general. A recent survey in Great Britain examined the relationship between smoking, health, and safety behaviors, and beliefs about health (Eiser, Sutton, & Wober, 1979). Controlling for sex, age and socioeconomic status, smokers were found to use seat belts significantly less while driving than either non-smokers or ex-smokers. In order to assess personal attitudes toward health, subjects were asked which of the following statements was most similar to their own belief: (1) if people want to do things which can cause sickness or injury to themselves, they have every right to do so; and (2) people have a moral responsibility to avoid doing things which can cause sickness or injury to themselves. Nearly 60% of smokers felt they had a right to risk their health while only one-third of non-smokers agreed with this notion. Thus, addictive behaviors may be seen as part of a more general behavior pattern involving personal health and safety. Eiser, Sutton, and Wober's (1979) study indicates that all such behaviors may have a common bond in relation to an individual's perceived right to put his health at risk and his expectations regarding the consequences of his behavior. The first belief system, however, appears to overshadow the second. Therefore, even if a smoker is aware of the health risks of smoking, he may continue because of a more basic attitude regarding his personal right to do as he pleases.

Second, addictions are related on a behavioral level. The use or abuse of one substance frequently serves to trigger the use or abuse of another substance. For example, alcohol consumption may serve as a stimulus cue for smoking and overeating. Actually, behavioral researchers (Polivy & Herman, 1976) have found a rather complex relationship between alcohol consumption and eating. Dieters tend to eat *more* food after ingestion of alcohol while non-dieters actually eat less after drinking. However, cognitions and moods were found to interact with this effect; that is, when dieters were given alcohol in a disguised form, increased eating did *not* occur. Thus, the effect of alcohol on eating appears related to a pharmacological-cognitive interaction. However, in a naturalistic setting with expectancy factors in full operation it appears that dieters are particularly prone to overeat while drinking alcohol. In this regard, it is interesting to note that even *small* doses of alcohol increase salivary and gastric secretions (Ritchie, 1965). Such secretions may be experienced as "hunger" or at least interpreted by the dieter as "hunger" and may induce eating.

Drinking has also been shown to increase the likelihood of smoking. The immediate effects of drinking on smoking include increasing the *rate* of smoking (Griffiths, Bigelow, & Liebson, 1976). It appears that smoking may potentiate the objective and subjective effects of alcohol and increase its overall reinforcement value. Along these lines, social drinkers have higher heart rates and higher adrenalin excretion when drinking *and* smoking as compared to when they were only drinking. Perhaps this higher level of arousal when cigarettes and alcohol are combined constitutes a more potent reinforcer than lower levels of arousal achieved by alcohol alone (Myrsten & Andersson, 1974). The same phenomenon is apparent when alcohol and certain psycho-active drugs are used in combination.

A *third* way in which addictions relate to one another involves their reciprocity; that is, a change in the pattern of use of one substance frequently results in a concomitant change in use of another substance. Unfortunately, this reciprocal relationship can be a negative one. For example, reduction or elimination of cigarette smoking often leads to increased eating and weight gain. In fact over one-third of ex-smokers gain a significant amount of weight after giving up cigarettes (NIH, 1977). This negative side effect can interfere with maintenance and produce a return to the smoking habit. Such patterns are not only important clinically from a maintenance standpoint but are also crucial when the overall health of the client is taken into consideration. For example, many alcoholics who successfully abstain from alcohol following treatment, report a concomitant increase in their smoking behavior. If this is found to be universally true, its import could be dramatic. Perhaps our alcoholism treatment methods are preventing cirrhosis of the liver, brain damage, and family disintegration while *increasing* the likelihood of emphysema, lung cancer, and atherosclerosis. Likewise, smoking programs could iatrogenically negatively affect eating habits, thereby exacerbating such conditions as diabetes and hypertension. The same phenomenon is apparent among ex-heroin addicts being maintained on methadone who increase their use of alcohol.

Common Ground: Clinical Process and Treatment Variables

It appears, from the standpoint of health, behavioral interactions, etiology, and clinical outcome that our clinical research efforts should be directed toward examining commonalities among addictive behaviors. The major areas where commonalities may exist include: (1) assessment and evaluation: (2) theoretical variables; and (3) clinical phenomena.

Assessment and Evaluation

One of the most obvious commonalities among addictions is the methods used to assess them and the problems inherent in this assessment. Objective assessment of addictive behaviors has, for all types of substance use, focused on three measurement categories: (1) self-reports and reports by others; (2) direct behavioral observations; and (3) physiological measures. In tracing the history of addictive behaviors assessment procedures, it is obvious that a great deal of time and energy has been lost by duplication of effort and lack of communication.

Part of the problem relates to the way in which substance abuses are viewed and the course of their historical roots. For example, since their inception, methadone maintenance programs have included an objective measure of progress in the form of urine ''surveillance'' (Dole & Nyswander, 1965). Such objective, systematic assessment has not been evident in alcoholism programs until very recently (Sobell & Sobell, 1972), and it is still not universally considered to be an essential element of alcoholism treatment programs. It seems inconsistent that grant-funding agencies refuse to fund drug abuse programs without such evaluation, but frequently consider behavioral assessment procedures as impractical, unnecessary, or a breach of patients' rights when used with alcoholics. Obviously, politics plays a role even with the addictions. Even the word ''surveillance'' in reference to drug abusers conveys the notion of a sinister group that must be watched. Alcoholics, on the other hand, are considered ''sick'' and in need of professional treatment. Thus, drug abuse is viewed, even by professionals, as a crime, alcoholism as a disease, smoking as a bad habit, and obesity as either simple gluttony and laziness, a learned behavior pattern, or a metabolic disorder. These different ways of conceptualizing addictive behavior patterns are more related to historical/political phenomena than to factual information. Unfortunately for clinicians and researchers interested in the commonalities and interrelationships among these habits, these viewpoints have affected assessment and treatment developments.

The need for systematic and objective assessment and evaluation in the field of the addictions is slowly becoming recognized. Generally, the types of measures used in assessing eating, smoking, drinking, and drug taking behaviors are quite similar.

Self-reports. Self-reporting or self-monitoring represents one of the most universal methods of addictive behaviors assessment. For example, alcoholics are requested to provide daily written records on amount of alcohol consumed, time of day when drinking occurred, and circumstances under which drinking occurred. Such records provide both baseline assessment of typical drinking patterns before treatment and an index of progress during and after treatment (Sobell & Sobell, 1973).

Similarly, clients in weight control and smoking programs are requested to keep records on consumption patterns in reference to date, time, place, activity, social interactions, and feelings or thoughts preceding eating or smoking episodes. Self-monitoring of cravings or urges to consume alcohol or drugs has also been utilized in order to pinpoint specific cues which trigger substance abuse (Epstein, Parker, & Jenkins, 1976).

Although self-reports are practical and easy to obtain, their reliability and validity must be assessed. This is usually accomplished by obtaining reports from friends or relatives. This is frequently a difficult clinical problem because clients are often hesitant to allow such corroboration of their reports. They may perceive this procedure as an invasion of privacy or as evidence that the treatment staff distrust them. This can pose a particular problem for substance abusers whose spouses or friends have attempted to "help" them in the past through close supervision and scrutiny. In these cases, monitoring of the client's behavior by the spouse may be perceived as coercion or annoyance. Such perceptions frequently trigger episodes of substance abuse (Miller, 1978). These difficulties can be overcome by using careful selection and training procedures (Miller, 1979).

In spite of the common clinical notion that substance abusers provide inaccurate information on their consumption patterns, Maisto, Sobell, and Sobell (1979) found that alcoholics' self-reports and collateral reports of their drinking were highly correlated. The correlation was the highest when patients were mostly abstinent or mostly intoxicated and lowest when drinking was more limited. When differences did occur, patients reported fewer "drunk" days than did friends or relatives. Maisto et al. (1979) concluded that alcoholics provide fairly reliable reports of their drinking and that obtaining drinking information from collaterals is an effective method of corroborating self-reports.

Miller, Crawford, and Taylor (1979) compared self-reports and "significant other" corroborative data obtained in four outcome studies of controlled drinking therapies. Clients and an average of 1.72 collaterals per client were asked to provide alcohol consumption information at pre-treatment, post-treatment, and a three-month follow-up. Data were converted into Standardized Ethanol Content (SEC) units, with one SEC equivalent to 0.5 ounces (15 ml) of absolute ethanol. While correlations between self and others reports ranged from .06 to .92, most were high. The highest correlations were obtained with more experienced interviewers. The investigators concluded that the overall correlations were strong and positive, supporting the validity of self-reports.

Similar data on the reliability of reports of eating behaviors by the obese are not as positive. Brownell, Heckerman, Westlake, Hayes, and Monti (1978) instructed weight control clients and their spouses to keep extensive eating behavior records on themselves and each other. Clients' ratings of their own eating behaviors were not correlated significantly with the spouses' ratings of the clients' behaviors. However, the correlation between the spouses' self-report and the clients' ratings of the spouses' behavior was high (r = .86). Thus, the couples agreed on what and how the non-obese spouse was eating but not on what and how the obese spouse was eating.

Collaborative research both on methods of self-monitoring and techniques for determining and enhancing reliability of self-reports is needed.

Direct Behavioral Observations. While direct behavioral observations of addictive habit patterns are not as practical as self-reports, they provide detailed information on consumption patterns that is highly reliable. Direct observations are obtained either via a simulated-analogue system or in the natural environment.

Analogue measures have been applied to most addictive behaviors. In fact, a taste rating task that was originally developed by Schachter (1971) to assess eating patterns surreptitiously was modified and used to analyze drinking (Marlatt, Demming, & Reid, 1973; Miller & Hersen, 1972), drug taking (Liberman 1968), and smoking (Briddell, Rimm, Caddy, & Dunn, 1979) patterns. The taste-rating task is presented to the subject as a taste experiment. During the assessment session, the subject is provided access to food, alcohol, drugs, or cigarettes depending on his particular problem habit. Subjects are instructed to drink, eat, or smoke as little or as much as they wish and then to rate the taste of each portion on various dimensions (e.g., sweet; sour). After the session is completed, the exact amount of each beverage consumed is calculated. In evaluating an aversion conditioning program with a drug abuser, Liberman (1968) allowed patients to choose between morphine, coffee, soft drinks, candy or cigarettes during the assessment session. Such analogue measures have been used in both basic behavioral research (Marlatt, Demming, and Reid, 1973) and as part of an evaluation system of therapeutic effectiveness (Miller, Hersen, Eisler, & Hemphill, 1973).

In addition to the absolute amount of a substance consumed, the patterning or topography of that consumption has been studied by direct observations. Sobell, Schaefer, and Mills (1972) compared the drinking patterns of alcoholics and social drinkers in a simulated bar setting. Not only did alcoholics consume more alcohol, but they also drank more straight versus mixed drinks, and consumed their drinks more quickly. The possibility that overeaters and heavy smokers can be differentiated from more controlled eaters and smokers on their consummatory "style" has also been investigated. It has long been assumed (especially by behavioral clinicians) that an obese eating style exists which is very similar to the alcoholic drinking style. Thus, dieters have been trained to take smaller bites of food, to lengthen the time between bites, and to chew food more carefully. In order to verify the validity of an obese eating style, investigators observed obese and nonobese individuals eating in restaurants. The results of these analyses have been extremely contradictory (Mahoney, 1975; Stunkard & Kaplan, 1977). While further research is needed, it now appears that the eating patterns of the obese may not differ significantly from those of the nonobese. This is not to say, however, that learning a slower, more controlled method of eating is not helpful in controlling overeating. Indeed, Miller and Sims (in press) found changes in eating style to be positively related to success at 12 months in a weight control program.

Experimental investigations of cigarette smoking style are limited in number. However, Moody, Griffith, and Averitt (1973) and Anderson (1973) found that patients with acute and chronic respiratory and heart disease demonstrated longer puff duration, greater puff volume, greater number of puffs, and longer smoking time per cigarette than non-patient control groups. They hypothesized that the way an individual smokes may be more important than the total number of cigarettes smoked. Frederiksen, Miller, and Peterson (1977) found that a detailed topographical analysis of smoking behavior can serve as a more accurate measure of the effectiveness of smoking control clinics than total cigarettes smoked, especially among participants who only reduce consumption. Decreasing cigarette consumption by 50%, for example, may have little meaning if there is a concomitant increase in puffs per cigarette, puff volume, or nicotine content of cigarettes. Since the amount of smoke an individual inhales is of prime importance in the health risk of smoking, Miller, Frederiksen, and Hosford (1979) have encouraged the use of the "inhalation index." This index is obtained by multiplying puff frequency and puff duration. It is interesting to note that the inhalation index remains high and stable for heavy smokers regardless of social conditions. The inhalation index of light smokers is low under social conditions and much higher when they smoke alone. Perhaps the smoking pattern of light smokers is controlled by external conditions while a heavy smoker's cigarette consumption is a function of internal cues (e.g., nicotine level). In any event, direct behavioral observations have added greatly to our knowledge of addictive behaviors and their patterning. Observations of more naturalistic settings in which individuals are consuming a combination of substances together (e.g., eating, smoking, and drinking at a cocktail party) would probably add greatly to our knowledge regarding the relationships among these habit patterns.

Physiological Monitoring. Techniques to assess physiological correlates of substance abuse have greatly enhanced the objectivity of addictions assessment. Drug dependence programs were the first to use physiological monitoring for treatment evaluation. Urine screening for drugs has proven to be a practical, reliable, and inexpensive assessment tool. Urine specimens are collected and analyzed either on a daily basis (Dole & Nyswander, 1965) or randomly (Goldstein & Brown, 1970). However, routine urine screening on a widespread basis can result in inaccuracies due to laboratory error. Trellis, Smith, Alston, and Siassi (1975) found that periodic feedback of false positives and false negatives to the toxicology laboratory increases accuracy of results. Such urine screenings provide an objective way of assessing treatment effectiveness and validating self-reports of drug use.

Analysis of blood/alcohol concentration via breath tests has been used extensively in the field of alcoholism. Blood/alcohol levels are probably a better index of overall impairment due to drinking than absolute amount of ethanol consumed. This is particularly true for females whose blood/alcohol concentration to a given amount of alcohol varies considerably as a function of menstrual cycle (Jones & Jones, 1978). Breath tests are convenient to obtain and correlate highly (.95) with blood tests (Dubowski, 1970). Breath testing for blood/alcohol level has been used to provide baseline information on an individual's drinking patterns, cooroborate self-reports, and evaluate treatment effectiveness (Miller, 1977). For example, Miller (1975) and Miller, Hersen, Eisler, and Watts (1974) used random breath tests to assess contingency management programs for Skid Row alcoholics. Subjects were called by telephone one hour prior to testing and the breath test was administered at the subject's home or place of employment.

Breath tests have also been used for training and evaluation in blood/alcohol discrimination training programs. In these programs clients are taught to estimate their own blood/alcohol level and then use this estimation skill to control alcohol consumption (Nathan, 1978). During training, clients are instructed to estimate their blood/alcohol level periodically while they are consuming fixed amounts of alcohol. They then focus on specific internal sensations such as numbness or tingling feelings associated with specific blood/alcohol levels. Breath tests provide an objective method of feedback on the accuracy of estimates and a method of evaluating clients' abilities to master these skills (Matthews & Miller, 1979). Since alcoholics are deficient in these estimation skills (Lansky, Nathan, & Lawson, 1978), the assessment of these skills through breath testing may serve as an easy and convenient method of screening alcoholics from a general population.

More recently, researchers of smoking behavior have evaluated the use of expired air carbon monoxide concentrations in assessing smoking programs. Carbon monoxide is a by-product of tobacco smoke that reacts to hemoglobin in the lungs to form carboxyhemoglobin (Horan, Hackett, & Linberg, 1978). Either blood or breath tests will detect carbon monoxide. Lando (1975) found statistically significant differences between ex-smokers and smokers on carbon monoxide concentration. Several investigators now stress the inclusion of this measure as part of the routine evaluation of smoking control programs (Frederiksen and Martin, 1979). As with physiological assessments of other addictions, carbon monoxide measures can also be used to validate self-reports of smoking. Lando (1975) found a correlation of .59 between self-reported cigarette consumption and carbon monoxide concentration. While the measure has some shortcomings (e.g., the concentration of carbon monoxide in the local atmosphere can exert a confounding influence), it represents a marked advance in the empirical analysis of smoking behavior.

The measurement of eating patterns has always appeared relatively straightforward. That is, an individual's body weight as measured by a scale seemed to be an adequate assessment tool for weight control programs. More recently, several investigators have questioned the use of body weight especially as a measure of success in weight control programs. Weight loss per se is often not the best measure of improvement for two reasons. First, there is not a high correspondence between weight loss and eating patterns (Brownell & Stunkard, 1978). In addition, water retention and the natural plateaus that occur during dieting markedly affect weight gain or loss. The increased emphasis on physical activity during dieting has added another dimension to this measurement problem (Miller, 1979). Exercise tends to build and firm muscle tissue. Since muscle weighs more than fat, muscle weight may replace fat weight and total weight lost may be relatively small. However, the individual may be slimmer and healthier even though the scale indicates no weight loss.

The ideal goal of obesity treatment is a reduction in *fat* weight, not overall body weight. The two most reliable methods of measuring body fat are total body immersion and skinfold measures. Total body immersion which requires immersion in a large tank of water is a function of total body weight divided by the weight of the water displaced. While this technique is highly accurate, it is expensive, time consuming, and impractical in many clinical settings. Estimates of subcutaneous fat can also be obtained from thickness of folds of skin in different areas of the body (Bailey, 1978). These measures are taken by means of skinfold calipers and are relatively easy to obtain. Durnin and Rahaman (1967) report correlations of .75 to .83 between skinfold measures and body fat density obtained by total immersion techniques.

Possible Theoretical Commonalities

Learning Theory

It is apparent that elements of learning are involved in the maintenance of addictive habit patterns. Various stimulus events set the occasion for the consumption of substances and reinforcing consequences increase the likelihood of this consumption. An obvious consideration, then, is that consuming substances is reinforced by both physiological and social events.

Contemporary behavioral researchers and clinicians contend that addictive behaviors are learned habits that are acquired and maintained by a wide array of sociological, psychological, and physiological factors (Miller & Eisler, 1977). Intervention, from a behavior modification perspective, focuses on four sequential and functionally related events. These are: (1) stimulus factors (i.e., antecedent cues): (2) mediational variables (i.e., attitudes and expectations); (3) consumption patterns, per se; and (4) outcome variables (consequences). Habitual substance abuse is explained on the basis of the relationship among these variables at any one point in time. Thus, a detailed description of the antecedent events, cognitive expectations, and consequent events could lead to an understanding of the mechanisms controlling addictive behaviors. Antecedents and consequences generally fall into the following categories: (1) situational (advertisements, bakeries, bars, time of day); (2) social (coaxing from friends, "help" from friends while dieting—"I knew this diet wouldn't last!"); (3) emotional (boredom, depression); (4) cognitive (expectations of "loss" of control); and (5) physiological (withdrawal symptoms, chronic back pain). Any one or a combination of these factors may precipitate abusive consumption patterns. Consequent events occuring immediately after substance use (e.g., changes in autonomic arousal patterns, increased attention from friends) help maintain the behavior via positive and negative reinforcement.

The goals of behavioral interventions consist of modifying social-environmental antecedents, teaching self-management techniques, and arranging a system of contingencies to reinforce abstinence or moderate substance use.

Many of the behavioral techniques used in the treatment of different addictive behaviors are similar. However, since there is little dialogue among clinicians and researchers in the substance abuse area, there is little sharing of clinical procedures. Clinical procedures useful in the obesity field may be effective with smokers and vice versa.

External Responsiveness

Several years ago Schachter (1971) postulated the notion that obese individuals are more responsive to *external* eating cues than internal ones. Time of day and the mere sight of food is considered more important in triggering eating among the obese than are internal "hunger" cues. Some studies indicate that the obese are less able to use internal sensations associated with hunger on which to base their eating. Perhaps these cues are not as strong in the obese or perhaps they are simply not discriminating them properly. Thus, it may be that the obese are more dependent on the external environment in imitating eating. However, as we shall see later, external responsiveness alone seems insufficient to explain eating in the obese. This is primarily due to the fact that the obese do, indeed, respond to internal cues at times, although they are often not *hunger* cues per se, but more generalized feelings of arousal. Thus, the problem may be one of deficient discrimination skills together with a tendency to mislabel non-hunger sensations as "hunger."

What makes this model more relevant to a discussion of the commonalities among addictions is that it bears a great deal of similarity to more recent research on alcohol abuse.

It has recently been found that *social* drinkers can learn to estimate blood/alcohol levels on the basis of *internal* sensations alone (Nathan, 1978). However, Nathan (1978) and his colleagues found that *alcoholics* can estimate blood/alcohol levels accurately *only* if continuous *external* feedback on accuracy is provided. Once feedback is discontinued, only alcoholics who have been provided with *external* reference points are able to estimate blood/alcohol level; that is, they must know such factors as amount and rate of consumption for their estimation. These investigators hypothesized that the alcoholic's lack of sensitivity to internal cues might be related to shifting levels of tolerance, a reduced sensitivity of peripheral receptor cells, or cognitive variables. (See Nathan's chapter in this volume for a more detailed discussion.)

Thus, over-dependence on external cues and misinterpretation or inability to recognize internal cues may be a characteristic of addicted individuals which interferes with habit control.

Arousal Theory

Another relevant model for substance abuse is arousal theory. For example, Tarter (1978) reviews several studies which indicate that alcoholics exhibit a failure to maintain arousal stability. This fluctuating arousal level creates a pattern of excessive physiological reactivity which, in turn, may be responsible for the alcoholic's difficulty in distinguishing interoceptive cues. In turn, difficulty in discriminating internal cues leads to deficiancies in applying appropriate cognitive labels to subtle variations in physiological states. Alcohol serves to increase autonomic arousal and reduce physiological reactivity. Perhaps it also helps the individual attain his optimum level of stimulation as suggested several years ago by Zuckerman (1964).

However, as we shall see in a moment, cognitions interact with these arousal variables and most probably, the combination of these factors determines consummatory behavior. Changes in arousal patterns may be interpreted as "craving" and lead to smoking, drinking, or drug abuse. Consumption of a substance, then, may reinstate a more optimum level of autonomic arousal for that particular individual. Thus, within this framework, either a reduction in stimulation as is experienced as boredom and depression or an increase in stimulation when excitement or anxiety is experienced may increase the likelihood of substance use. At least it might set the occasion for such use if certain environmental stimuli and cognitive labels are present. Clinically, Leon and Chamberlain (1973) report corroborating evidence for this phenomenon. They found that dieters who had regained weight lost a year previously were most likely to eat in response to emotional arousal whether that arousal was positive (such as excitement and extreme happiness) or negative (such as boredom or loneliness). In contrast to this eating pattern, non-overweight individuals were more likely to eat in response to hunger and enjoyment of food.

A recent study by Judith Rodin (1978) at Yale has relevance to this arousal notion. She and her colleagues found that the mere sight of appetizing foods, regardless of the level of food deprivation at the time, led to increased physiological arousal in the obese. One specific element of this arousal pattern was an increased output of insulin. Insulin, of course, functions to lower the blood sugar level. In turn, a lowered blood sugar level is often associated with feelings of fatigue, weakness, and cravings for food, particularly simple carbohydrate foods such as sweets. This state of hypoglycemia can lead directly to eating in an attempt to normalize the blood sugar level and reduce feelings of fatigue.

Clinically, reports have appeared in which reduction in arousal associated with alcohol, food, or cigarette cues is used as part of the overall treatment plan. Strickler, Bigelow, and Wells (1976) used relaxation training to reduce muscle tension responses (craving?) of abstinent alcoholics to alcohol related stimuli. Seven abstinent alcoholics (all taking Antabuse) were instructed to use relaxation procedures while listening to an audiotape recording of a problem drinker in a bar. The recording consisted of various sounds (e.g., ordering drinks, ice tinkling in glasses, etc.) typical of a barroom scene. A control group of seven abstinent alcoholics who had not received relaxation training were exposed to the same experience with instructions to relax. Electromyographic (EMG) recordings of muscle tension levels in the frontalis muscle revealed that subjects using relaxation training were able to lower their muscle tension levels significantly in response to alcohol related cues while control subjects were not. Thus, relaxation training was used to help abstinent alcoholics cope with arousal producing stimuli which they reported to increase the likelihood of their drinking.

In a stimuli vein, Hodgson and Rankin (1979) postulated that craving and addictive behavior is analogous to fear and avoidance behavior and thus is amenable to extinction procedures. Extinction may decrease arousal to alcohol cues and thus decrease the probability of drinking. They used a technique known as cue exposure with a 43-year-old manual laborer who had been drinking excessively for 17 years. Historically, the consumption of one vodka was enough to establish a strong desire for further alcohol consumption. Over several days the subject was given priming doses of either 40 ml or 80 ml of vodka with no ice or mix. Throughout the day measures were taken on mood, subjective estimates of craving and desire to drink, pulse, and blood/alcohol concentration. After consuming the drink, the subject was instructed to resist the desire to drink further. Over a period of cue exposure with no opportunity to drink further, the subject's desire for a drink after the priming dose decreased gradually. In addition, his expectations of unpleasant feelings decreased over time. After the sixth session the subject experienced no further cravings in the four-hour period subsequent to receiving the priming dose. Clinically, the subject was followed up for six months. During this time he drank on only six occasions, each time terminating his drinking voluntarily soon after he began. This voluntary cessation of drinking had *never* occurred during the three years prior to the cue exposure.

Similarly, Miller (1979) has described the use of this extinction procedure with smokers. After a period of abstinence, during which cigarette cues (cigarettes, ashtrays, cigarette advertisements, cigarette machines) are avoided, the client is systematically reintroduced to situations which have been associated with smoking. Exposure is repeated until arousal and subjective feelings of cravings diminish. Reexposure to food cues for obese clients is accomplished in a similar manner. For example, a client might be accompanied to MacDonalds, at first under relatively "safe" conditions. Safe conditions might include: (1) immediately after a meal; (2) in the company of a supportive friend who is aware of the dieter's goals; or (3) in the company of the clinician. The dieter is instructed to sit in the restaurant, attend to the visual and gustatory food cues, and perhaps order a diet drink. Conditions under which food cue exposure occur are expanded gradually until cravings decrease.

Clinically, reducing the arousal value of a substance is only one element of treatment. Alternative methods of altering arousal states and enhancing feelings of self-efficacy must be developed. For example, relaxation and exercise constitute healthy alternatives to abuse which also modify arousal levels.

The effects of relaxation and meditation on addictive habit patterns has been investigated in several studies. Significant decreases in alcohol, tobacco, and marijuana use have been reported following the regular use of transcendental meditation (Lazar, Farwell, & Farros, 1977; Monahan, 1977; Shafii, Lavely, & Jaffe, 1974). Consistent practice of meditation also appears to be associated with decreased caloric intake and weight loss of obese individuals (Saxena and Saxena, 1977).

Steffen (1974) examined the relationship between relaxation training and drinking behavior under controlled laboratory conditions. Four alcoholics were taught muscle relaxation with the aid of electromyographic (EMG) biofeedback. During training, patients received continuous feedback on muscle activity in the frontails muscle of the forehead. Control phases were included during which relaxation training was not provided. Drinking was measured prior to and after training by allowing access to an unlimited supply of bourbon. Muscle relaxation training resulted in lowered blood/alcohol levels and reports of decreased anxiety. Placebo conditions had no effect on drinking.

In one of the most controlled investigations in this area, Marlatt, Pagano, Rose, and Marques (1976) studied the influence of different relaxation training techniques on drinking behavior. Subjects were young, male, heavy drinkers. Drinking was assessed before, during, and after training. Subjects were randomly divided into four groups. Group 1 received a meditational-relaxation technique emphasizing a passive attitude, muscle relaxation, and the subvocal repetition of a word (Benson, 1975). Group 2 subjects were taught progressive muscle relaxation as described by Wolpe (1958). Group 3 subjects were instructed to rest each day, reading pleasant and relaxing books. Group 4 was given no special instructions. Alcohol consumption decreased for all relaxation groups, but not for the control group. Alcohol intake for the meditation-relaxation group decreased by 50%. The regular practice of relaxation was associated with enhanced feelings of self-efficacy.

The relationship between exercise and addictive behaviors has been studied primarily in relation to alcohol abuse and obesity. Regular strenuous physical activities such as running, bicycling, handball, raquetball, and swimming are both psychologically and physiologically incompatible with regular excessive alcohol consumption (Miller, in press). One reason for the incompatibility is that alcohol leads to decreased oxygen uptake, reduced heat tolerance, reduced muscle contractile strength, and impaired coordination (Glover & Shepherd, 1978). Negative consequences of excessive drinking are immediately apparent because they impair fitness and the ability to perform physical activities. This is extremely relevant if alcohol abuse is viewed from a social learning reinforcement standpoint. Engaging in regular physical activity enhances the negative consequences of heavy drinking and allows for such consequences to be experienced *immediately* after alcohol is consumed. Typically, negative effects of drinking are so delayed that they have little influence over drinking behavior.

Running, for example, also tends to reduce negative mood states such as anxiety, depression, and feelings of worthlessness. Such feelings are often associated with episodes of excessive drinking (Miller, 1979). Gary and Guthrie (1972) reported improvements in feelings of self-esteem, anxiety, sleeping patterns and cardiovascular functioning of alcoholics after a physical fitness program in which patients jogged one mile per day.

Regular physical activity also has a positive influence on patterns of overeating both with children and adults. In one of the few studies of this nature with children, Epstein, Masek, and Marshall (1978) increased activity patterns in a school program for obese children by means of structured activities and verbal praise for exercising. The results indicated that the correlation between activity and changes in food intake was .90. It was found that the greater the activity, the greater the decreases in caloric intake. Timing of physical activity also seemed important. Exercise before a meal tended to suppress eating at that meal.

The importance of exercise in modifying eating patterns and weight losses of obese adults has recently been investigated. Stalones, Johnson, and Christ (1978) compared exercise and a self-managed contingency treatment with 44 obese patients. At a one-year follow-up, exercise was found to be a more influential factor in weight loss than behavior modification treatment procedures. Miller and Sims (in press) compared successful (mean weight loss equals 58 lbs) versus unsuccessful (mean weight loss equals 7 lbs) patients one year after participation in an intensive weight control program. The regular practice of aerobic exercise (walking, jogging, swimming, aerobic dancing, bicycling) was significantly related to successful weight loss. While 90% of successful patients engaged in regular aerobic activities only 21% of the unsuccessful patients exercised on a regular basis.

The exact nature of the positive influence of exercise on habit change is unclear. Certainly, with weight control, the influence can be direct in terms of caloric expenditure. The effect may also be indirect in terms of enhanced feelings of psychological well-being. Regular aerobic exercise decreases negative affect states such as anxiety and depression that often interfere with motivation and self-control (Kostrubala, 1976).

Aerobic exercise can become as addictive as substance abuse. Glasser (1976) has described running as a "positive addiction" to counteract other unhealthy addictions. Kostrubala (1976), a psychiatrist who uses running as part of his therapy, describes the similarities between exercise as an addiction and substance abuse as an addiction. For example, runners develop "tolerance" similar to alcohol and drug abusers in that running produces a desire to increase the mileage (dosage?) in order to experience positive effects. Even symptoms of "withdrawal" are observed in runners when they are unable to run due to injury or circumstance. That is, when deprived of running these "addicts" become restless, agitated, and irritable (Glover & Shepherd, 1978).

Clinical Phenomena

Degree of Dependence

The degree to which an individual is physically and/or psychologically dependent on a substance is an important clinical phenomenon that is common to all substance abuse patterns. Of course, some substances such as alcohol and certain drugs are physiologically addicting while others such as high calorie foods involve only psychological dependence. However, the subjective experiences of physical versus psychological withdrawal symptoms are similar and, clinically, the differentiation of these reactions is purely academic. The *degree* to which an individual is dependent, however, may have important clinical implications.

In recent years, investigators have attempted to clarify and measure this dependence phenomenon. For example, Edwards and Gross (1976) point out that dependence on alcohol is an important dimension apart from problems related to drinking. They describe the components of the dependence syndrome as follows: "A narrowing in the repertoire of drinking behaviors;

salience of drink-seeking behavior; increased tolerance to alcohol; repeated withdrawal symptoms; repeated relief or avoidance of withdrawal symptoms by further drinking; subjective awareness of a compulsion to drink; reinstatement of the syndrome after abstinence'' (Edwards & Gross, 1976). Number or extent of alcohol related problems (e.g., incarceration, hospitalizations, divorce) are not necessarily predictive of degree of dependency. Unfortunately, most alcoholism questionnaires combine these two dimensions. Recently, Hodgson, Stockwell, Rankin, and Edwards (1978) and Stockwell, Hodgson, Edwards, Taylor, and Rankin (1979) described the development and utility of the Severity of Alcohol Dependence Questionnaire (SADQ). Alcoholics are asked to respond to questions in five major categories: (1) physical symptoms of withdrawal; (2) affective symptoms of withdrawal; (3) craving and withdrawal relief drinking; (4) typical daily consumption; and (5) rapidity of reinstatement of symptoms after a period of abstinence. Responses to questions in each of these areas correlate highly with one another. Total score on this scale also correlated highly with ratings of dependence obtained from clinical interviews.

This research group has found that severity of dependence has important implications for the understanding of cravings, controlled drinking, and response to treatment. For example, Hodgson, Rankin, and Stockwell (1979) tested the notion that after a period of abstinence, the consumption of alcohol can trigger a craving for more. This notion has been quite controversial in the literature with evidence both for and against this loss of control notion (Keller, 1972; Ludwig, Wikler, & Stark, 1974). Hodgson, et al. (1979) administered priming doses of no alcohol, 15 ml of 65 proof vodka, and 150 ml of vodka to abstinent alcoholics. Overall, consumption of these doses did not trigger cravings for further alcohol. However, a different pattern was evident when severity of dependence was evaluated. It was evident that craving was primed in the severely dependent groups, but not in the less dependent groups. Thus, severity of dependence may be a significant clinical dimension that may have predictive value in clinical situations. In this regard, Orford, Oppenheimer, and Edwards (1976) found that severely dependent alcoholics were less likely to achieve a controlled drinking pattern than were the less severely dependent. After treatment, the most severely dependent alcoholics were more likely to be abstinent or drinking in an uncontrolled fashion.

In a further analysis, Hodgson, Rankin, and Stockwell (1978) found severity of dependence related to the behavioral measures of quantity consumed and speed of consumption. After a priming dose of alcohol, severely dependent alcoholics consumed more of additional alcoholic beverages and consumed those drinks more rapidly than they did with no priming dose. Alcoholics labeled as moderate or low on the severity of dependence did not show this trend.

Measurement of severity of dependence among cigarette smokers has also proven to be clinically useful. Fagerstrom (1978) developed the Tolerance Questionnaire to assess degree of physical dependence in smokers. This is an eight-item scale that includes questions on quantity of consumption, brand smoked, tendency to inhale, early morning smoking, and ability to refrain from smoking due to circumstances (e.g. in church or illness). Scores on this test were correlated with physiological indicators of physical dependence. These included: (1) a withdrawal response defined as a change in body temperature; (2) degree of acquired increase in tolerance defined as heart rate increase while smoking a cigarette; and (3) initial tolerance defined as heart rate increase for ex-smokers while smoking a cigarette. Degree of physical dependence was positively correlated with decreases in body temperature after smoking termination and smaller increases in heart rate after smoking. This brief questionnaire, then, is related to physiological aspects of dependence. Such a questionnaire could be most helpful in examining the relationship between dependence and such therapeutic considerations as gradual quitting versus sudden total abstinence or the utility of nicotine chewing gum.

Similar measures of dependence on food or certain types of food could be relevant to the study and treatment of obesity. For example, some individuals experience severe "withdrawal" symptoms while dieting such as headaches, fatigue, irritability, tension, dizziness, and inability to concentrate. The measurement of this dimension may help to predict response to dieting and help to pinpoint which type of weight control program might be most beneficial. Such considerations may also be important in weight maintenance. For example, perhaps individuals who are severely dependent on sugar should refrain totally from sweets while a less dependent individual could eat a candy bar occasionally with no further desire to eat.

Another aspect of degree of dependence relates to attitudes and expectancies. For example, smokers who perceive themselves as being "addicted" to cigarettes are less likely to even attempt to quit smoking than those who do not consider themselves addicted (Eiser, Sutton, & Wober, 1977). Perceived degree of dependency may be as important, if not more important, than *actual* degree of dependency. Caddy (1978) found that heavy drinking college students were more likely to believe that alcoholism is an inherited disease, outside of an individual's control, than were light or moderate drinkers. In addition, alcoholics were also more likely to believe this notion than was the general population. The interaction between these beliefs and scores on degree of dependence measures should be further investigated.

Indeed, several investigators have demonstrated that expectations regarding craving and "loss of control" are important determinants of behavior. Marlatt, Demming, & Reid (1973) have demonstrated that the priming effect mentioned previously is a function of an individual's expectations and not of whether he or she has consumed an alcoholic beverage.

Cognitive Style

An interesting and potentially significant commonality among addictive behaviors is the cognitive style associated with them. Certain self-statements appear to be related to the probability of abstinence versus abuse. The most commonly reported cognitive factors related to the excessive consumption of food, cigarettes, alcohol, and drugs are: (1) expectations regarding substance use and abuse; (2) the Abstinence Violation Effect; and (3) thoughts regarding self-efficacy.

Several studies have indicated that the overconsumption of alcohol and food can be triggered more by expectancies than by internal physiological processes. For example, Marlatt, Demming, and Reid (1973) studied the "loss of control" hypothesis with alcoholics. This hypothesis implies that once an alcoholic consumes even a small amount of alcohol, he or she will not be able to discontinue drinking voluntarily (perhaps because the first drink triggered a physiological craving for more). Alcoholics and social drinkers were allowed to drink beverages under two different expectancy conditions. Half the subjects in each group were told that the beverages contained alcohol while the other half were told that they were consuming nonalcoholic drinks. Actually, half the subjects in each group received alcoholic beverages and half received nonalcoholic ones. Amount of alcohol consumed by the alcoholics was related to their expectancy and not to the contents of the drinks. That is, if they thought they were drinking alcohol, they drank more than if they thought they were drinking nonalcoholic beverages. In a similar experiment analyzing the relationship between alcohol and food, Polivy and Herman (1976) found psychological set to be extremely influential in determining eating behavior. Dieters ate more food after consuming alcohol only if they *thought* they were drinking alcohol. When they were given alcohol and told it was a nonalcoholic drink, overeating did not occur.

The expectancy that excessive consumption of a substance will lead to positive as opposed to negative consequences also effects addictive behaviors. A problem drinker might expect that by drinking, he or she will become more outgoing, less tense, and more adept sexually. To examine this expectancy phenomenon, Wilson and Lawson (1976) used an experimental design similar to the one by Marlatt, et al. (1973) reported above. They found that alcohol itself had no effect on sexual arousal. As with other studies on alcohol and expectancy, subjects who believed thay had consumed alcohol showed a more significant sexual response than those who believed they were consuming a nonalcoholic beverage.

Thus, it appears that an individual's beliefs about substances and their effects exert a strong influence on consumption patterns.

In analyzing the relapse process related to alcohol abuse, Marlatt (1978) describes the abstinence violation effect which appears to be a commonly observed phenomenon with all addictive behaviors. The effect was developed to account for relapse situations of the type described below:

A middle aged man quit smoking successfully for two weeks. After a very stressful day, he smokes one cigarette to calm himself. He immediately labels himself as a "smoker," feels as though he's "blown" his no-smoking program, and feels he can smoke as much as he wants until his next inclination to quit smoking.

Dieters are also notorious for this dichotomous reasoning (Miller, 1979); that is, one is either on a strict diet or on no diet at all. Marlatt (1978) has postulated that this Abstinence Violation phenomenon is most likely to occur when an individual is committed to an extended period of abstinence and the consummatory behavior occurs during this period of time. Further, two cognitive elements seem to be involved. First, a cognitive dissonance effect occurs which is experienced as guilt for having succumbed to temptation. Second, a personal attribution effect occurs in which the consummatory behavior is attributed to personal failure (i.e., lack of will power) as opposed to a situation of circumstance. This effect and its analysis is being explored further by Marlatt and his colleagues and could have important implications for clinical treatment. (The chapter by Cummings, Gordon and Marlatt in this volume describes the application of this and other principles to the prevention of relapse in addictive behaviors.)

Finally, the concept of *self-efficacy* has been discussed by Bandura (1977) as it relates to habit changes. He reviews a great deal of evidence to suggest that an individual's expectations of his or her own personal competency (i.e., self-efficacy) are primary determinants of whether newly learned behaviors will be initiated and how long they will be maintained. Bandura further postulates that the most powerful treatment methods will be those with the greatest impact on the level and strength of an individual's self-efficacy cognitions.

Unfortunately, little controlled experimentation or even systematic clinical evaluations are available in applying this concept to addictive behaviors. Mahoney and Mahoney (1975) have discussed the need for modifying the self-defeating private monologues of dieters to provide them with more positive expectations regarding success. Clients are instructed to recognize and monitor negative efficacy statements and to replace them with positive ones. For example, statements such as "I just don't have the will power" are changed to "There's no such thing as will power—just poor planning. If I make a few improvements here and there, and take things one at a time, I can be successful." These investigators (Mahoney & Mahoney, 1975) have reported that changes in these self-expectancies in addition to modifications in perfectionistic standards related to "cognitive claustrophobia" (similar to Marlatt's Abstinence Violation Effect) were extremely important in determining twelve month success in a behavioral weight control program.

Miller and Sims (in press) also found that cognitive changes in self-efficacy were related to success among obese individuals. These investigators found that over 75% of successful clients (mean weight loss of 58 lbs) had made changes in self-efficacy cognitions (e.g., high frequency of such statements as "I *can* lose weight" or "I *do* have the ability to control my behavior") at a one-year follow-up. Only one-third of the unsuccessful clients (mean weight loss of seven lbs) had changed their thinking patterns. The weight control program described by these investigators included special training to enhance self-efficacy feelings. Clients were taught self-management skills and given repeated practice at implementing these skills in food related situations. In addition, sessions were conducted on cognitive rehearsal of successful self-control over food together with the repetition of positive efficacy statements, such as "I am in complete control over my eating behavior."

Conclusions and Future Trends

While progress is apparent in the study of substance abuse, more research is needed on the commonalities and differences among the addictions. While the developement of a common theory of addiction is an intriguing notion, it is important not to lose sight of essential differences among substances and their effects. Individual pharmacological effects and physical addiction phenomena certainly influence the factors maintaining addiction and the clinical treatment process.

There are current indications in the research literature that both the methodology and content of research on addictive behaviors is changing for the better. From the methodological standpoint, the assessment and evaluation of addictive behaviors has become more objective and systematic. Early studies relied exclusively on self-report data with no attempt to establish the validity or reliability of such reports. Even treatment evaluation studies utilized subjective evaluations of very short duration. For example, many of the early treatment data in the weight control field were based on follow-up information of no longer than eight to ten weeks duration (see Chlouverakis, 1976 for review). A minimum of six to 12 months for follow-up is now considered a necessity by most investigators since relapse during the first six months after treatment is high. In fact, the state-of-the-art of alcoholism and weight control research, in particular, has emphasized the importance of long-term two and three year follow-up studies (Sobell & Sobell, 1974; Gotestam, 1979). Current research is also characterized by more sophisticated methodology in terms of control groups and blind analysis of results. (Caddy, Addington & Perkins, 1979; Sobell & Sobell, 1976).

The content of addictions research is also changing gradually and becoming more clinically relevant than was once the case. It is interesting to note, however, that this trend toward relevance has occurred almost in opposite directions with different addictions. The alcoholism literature has long been characterized by studies of older, male Skid Row alcoholics. Since only 5% of alcoholics are of this Skid Row type, more recent studies have begun to focus on younger less chronic male and female problem drinkers (i.e. the majority of those who abuse alcohol). Weight control investigators, on the other hand, have been notorious for using slightly overweight college students as subjects for studies. This fact has led to concern over whether the results of treatment techniques (particularly behavioral ones) can be generalized to clinical populations who are generally older and more overweight. Recently, however, studies have focused on a wider age range of patients who are more severely overweight, i.e., 25% to 50% above ideal weight. These trends have resulted in more meaningful data on the treatment of addictions. In addition, they help to bridge the gap between research and treatment. Clinicians often have a tendency to discount treatment research as being trivial or irrelevant. Studies on the addictive patterns of "real" clinical populations in "real" clinical settings have begun to counteract these attitudes. Familiarity with the research literature is especially important in the addictions field since it is fraught with quackery and fad treatment techniques.

While a few investigators have studied the interactions among addictions (Polivy & Herman, 1976; Griffiths, Bigelow & Liebsen, 1976) such studies are relatively rare. This state of affairs seems ironic when one considers that the use and abuse of more than one substance at a time is more typical than is a single addiction. Perhaps, we have overemphasized studies of chronic, single substance abusers to the exclusion of the more commonplace polysubstance abuser who has a less severe problem. For example, a 42-year-old businessman who drinks, eats and smokes to excess may differ significantly in his use and abuse patterns from what would be expected based on the addictions research literature. He may just as likely receive treatment via a weight control program, a smoking clinic or a center for problem drinkers. It is highly probable that each program will focus on either eating, drinking, *or* smoking but not the interaction of the three. As was noted earlier in this chapter, such focal treatment may decrease one addiction (e.g., smoking) but inadvertantly increase another (e.g., eating). Joint addictions centers focusing on habit control in several areas could provide an excellent laboratory for the study of addictions interaction. Miller (1980) notes that a total health approach may be a more appropriate way of viewing addictive behaviors; that is, the target of intervention becomes *any* substance use or abuse habit pattern that negatively influences health. Total health treatment would serve to deemphasize labels (e.g., addict; alcoholic) and stereotypes associated with those labels. In fact, such an approach would probably be more acceptable to the general public since such terms as "alcoholism" or "drug addiction" often lead to the offhand rejection of participation by potential patients. This is not to say that the issues of substance use and abuse should be disguised or avoided. Rather, they should be put into perspective with other related social and health problems to achieve maximum impact from intervention efforts.

The study and treatment of addictions *together* has several practical advantages. Certain practical clinical problems are common to several different addictions. For example, the phenomenon of high attrition rates has been reported in the treatment of smoking, weight control, alcoholism, and drug abuse. Since drop-out during both treatment and follow-up is such a common problem, clinicians and researchers would save time and effort by working jointly on a solution. Other clinical issues such as self-assessment, modeling influences, relapse, and maintenance lend themselves to similar joint analyses.

Finally, prevention is particularly amenable to a coordinated approach. This is especially true when self-management techniques (Miller, 1979) are taught to enable individuals to control internal and external cues triggering substance use and to develop healthier alternatives to substance use, regardless of the substance being used.

References

Anderson, W. H. Smoking history and puff profile care service at the University of Louisville—A successful explant. In *Proceedings of the University of Kentucky Tobacco and Health Research Institute*. Lexington, Kentucky: University of Kentucky, 1973, 63-69.

Bailey, C. *Fit or fat*. Boston: Houghton Mifflin Co., 1978.

Bandura, A. Self-efficacy: Toward a unifying theory of behavior change. *Psychological Review*, 1977, **84**, 191-215.

Benson, H. *The relaxation response*. New York: William Morrow Co., 1975.

Bridell, D. W., Rimm, D. C., Caddy, G. R., & Dunn, N. J. Analogue assessment, affective arousal, and the smoking taste test. *Addictive Behaviors*, 1979, **4**, 287-295.

Brown, K. E., & Campbell, A. H. Tobacco, alcohol, and tuberculosis. *British Journal of Diseases of the Chest*, 1961, **55**, 150-158.

Brownell, K. D., Heckerman, C. L., Westlake, R. J., Hayes, S. C., & Monti, P. M. The effect of couples training and partner cooperativeness in the behavioral treatment of obesity. *Behaviour Research and Therapy*, 1978, **16**, 323-333.

Brownell, K. D., & Stunkard, A. J. The behavioral treatment of obesity in children. *American Journal of Children's Diseases*, 1978, **132**, 403-412.

Brownell, K. D., Stunkard, A. J.: Behavior therapy and behavior change: Uncertainties in programs for weight control. *Behavior Research and Therapy*, 1978, **16**, 301-303.

Brunswick, A. F. Adolescent health in Harlem: Correlates of drinking among black teenagers. Unpublished manuscript, Columbia University, 1973.

Caddy, G. R., Addington, H. J., & Perkins, D. Individualized behavior therapy for alcoholics: A third year independent double-blind follow-up. *Behavior Research and Therapy*, 1978, **16**, 345-362.

Caddy, G. R., Goldman, R. D., & Huebner, R. Group differences in attitudes towards alcoholism. *Addictive Behaviors*, 1976, **1**, 281-286.

Chlouverakis, C. Dietary and medical treatments of obesity: An evaluative review. *Addictive Behaviors*, 1975, **1**, 3-21.

Dole, V. P., & Nyswander, M. A., medical treatment for heroin addiction. *Journal of the American Medical Association*, 1965, **193**, 648.

Dubowski, K. M. Studies in breath alcohol analysis: Biological factors. *Z Rechtsmedicine,* 1975, **76**, 93-117.

Durnin, J. V., & Rahaman, M. M. The assessment of the amount of fat in the human body from measurements of skinfold thickness. *British Journal of Nutrition,* 1967, **21**, 281-289.

Edwards, G., & Gross, M. M. Alcohol dependence: Provisional description of a clinical syndrome. *British Medical Journal.* 1976, **1**, 1058-1061.

Eiser, J. R., Sutton, S. R., & Wober, M. "Consonant" and "dissonant" smokers and the self-attribution of addictions. *Addictive Behaviors,* 1978, **3**, 99-106.

Epstein, L. H., Masek, B., & Marshall, W. Pre-lunch exercise and lunchtime caloric intake. *The Behavior Therapist,* 1978, **3**, 15.

Fagerstrom, K. Measuring degree of physical dependence to tobacco smoking with reference to individualization of treatment. *Addictive Behaviors,* 1978, **3**, 235-241.

Frederiksen, L. W., & Martin, J. E. Carbon monoxide and smoking behavior. *Addictive Behaviors,* 1979, **4**, 21-30.

Frederiksen, L. W., Miller, P. M., & Peterson, G. L. Topographical components of smoking behavior. *Addictive Behaviors,* 1977, **2**, 55-61.

Gary, V., & Guthrie, D. The effect of jogging on physical fitness and self-concept in hospitalized alcoholics. *Quarterly Journal of Studies on Alcohol,* 1972, **33**, 1073-1078.

Glasser, W. *Positive addictions.* New York: Harper & Row, 1976.

Glover, B., & Shephard, J. *The runner's handbook,* New York: Penguin Books, 1978.

Goldstein, A., & Brown, B. W. Urine testing schedules in methadone maintenance treatment of heroin addiction. *Journal of the American Medical Association,* 1970, **214**, 311-315.

Gotestam, K. G. A three year follow-up of a behavioral treatment for obesity. *Addictive Behaviors,* 1979, **4**, 179-183.

Griffiths, R. R., Bigelow, G. E., & Liebson, I. Facilitation of human tobacco self-administration by ethanol: A behavioral analysis. *Journal of the Experimental Analysis of Behavior,* 1976, **24**, 279-292.

Heyden, S., Cassel, Bartel, A.,Tyroler, H. A., Hames, C. G., & Cornoni, J. C. Body weight and cigarette smoking as risk factors, *Archives of Internal Medicine,* 1971, **128**, 915-918.

Hirayama, T. A prospective study on the influence of cigarette smoking and alcohol drinking on the death rate for total and selected causes of death in Japan. *Smoke Signals,* 1970, **16**, 1-6.

Hodgson, R. J., & Rankin, H. J. Modification of excessive drinking by cue exposure. *Behavior Research and Therapy,* 1976, **14**, 305-307.

Hodgson, R., Rankin, H., & Stockwell, T. Craving and loss of control. In P. Nathan, G. A. Marlatt, and T. Loberg (Eds.). *Behavioral and experimental approaches to alcoholism.* New York: Plenum Press, 1978.

Hodgson, R., Rankin, H., & Stockwell, T. Alcohol dependence and the priming effect. *Behavior Research and Therapy,* 1979, **17**, 379-387.

Hodgson, R., Stockwell, T., Rankin, H., & Edwards, G. Alcohol dependence: The concept, its utility and measurement. *British Journal of Addiction,* 1978, **73**, 339-342.

Horan, J. J., Hackett, G., & Linberg, S. E. Factors to consider when using expired air carbon monoxide in smoking assessment. *Addictive Behaviors,* 1978, **3**, 25-28.

Jones, B. M., & Jones, M. K. Women and alcohol: Intoxication, metabolism, and menstrual cycle. In M. Greenblatt & M. A. Schuckit (Eds.), *Alcoholism problems in women and children*. New York: Grune and Stratton, 1976.

Keller, M. On the loss of control phenomenon in alcoholism. *British Journal of Addiction*, 1972, **67**, 153-166.

Kostrubala, T. *The joy of running*. Philadelphia: J. B. Lippincott, 1976.

Lando, H. A. An objective check upon self-reported smoking levels: A preliminary report. *Behavior Therapy*, 1975, **6**, 547-549.

Lanskey, D., Nathan, P. E., & Lawson, D. Blood alcohol level discrimination by alcoholics: The role of internal and external cues. *Journal of Consulting and Clinical Psychology*, 1978.

Lazar, Z., Farwell, L., & Farwell, J. T. The effects of the Transcendental Meditation program on anxiety, drug abuse, cigarette smoking, and alcohol consumption. In D. W. Orme-Johnson & J. T. Farrow (Eds.), *Scientific research on the Transcendental Meditation program: Collected papers*. Livingston Manor, N. Y.: MIU Press, 1977.

Leon, G. R., & Chamberlain, K. Emotional arousal, eating patterns, and body image as differential factors associated with varying success in maintaining a weight loss. *Journal of Consulting and Clinical Psychology*, 1973, **40**, 474-480.

Liberman, R. Aversive conditioning of drug addicts: A pilot study, *Behavior Research and Therapy*, 1968, **6**, 229-231.

Ludwig, A. M., Wikler, A., & Stark, L. H. The first drink. *Archives of General Psychiatry*, 1974, **30**, 539-547.

Mahoney, M. J.: The obese eating style: Bites, beliefs and behavior modification. *Addictive Behaviors*, 1975, **1**, 47-53.

Mahoney, M. J., & Mahoney, K. Treatment of obesity: A clinical exploration. In B. J. Williams, S. Martin, & J. P. Foreyt (Eds.) New York: Brunner/Mazel, 1976.

Maisto, S. A., Sobell, L. C., & Sobell, M. B. Comparison of alcoholics' self-reports of drinking behavior with reports of collateral informants. *Journal of Consulting and Clinical Psychology*, 1979, **47**, 106-112.

Marlatt, G. A., Craving for alcohol, loss of control, and relapse: A cognitive-behavioral analysis. In P. Nathan, G. A. Marlatt, & T. Loberg (Eds.) *Alcoholism: New directions in behavioral research and treatment*. New York: Plenum Press, 1978.

Marlatt, G. A., Demming, B., & Reid, J. B. Loss of control drinking in alcoholics: An experimental analogue. *Journal of Abnormal Psychology*, 1973, **81**, 233-241.

Marlatt, G. A., Pagano, R. R., Rose, R. M., & Marques, J. K. The effects of meditation upon alcohol consumption in male social drinkers. Unpublished manuscript, University of Washington, 1976.

Matthews, D. B., & Miller, W. R. Estimating blood alcohol concentrations: Two computer programs and their applications in therapy and research. *Addictive Behaviors*, 1979, **4**, 55-60.

Miller, P. M. A behavioral intervention program for chronic public drunkness offenders. *Archives of General Psychiatry*, 1975, **32**, 915-922.

Miller, P. M. *Behavioral treatment of alcoholism*. New York: Pergamon Press, 1976.

Miller, P. M.: *Personal habit control*. New York: Simon & Schuster, 1978.

Miller, P. M. Practical issues in obesity treatment outcome evaluation. Paper presented at the meeting of the Southeastern Psychological Association, New Orleans, 1979.

Miller, P. M. Behavioral strategies for reducing drinking among young adults. In M. E. Chafety & H. T. Blane (Eds.), *Youth, alcohol, and social policy.* New York: Plenum Press, 1980.

Miller, P. M., & Eisler, R. M. Assertive behavior of alcoholics: A descriptive analysis. *Behavior Therapy,* 1977, **8,** 146-149.

Miller, P. M., Frederiksen, L. W., & Hosford, R. L. Social interaction and smoking topography in heavy and light smokers. *Addictive Behaviors,* 1979, **4,** 147-153.

Miller, P. M., & Hersen, M. Quantitative changes in alcohol consumption as a function of electrical aversive conditioning. *Journal of Clinical Psychology,* 1972, **28,** 590-593.

Miller, P. M., Hersen, M., Eiseler, R. M., & Watts, J. G. Contingent reinforcement of lowered blood/alcohol levels in an outpatient chronic alcoholic. *Behaviour Research and Therapy,* 1974, **12,** 162-263.

Miller, P. M., & Mastria, M. A. *Alternatives to alcohol abuse.* Champaign, Ill: Research Press, 1977.

Miller, P. M., & Sims, K. L. Evaluation and component analysis of a comprehensive weight control program. *International Journal of Obesity,* in press.

Miller, W. R., Crawford, V. L., & Taylor, C. A. Significant others as corroborative sources for problem drinkers. *Addictive Behaviors,* 1979, **4,** 67-70.

Moody, P. M., Griffiths, R. B., & Averitt, J. H. Smoking history and puff profiles of hospital patients. *Proceedings of the University of Kentucky Tobacco and Health Research Institute.* Lexington, Kentucky: University of Kentucky, 1972, 22-49.

Monahan, R. J. Secondary prevention of drug dependence through the transcendental meditation program in metropolitan Philadelphia. *International Journal of the Addictions,* 1977, **12,** 629-784.

Myrsten, A. L., & Anderson, K. Interactions between effects of alcohol intake and cigarette smoking during acute alcohol intoxication and hangover. Unpublished manuscript, University of Stockholm, 1974.

Nathan, P. E. Studies in blood alcohol level discrimination. In P. E. Nathan, G. A. Marlatt, & T. Loberg (Eds.) *Alcoholism: New directions in behavioral research and treatment,* New York: Plenum Press, 1978.

National Institute of Health. The smoking digest. Washington, D.C.: Office of Cancer Communications, 1977.

Orford, J., Oppenheimer, E., & Edwards, G. Abstinence or control: The outcome for excessive drinkers two years after consultation. *Behaviour Research and Therapy,* 1976, **14,** 409-418.

Polivy, J., & Herman, C. P. Effects of alcohol on eating behavior: Influence of mood and perceived intoxication. *Journal of Abnormal Psychology,* 1976, **85,** 601-606.

Ritchie, J. M. The aliphatic alcohols. In L. S. Goodman & A. Gilman (Eds.) *The pharmacological basis of therapeutics.* New York: Macmillan, 1965.

Rodin, J. Has the internal versus external distinction outlived its usefulness? Paper presented at the meeting of the Second International Congress on Obesity. Washington, D.C. 1977.

Saxena, R. P., & Saxena, U. Loss of weight in obese patients who regularly elicited the relaxation response. *Journal of Chronic Disease and Therapeutic Research,* 1977, **1,** 32-35.

Schachter, S. *Emotion, obesity, and crime.* New York: Academic Press, 1971.

Schaeffer, H. H., Sobell, M. B., & Mills, K. C. Baseline drinking behaviors in alcoholics and social drinkers: Kinds of sips and sip magnitude. *Behavior Research and Therapy,* 1971, **9**, 23-27.

Shafii, M., Lavely, R. A. & Jaffe, R. D. Meditation and marijuana. *American Journal of Psychiatry,* 1974, **131**, 60-63.

Sobell, M. B., Schaeffer, H. H., & Mills, K. C. Differences in baseline drinking between alcoholics and normal drinkers. *Behavior Research and Therapy,* 1972, **10**, 257-267.

Sobell, L. C., & Sobell, M. B. A self-feedback technique to monitor drinking behavior in alcoholics. *Behavior Research and Therapy,* 1972, **11**, 237-238.

Sobell, M. B., & Sobell, L. C. Individualized behavior therapy for alcoholics. *Behavior Therapy,* 1973, **4**, 49-72.

Sobell, M. B., & Sobell, L. C. Second year treatment outcome of alcoholics treated by individualized behavior therapy: Results. *Behavior Research and Therapy,* 1976, **14**, 195-215.

Stalones, P. M., Johnson, W. G., & Christ, M. Behavior modification for obesity: The evaluation of exercise, contingency management, and program adherence. *Journal of Consulting and Clinical Psychology,* 1978, **46**, 463-469.

Steffan, J. J. Electromyographically induced relaxation in the treatment of chronic alcohol abuse. *Journal of Consulting and Clinical Psychology,* 1974, **43**, 275-279.

Stockwell, T., Hodgson, R., Edwards, G., & Rankin, H. The development of a questionnaire to measure severity of alcohol dependence. *British Journal of Addiction,* in press.

Strickler, D., Bigelow, G., & Wells, D. Electromyograph responses of abstinent alcoholics to drinking related stimuli: Effects of relaxation instructions. Paper presented at the meeting of the Association for Advancement of Behavior Therapy, New York, 1976.

Stunkard, A. J., & Kaplan, P. Eating in public places: A review of reports of the direct observations of eating behavior. *International Journal of Obesity.* 1977, **1**, 89-101.

Tarter, R. E. Etiology of alcoholism: Interdisciplinary integration. In P. Nathan, G. A. Marlatt, & T. Loberg (Eds.) *Alcoholism: New Directions in behavioral research and treatment.* New York: Plenum Press, 1978.

Trellis, E. S., Smith, F. F., Alston, D. C., & Siassi, I. The pitfalls of urine surveillance: The role of research in evaluation and remedy. *Addictive Behaviors,* 1975, **1**, 83-88.

Walton, R. G. Smoking and alcoholism: A brief report. *American Journal of Psychiatry,* 1972, **128**, 1455-1459.

Wilson, G. T., & Lawson, D. M. Expectancies, alcohol, and sexual arousal in male social drinkers. *Journal of Abnormal Psychology,* 1976, **85**, 587-594.

Wolpe, J. *Psychotherapy by reciprocal inhibition.* Stanford: Stanford University Press, 1958.

8
Relapse: Prevention and Prediction

Claudette Cummings, Judith R. Gordon, and G. Alan Marlatt

University of Washington
Seattle, Washington 98195

Introduction

The plan of this chapter is threefold. First, a brief review of the literature and theoretical conceptualizations of addiction and relapse will be presented. Next, an alternative relapse model will be described and related to research on five addictive behaviors: abuse of alcohol, opiates, nicotine, uncontrolled eating, and compulsive gambling. Finally, with the intent of providing guidelines for both practitioners and researchers, an approach to relapse prevention will be proposed.

Theories of Addiction and Relapse

We live in a consummatory society. The cultural norms since World War I have defined personal success in terms of unregulated acquisition of material goods and the pursuit of immediate pleasure. Perhaps with the added factors of greater leisure time and increased environmental stressors, large numbers of people have developed dependent relationships with drugs, alcohol, food, and gambling. However, the problem of addiction is not unique to the 20th century. Three major models which span many generations have been developed in an attempt to explain the etiology of addiction. Chronologically, these are the moral model, the disease model, and the social-learning model.

Historically, alcohol and drug addicts were viewed as being morally depraved and were incarcerated on the basis of unredeemable character. The moral model prevailed throughout the 19th century and was an active force in the temperance movement in the United States, culminating in the prohibition era (Tongue & Blair, 1975). The second model conceptualizes addiction as a disease and implies that all addictive substances are addictive through some underlying physiological mechanism. Like the sinful addict, the sick addict is seen as having no control over the addiction, but is at the mercy of physiological craving. The result is uncontrolled use and eventual physical tolerance (Jellinek, 1960). Relapse, in the circular logic of this theory, is interpreted as a symptom of the re-emerging disease.

However, according to current nomenclature (DSM III, 1980), substance abuse is classified by effects on psychological as well as physiological functioning. *Substance-Induced Organic Mental Disorders* are caused by the direct impact of various substances on the central nervous system. *Substance-Use Disorders* result in the behavioral changes attributed to taking substances that affect the central nervous system (psychological dependence shown by loss of control and substance dependence shown by tolerance and/or withdrawal).

Within the past two decades, an alternative model of the mechanisms of addiction and relapse was developed within the framework of social learning theory (Bandura, 1969). Proponents of this model view addictive behaviors as learned behavior disorders which are best understood through the principles of social learning, cognitive psychology, and behavior modification. Both classical (Pavlovian) and instrumental (operant) learning are applied to the development and maintenance of addictive behavior.

In Pavlov's classical conditioning paradigm, a neutral stimulus is repeatedly paired with an unconditioned stimulus that naturally elicits an unconditioned response. After repeated trials, the neutral stimulus becomes a conditioned stimulus and is capable of eliciting a conditioned response (Pavlov, 1927). From this perspective, dependence or "craving" for a drug can be explained by classical conditioning. Initially, craving occurs during the withdrawal syndrome and becomes associated with the stimuli (interoceptive bodily sensations and/or exteroceptive cues) present during withdrawal. If, at some future time, the abstinent addict is exposed to the stimuli previously paired with the experience of withdrawal (e.g., physiological arousal, presence of drug-taking friends, environmental/ritual settings of past drug use, etc.) then he or she will experience the conditioned response of craving (Ludwig & Wickler, 1974). This conditioned craving will now act to motivate the individual to seek relief through substance use. Craving may eventuate in "loss of control" consumption to the extent that the first drink (or cigarette, or heroin "fix") produces additional craving for the drug and an inability to voluntarily inhibit further consumption. In the case of alcohol, "This first drink, then would act like an 'appetizer,' stimulating hunger (craving, as a conditioned withdrawal response) even further because it has become sequentially conditioned to later consumption of an 'entree' (intoxication)" (ibid, p. 128). However, we propose that to explain the cause of relapse on the basis of an unobservable, internal response (craving) inferred from loss of control. The disease model is similarly tautological in inferring the presence of the disease of addiction on the basis of loss of control. In the absence of physiological or biochemical measures to assess craving, the concept of craving offers little power to predict and prevent relapse (Marlatt, 1978).

Recent evidence is accumulating in support of a classical conditioning learning interpretation of drug tolerance. Briefly stated, the central nervous system tends toward homeostasis by automatically compensating for the unconditioned systemic effects of a drug through the initiation of internal opponent processes (i.e., drug compensatory responses) (cf. Solomon & Corbit, 1974). Each time the drug is taken in the presence of an initially neutral stimulus, this stimulus precedes both the unconditioned effect of the drug and the reflexive physiological drug compensatory response. Over the course of successive pairings of this initially neutral stimulus with the compensatory response, the stimulus acquires, through the process of classical conditioning, the ability to elicit the compensatory responses. Three important effects of this process are: (1) the conditioned stimulus can elicit the compensatory response; (2) the compensatory response attenuates the unconditioned effect of the drug; and (3) therefore, the organism must increase the drug dose to restore the pre-tolerant (and presumably desired) drug effects. For example, compensatory responses have been conditioned in dogs that are administered anticholinergic drugs (Lang, Brown, Gershon, & Korol, 1966). After repeated injections of anticholinergic drugs which inhibit salivation, these dogs showed hypersalivation when injected with a saline placebo. Similar "paradoxical" conditioned responses have been demonstrated in animals administered epinephrine (Subkov & Zilow, 1937) and hyperglycemic agents (Deutch, 1974; Russek & Pina, 1962). Further animal research strongly supports the conceptualization of morphine tolerance as a classically conditioned, learned response (Siegel, 1975; 1976; 1977). Although there is currently no direct human experimental research investigating the issue of behavioral tolerance as a learned compensatory response, conditioned agonist effects have been experimentally produced in addicts who were given a narcotic antagonist (O'Brien, Tests, Ternes, & Greenstein, 1978).

Similarly, operant learning can also explain drug tolerance. Many psychoactive drugs interfere with behavior in general and reinforcement-seeking behavior in particular. This interference with reinforcement-seeking behavior motivates the organism to learn compensatory responses to ameliorate this interference. For example, alcohol causes ataxia which can interfere with reinforcement-seeking behavior. Animals made to walk a treadmill to avoid foot shock while intoxicated become behaviorally tolerant whereas animals given equivalent amounts of ethanol and treadmill practice but separated in time do not become behaviorally tolerant (Wenger, Berlin, & Woods, 1979; Wenger, Tiffany, & Woods, 1979). This research has not yet been extended to behavioral tolerance in humans. Presumably, organisms self-administering drugs for their reinforcement properties will develop tolerance by increasing the amount of drug self-administered, thereby placing themselves at risk for both physiological and psychological dependence.

The popularly-held tension reduction hypothesis provides an example of an operant analysis of alcohol consumption. This theory states that alcohol is reinforcing due to its tension reduction properties (Conger, 1956). The results of attempts to validate this theory have been contradictory; many of these studies were conducted on animals (Cappell & Herman, 1972), so that applicability to humans is in doubt. The human literature on the tension reduction hypothesis is equally confusing, due to a number of conceptual and methodological problems (Marlatt, 1976a). Tension has been defined variously as anxiety, stress, depression, and other dysphoric states and has been assessed using relatively unrefined measures ranging from self-report (Kastl, 1969; Warren & Raynes, 1972; Williams, 1966) to ratings made by observers (Berg, 1971; Nathan & O'Brien, 1971). Direct physiological measures are rarely employed and when they are it appears that blood alcohol levels are positively correlated with muscle tension but negatively correlated with subjectively rated tension (Steffen, Nathan, & Taylor, 1974).

The dose administered is a critical factor to consider when evaluating the literature on alcohol as a tension reducer. Growing evidence suggests a biphasic arousal response to alcohol, and many of the contradictory human findings on the tension reduction hypothesis may be due to a failure to control for whether the subject's blood alcohol level is rising or falling. At low to moderate doses, alcohol acts as a stimulant on central nervous system functioning (Grenell, 1972; Himwich & Callison, 1972) and motor-perceptual performance (Moskowitz & DePry, 1968). As the dose increases, the effects of alcohol are likely to be experienced as depressant in quality (Cameron, 1974; Russell & Mehrabian, 1975). At extremely large doses, narcosis and eventual death by respiratory paralysis occur (Madden, Walker, & Kenyon, 1976). In light of these findings, the reinforcing properties of alcohol may be due not to the eventual depressant effects (e.g., "tension reduction") but to the emotional and physiological "high" corresponding to the ascending blood alcohol level. In addition to these biphasic effects, the parameters of the setting in which the drug is used and the individual's psychological set must be included in any theoretical understanding of a drug's experiential effect.

Schachter's two-factor theory of emotions argues that a drug's effects are a joint function of the pharmacological arousal and the cognitive/environmental context in which the pharmacological arousal occurs (Schachter, 1964). Cognitive labeling of an emotional state may hold even in the absence of pharmacologically induced arousal (Valins, 1966). This attribution process, occurring in an appropriate, socially defined context regardless of actual ingested substance, is a major contributor to the drug's subjective quality.

Moreover, the short-term effects attributable to a drug appear, in part, to reflect the user's expectancies about the effects of the drug. In an attempt to control for the influence of expectancy on the labeling of emotions, the inclusion of a placebo control in drug research has become a common procedural condition to assess the relative contributions of the drug's "active" ingredient (i.e., chemical-physiological interaction) and the drug's "inactive" placebo effect. Enlarging on this design and on previous alcohol research using placebo conditions (Merry, 1966; Williams, 1970), Marlatt, Demming, and Reid (1973) employed the *balanced placebo design* in an analogue study of loss of control drinking. Under the guise of a "taste-rating" task, alcoholic subjects and social drinker control subjects were instructed to rate the taste of a beverage in one of four independent conditions in which they expected to receive either alcohol or tonic water alone, and then actually received either a vodka and tonic mixture or plain tonic water. This paradigm controls not only for the effects of the beverage administered (the traditional placebo versus active ingredient condition), but also for the subject's expectancies about what he is drinking. The results showed that the only condition that significantly influenced the amount of beverage consumed was the expect-alcohol condition, regardless of the actual alcohol content of the drinks consumed. Both alcoholics and social drinkers consumed more beverage when they were led to believe the drinks contained alcohol. Since that study, a number of experiments have been published using this balanced placebo design with alcohol, and the reader is referred to a recent critical review of these studies (Marlatt & Rohsenow, 1980). At least with regard to such specific social behaviors as aggression, anxiety, humor, and sexual arousal, the expectancy that one is receiving alcohol overrides the pharmacological effects of alcohol (at low dose levels), and seems to support a culturally learned perspective:

When a man lifts a cup, it is not only the kind of drink that is in it, the amount he is likely to take and the circumstances under which he will do the drinking that are specified in advance for him, but also whether the contents of the cup will cheer or stupify . . . induce affection or aggression, guilt or unalloyed pleasure. These and many other cultural definitions attach to the drink, even before it touches the lips. [Mandelbaum, 1965]

The role of expectancy in the perceived effects of alcohol may have important implications for the control and prediction of alcoholic relapse insofar as it pinpoints the significance of psychological factors as they interact with the pharmacological action of alcohol. According to this view, the reinforcing quality of alcohol for the experienced user may not be based on the satiation of biochemically mediated craving but rather on the expectation of certain behavioral effects. This has important treatment implications, for if the determinants of alcohol use (and perhaps also other drug use) are not primarily physiological, then cognitive-behavioral interventions would be the treatment of choice as compared to drug therapies which risk pharmacological side effects and additional drug dependence (e.g., methadone maintenance programs). Equally significant, the treatment goal of controlled social use clearly becomes a viable alternative to abstinence when psychological factors are seen to play a primary role in mediating pharmacological effects.

In a review article comparing relapse rates across time from 84 separate smoking programs, an alcohol treatment program, and a heroin treatment program, comparable relapse curves emerged; by 90 days, approximately 66% of the clients in all three drug categories had relapsed (Hunt, Barnett, & Branch, 1971). The similarity of the high relapse rates suggests that there may be common psychological processes underlying addictive behaviors that are independent of the particular substance or response. Maintenance of positive change has emerged as the key issue in this area.

One approach to the maintenance problem, sometimes called the "shotgun" approach, involves the development of bigger and better treatment programs consisting of multi-modal, broad spectrum packages. The assumption of this approach is that the degree of outcome success will vary directly with the number of treatment components. A second major approach has been the development of self-control procedures, in which the client is trained to self-administer a program of assessment and intervention. A key assumption of this approach is that the client can be trained to become his or her own therapist and will therefore be able to implement procedures to maintain changes in behavior long after the formal treatment program has ended. Despite the advances in knowledge and some increase in long-term successes associated with the development of both broad-spectrum intervention programs and self-control strategies (Best & Block, in press; Gotestam, Melin, & Ost, 1976; Hamburg, 1975; Sobell & Sobell, 1973), we are still relatively naive about relapse, the point at which behavioral change fails to maintain and treatment effects decay. Since treated individuals have a high probability of experiencing a relapse, our position is that strategies aimed at preventing and coping with relapse should be an essential part of any treatment program. The remainder of this chapter will be devoted to describing our conceptualization of the relapse phenomenon, reviewing our research findings on the determinants of relapse, and presenting a relapse prevention program of intervention strategies suggested by the model and research.

Cognitive-Behavioral Model of Relapse

In recent years, we have been developing a theoretical framework from which to conceptualize and ultimately treat relapse (Marlatt, 1978; Marlatt &

Gordon, 1980). The behaviors of interest in this working model are what might be called ''indulgent behaviors.'' The relationship of these behaviors to an underlying physiological need state is less exact than is usually intended by the term ''addictive behaviors.'' Indulgent behaviors temporarily give rise to positive feelings in the individual but in the long run produce detrimental effects that may be physical, social, economic, or psychological in nature. The relapse model attempts to describe the individual's reaction to a relapse and to examine the relationship between the first relapse episode and subsequent use.

First formulated as a perspective on alcohol addiction and relapse, the relapse model seems applicable to a variety of indulgent behaviors. At this point, we are expanding the definition of relapse beyond the ingestion of drugs to include any violation of a self-imposed rule governing consummatory behavior. In this framework, going off a diet, or gambling, drinking alcohol, smoking cigarettes, or injecting heroin after a period of abstinence are all instances of relapse and are relevant behaviors to include in an analysis of the relapse phenomenon.

During abstinence, or adherence to the self-imposed rule, following either a professional treatment or a self-help program, we assume that the individual experiences a sense of *personal control* over the target behavior. The longer the period of abstinence, the greater will be this perceived sense of ability to cope with situations previously associated with the addictive behavior. However, even when the abstinent individual's commitment is strong and the perceived sense of personal control is growing the person may inadvertently be making ''mini-decisions'' that begin a chain of behaviors which may set the stage for a relapse to occur. Unlike the conscious decision to stop the indulgent behavior, these mini-decisions may appear unrelated to any decision to indulge. Such mini-decisions are illustrated by the abstinent alcoholic who just happens to get off the bus in front of a liquor store, or the ex-smoker who keeps a pack of cigarettes around the house just in case friends drop by who might ask for a cigarette, or the reformed gambler who goes along with friends to a tavern where gambling is legal. We have termed these decisions ''Apparently Irrelevant Decisions'' (AIDs), (Marlatt, 1979) to express their seemingly irrelevant connection with the eventual relapse episode. Nevertheless, these AIDs increase the likelihood that the individual will encounter a *high-risk situation* that may trigger a relapse (Fig. 8.1).

These high-risk situations are associated with a history of use of the addictive behavior as a coping response and thus represent a critical choice point for the individual. If the individual is able to execute an adaptive *coping response* and master this source of potential danger, his sense of self-control should increase and the expectation of being able to cope should generalize to future high-risk situations. In a discussion of psychological expectations, Bandura (1977) has coined the term *self-efficacy* to describe this expectation of self-control, as differentiated from outcome-expectation. An outcome-expectation is the belief that the outcome of one's behavior will have the intended results. In contrast, an efficacy-expectation is the confidence in one's ability to pro-

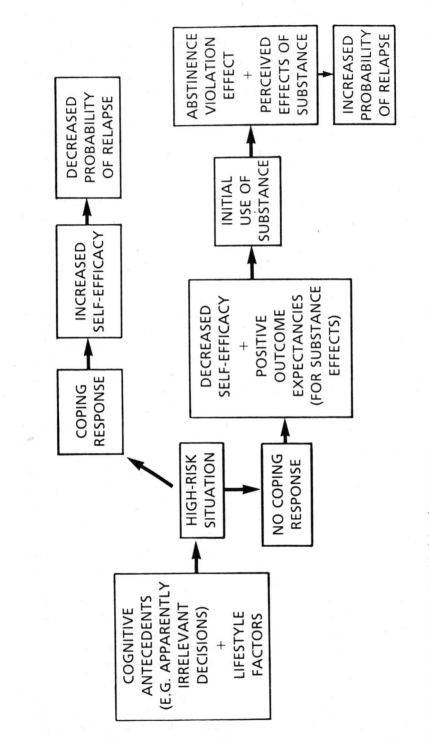

Fig. 8.1. Cognitive-behavioral model of the relapse process.

duce the desired behaviors. For example, a heroin addict may believe that the outcome would be better for his health if he did *not* put a needle in his vein (outcome-expectation), yet feel unsure of his ability to resist, therefore doubting his self-efficacy in achieving the outcome. If the individual has experienced the hazardous situation without relapsing, we predict that the probability of relapse should decrease. In addition, the longer the period of abstinence the greater the individual's perception of self-efficacy.

At some point, most abstinent persons will encounter a high-risk situation that they are unprepared for. If the individual does not or cannot perform an adequate coping response either due to lack of skills and/or to inhibition of skills due to anxiety, fear, or some other behavior-blocking emotion, we predict an immediate decrease in self-efficacy, a concomitant increase in feelings of helplessness, and a tendency to "give in" to the situation. In addition, the temptation to relapse will grow stronger if the person has positive outcome expectancies about the indulgent behavior's effectiveness as a coping response. For many people, taking a drink, eating something sweet, or smoking a cigarette has been long associated with coping with stress. "I can't handle this without a drink," or "I need a cigarette to relax," are common responses to difficult events. When faced with the opportunity to indulge, most people remember only the positive effects of the behaviors (the "glow" from the first drink, the nicotine "high" from a long drag on a cigarette, the thrill of winning at the craps table, the delicious taste of German chocolate cake) and selectively repress/forget the negative outcome (the hangover, gasping for breath in the early morning hours, the unattractive bulges underneath slacks, the destitute feeling after having gambled away one's savings). Thus, if the individual fails to cope adequately with a high-risk situation, has a decreased sense of personal power, and believes that the indulgent behavior will enhance feelings of control, the stage is set for relapse.

The requirement of abstinence reads like an edict; there are no qualifying conditions, no moderating clauses, but only the proclamation that "THOU SHALT NOT . . ." What happens to the individual after drinking the first sip of alcohol, betting a buck on the World Series, or eating the oh-so-small sugar cookie? The vow of abstinence is immediately and irrevocably violated. We have postulated an Abstinence Violation Effect (AVE) to account for the individual's response to this transgression of an absolute rule (Marlatt, 1978). The intensity of this cognitive and affective reaction will vary as a function of several factors, including the prior degree of effort or personal commitment to maintain abstinence, the duration of the abstinence period (the longer the duration, the greater effect), and the overall value or importance of the behavior to the individual involved. The model proposes two components to the AVE: (a) a cognitive dissonance component; and (b) a personal attribution effect.

In classical dissonance theory (Festinger, 1964), cognitive dissonance develops out of the disparity between an individual's cognitions about himself (e.g., as an abstainer) and his subsequent behaviors that are incongruent with those cognitions (e.g., engaging in the forbidden behavior). We predict that this dissonance will vary in degree as a function of the length of abstinence, and the amount of personal and public commitment to abstain. This internal conflict acts as a source of motivation to engage in behaviors (or cognitions) that will reduce the dissonance. Insofar as the target behavior has been used as a coping response to deal with stress in the past, continued performance of the behavior after the first "slip" is hypothesized to reduce the dissonant feelings of guilt, tension, and anxiety. Alternatively, the individual can reduce the dissonance by changing his or her self-image to be aligned with the overt behavior ("I guess I'm not cured, the disease has still *got* me," "Gambling must still be in my blood").

The second component of the AVE is a self-attribution effect (Jones, Kanouse, Kelley, Nisbett, Valins, & Weiner, 1972) whereby the person attributes the cause of the relapse to internal weakness and personal failure rather than to the external situation. Most abstinent individuals feel proud of their abstinence and therefore feel responsible for their relapse. Often people draw inferences about their own traits, attitudes, and motives from the observation of their own behavior (Bem, 1972). To the extent that the individual feels personally responsible for "giving in," attribution theory would predict that he or she would attribute this failure to internal, personal causes (Weiner, Frieze, Kukla, Reed, Rest, & Rosenbaum, 1971). This self-attribution provides the individual with a facile explanation for past inabilities to remain abstinent and an excuse for and a prediction of continuing to indulge (Eiser, Sutton, & Wober, 1978). Consequently, self-efficacy regarding future high-risk situations is decreased, and the expectation of failure will tend to substantiate and fulfill the adage: "Once an addict, always an addict."

A final factor to be considered in the relapse process is the subjective effect of the substance or the indulgent behavior as experienced by the user. While these effects will differ with the particular drug or behavior, many drugs act in such a way as to produce an initial "high" or state of arousal which is interpreted as a pleasant or euphoric state by the user. Both alcohol and tobacco, for example, produce an initial state of physiological arousal (increased heart rate and other autonomic reactions) which may be subjectively experienced by the user as an increase in energy or power. Many psychoactive drugs seem to have a biphasic effect in this regard: the first state is experienced as an excitatory "high" or "upper" (Docter, Naithoh, & Smith, 1966; Garfield & McBrearty, 1970), while subsequent doses cause depressant effects (Bach-Y-Rita, Lion, & Ervin, 1970; Ritchie, 1965). The initial increase in physiological arousal may be labeled by the user as a feeling of enhanced power or control (McClelland, Davis, Kalin, & Wanner, 1972). If this reaction occurs, the use of the substance to counter the individual's prior feelings of decreased self-efficacy or personal powerlessness in the high-risk situation is strongly reinforced. Taken together, the cumulative effects of the AVE coupled with the reinforcing perceived effects of the drug or consummatory response greatly increase the probability that the first slip will be followed by a full relapse or return to habitual patterns of use within a relatively short period of time. The relapse model provides an explanation for the power of the relapse phenomenon to affect subsequent responses. The following section reviews empirical findings on relapse determinants, and the final sections on intervention integrates them with the conceptual model of relapse.

Determinants of Relapse: High-Risk Situations

Recently, we have devised a classification scheme to categorize the situational factors and emotional states that immediately precede a relapse (Marlatt & Gordon, 1980). Open-ended questions regarding reasons for relapse have been content-analyzed by trained coders (88% reliability agreement) into the primary determinants of relapse. Responses to questions such as the following were analyzed: (a) "When I took my first drink (or cigarette, or fix of heroin, or ate in an uncontrolled manner, or gambled) the situation was as follows . . ."; (b) "What would you say was the *main reason* for taking the first drink?"; (c) "Describe any particular circumstances or set of events, things which happened to you in the outside world, which triggered off your need or desire to take the first drink."; (d) "Describe any inner thoughts or emotional feelings (things within you as a person) that triggered off your need or desire to take the first drink."

In an attempt to differentiate relapse episodes into categories of high-risk situations, relapses were content-analyzed into two major classes: intrapersonal/environmental determinants and interpersonal determinants, with eight subcategories (five within intrapersonal determinants, and three within interpersonal determinants). The categories for classification of relapse episodes were as follows:

1. *Intrapersonal/Environmental Determinants:* Includes all determinants which are primarily associated with intrapersonal factors (within the individual), and/or reactions to nonpersonal environmental events: (a) coping with negative emotional states (e.g., frustration, anger, depression, etc.); (b) coping with negative physiological/physical states (associated with prior substance use, as well as other negative, non-drug-related physical states); (c) enhancement of positive emotional states; (d) testing personal control (use of the substance to "test" one's ability to engage in controlled or moderate use, tests of "will-power"); (e) giving in to temptations or urges (substance use in response to subjective desire).

2. *Interpersonal Determinants:* Includes determinants which are primarily associated with interpersonal factors, due to the presence or influence of other individuals as part of the precipitating event: (a) coping with interpersonal conflict (e.g., frustration, anger, jealousy, etc.); (b) social pressure; (c) enhancement of positive emotional states.

Results: Determinants of Relapse in Alcoholics, Smokers, Opiate Addicts, Compulsive Gamblers, and Uncontrolled Eaters.

Relapse episodes taken from eight separate abstinence-oriented treatment programs with a total of 327 subjects were content-analyzed from open-ended questions regarding the reasons for relapse. Five addictive behaviors were represented: drinking, smoking, opiate use, compulsive gambling, and uncontrolled eating. The alcohol group consisted of 70 male chronic alcoholics (mean age, 45) drawn from two inpatient treatment programs (48 from a state hospital inpatient program and 22 from an inpatient V.A. hospital program). Relapse for this group was defined by any use of alcohol after being abstinent. The smoking group consisted of 64 male and female smokers (mean age, 30) from two outpatient programs. Relapse here was defined as any cigarette smoked following a minimum of three days of total abstinence. The heroin addicts consisted of 135 male addicts (mean age, 30) from two outpatient drug treatment programs (16 from a V.A. drug dependency treatment methadone maintenance program and 129 from a Washington State Evaluation-of-Services program; hereafter referred to as V.A. and W.S., respectively. Relapse for the heroin addicts was defined differently for the two groups. In the W.S. (N = 129) sample, relapse was considered to have occurred if the individual consumed *any* opiate, whereas for the V.A. sample (N = 16) who were already on maintenance doses of methadone as part of treatment, relapse was defined as the use of any illicit drug after at least a 30-day period of abstinence. The gambling sample consisted of 19 male gamblers from the Gambler's Anonymous organization in eight major U.S. cities (mean age, 38). Relapse was defined as any gambling after a period of abstinence. The uncontrolled eaters consisted of 29 females from an outpatient weight reduction program (mean age, 38). Relapse was defined by uncontrolled eating for a 24-hour period during which they did not use any of the three behavioral methods they relied on most to control their weight. The gambling, weight, and V.A. heroin subjects were all administered an identical questionnaire, appropriately worded for the addictive behavior under study. The remaining groups received different questionnaires that included open-ended questions asking for a description of the situation surrounding relapse, main reasons for relapse, etc. We believe that the questions eliciting the open-ended descriptions of the relapse episodes are roughly comparable and hence justify this comparative analysis.

Table 8.1 presents the results of the relapse episodes content-analyzed according to the primary determinant. When examining the combined results across all groups, the relapses were found to be split roughly in half, with 52% falling into Intrapersonal Determinants and 48% falling into Interpersonal Determinants. 72% of all relapses can be accounted for by just three

Table 8.1. Analysis of Relapse Situations with Alcoholics, Smokers, Heroin Addicts, Gamblers, and Uncontrolled Eaters

Situation	Alcoholics (N=70)	Smokers (N=64)	WS Addicts (N=129)	VA Addicts (N=16)	Gamblers (N=19)	Uncontrolled Eaters (N=29)	Total (N=327)
INTRAPERSONAL DETERMINANTS	**61%**	**50%**	**45%**	**75%**	**79%**	**46%**	**52%**
Negative Emotional States	38%	37%	19%	19%	47%	33%	30%
Negative Physical States	3%	2%	9%	50%	—	—	7%
Positive Emotional States	—	6%	10%	6%	—	3%	6%
Testing Personal Control	9%	—	2%	—	16%	—	3%
Urges and Temptations	11%	5%	5%	—	16%	10%	6%
INTERPERSONAL DETERMINANTS	**39%**	**50%**	**55%**	**25%**	**21%**	**52%**	**48%**
Interpersonal Conflict	18%	15%	14%	6%	16%	14%	15%
Social Pressure	18%	32%	36%	19%	5%	10%	27%
Positive Emotional States	3%	3%	5%	—	—	28%	6%

303

categories: Negative Emotional States (30%), Social Pressure (27%), and Interpersonal Conflict (15%).

At least 72% of all relapses were associated with negative situations, suggesting that relapse may represent a response to stress. In contrast, only 12% of relapses were due to Positive Emotional States (combining both Intrapersonal and Interpersonal Determinants). Determinants that were consistent across groups will be described first, followed by a discussion of determinants specific to particular behaviors.

Negative Emotional States

The greatest number of relapses were found to fall within this category, which includes all relapses associated with negative emotional reactions either to noninterpersonal, environmental events or to interpersonal situations that have occurred some time previously. For example, a smoker from our sample reported, "It had been raining continually all week. Saturday morning, I walked down to the basement to do laundry and I found the basement filled with a good three inches of water. To make things worse, as I went to turn on the light to see the extent of damage, I got shocked from the light switch. Later that same day, I was feeling real low and knew I had to have a cigarette after my neighbor, who is a contractor, assessed the damage at over $4,000. I went to the store and bought a pack."

Social Pressure

The second most frequent relapse determinant was social pressure, which includes both direct interpersonal coercion aimed at pressuring the abstinent individual to engage in the addictive behavior and indirect social pressure. Indirect pressure usually occurs as a result of finding oneself in a social context where everyone else is using the substance and perceiving oneself to be behaving in an inappropriate social manner if one does not "do as the Romans do." An alcoholic in our sample wrote, "I went to my supervisor's house for a surprise birthday dinner for him. I got there late and as I came into the living room everyone had a drink in hand. I froze when his wife asked me what I was drinking. Without thinking I said, 'A J&B on the rocks'."

Interpersonal Conflict

This was the third largest category. Disagreements and negative confrontations appear to be very high-risk situations, perhaps in part because interpersonal conflicts seem to provide a widely sanctioned excuse for indulging. Also, the individual may use the interpersonal problem to justify attributing some of the responsibility for his or her behavior to someone else. "I came home late from a horrible day on the road and hadn't stepped in the house five minutes before my wife started accusing me of gambling on the horses.

Racetrack, hell! I told her if she didn't believe me I'd give her a real reason to file for divorce. That night I spent $450 at Longacres.''

An examination of the relapse determinants by groups reveals some unique patterns emerging out of the general relapse profile described above.

Negative Physical States

Negative physical states were relatively infrequent as determinants of relapse except in the V.A. sample (N = 16) of heroin addicts. The two heroin groups are presented separately because they showed different patterns of relapse—a disproportionately high percentage of the V.A. addicts relapsed due to negative physical states (50%) compared to the low percentage of the larger W.S. sample (N = 129) of addicts (9%). The V.A. sample relapsed with a variety of illicit drugs versus only opiate relapse in the W.S. sample. Because of this important difference, we further analyzed the V.A. sample according to the *kind* of drug relapsed with and found that of the 50% relapses due to negative physical states, opiate relapse in this category accounted for 14% of all relapses, barbiturates for 29%, both opiates and barbiturates taken simultaneously during relapse for 7%, and amphetamines for 0%. This separate analysis thus revealed more similar percentages for the opiate relapses due to negative physical states for the two heroin groups: 14% for the V.A. sample and 9% for the W.S. sample. Clearly, relapses involving opiates do *not* occur primarily in response to somatic discomfort.

Testing Personal Control

It is intriguing that alcoholics (9%) and gamblers (16%) constituted the largest percentage of relapses for this determinant. In the traditional view, alcoholism is seen as a disease over which the alcoholic has *no* control. This assumption is formalized in the Alcoholics Anonymous doctrine, which the Gamblers Anonymous organization has overtly used as their guiding philosophy:

The first small bet to a problem gambler is like the first small drink to an alcoholic. Sooner or later he falls back into the same old destructive pattern. Once a person has crossed the invisible line into irresponsible gambling he *never* seems to regain control. After abstaining a few months some of our members have tried some small-bet experimentation, always with disastrous results. The old obsession inevitably returned . . . We know that no real compulsive gambler ever regains control. All of us felt at times we were regaining control, but such intervals—usually brief—were inevitably followed by still less control, which led in time to pitiful and incomprehensible demoralization. We are convinced to a man that gamblers of our type are in the grip of a *progressive illness*. Over any considerable period of time we get worse, never better. [Gamblers Anonymous Handbook, 1976, pp. 3 and 13]

We interpret the relatively large percentage of relapses due to testing of personal control in the two groups as reflecting a vulnerability directly fostered by the shared philosophy of the two treatment programs. These people seem to be testing the cardinal principle that the individual must admit powerlessness over drinking or gambling and explicitly acknowledge the impossibility of ever engaging in the behavior in a controlled manner. To quote from one of our gambler's relapse episodes: "I gambled just to see if I could start and stop when I wished; just to see if I could control it." This illustrates a salient inconsistency in the disease model in that any addictive behavior, whether or not it involves use of a pharmacological agent, is conceptualized as a disease. It seems more parsimonious to attribute relapse to a common psychological factor than to attribute both alcoholism, which involves a drug, and gambling, which does not involve a drug, to a "progressive illness."

Interpersonal Positive Emotional States

Although this determinant accounted for a small percentage of alcoholic, smoking, gambling, and heroin relapses, 28% of the uncontrolled eaters fell into this relapse category. Sharing food is a culturally acceptable, reinforced, and valued means of promoting and deepening social contact, and perhaps the obese group is more at risk for this category by the very nature of the substance consumed. A relapsed dieter wrote, "It is easiest to eat when people around me are eating, when social aspects seem to focus around meals. It is easier to make meals a 'let's-get-together' time."

Relapse Prevention: Implications for Treatment

Most traditional abstinence-oriented treatment programs do not address themselves to the relapse question. To the extent that treatment success is synonymous with 100% abstinence, the client may infer that he or she has no control over the addictive behavior. Therefore, if the client "loses control" through one slip, this may be interpreted as proof of lack of control, and of an inability to regain control, thus undermining motivation to make an attempt at control. In other words, the person has defined himself or herself as a helpless victim.

In Alcoholics Anonymous and Gamblers Anonymous, this abnegation of personal control is stated in the organizations' formal "steps toward recovery": "We believe that a Power greater than ourselves can restore us to a normal way of thinking and living and we make a decision to turn our will and our lives over to the care of this Power . . ." (Gamblers Anonymous Handbook, 1976, p. 4). The group itself is invested with power which the client is encouraged to call upon if he or she feels weakened by the need to use. In our view, these two organizations foster dependency on the group and God that serves as the "cure" for the disease. This conversion to group support and external control makes therapeutic sense as a means of substituting dependency in place of the addiction. However, little if any behavioral advice is given to the client about what to do when he or she encounters a high-risk situation for relapse. These programs avoid the issue of breakdown of abstinence perhaps because they lack an understanding of the relapse process and the requisite behavioral skills necessary to handle such situations. In place of skills to prevent relapse or moderate the effects of relapse if it occurs, slogans are presented that unfortunately sound more like dogmatic tenets or axioms than like self-instructional or coping statements. "Don't tempt or test yourself" (Gamblers Anonymous Handbook, 1976, p. 17), "You are one drink away from a drunk," etc.

It is important to acknowledge that organizations like Alcoholics Anonymous and Gamblers Anonymous are successful with some people who wish to adopt the goal of abstinence *and* who don't drop out (although few dropout rate statistics are available from these organizations). However, for many people, the cost of abstinence is too big a price to pay in terms of either social isolation or a philosophical admission that they cannot control their behavior. Clearly, this group-support based, disease-victimization model is appropriate for a percentage of people struggling to control their indulgent behavior, but it appears equally clear that for a significant number of people unable or unwilling to follow the traditional treatment, an adaptive, skills-oriented treatment is preferable. A project funded by the National Institute on Alcohol Abuse and Alcoholism to assess the effectiveness of a variety of abstinence-oriented alcohol treatment programs found at an 18-month follow-up that approximately 25% of the clients were drinking "normally," and that less than 10% were able to maintain abstinence after two years (Armor, Polich, & Stambul, 1976). A recent review cites 74 studies documenting controlled "social drinking" by former alcoholics (Pattison, Sobell, & Sobell, 1977). Controversy over abstinence and controlled use exists regarding heroin and nicotine use as well. Ideally, clients should be offered the choice between abstinence and controlled use when techniques whose effectiveness has been demonstrated are available. Further research is also needed to determine if there are reliable ways of matching clients and treatment approaches.

Points of Intervention for Prevention of Relapse

Figure 8.2 depicts the cognitive-behavioral model of relapse with points of intervention for each stage of the process.

Apparently Irrelevant Decisions. Many clients are able to provide retrospective accounts of a chain of mini-decisions, expectations, and rationalizations that precede a relapse.

It seems possible that some individuals engage in a series of mini-decisions, or AIDs, that set the stage for relapse. An abstinent alcoholic may, for ex-

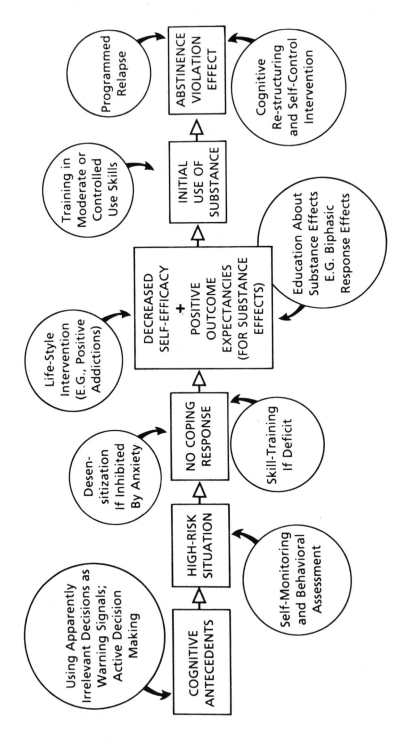

Fig. 8.2. Points of intervention for prevention of relapse.

ample, decide that at a certain point it is safe to have liquor around the house for guests who may drop by. Although the alcoholic in this instance may deny that this decision has any effect in terms of increasing the probability of relapse, this behavior usually does move the individual one step closer to the brink of relapse. With some of our clients, it seems clear that they engage in a number of such AIDs which culminate in a situation of such high temptation and risk that it would take a moral Superman to resist. When this occurs, the relapse may be justified as an inevitable giving in to overwhelming situational circumstances (e.g., an abstinent gambler who takes a vacation in Reno). In the relapse prevention approach, we try to train the client to recognize the nature and function of these AIDs, and to respond to such cognitive processes as early warning signals that indicate an increased probability of relapse. Rationalizations and mini-decisions of this kind are labeled with a "red flag" (discriminative stimulus), to warn the person of impending danger. The AID becomes a signal that the person must stop and closely examine the motivations for his or her actions. At this point, the client is urged to take the following steps: (a) to recognize the AID as a decision, and to assume responsibility for this choice (i.e., avoid denial of its influence and its relation to relapse); and (b) to review the criteria for making the decision to abstain or to adhere to a fixed program of moderation in the light of the current situation. A renewed decision in the form of a commitment to go "back on the program" is the goal of this intervention. If clients can be taught to respond to these AIDs as warning signals, they may be able to come up with a constructive alternative response. Forewarned is forearmed.

High-Risk Situations. On the basis of the analysis of relapse episodes, specific high-risk situations both within and across addictions are evident. The client and therapist should identify these situations in order to either avoid them or cope with them. Here, it is necessary to establish a functional relationship between the environment and the client's behavior so that the client learns to recognize cues associated with an increased likelihood of relapse. Such stimuli may come from the environment (e.g., walking past a favorite bar, turning accidentally to the horse racing page in the newspaper), from the individual's cognitive strategies (images, fantasies, and expectations concerning the use and effects of the taboo substance or activity), or from physiological state changes (arousal feelings of frustration or anger which the person labels as "craving").

The targeting of high-risk situations must be done individually due to the uniqueness of each client's personal history and learning experiences. Ideally, this would involve having the client self-monitor his or her indulgent behavior before a detoxification or treatment program has begun. Using standard self-monitoring procedures (McFall, 1977) the client can record a baseline consumption frequency, settings of use, mood, and so on. As an adjunct to, or in place of, self-monitoring if detoxification has begun, the use of paper and pencil inventories are helpful, such as the Drinking Profile (Marlatt, 1976b). Taken together, both in vivo self-monitoring and retrospective accounts give critical information concerning the situations likely to be associated with the greatest psychological payoff for a particular client and hence providing the greatest risk or temptation to relapse.

The assessment process may yield one of three outcomes. If the client's repertoire includes an adequate coping response for a given high-risk situation, the therapist can reinforce the client for utilizing this response, thereby enhancing the expectation of success, increasing the sense of self-efficacy, and decreasing the probability of a relapse. On the other hand, the client either may not have the requisite skills to deal with the high-risk situation, or his or her behavioral repertoire may contain adequate coping responses which are inhibited because of anxiety or fear. Once the high-risk situations have been defined and a behavioral assessment has been made of the client's existing means of coping effectively with these situations, a program can then be implemented to help the client acquire the necessary skills and self-control strategies.

No Coping Response. If the client does not have the necessary skills, the therapist must use techniques to develop these coping responses. The literature on skill training with alcoholics (O'Leary, O'Leary, & Donovan, 1976) and drug addicts (Van Hasselt, Hersen, & Milliones, 1976) is encouraging. One prototypic assessment procedure for alcoholics, which could easily be generalized to any indulgent behavior, is the *Situational Competency Test* (Chaney, O'Leary, & Marlatt, 1978). After assessing chronic alcoholics' skill deficits on the basis of self-reported situations that were difficult to handle without using alcohol, these patients were verbally presented with hypothetical high-risk situations (e.g., frustration and anger, other negative emotional states, etc.). Through the use of modeling, behavioral rehearsal, and successive approximations, these clients' coping responses to the hypothetically posed high-risk situations improved to criterion levels. At a one-year follow-up, these clients when compared with controls were able to generate and maintain appropriate behavioral skills which resulted in significantly less frequent and severe relapse episodes. Similar procedures can be used with assertion training (Miller & Eisler, 1977), communication skill training, and other behavioral strategies. Finally, the therapist can increase the generalization of these coping skills by instructing the client to practice these newly acquired skills in vivo, perhaps with the therapist or supportive friend present (Eisler, Hersen, Miller, & Blanchard, 1975), as well as teaching the client general problem-solving strategies (D'Zurilla & Goldfried, 1971) so that new high-risk situations can be dealt with effectively.

Alternatively, the client's problems may involve the inhibition of coping skills by anxiety (e.g., caused by social pressure). In this case desensitization to pair the feared stimuli with an incompatible response (e.g., deep muscle relaxation, Bernstein & Borkovec, 1973), or cognitive restructuring of anxiety-producing self-statements (Ellis & Grieger, 1977; Meichenbaum, 1977) may be used.

Decreased Self-Efficacy. Since low self-efficacy or a sense of helplessness is hypothesized to be a significant factor in precipitating relapse, skill training and anxiety reduction are viewed as effective interventions for coping with specific high-risk situations that threaten the individual's self-efficacy. A more global intervention may also be required to impart and stabilize a general sense of self-efficacy.

Many people live in a state of imbalance between pleasure and responsibility, delaying engaging in activities that are pleasurable rather than obligatory until Saturday night or an annual two-week vacation. The ensuing sense of deprivation often leads to attempts to "compensate" by excessive indulgence in drugs, food, or any behavior with short-term payoffs even when long-term effects may be harmful. Marlatt and Gordon (1980) have developed a *want/should* ratio to index the proportion of "wants" (activities intrinsically rewarding) to "shoulds" (activities performed out of a sense of duty or obligation). It is proposed that the closer this ratio is to unity, the more balanced the person's lifestyle will be , leading to a greater sense of personal control, choice, and self-efficacy.

Self-monitoring provides a means of assessing the "want/should" ratio. Daily activities are recorded and rated according to whether the individual perceives them as wants, shoulds, or some combination (using, e.g., a scale of 1-7 where 1 is a total "should" and 7 is a total "want"). After doing this for several typical weekdays and weekends, awareness of how time is being spent should be sufficient so that the therapist and client can restructure the day or week so as to better balance this "life-style ledger." For most individuals trying to control an indulgent behavior, this activity may be one of the few "wants" in a long day of "shoulds." The purpose of this intervention is to replace the addictive behavior with something which has a similar functional value to the individual but is a more adaptive form of self-indulgence or reward.

Data from our laboratory (Marlatt & Marques, 1977) indicate a significant reduction in alcohol use (approximately 50% drop from baseline) in heavy social drinkers who were involved in six weeks of either progressive muscle relaxation training, meditation training (Benson, 1975), or a "bibliotherapy" (quiet reading periods) group when compared to a no-treatment control. All groups showed a significant shift to internal locus of control during the treatment period. Apparently taking regular "time-out" periods each day to relax, meditate, or read an enjoyable book both reduces alcohol consumption and increases self-efficacy. A weight reduction client wrote: "Something that has really helped with keeping my eating under control is what I would call balancing out my lifestyle. I've always taken on much more responsibility than

I can handle which brings on anxiety (i.e., eating). I'm learning to balance out work with recreation. Plus I spend time each day in silence—alone to pray and meditate.'' Similarly, previous research has reported that regular meditation results in decrements in self-reported substance usage (Benson, 1974; Shafii, Lavely, & Jaffe, 1974, 1975). If alcoholics increase their drinking after a stress condition more than social drinkers (Miller, Hersen, Eisler, & Hilsman, 1974), and if meditation can serve as an intervention for stress reactivity (Goleman & Schwartz, 1976), then perhaps meditation provides the individual with a global perception of power to cope with stressful high-risk situations.

Recently, the concept of "positive addictions" has been developed by Glasser (1976). Like negative addictions, positive addictions are habit-forming, but the long-term consequences are positive rather than negative. Such activities as jogging, swimming, yoga, and meditation could be viewed as being positively addicting to the extent that once individuals are addicted they experience withdrawal-like symptoms if they do not engage in the activity and possibly become tolerant to the activity in the sense of requiring longer periods of involvement before experiencing pre-tolerant effects.

As an alternative or adjunct to specific activities, we prescribe for some clients taking at least one-half hour of "self-time" each day. The first few minutes are spent meditating or sitting quietly in an effort to identify what one's particular "wants" are at that time. If the client is physically tired but mentally alert, a form of indulgence like reading, listening to or playing music, or working on a hobby might prove more satisfying than strenuous physical activity, which would be more appropriate when the person is rested. Recent research suggests the possibility that therapeutic activities designed to reduce anxiety (i.e., meditation, active sports, etc.) should be assigned on the basis of the psychophysiological system implicated in the anxiety response. For example, physical exercise may be the intervention of choice for somatic anxiety, whereas mantra meditation may be more appropriate for anxiety caused by obsessive-compulsive worrying (Davidson, 1978).

The issue most crucial to self-efficacy is the emphasis on the client's personal choice and ultimate autonomy in the decision-making process involved in relapse. If we indoctrinate the individual to assume a victim role in which he is basically helpless, sick, buffeted by external forces, and without self-control, the end result will be a person without significant freedom of choice, unable to adapt flexibly to novel situations, and dependent on sources of control outside of himself. We are arguing that by increasing people's perception of having control, decision-making power, or choice in any given moment or during any chain of events, their willingness to assume responsibility for their actions will increase and this will increase the probability of making decisions congruent with their treatment goal.

Positive Outcome Expectancies for Substance Effects. After a period of abstinence, the individual may forget the negative consequences and remember only the positive aspects of engaging in the addictive behavior.

Although education about long-term health risks involved in excessive nicotine, alcohol, heroin, and food intake functions as a relapse deterrent for some people, a study investigating smoking cessation found that fears about the health risks of smoking were unrelated to the success of attempts at stopping smoking (Eisler, Sutton, & Wober, 1978). In addition to information about psychological and physical health risks, education about both the dose-dependent effects of the particular substance over time and the role of expectancy effects should be part of the treatment.

Positive expectancies for substance effects can be attributed to the immediately reinforcing qualities of the initial physiological arousal and subjective "high" produced by many psychoactive drugs. Because the negative effects of the biphasic response occur after the positive effects, the immediate positive effects act as the major reinforcer. Clients need to be informed of the opponent nature of many drugs' actions, as well as of the eventual adverse effects, such as respiratory depression and vomiting (Calne, 1978), fall in hormone level production with heroin use (Martin, Jasinski, Haertzen, Kay, & Jones, 1973; Mirin, Mendelson, Ellingboe, & Meyer, 1976), behavioral stupor and physiological depression with alcohol use (Docter, et al., 1966), and decreases in skeletal muscle tone and EEG changes in nicotine use (Domino, 1973; Larsen & Silvett, 1975; Russell, 1976), as well as the long-term health risks of smoking (U.S.P.H.S. 1976). The drug's pharmacological effects also interact with the individual's psychological set, and with the length of abstinence. Lienert and Traxel (1959) found that alcohol's sedating effects were more pronounced under conditions of high emotionality. Similarly, tolerance to alcohol after a period of abstinence is usually lowered, thereby magnifying the effects of alcohol during the relapse episode (Maisto, Henry, Sobell, & Sobell, 1978).

Initial Use of Substance. In spite of the best efforts and intentions of therapist and client alike, many clients may experience a slip. As a preventive strategy, they need behavioral skills and cognitive strategies to help control the magnitude of the slip so that it does not initiate a full-blown return to pretreatment consumption levels. Controlled use techniques have been applied primarily to the alcohol and obesity areas while less has been done for controlled use of narcotics (Harding & Zinberg, 1977), or nicotine (Frederiksen & Peterson, 1976). Nonetheless, a package of skills are being developed which appear to have common utility across a variety of addictions.

Teaching the client to self-monitor the amount of substance used or behavior engaged in is essential to controlled use. Blood alcohol level discrimination training with alcoholics has been attempted through aversive conditioning (Lovibond & Caddy, 1970) and biofeedback (Silverstein, Nathan, & Taylor, 1974). However, alcoholics seem less able to relate internal, visceral-based sensations (e.g., dizziness, tingling of the skin) than external cues (e.g., number of drinks consumed per unit time) to their blood-alcohol levels. Consequently, at least with alcoholics, training in self-monitoring should emphasize attention to external sources of information (Nathan, 1978). Individual monitoring of consumption once relapse occurs is also possible with obese persons by discrimination training of calorie intake (Polivy, 1976). A variety of rate reduction techniques include limitations on the frequency and duration of sips and bites, kind of beverage or food consumed (mixed drinks, low calorie foods) (Sobell, Schaeffer, & Mills, 1972; Stuart & Davis, 1972), and contingency management training (Frederiksen & Peterson, 1976; Mann, 1972), among others. Most of the work on controlled use has been done with training alcoholics to control their alcohol consumption, and the interested reader should consult the following references for a more complete review of controlled drinking techniques (Marlatt & Nathan, 1978; Miller & Mastria, 1977; Miller & Munoz,, 1976; Sobell & Sobell, 1978) as well as the chapter by Miller and Hester in this volume. Creative controlled use techniques could be developed to apply to gambling, using similar behavioral skills such as limiting the amount of money wagered on any one bet or spacing bets by limiting the absolute number of bets per unit time.

We suggest for all addictive behaviors that the client be instructed to wait at least 20 minutes after the initial urge to relapse before acting on any decision to do so. This focuses the client's attention on the decision-making process and introduces the elements of control and choice. In addition, since the delay has the effect of temporally separating the triggering event from the relapse, the reinforcing qualities of using the indulgent behavior to cope with stress may be reduced.

The client may practice these controlled-use skills during relapse and *still* have a strong deleterious cognitive/affective reaction that may weaken the chances of resisting further relapse. The final treatment component intervenes at this point.

Abstinence Violation Effect (AVE). As a conservative therapeutic stance, the therapist should assume that if relapse occurs the client will experience the AVE to some degree. A gambler wrote: "I knew I was doing something I shouldn't have been doing. Nevertheless, I felt powerless, like there was nothing I could do to stop it. I had been contemplating it for a long time and I don't think I realized the severity of it 'till it was too late. I had tremendous guilt about it. It didn't matter whether the bet lost or won—the damage was done." It is therefore necessary to prepare the client for this effect. By educating the client about the components of the AVE and providing techniques for restructuring this cognitive reaction, the therapist can help the client to cope with the AVE without succumbing to a total relapse. The occurrence of a slip does not mean that the client has failed. It is used to gather important information about the antecedent events likely to elicit a recurrence of the indulgent behavior. This approach allows the client to practice alternative coping responses for future situations, thus increasing self-efficacy and redefining the slip as a learning experience.

Two possible approaches to preparing clients to cope more effectively with a slip are the relapse rehearsal and the programmed relapse. A relapse rehearsal may be covert or actual. The client is asked to either imagine or act out, without actually using the substance or response, a high-risk situation in which the outcome is a decision to indulge. The cognitive/affective reactions can then be articulated and restructured and a coping response to bring the behavior back under control can be imagined or acted out.

A more dramatic technique is the programmed relapse, which we have recommended for individuals for whom a relapse appears to be so imminent that a supervised relapse is judged more helpful in defusing the perceived threat and demystifying the power of the behavior or substance. Viewed as a "fire drill" or dress rehearsal, the therapist sets the time and place of the relapse in order to reduce the self-attribution of the AVE and to remove the relapse response from the situation the client is reacting to. The therapist is present during this programmed relapse to coach the client to practice the controlled use skills previously taught and to monitor the client's cognitive reactions to the relapse, supplying rational, alternative interpretations in case the client is unable to do so. While this technique is currently being investigated systematically, it seems reasonable that a practice relapse should provide the client with a preview of potential pitfalls, thus indicating appropriate self-corrective measures in the areas of behavioral skills, emotional reactions, or cognitive attributions.

Concluding Remarks and Future Directions

In this chapter we have presented a model which conceptualizes relapse as a process consisting of discrete sequential steps beginning with the decision to abstain, proceeding to the actual relapse episode, and culminating in the affective and cognitive reactions to the relapse. By viewing relapse not as a strictly binary, abstinence-nonabstinence event but rather as one that occurs along a continuum, more sophisticated strategies for relapse prevention emerge. To use a metaphor, we could liken controlling an addictive behavior to a car trip with clear points of departure (i.e., the decision to abstain) and arrival (i.e., abstinence or controlled use). The trip covers varied terrain which may or may not be familiar to the individual. The importance of a cognitive map delineating rough roads, dangerous curves, critical intersections, and alternative routes is self-evident, and the input of an instructor, guide, or experienced traveler would be invaluable. Additional relevant travel information could be gained by knowledge of the extent to which the car and driver's current level of functioning match the demands of the trip. By assessing these strengths and weaknesses *before* beginning the trip, the individual is better prepared to drive in accordance with the limitations of his or her skills, his or her vehicle, and the realities of the geography and general environmental factors. Short practice runs might also be useful.

Diverse ideas and research findings have been integrated into the relapse model described here, which now requires further empirical testing. It is necessary specifically to determine the effectiveness and parameters of the proposed interventions, and on a broader level to continue to investigate the validity of the notion that there are common denominators across addictions, and that many of these factors may be primarily psychological in nature. A number of pivotal issues need to be addressed in future research on this topic.

Foremost among these issues is the question of which addictive behavior problems will benefit most from an education/skill training approach, as contrasted with a traditional disease model treatment approach. A series of outcome studies are necessary in which the criterion of treatment success or failure is expanded to include relative degrees of relapse as defined by the amount of substance used or behavior engaged in per unit time. Further, within a skill training outcome study, the model's assumptions must be empirically validated. One methodological approach would be to predict the course of relapse (i.e., no relapse, one slip, initial heavy use followed by a return to abstinence, controlled social use, etc.) on the basis of the parameters of the model (i.e., skill level, degree of perceived self-efficacy at treatment termination, want/should lifestyle ratio, outcome expectancies for substance use, determinant of first relapse, degree of AVE at time of first slip, etc.). These relapse-prediction studies could be done both within and across various addictive behaviors, thereby establishing factors common to the addictive process and their relative contributions to eventual relapse. Results from this line of research would yield an important guide for treatment planning. On the basis of the client's characteristics, length of prior substance use and abstinence, type of addictive behavior involved, skill deficits, and other related factors, the client could be informed about which environmental situations and affective and cognitive factors are predicted to be asociated with relapse. Specific interventions tailored to the individual could then be generated in advance of the problematic situations, thus increasing the probability of preventing relapse and protecting positive changes from decay.

We believe that, as our understanding of the interplay and relative contributions of psychosocial, pharmacological, and physiological factors associated with addictive behaviors grows, people can, with increased knowledge and training, learn to control their behavior. In contrast with the traditional view of the ''addict'' as a helpless pawn of an underlying disease or physiological addiction mechanism, the relapse prevention model provides a self-control framework in which the individual is given the appropriate skills and associated cognitions to assume responsibility for and maintain control of the target behavior.

References

Armor, D. J., Polich, J. M., & Stambul, H. B. *Alcoholism and treatment* Report #R-1739 NIAAA. Santa Monica, California: Rand Corp, 1976.

Bach-Y-Rita, G., Lion, J., & Ervin, F. Pathological intoxication: Clinical and electroencephelographic studies. *American Journal of Psychiatry* 1970, **127**:698-703.

Bandura, A. *principles of behavior modification*. New York: Holt, Rinehart & Winston, 1969.

Bandura, A. Self-efficacy: Toward a unifying theory of behavioral change. *Psychological Review* 1977, **84**:191-215.

Bem, D. J. Self-perception theory. In: L. Berkowitz (Ed.) *Advances in Experimental Social Psychology* Vol. 6. New York: Academic Press, 1972.

Benson, H. Decreased alcohol intake associated with the practice of meditation: A retrospective investigation. *Annals of the New York Academy of Sciences*, 1974, **233**:174-177.

Benson, H. *The Relaxation Response*. New York: William Morrow & Co., 1975.

Berg, N. L. Effects of alcohol intoxication on self-concept. *Quarterly Journal of Studies on Alcohol*, 1971, **32**:442-453.

Bernstein, D. & Borkovec, T. *Progressive Relaxation Training: A manual for the helping professions*. Champaign, Illinois: Research Press, 1973.

Best, J. A. & Block, M. Compliance in the control of smoking. In: R. B. Haynes, D. W. Taylor, & D. L. Sackett (Eds.) *Compliance with therapeutic and prevention regimens*. Baltimore: Johns Hopkins University Press (in press).

Calne, D. B. Pain and analgesic mechanisms. In: M. A. Lipton, A. Di Mascio, & K. F. Killam (Eds.) *Psychopharmacology: A generation of progress*. New York: Raven Press, 1978.

Cameron, D. The psychopharmacology of social drinking. *Journal of Alcoholism*, 1974, **9**:50-55.

Cappell, H. & Herman, C. P. Alcohol and tension reduction: A review. *Quarterly Journal of Studies on Alcohol*, 1972, **33**:33-64.

Chaney, E. F., O'Leary, M. R., & Marlatt, G. A. Skill training with alcoholics. *Journal of Consulting and Clinikal Psychology*, 1978, **46**(5): 1092-1104.

Conger, J. J. Alcoholism: Theory, problem and challenge. II. Reinforcement theory and the dynamics of alcoholism. *Quarterly Journal of Studies on Alcohol*, 1956, **17**:296-305.

Davidson, R. J. Specificity and patterning in biobehavioral systems. *American Psychologist*, May, 1978, 430-436.

Deutsch, R. Conditioned hypoglycemia: A mechanism for saccharin-induced sensitivity to insulin in the rat. *Journal of Comparative and Physiological Psychology*, 1974, **86**:350-358.

Docter, R., Naitoh, P., & Smith, J. Electroencephalographic changes and vigilance behavior during experimentally induced intoxication with alcoholic subjects. *Psychosomatic Medicine*, 1966, **28**, 605-615.

Domino, E. F. In W. L. Dunn, Jr. (Ed.) *Smoking Behavior: Motives and Incentives*. Washington D. C.: Winston Press, 1973.

D'Zurilla, T. J. & Goldfried, M. R. Problem solving and behavior modification. *Journal of Abnormal Psychology,* 1971, **78,** 107-126.

Eiser, J. R., Sutton, S. R., & Wobel, M. 'Consonant' and 'dissonant' smokers and the self-attribution of addiction. *Addictive Behaviors,* 1978, **3,** 99-106.

Eisler, R. M. Hersen, M., Miller, P. M., & Blanchard, E. B. Situational determinants of assertive behavior. *Journal of Consulting and Clinical Psychology,* 1975, **43,** 330-340.

Ellis, A. & Grieger, R. *Handbook of rational emotive therapy.* New York: Springer Publishing Company, 1977.

Festinger, L. *Conflict, decision and dissonance.* Stanford: Stanford University Press, 1964.

Frederiksen, L. W. & Peterson, G. L. Controlled smoking: Development and maintenance. *Addictive Behaviors,* 1976, **1,** 193-196.

Gamblers Anonymous Handbook. P.O. Box 17173, Los Angeles, California, 90017, 1976.

Garfield, Z. & McBrearty, J. Arousal level and stimulus response in alcoholics after drinking. *Quarterly Journal of Studies on Alcohol,* 1970, **31,** 832-838.

Glasser, W. *Positive Addictions.* New York: Harper & Row, 1976.

Goleman, D. J. & Schwartz, G. E. Meditation as an intervention in stress reactivity. *Journal of Consulting and Clinical Psychology,* 1976, **44**(3), 456-466.

Gotestam, R. G., Melin, L., & Ost, L. Behavioral techniques in the treatment of drug abuse: An evaluative review. *Addictive Behaviors,* 1976, **1,** 205-225.

Grenell, R. G. Effects of alcohol on the neuron. In: B. Kissin & H. Begleiter (Eds.) *The biology of alcoholism* Vol. 2. New York: Plenum Press, 1972.

Hamburg, S. Behavior therapy in alcoholism: A critical review of broad-spectrum approaches. *Journal of Studies on Alcohol,* 1975, **36,** (1), 69-87.

Harding, W. M. & Zinberg, N. E. The effectiveness of the subculture developing rituals and social sanctions for controlled drug use. In: B. M. Du Toit (Ed.) *Drugs, rituals, & altered states of consciousness.* Rotterdam: A. A. Balkema, 1977.

Hamwich, H. E. & Callson, D. A. The effects of alcohol on evoked potentials of various parts of the CNS of the cat. In: B. Kissin & H. Begleiter (Eds.) *The biology of alcoholism* Vol. 2, New York: Plenum Press, 1972.

Hunt, W. A., Barnett, L. W., & Branch, L. G. Relapse rates in addiction programs. *Journal of Clinical Psychology,* 1971, **27,** 455-456.

Jellinek, E. M. *The disease concept of alcoholism.* Highland Park, New Jersey: Hillhouse Press, 1960.

Jones, E. E., Kanouse, D. E., Kelley, H. H., Nisbett, R. E., Valins, S., & Weiner, B. (Eds.) *Attribution: Perceiving the causes of behavior.* Morristown, New Jersey: General Learning Press, 1972.

Kastl, A. J. Changes in ego functioning under alcohol. *Quarterly Journal of Studies on Alcohol,* 1969, **30,** 371-383.

Lang, W. J., Brown, M. L., Gershon, S., & Korol, B. Classical and physiologic adaptive conditioned responses to anti-cholenergic drugs in conscious dogs. *International Journal of Neuropharmacology,* 1966, **5,** 311-315.

Larson, P. S. & Silvette, H. *Tobacco: Experimental and clinical studies.* Supplement 3. Baltimore: Williams & Wilkins, 1975.

Lienert, G. A. & Traxel, W. The effects of meprobamate and alcohol on galvanic skin response. *Journal of Psychology,* 1959, **48,** 329-334.

Lovibond, S. H. & Caddy, G. R. Discriminated aversive control in the moderation of alcoholic drinking behavior. *Behavior Therapy,* 1970, **1,** 437-444.

Ludwig, A. M. & Wikler, A. "Craving" and relapse to drink. *Quarterly Journal of Studies on Alcohol,* 1974, **35,** 108-130.

Madden, J. S., Walker, R., & Kenyon, W. H. *Alcohol and drug dependence.* New York and London: Plenum Press, 1976.

Maisto, S. A., Henry, R. R., Sobell, M. B., & Sobell, L. C. Implications of acquired changes in tolerance for the treatment of alcohol problems. *Addictive Behaviors,* 1978, **3,** 51-55.

Mandelbaum, D. G. Alcohol and culture. *Current Anthropology,* 1965, **6,** 281-294.

Mann, R. A. The behavior-therapeutic use of contingency contracting to control an adult behavior problem: Weight control. *Journal of Applied Behavior Analysis,* 1972, **5,** 99-109.

Marlatt, G. A. Alcohol, stress and cognitive control. In: I. G. Sarason & C. D. Spielberger (Eds.) *Stress and anxiety.* Vol. 3. Washington D. C.: Hemisphere Publishing Company, 1976a.

Marlatt, G. A. The Drinking Profile: A questionnaire for the behavioral assessment of alcoholism. In: E. J. Mash & L. G. Terdal (Eds.) *Behavior therapy assessment: Diagnosis, design, and evaluation.* New York: Springer, 1976b.

Marlatt, G. A. Craving for alcohol, loss of control, and relapse: A cognitive behavioral analysis. In: P. E. Nathan, G. A. Marlatt, & T. Løberg (Eds.) *Alcoholism: New directions in behavioral research and treatment.* New York: Plenum Publishing Co., 1978.

Marlatt, G. A. Alcohol use and problem drinking: A cognitive-behavioral analysis. In: P. C. Kendall and S. P. Hollon (Eds.) *Cognitive-behavioral interventions: Theory, research and procedures.* New York: Academic Press, 1979.

Marlatt, G. A., Demming, B., & Reid, J. B. Loss of control drinking in alcoholics: An experimental analogue. *Journal of Abnormal Psychology,* 1973, **81,** 233-241.

Marlatt, G. A. & Gordon, J. R. Determinants of relapse: Implications for the maintenance of behavioral change. In: P. Davidson & S. Davidson (Eds.) *Behavioral medicine: changing health lifestyles.* New York: Brunner/Mazel, 1980.

Marlatt, G. A. & Marques, J. K. Meditation, self-control and alcohol use. In: R. B. Stuart (Ed.) *Behavioral self-management: Strategies, techniques, and outcomes.* New York: Brunner/Mazel, 1977.

Marlatt, G. A. & Nathan, P. E. (Eds.) *Behavioral Approaches to alcoholism.* New Brunswick, N. J.: Center of Alcohol Studies, 1978.

Marlatt, G. A. & Rohsenow, D. J. Cognitive processes in alcohol use: Expectancy and the balanced placebo design. In: N. K. Mello (Ed.) *Advances in substance abuse: Behavioral and biological research.* Greenwich, Conn.: JAI Press, 1980.

Martin, W. H., Jasinski, D. R., Haertzen, C. A.; Kay, D. C.; & Jones, B. E. *Archives of General Psychiatry,* 1973, **28,** 286-295.

McClelland, D. C., Davis, W. M., Kalin, R., & Wanner, E. *The drinking man.* New York: Free Press, 1972.

McFall, R. M. Parameters of self-monitoring. In: R. B. Stuart (Ed.) *Behavioral self-management: Strategies, techniques, and outcomes.* New York: Brunner/Mazel, 1977.

Meichenbaum, D. H. *Cognitive behavior modification.* New York: Plenum Press, 1977.

Merry, J. The "loss of control" myth. *Lancet,* 1966, **1,** 1257-1258.

Miller, P. M. & Eisler, R. M. Assertive behavior of alcoholics: A descriptive analysis. *Behavior Therapy,* 1977, **8,** 146-149.

Miller, P. M., Hersen, M., Eisler, R. M., & Hilsman, G. Effects of social stress on operant drinking of alcoholics and social drinkers. *Behavior Research and Therapy,* 1974, **12,** 67-72.

Miller, P. M. & Mastria, M. A. *Alternatives to alcohol abuse: A social learning model.* Champaign, Illinois: Research Press, 1977.

Miller, W. R. & Munoz, R. F. *How to control your drinking.* Englewood Cliffs, New Jersey: Prentice Hall, 1976.

Mirin, D. M., Mendelson, J. H., Ellingboe, J., & Meyer, R. E. *Psychoneuroendocrinology,* 1976, **1,** 359-369.

Moskowitz, A. & DePry, D. Differential effect of alcohol on auditory vigilance and directed-attention tasks. *Quarterly Journal of Studies on Alcohol,* 1968, **29,** 54-63.

Nathan, P. E. Studies in blood alcohol level discrimination. In P. E. Nathan, G. A. Marlatt, & T. Løberg (Eds.) *Alcoholism: New directions in behavioral research and treatment.* New York: Plenum Press, 1978.

Nathan, P. E. & O'Brien, J. S. An experimental analysis of the behavior of alcoholics and non-alcoholics during prolonged experimental drinking: A necessary precursor of behavior therapy? *Behavior Therapy,* 1971, **2,** 455-476.

O'Brien, C. P., Testa, T., Ternes, J., & Greenstein, R. Conditioning effects of narcotics in humans. *Behavioral tolerance: Research and training implications.* Department of HEW Public Health Service, NIDA Research Monograph 18, 1978.

O'Leary, D. E., O'Leary, M. R., & Donovan, D. M. Social skill acquisition and psychosocial development of alcoholics: A review. *Addictive Behaviors,* 1976, **1,** 111-120.

Pattison, E. M., Sobell, M. B., & Sobell, L. C. *Emerging concepts of alcohol dependence.* New York: Springer Publishing Co., 1977.

Pavlov, I. P. *Conditioned reflexes* (Translation by G. V. Amrep). London: Oxford University Press, 1927.

Polivy, J. Perception of calories and regulation of intake in restrained and unrestrained subjects. *Addictive Behaviors,* 1976, **1,** 237-243.

Ritchie, J. M. The aliphatic alcohols. In: L. S. Goodman & A. Gilman (Eds.) *The pharmacological bases of therapeutics.* New York: Macmillan, 1965.

Russek, M. & Pina S. Conditioning of adrenaline anorexia. *Nature,* 1962, **193,** 1296-1297,

Russell, J. A. & Mehrabian, A. The mediating role of emotions in alcohol use. *Quarterly Journal of Studies on Alcohol,* 1975, **36,** 1508-1536.

Russell, M. A. H. In R. J. Gibbins, Y. Israel, R. F. Kalant, W. Popham, W. Schmidt, & R. G. Smart (Eds.) *Recent advances in alcohol & drug problems,* Vol. 3. New York: Wiley & Sons, 1976.

Schacter, S. The interaction of cognitive and physiological determinants of emotional states. In: L. Berkowitz (Ed.) *Advances in experimental social psychology.* New York: Academic Press, 1964.

Shafii, M., Lavely, R., & Jaffe, R. Meditation and marijuana. *American Journal of Psychiatry,* 1974, **131,** 60-63.

Shafii, M., Lavely, R., & Jaffe, R. Meditation and the prevention of alcohol abuse. *American Journal of Psychiatry,* 1975, **132,** 942-945.

Siegel, S. Evidence from rats that morphine tolerance is a learned response. *Journal of Comparative and Physiological Psychology*, 1975, **89**, 498-506.

Siegel, S. Morphine analgesic tolerance: Its situation specificity supports a Pavlovian conditioning model. *Science*, 1976, **193**, 323-325.

Siegel, S. Morphine tolerance acquisition as an associative process. *Journal of Experimental Psychology*, 1977, **3**, 1-13.

Silverstein, S. J., Nathan, P. E., & Taylor, H. A. Blood alcohol level estimates and controlled drinking by chronic alcoholics. *Behavior Therapy*, 1974, **5**, 1-15.

Sobell, M. B., Schaeffer, H. H., & Mills, K. C. Differences in baseline behavior between alcoholics and normal drinkers. *Behavior Research and Therapy*, 1972, **10**, 257-269.

Sobell, M. B. & Sobell, L. C. Alcoholics treated by individualized behavior therapy: One-year treatment outcome. *Behavior Research and Therapy*, 1973, **11**, 599-618.

Sobell, M. B. & Sobell, L. C. *Behavioral treatment of alcohol problems*. New York: Plenum Press, 1978.

Solomon, R. L. & Corbit, J. P. *Psychological Review*, 1974, **81**, 119-145.

Steffen, J., Nathan, P., & Taylor, H. A. Tension-reducing effects of alcohol: Further evidence and some methodological considerations. *Journal of Abnormal Psychology*, 1974, **83**(5), 542-547.

Stuart, R. B. & Davis, B. *Slim chance in a fat world*. Champaigne, Illinois: Research Press, 1972.

Subkov, A. A. & Zilov, G. N. The role of conditioned reflex adaptation in the origin of hyperergic reactions. *Bulletin de Biologie et de Medicine Experimentale*, 1937, **4**, 294-296.

Tongue, E. & Blair, B. Proceedings of the 31st International Conference on Alcoholism and Drug Dependence. Appendix 1. Lausanne, 1975.

United States Public Health Service. *The health consequences of smoking*, 1975 DHEW Publication No. CDC-76-8704, U.S. Government Printing Office, 1976.

Valins, S. Cognitive effects of false heart-rate feedback. *Journal of Personality and Social Psychology*, 1966, **4**, 400-408.

Van Hassett, V. B., Hersen, M., & Milliones, J. Social skill training for alcoholics and drug addicts: A review. *Addictive Behaviors*, 1978, **3**, 221-233.

Warren, G. H. & Raynes, A. E. Mood changes during three conditions of alcohol intake. *Quarterly Journal of Studies on Alcohol*, 1972, **33**, 979-989.

Weiner, B., Frieze, I., Kukla, A., Reed, L., Rest, S., & Rosenbaum, R. M. *Perceiving the causes of success and failure*. Morristown, New Jersey: General Learning Press, 1971.

Wenger, J. R., Berlin, V. & Woods, S. C. Learned tolerance to the behaviorally disruptive effects of ethanol. *Behavioral and Neural Biology*, in press.

Wenger, J. R., Tiffany, T., & Woods, S. C. A comparison of learned and unlearned factors in the acquisition of behavioral tolerance to ethanol and sedative-hypnotic drugs. In: K. Eriksson, J. D. Sinclair, K. Kiianmaa, & A. A. Pawlowski, *Animal models in alcohol research* New York: Academic Press, in press.

Williams, A. F. Social drinking, anxiety, and depression. *Journal of Personality and Social Psychology*, 1966, **3**, 689-693.

Williams, T. K. The ethanol-induced loss of control concept in alcoholism. Unpublished doctoral dissertation. Western Michigan University, 1970.

Author Index*

*In multiple author citations all authors have been listed as occurring on a given page even though only the first author's name may actually appear on that page (e.g., Vogler et al., 1977).

Special thanks are due to Joan Block, Juliette Lagassé and Mary Johnson for their assistance in preparation of this index.

Subject Index

About the Contributors

William R. Miller received his Ph.D. in clinical psychology in 1976 from the University of Oregon, and is currently Associate Professor of Psychology at the University of New Mexico in Albuquerque. Since 1974, his principal research interest has been the treatment of problem drinkers. He has coauthored two volumes on the subject, *How to Control Your Drinking* (1976, with Ricardo F. Muñoz) and *Understanding Alcoholism and Problem Drinking* (1977, with Sam Hamburg and Vitale Rozynko). He is also the editor of Pergamon's 1980 monograph, *Recent Advances in Addictions Research,* and has authored or coauthored more than 30 articles, chapters and papers on the addictive behaviors and other topics.

Richard A. Brown is a doctoral candidate in clinical psychology at the University of Oregon. He has been active in smoking treatment and research for the past five years at the University of Maryland and at Oregon. Among his other research interests are community psychology and the cognitive/behavioral treatment of depression.

Edward J. Callahan received his Ph.D. in 1972 from the University of Vermont. He currently teaches at West Virginia University after having spent four years at the Camarillo Neuropsychiatric Institute Research Program (UCLA). While there, he founded the Heroin Antagonist and Learning Therapy (HALT) Project which has successfully combined behavioral therapy and narcotic antagonist therapy for heroin addiction. Dr. Callahan has served as a member of the board of editors for the *Journal of Applied Behavior Analysis* and on the board of directors for the Association for Advancement of Behavior Therapy.

Claudette Cummings is currently an advanced doctoral student in clinical psychology at the University of Washington, where she is specializing in a psychophysiological approach to addiction problems.

Judith R. Gordon is currently a Research Associate in the Department of Psychology at the University of Washington. She received her doctoral degree from the same university in 1978 and is actively involved in research applying a relapse prevention approach to smoking cessation. She also maintains a private practice in psychology in the Seattle area.

Reid K. Hester received his Ph.D. in clinical psychology from Washington State University and completed his clinical internship at the Veterans Administration Medical Center in Albuquerque, New Mexico. His research has included explorations of neuropsychological impairment in alcoholics. He is currently with Advanced Health Systems, Inc., in Glendale, California.

Edward Lichtenstein is Professor of Psychology and past Director of Clinical Training at the University of Oregon in Eugene. He received his Ph.D. from the University of Michigan in 1961. Since 1965 his research has centered on the development of effective methods for physicians and therapists to help their patients stop smoking, and he has recently begun research on the prevention of smoking among teenagers. His numerous publications include two books: *How to Become an Ex-Smoker: A Comprehensive Program for Permanent Smoking Control* (with Brian Danaher) and the newly released *Psychotherapy: Approaches and Applications.*

G. Alan Marlatt is Professor of Psychology at the University of Washington in Seattle. Previously, he taught at the Universities of Wisconsin and British Columbia, having received his degree in clinical psychology from Indiana University in 1968. He has served as co-editor of two books on behavioral approaches to alcohol problems and is currently conducting research on cognitive-behavioral approaches with a variety of addictive behaviors. He serves on the editorial board of several journals, including the *Journal of Abnormal Psychology, Cognitive Research and Therapy,* and *Addictive Behaviors.*

Peter M. Miller is Director of the Sea Pines Behavioral Institute on Hilton Head Island, South Carolina. He is also Clinical Professor in the Department of Psychiatry and Behavioral Sciences of the Medical University of South Carolina. Dr. Miller has authored more than 50 research articles on behavior modification. He has written three books, *Behavioral Treatment of Alcoholism, Alternatives to Alcohol Abuse,* and *Personal Habit Control.* He is Editor-in-Chief of *Addictive Behaviors,* a research journal specializing in alcoholism, drug abuse, obesity, and smoking.

Peter E. Nathan is Professor and Director, Alcohol Behavior Research Laboratory, Rutgers University, as well as Chairman of the Department of Clinical Psychology at the University's Graduate School of Applied and Professional Psychology. He has been involved in alcoholism research from the behavioral perspective since 1967, when he established one of the first in-patient behavioral research laboratories in the country at Boston City Hospital. He is Associate Editor of *American Psychologist* and has published widely on alcoholism and other topics within clinical psychology.

G. Terence Wilson is Professor of Psychology at the Graduate School of Applied and Professional Psychology at Rutgers University. He is President of the Association for Advancement of Behavior Therapy, Editor of the *Annual Review of Behavior Therapy,* and Associate Editor of the *Journal of Applied Behavior Analysis* and *Cognitive Therapy and Research.* He has coauthored five books on behavior therapy and psychotherapy, as well as numerous professional articles and chapters.